D1569813

ON SOCIAL RESEARCH AND
ITS LANGUAGE

THE HERITAGE OF SOCIOLOGY

A Series Edited by Donald N. Levine

Morris Janowitz, *Founding Editor*

PAUL F. LAZARSFELD

ON SOCIAL
RESEARCH AND ITS
LANGUAGE

Edited and with an Introduction by
RAYMOND BOUDON

THE UNIVERSITY OF CHICAGO PRESS
Chicago and London

RAYMOND BOUDON is professor of sociology at the Sorbonne and a member of the Institute de France. He is the author of numerous books including *A Critical Dictionary of Sociology* and *The Analysis of Ideology*, both published by the University of Chicago Press.

The University of Chicago Press, Chicago 60637
The University of Chicago Press, Ltd., London
© 1993 by The University of Chicago
All rights reserved. Published 1993
Printed in the United States of America
02 01 00 99 98 97 96 95 94 93   1 2 3 4 5

ISBN (cloth): 0-226-46961-1
ISBN (paper): 0-226-46963-8

Library of Congress Cataloging-in-Publication Data

Lazarsfeld, Paul Felix.
    On social research and its language / Paul F. Lazarsfeld : edited and with an introduction by Raymond Boudon.
        p.   cm. — (The Heritage of sociology)
    "Writings of Paul F. Lazarsfeld" : p.
    Includes bibliographical references (p.   ) and index.
        ISBN 0-226-46961-1. — ISBN 0-226-46963-8 (pbk.)
        1. Social sciences—Methodology. 2.   Sociology—Methodology.
    I. Boudon, Raymond.   II. Title.   III. Series.
    H61.L352   1993
    300′.1′9—dc20   93-12748
                                                         CIP

Contents

Acknowledgments

I am deeply grateful to the University of Chicago Press for giving me the responsibility of putting together this selection of Lazarsfeld's works. I greatly appreciate this opportunity of again reading the texts of a friend and most admired teacher.

I am particularly indebted to Professor Donald Levine. Without his help, care, and kindness in making a variety of arrangements, this project could not have been possible. Also I thank him for his always perceptive comments and criticisms on my introductory text.

On this side of the Atlantic, Annie Devinant helped me enormously in the collection and selection of Lazarsfeld's texts, in the arrangement of the contents, in the compilation of the bibliography, and the index.

I acknowledge my debt to all those who helped to see this book through.

Raymond Boudon
Paris 1992

Introduction

Georg Simmel once raised a very Lazarsfeldian question: How is it possible to measure the importance of a great man, of a historical event, or of an intellectual or artistic work (Simmel 1907)? The concept of importance is obviously multidimensional, but one way of "measuring" it, suggests Simmel, is to look at someone's impact counterfactually. For example, one can estimate the influence of a composer by showing that without his contributions, a good deal of significant later music would not have been created.

Paul Lazarsfeld's work is important in this sense and in others. Without him, sociology would undoubtedly look otherwise. We would probably not use the expression "survey research," nor would survey research be practiced so widely around the world. We would not know what the word "panel" means in Lazarsfeldian language or be using the design covered by this label. It is also unlikely that we would be reading the *Journal of Mathematical Sociology*. To Lazarsfeld's name a number of words can be associated which were previously unknown or at least unknown in the sense he gave them, and which appear now in the index of any handbook of sociology or sociological methods. These words correspond to new research procedures or techniques, like "panel" and "contextual analysis," or "latent structure analysis"; to new theories, like the famous "two-step flow"; to new "paradigms" (using Kuhn's notion), like the style of research Lazarsfeld called "empirical social research."

Lazarsfeld's influence was strong, not only on the language of social research, but also on its institutions. Without him, institutes of applied social research throughout Eastern and Western Europe, in Asia, and in America would not look the way they do or be as numerous as they are; nor would they have the same history. In particular, the explosion of survey research centers in the fifties and sixties was made possible, at least in part, by Lazarsfeld's influence and authority.

Finally, many of Paul Lazarsfeld's books and articles have become classics: His publications on consumer and voting behavior, the influence of the media, and the psychosociological effects of unemployment are referred to and quoted by most contemporary sociologists writing on the same topics. *The People's Choice* (1944e) and *Voting* (1954g) are present in the minds and on the shelves of most sociologists. No handbook on media research could omit mentioning *Personal Influence* (1955j). Even his older books, originally written in German, for example, *Jugend und Beruf* (1931) and *Die Arbeitslosen von Marienthal* (1933b), inform modern works on occupational choice and unemployment. Indeed, a striking feature of Lazarsfeld's work is its great unity of inspiration. The main intuitions that were to guide him throughout his intellectual life were clearly articulated in his first works.

Lazarsfeld's Intellectual History

Paul Lazarsfeld was born in Vienna in 1901. His father was a lawyer and a friend of the innovative socialist leaders of the city. The Lazarsfeld children occasionally spent their vacation time at the home of Rudolf Hilferding, the well-known physician and Marxist economist. This family context helps to explain why Paul developed an early interest in social life and human action in addition to science.

As a student at the University of Vienna, Paul studied *Staatswissenschaft*—law, political theory, government, and economics—and mathematics. Influenced by the people he met in the "Lazarsfeld salon" presided over by his mother, he became active in the Socialist Student Movement. At the same time, he continued to pursue scientific interests. Through the physicist Friedrich Adler, he became familiar with Albert Einstein's relativity theory, Ernst Mach's empiriocriticism, and Henri Poincaré's writings. Significantly, these men were not only eminent scientists but great philosophers of science (Zeisel 1979, p. 10), filling two roles that Lazarsfeld came to see as essential to each other. He was convinced of the importance of "the idea that 'the clarification' [of the scientific language] is a road to discovery" (Lazarsfeld 1968c, p. 273). This principle immediately calls to mind the Vienna Circle. Although Lazarsfeld had no real contact with that group, his own ideas were in many ways close to the teachings of its members.

In 1923, the psychologists Karl and Charlotte Bühler were appointed by the University of Vienna to build up a new department of psychology. The Bühlers had come to the university from the Pedagogical Institute of Vienna, which received the bulk of its funds from the socialist city hall. They were part of what was known as the Würzburg school of psychology, which held that the analysis of human *action* should be the main topic of modern psychology. After their appointment to the university, Lazarsfeld became the Bühlers' assistant, first teaching statistics, then psychology and social psychology as well. By 1925, he was also teaching in a *Gymnasium* in Vienna, having completed his Ph.D. in applied mathematics with a dissertation on the trajectory of the planet Mercury (Girard 1976, p. 379).

But Lazarsfeld very soon started branching out from teaching. In 1927 he founded the *Wirtschaftspsychologische Forschungstelle*, a center of applied social research in Vienna, the first such institution in Europe (1968c, p. 274). Karl Bühler was its first president. As its name indicates, the center was chiefly concerned with the "psychology of economics." Thanks to its facilities, Lazarsfeld undertook his first book, *Jugend und Beruf* (1931b), a study on occupational choices in which he used a statistical approach to explore psychological processes. He also wrote a handbook of statistical methods for teachers and psychologists, the first of its type in Europe (1929b). At the same time, he was conducting market studies. Though market research is oriented toward a practical demand from business, Lazarsfeld perceived immediately that such studies are useful for exploring general human decision-making. Around 1930, he began to organize his study on unemployment in Marienthal with the help of Marie Jahoda and Hans Zeisel. The final definition of the study resulted from a discussion between Lazarsfeld and the socialist leader Otto Bauer (1933b).

The Marienthal study was to prove crucial in Lazarsfeld's career, since it attracted the attention of the Paris representative of the Rockefeller Foundation. In 1932, Lazarsfeld obtained a Rockefeller fellowship, arriving in the United States in September 1933. Soon afterward, political events at home began to overtake him. In 1934, he learned that the Socialist party had been outlawed in Austria. As a result, he lost his position in the secondary school system there, keeping only a vague position as assistant at the University of Vienna. By the end of his fellowship in the fall of 1935, most of his family had been arrested. There seemed little choice but for him to stay in the United States. Robert Lynd, the author of *Middletown* (1929), at that time professor of sociology at Columbia University, helped him to find a job as the director of a research institute at the University of Newark, which Lazarsfeld would develop along the model of the *Forschungstelle* he had created in Vienna.

In 1937, only a year after his ground-breaking work in Newark, Lazarsfeld founded the third of his university research centers—this time at Princeton, where the Rockefeller Foundation had decided to create an "Office of Radio Research." Its objective was to study the effect of radio on American society. Before the end of 1937, the office had moved with Lazarsfeld to Columbia University, where within a few years he was appointed associate professor. By 1944, the Columbia Office of Radio Research had become the Bureau of Applied Social Research, reflecting the more diversified research interests of its members (Zeisel 1976–77, p. 557; Lazarsfeld 1968c, p. 276).

The research on radio conducted by Lazarsfeld produced three volumes edited with Frank Stanton (1941m, 1944h, 1949i). This series was completed in 1948 by *Radio Listening in America,* a book published with Patricia Kendall. This interest in the influence of the media, radio first and newspapers later, appears also in Lazarsfeld's studies on political behavior, notably in *The People's Choice* and *Voting.* Indeed, *Personal Influence* represents a kind of synthesis and coronation of Lazarsfeld's work on this topic.

Both because of his own strongly articulated personal interests and as a result of his widening reputation regarding the topics he chose to investigate, Lazarsfeld is known for detailed work on a limited number of substantive fields: voting, consumer behavior, and media research. His Austrian studies were products of the local political and economic context, just as *The Academic Mind* (1958c) grew out of the particular circumstances of the McCarthy years.

Beyond this empirical approach, Lazarsfeld was convinced that social research should clarify and codify its practices and its language. Thus, for him, methodology was a discipline in itself. Out of this conviction came such works as *The Language of Social Research* (1955k; 2d ed. 1972l). In particular, Lazarsfeld tried to develop the use of mathematical language in sociology. The papers collected in *Mathematical Thinking in the Social Sciences,* edited by Lazarsfeld (1954e), describe the potential of the association between mathematics and the social sciences. *Latent Structure Analysis,* written with Neil Henry (1968g), presents Lazarsfeld's own main contribution to this subfield.

Along with this interest in methodology, Lazarsfeld had a deep concern for the applications of sociology, as he made clear in his 1962 address to the American Sociological Association (1926b). *The Uses of Sociology* (1967d), edited with William Sewell and Harold Wilensky, can be seen as the culmination of Lazarsfeld's efforts to define the scope and identify the ways of applied versus theoretical sociology.

Lazarsfeld once wrote that he had become a sociologist simply because he was appointed to a chair of sociology that happened to be vacant at Columbia. Because of his diverse intellectual and professional interests, Lazarsfeld always sought to develop closer relationships between the various social sciences. From his Viennese years, he was persuaded that a unique scientific method is valid for all sciences, and he tended to see the division of labor within the human sciences as being more institutional than intellectual. This attitude led him to a nominalist conception of sociology, which helps to explain why, as we shall see, on a number of issues he devised solutions from several disciplines—not only mathematics and sociology, but psychology. Furthermore, although he was well aware that his "empirical" sociology was not traditional, he had a strong sense of continuing a style of research that reached back to Quetelet and Le Play. As we shall see in more detail below, he devoted no small amount of energy to the history of social research.

By the 1960s, Lazarsfeld had become a dominant figure in the social sciences. Perhaps only Talcott Parsons enjoyed a similar standing, although it must also be said that Lazarsfeld's long intellectual association with Robert Merton contributed to his influence in no small part, bringing together a unique methodological sophistication on one side and theoretical insight on the other (Coleman 1972, pp. 400–401). Lazarsfeld's reputation was acknowledged not only in the United States, but in Europe as well, particularly where he had been directly active in the development of social research. He helped to found the Vienna Institute of Advanced Studies in the Social Sciences. In France, he was twice appointed as a visiting professor at the Sorbonne, in 1963 and 1968.

Lazarsfeld's intellectual and scientific importance were acknowledged by a number of distinctions. He was a member of the United States National Academy of Sciences and of the National Academy of Education and received honorary degrees from the Universities of Chicago, Vienna, the Sorbonne, Yeshiva, and Columbia. At Columbia, he also held the newly established chair of Quetelet Professor of Social Science (Zeisel 1979, p. 21). That he was made responsible for the chapter on sociology in the world survey on the social sciences completed under the auspices of UNESCO (Lazarsfeld 1970d) confirms his status as one of the leading sociologists of his day.

Paul Lazarsfeld died on August 30, 1976. The day before his death, he was able to review the manuscript of a collection of essays in honor of his seventy-fifth birthday, presented to him by some of his former students (Barton 1976).

Lazarsfeld's Main Intuitions

The Analysis of Action

Lazarsfeld always insisted upon the influence of the Bühlers on his intellectual development (1968c). From them came one of the ideas at the center of his work—that the analysis of action should be a main objective of the social sciences as well as of psychology and social psychology. In "Some Historical Notes on the Empirical Study of Action" (1953e), he describes how the intellectual climate in Vienna led him to concentrate his interests on the processes of decision, how the circumstances led him to study consumer decisions, and how he was led to the particular style of research he calls "the empirical analysis of action." This "empirical study of action" was defined against a number of schools of psychology dominant at the time he started to develop his own intellectual program.

Thus, from the teachings of Alfred Adler, a psychoanalyst he came to know through his mother, Lazarsfeld became familiar with the argument that motivations were always to some extent unconscious. He does not seem to have retained from psychoanalysis more than this easily acceptable idea, however. It can be recalled in this respect that classical action sociologists like Weber and Simmel had already defended the view that the reasons moving a social actor might be unknown to that actor. But Lazarsfeld had to reconcile this view with the school of psychology known as behaviorism.

According to orthodox behaviorism, the very notion of action is rejected as scientifically inadequate, since it entails a description of subjective, unobservable states. As Gellner (1987) has noted, behaviorism is the psychological version of the epistemological view that science should, by definition, exclude from its language any statement dealing with unobservable entities. The anthropological version of this general program is exemplified by Malinowski's empiricism, the philosophical by Carnap's physicalism, the physical by Mach's empiriocriticism (a point of Mach's philosophy that apparently did not draw Lazarsfeld's attention), and the sociological by Lundberg's positivism.

In "Concept Formation and Measurement in the Behavioral Sciences: Some Historical Observations" (1966b), Lazarsfeld presents a detailed discussion of behaviorism. One of his main points is that the ideal of behaviorism—to exclude unobservable variables—was violated from the outset by the Weber-Fechner law, since the very notion of the intensity of sensations is an hypothetical construct. The intellectual evolution of Tolman led Lazarsfeld to the same conclusion. Tolman started as a specialist of animal psychology. Though originally attracted by behaviorism, he soon realized that it was impossible to describe animal behavior without using such concepts as "prudence" or "fear." For this reason, Tolman had no problems contributing to Parsons's and Shils's theory of action, although this theory was incompatible with orthodox behaviorism. In the same fashion, another behaviorist, Hull, discovered very soon that introducing intervening unobservable variables is an indispensable scientific move, crucial to interpreting the relationships between observable variables.

But if Lazarsfeld saw clearly that "action" was a valid substitute for "behavior" as the primary objective of the psychological and social sciences, and also that the notion of a *scientific* approach to action is far from being incompatible with the mobilization of unobserved variables and entities, he was at the same time eager to avoid arbitrariness in his analysis. In other words, he sought to develop a style of research that would avoid two opposite pitfalls: the rigidity of Wundt's psychophysics and the overflexibility of introspective psychology. In short, he kept to the scientific ideal of behaviorism, but rejected its means. His approach to the study of action may thus be described as experimental or quasi-experimental.

The fact that motivations are normally unconscious opened a crucial methodological question for Lazarsfeld: How is one to find the proper means to reconstruct them? As early as 1931, during the preparation of his study *Jugend und Beruf*, he realized that subjects seem to answer direct questions almost arbitrarily. He determined that since motivations are in many circumstances unconscious, access to them cannot be guaranteed, except in some marginal cases, by asking people point blank "Why did you do that? " or "Why do you think or believe that?" In other words, to use the title of one of his articles, asking why is an *art* (1935a) and apparently minor variations in the ways a question is asked can lead a subject to different answers.

For example, if a subject is asked, "Why do you buy flowers?" he tends to give stereotyped and socially acceptable answers. By contrast, when he is asked, "Why did you buy *these* flowers?" the answers are much more informative. The subject tends to mention the particular circumstances which have led him to buy flowers. Similarly, when a subject is asked why she has bought such-and-such type of shoes, her answers vary depending on whether the question is asked shortly after she bought the shoes or some time later. The researcher can therefore provoke answers that lead either to the deep motivations of the subject or, alternatively, to superficial social motivations. Moreover, the way a subject perceives and evaluates an object, far from being stable, may change over time. From such market studies, Lazarsfeld became convinced that a systematic analysis of the variation of the answers with the form of the questions, the conditions of the interview, and so on, would lead to a better evaluation of the answers (Zeisel 1968, pp. 10–11). Reflecting on "the art of asking why" would lead to interesting psychological insights. For Lazarsfeld, methodology and theory, as well as methodology and the production of new knowledge, went hand in hand.

It is in this light that we must understand his statement that there is a "methodological equivalence" between buying soap and voting for the Socialist party. The comparison, which I mentioned in the obituary I wrote on Lazarsfeld for the French newspaper *Le Monde* (Boudon 1976), should be seen as humorous and didactic rather than literal and provocative. Lazarsfeld was simply arguing that progress in the scientific understanding of human action can be gained by analyzing any type of decision, for human action is always complex, even when its goals appear simple or prosaic.

Lazarsfeld also perceived early on from his market studies, as well as from more academically "respectable" analyses, that a given situation normally gives birth to several types of response—a point borne out by his study on Marienthal. At the time of the study, more than 20 percent of the population of this small city close to Vienna were unemployed. Though the people in the sample seemed much alike and were all in a similar economic situation, their reactions to that situation were diverse. In some cases, unemployment had the effect of making family links stronger, in some cases weaker. As Simmel observes in his *Probleme der Geschichtsphilosophie* (1907), opposite responses to a given situation may be equally "understandable." This point led Lazarsfeld to the conclusion that identifying types of answers is important in empirical research. He also derived from his Marienthal study the idea that each type has its own coherence, more precisely, that it should be described by a combination of convergent features. For example, he identifies in his Marienthal study the "proletarian consumer," describing him as follows:

> Less psychologically mobile, less active, more inhibited in his behavior. The radius of stores he considers for possible purchases is smaller. He buys more often at the same store. His food habits are more rigid and less subject to seasonal variations. As part of this reduction in effective scope the interest in other than the most essential details is lost; requirements in regard to quality, appearance and other features of merchandise are the less specific and frequent the more we deal with consumers from low social strata. (1968c, p. 280).

These insights gained from psychology may explain in part Lazarsfeld's rejection of the models of action used by Austrian economists. Austria is the country where Carl Menger flourished, and Lazarsfeld knew Osker Morgenstern, like himself an immigrant to the United States. But their *a priori* approach seemed to him artificial. The economists gave their *homo economicus* a uniform, *a priori,* simple rational psychology, while as Lazarsfeld knew from his own efforts, any "empirical" study shows that several types of answers to a situation can always be identified. The economists underestimated the multidimensionality of motivations and exaggerated the utilitarian aspects of action.

More curiously, Lazarsfeld never devoted much attention to the theories of action used by historians and also by action sociologists like Tocqueville, Pareto, Weber, or Simmel. Their style of sociology has beyond doubt produced theories which can be called scientific, though they too use an *a priori* approach in their analyses. But their approach must be distinguished from that of the neoclassical economists and of today's so-called rational choice theorists. The classical sociologists used a flexible theory of action where, for example, the affective or cognitive dimensions of action were taken into account as well as its utilitarian dimension.

It is not clear why Lazarsfeld disregarded this type of approach, in spite of its evident importance to sociology past and present. One explanation may be that he was too unfamiliar with macrosociology. He was also more interested in real human beings than in the abstract "actors" manipulated by historians and macrosociologists. Though Tocqueville's Americans in *Democracy in America* are much more complex psychologically than the *homo economicus* of the rational choice theorists, they are still highly stylized. Interestingly enough, in his reflections on Max Weber, Lazarsfeld appears very pleased to observe that, in his empirical studies, the German sociologist paid attention to concrete psychological questions, such as the stabilizing effects of marriage. But he wonders at the same time why this type of research appears to be so marginal in Weber's work and proposes—very prudently—to explain this inconsistency with the help of psychoanalytic theory: Weber perhaps resisted the attraction he felt toward psychology because of his mental problems. Apparently, Lazarsfeld did not realize that Weber's main works were also full of psychological analyses, conjectures, and theories. Probably because this work was intuitive, Lazarsfeld felt it did not deserve his attention.

The differences that Lazarsfeld saw between his own work and

that of the classical sociologists underscores the fact that he envisioned
a new direction for sociology. In short, Lazarsfeld began the definition
and institutionalization of an original and flexible approach to the
social sciences. As we shall see, he would apply his "empirical social
research" to a number of complex subjects and equip it with an ever-
growing methodological toolbox.

Empirical Social Research

If the expression "empirical social research" (ESR) is taken literally,
Lazarsfeld was not the first to employ the approach. The French sociologist Le Play, to whom Lazarsfeld (1961b) devoted much attention,
also used standardized observation procedures in his analysis of the
living conditions of European workers' families; Tarde ([1886] 1924)
raised a number of questions about the growth and the differential
frequency of crime using standardized statistical data; and Durkheim
(1897) proposed to distinguish four types of suicide which he identified with the help of statistics from a number of European countries.
The sociologists of the Chicago school—notably Park and Burgess
and Thomas and Znaniecki—also explored many types of social phenomena, from the conditions of living prevailing in the big industrial
cities to the development of marginality or the integration of immigrants, using data generated by methodical observational procedures.

But in spite of their historical interest for the social sciences—a
topic to which we shall return—these works do not really correspond
to what Lazarsfeld calls ESR. Le Play's observations were largely descriptive. He aimed essentially at answering questions of the *what* and
how type: How do people live? What do they consume? By contrast,
ESR is mainly concerned with questions of the *why* type: Why do
voters vote as they do? When ESR does ask questions of the *how*
type, they refer to processes rather than static pictures: How do consumers make up their minds in favor of a given product? How and to
what extent are voters influenced by political campaigns? True, Tarde,
Durkheim, and Quetelet used official statistical data, and Thomas and
Znaniecki's work *The Polish Peasant* (1918) also rests upon official
documents, letters, and interviews. But while Lazarsfeld always recognized the importance of such sources, he felt that on many subjects
quantitative data could not answer the questions sociologists should
be asking—hence his conviction that sociologists should learn to build
appropriate observational designs and collect data in a methodical
fashion, as is done in the so-called hard sciences.

ESR was regularly faced with an objection resting on a misunderstanding. To many people, the very notion of "empirical" social re-

search implied an antipathy toward "theory." This interpretation was reinforced in the sixties, when "positivism" became a favorite target. Now, while Lazarsfeld saw the defects of what sociologists generously called theory, he always defended the idea that ESR cannot dispense with theory. On the contrary, he insisted, since the main objective of ESR is to understand human action, it is confronted with the crucial task of creating explanatory concepts. However, I should mention here what appears to me as a limitation of Lazarsfeld's notion of theory. To him, theory essentially means conceptualization. It is ironic to note that Parsons embraced a similar conception of theory, inasmuch as he deemed it appropriate for sociological theory in the 1950s to be working at the level of constructing a system of interrelated concepts, and devoted a good part of his own work to the elaboration of such "categorical systems." At any rate, Lazarsfeld did not pay much attention to the fact that, in the hard sciences, theories often take the form of deductive systems or generative models. For example, Zetterberg (1954) tried to axiomatize Durkheim's *Division of Labour*. Many pages of Tocqueville or, say, Weber could be axiomatized in the same fashion (Boudon 1990, 1991b; Pawson 1989). It is easy to show that many classical analyses can be translated into more or less sophisticated generative models or theories as they are usually understood in the hard sciences.

What, then, in Lazarsfeld's view was the relationship of ESR to sociology? First of all, it must be remembered that when Lazarsfeld first became interested in the human sciences, sociology proper did not exist in Vienna: psychology was the only human science to have been established to any degree (Zeisel 1979, pp. 10–15; Zeisel 1968, pp. 4–5). Lazarsfeld's intellectual inclinations were understandably toward psychology rather than sociology. Furthermore, although he was generally very prudent when he passed judgment on the state of the sociological art, it can easily be seen from his writings that he felt the label "sociology" encompassed a number of very heterogeneous activities. Sometimes, as in the essay on macrosociology (1970d, pp. 76–90), he failed to hide that he found mainstream sociology disappointingly vague and very far from the scientific ideal he had had in mind since his Vienna *Lehrjahre*. In that article, he argued— politically but clearly—that most current macrosociological production fell into the descriptive tradition of "social analysis," indicating that he had trouble finding in the macrosociological writings of his time articulate and testable hypotheses and assumptions.

Lazarsfeld saw two trends in the dominant sociology of his time. On the one hand there was what he called "social analysis," that is, essays in the style of C. Wright Mills, which, it seemed to him, were primarily of literary value. On the other was sociological "theory" in the style of Parsons. Rightly, I think, Lazarsfeld believed that theory in such works as *The Structure of Social Action* ([1937] 1968) has little to do with the theory represented in the natural sciences. For this reason, he always stressed the importance of Merton's notion of "middle range theory" (Boudon 1991a). But Lazarsfeld had to be cautious and diplomatic toward mainstream sociology, and it is possible he used the expression ESR rather than the more explicit "empirical sociology," to downplay their competition.

Lazarsfeld characterized ESR as a "research style," and he considered it his main contribution to the practice of sociology (1968c, p. 277). But the ESR paradigm was for him more than intrinsically interesting. He also hoped to raise the level of scientific expectations and consciousness among sociologists and—by stressing the idea that sociology, like any scientific discipline, should aim at producing controlled knowledge—to give it a more satisfactory direction.

Methodology

Certainly, one of the ideas most closely associated with Lazarsfeld's name is that of "methodology." It is important to understand its meaning clearly, for, as he frequently complained, "methodology" is often confused with "technology." The latter is a label for the toolbox used by sociologists in their empirical studies. It includes, for example, the various statistical methods used by data analysts and the standardized rules for the elaboration of questionnaires. These tools are the *product* of methodology in the sense that they all derive from actual questions or problems met by empirical research in the course of its development. Thus correlation coefficients originated from the need to define a valid measure of the influence of one variable on another or, more generally, the strength of the association between two or more variables. But such techniques should not be confused with methodology.

While technology is a standardized, and to that extent dead, product of methodology, methodology itself should be apprehended as a much more flexible activity, resting on general intellectual attitudes and orientations rather than on rules or principles. To make his notion of methodology clearer, Lazarsfeld assimilated it with a more familiar process: literary, or rather musical, criticism (for, as a good Viennese, Lazarsfeld considered himself more educated in music than in *belles lettres*). He insisted repeatedly that criticism is a fundamental activity, perhaps even more in the sciences than in the arts. In his memoir

(1968c), he describes vividly the significance for him of the fact that Einstein's relativity theory was generated less by the failure of the Michelson-Morley experiment than by Einstein's criticism of the notion of simultaneity. While common sense gives "simultaneity" an absolute meaning, Einstein demonstrated that it has no meaning when it is applied to two bodies moving at high speeds relative to one another. In this way, the critical analysis of a word precipitated a scientific revolution.

The critical analysis of words is as essential in social research as in physics. Lazarsfeld's reflections on the art of asking "why" sprang from the polysemous character of that familiar word. "Cause," another familiar and indispensable term, is also far from being unambiguous. Consequently, it is not always easy to determine whether a set of statistical data supports a causal statement or not. Hume raised the question as to which data would be needed before one could consider a statement like "X causes Y" as valid and answered the question in a radically negative fashion. Kant's criticism, which Lazarsfeld presents as another illustration of his ideal of methodology, was directed toward Hume's answer. Lazarsfeld's writings on causal inference, like those of Simon (1957) on the same topic, are continuations of this classical methodological discussion and good illustrations in themselves of the notion of methodology.

It is necessary to stress, against a current misunderstanding, that methodology is not a normative concept. Methodology does not aim to answer questions of the type "What should be done?" It proposes instead to look at convincing studies in order to understand why they are convincing, why they appear to generate genuine new knowledge. In that respect, Lazarsfeld's comparison of methodology and criticism is illuminating. In the arts, criticism aims to clarify the reasons a particular picture or quartet have come to be considered "great," why they are "breathtaking," not to teach how to write a good quartet or paint a good picture. In other words, the latent objective of the criticism is to try to disentangle the objective correlates of intersubjective aesthetic feelings. In the same way, methodology, as applied to the social sciences, aims at bringing into daylight the objective correlates of intersubjective feelings like "X's theory on Y is convincing (or not)," "the statement 'X causes Y' is convincing, given the set of data D," and so on. For this reason, Lazarsfeld repeatedly proposed *l'explication de texte* in the French tradition as the model or, if I may say so, the method *par excellence* of methodology. An *explication de texte* strives to show how a text is built, why it works so well—or so badly—although criticism in the negative sense is not the aim of

methodology, and it is certainly less fruitful than criticism in the positive sense. Lazarsfeld summarized his view on methodology by a simple formula: "The sociologist studies man in society: The methodologist studies the sociologist at work" (1959b, p. 39).

The value of methodology is twofold: First it has a theoretical
interest. It generates technical tools, such as the statistical instruments
I mentioned. Just as logic originates from a codification of the rules
used in ordinary thinking, many statistical tools were born from the
clarification and systematization of the rules of inference used in everyday life, and in research. But of course, methodology also has a
practical interest, since it makes research more effective, more reliable,
able to solve more complex problems. Moreover, the codification of
inferential rules that results from methodology makes the development, transmission, and diffusion of those rules more likely. So the
institutionalization of methodology generates a chain reaction, con-
solidating through a number of channels the cognitive efficiency of
the social sciences.

To see Lazarsfeld's notion of methodology at work, we can turn
to an example which he himself (1959b) borrowed from Clausen
(Clausen and Kohn 1954). Very often, sociologists use variables defined not on individuals but on administrative or geographical units.
Thus it is possible to study the correlation between the diffusion of
mental diseases and standards of living, taking as units, for instance,
the neighborhoods of a city, in order to determine whether mental
diseases tend to be more frequent when the standard of living is lower.
Suppose the correlation is high. The crucial methodological question
is whether, without further information, this finding can be interpreted causally: Conditions of living are responsible for the emergence
of mental diseases. The answer is no. This causal interpretation is
only one among others, for it is also possible to suppose that, when
people succumb to a mental illness, their occupational lives become
disorganized and some of them will as a consequence move to poorer
areas. One can assume as well that some types of mental disease are
produced, not by the conditions of living itself, but by the style of
social relations prevailing in poor areas. Under this assumption, the
correlation would be due, not to the personal situation of the subjects,
but to the characteristics of the neighborhood itself. Furthermore, as
is now well known, a correlation can be high when it is computed at
the collective level and zero or even negative, at least in theory, when
computed at the individual level.

Lazarsfeld not only defined methodology as a new discipline, the
methodology of ESR in particular, he also brought into existence

many of its most effective instruments. His contributions bear first on the language of variables. The importance he assigned to this topic can easily be understood. Because survey research is a main dimension of the general ESR paradigm, the basic information available to sociological analysis often takes the form of statistical distributions. Lazarsfeld explored the issue of how such data should be analyzed to reconstitute the psychosociological processes they are the product of. How, for instance, in the example from Clausen referred to above, is one to make a grounded choice between alternative interpretations? This question gave birth to papers like "The Interpretation of Statistical Relations as a Research Operation" and similar essays in *The Language of Social Research* (1955k). His writings on this subject inspired many methodological and technological researches in the sociological community. The methods of so-called causal analysis as well as of multivariate analysis, for example, the now popular log-linear models, would probably not have been developed and used so extensively without the pioneering work of Lazarsfeld.

Lazarsfeld never used a technique in a mechanical fashion. Because his objective was always to understand human action, when he found, say, a correlation between two variables, he never forgot that a joint distribution defines, beside the majority of cases contributing to the correlation, a minority of subjects representing "deviant cases." Since correlations observed by sociologists are generally weak, as Lazarsfeld repeatedly noted, that minority is often large. To him, these deviant cases were as important as the others. He never treated them, in the statistical fashion of many sociologists, as the uninteresting effect of random factors. On the contrary, he saw them as methodologically strategic: Analyzing the reasons for their statistical "deviance" was a way of refining the analysis of the psychosociological processes responsible for the statistical data.

Clearly, Lazarsfeld's methodology was not limited to quantitative analysis. The art of building typologies, of systematizing them by analyzing their underlying dimensions and projecting them into an attribute space, and the devising of overarching concepts ("matrix formula")—like Weber's "bureaucracy" or Durkheim's "anomie" —inspired several of his best-known papers. It should be noted that all these concerns can be found *in statu nascendi* in his Marienthal study, in which he noticed that the same cause (unemployment) can have opposite effects (reinforcement vs. destruction of the nuclear family). The first effect was *less frequent* than the second but perhaps *more interesting,* because of the insight it gave into complex processes and decisions. Even in Lazarsfeld's very early work, he employed the strategies that would define his methodology—not only the notion of deviant cases, but also the idea that typologies and matrix formulas are essential mental bridges between the means of ESR (observational data) and its objective (understanding human action).

In the process of conceptualization, the recurrent problem of measuring unobservable variables led Lazarsfeld to a variety of technical solutions. For example, the notion that people can be ranked in terms of their status is a familiar and indispensable one. But it is generally difficult to identify the variables most closely related to status, a mental and social construct which cannot itself be directly measured. How can one assure that the observable variables (or indicators) of status are statistically valid? Lazarsfeld determined that statistical relationships seem to remain stable when unobserved variables are measured by different sets of plausible indicators, a solution he called the "interchangeability of indices."

Scale analysis offers another answer to the same problem. Scaling was not invented by Lazarsfeld. Indeed, at the beginning of the century, Binet and Simon (1905), for example, had already addressed the issue of how to measure unobservable variables (such as "intelligence") with observable data. But Lazarsfeld certainly stimulated the development of scale analysis and, more generally, of measurement techniques and introduced into sociology methodological problems long familiar to psychologists.

This idea of measuring unobserved variables with the help of indicators also led Lazarsfeld to the mathematical tools of latent structure analysis (LSA). At core, LSA is close to Spearman's (1904) unifactorial or Thurstone's (1947) multifactorial analysis. The "trick" common to all these techniques is that while the correlations between unobserved variables and indicators cannot be directly measured, they can, provided adequate assumptions are introduced, appear as unknowns in sets of equations where the known quantities are represented by the correlations between the indicators. When these equations can be solved, the validity of the indicators—their correlation with the latent variables—can be measured. LSA is actually little used in social research today. But from the viewpoint of the history of ideas, it offers a fascinating glimpse of how questions met in the course of Lazarsfeld's projects fueled the development of sophisticated instruments of empirical research.

The importance of Lazarsfeld's contributions to quantitative analysis in the social sciences gave birth to the legend of his quantomania, a myth which can be easily refuted. The problem of the measurement of unobservable variables inspired LSA, but also a number of entirely nonmathematical and nonquantitative developments, for example, in Lazarsfeld's writings on typologies and attribute spaces, where he develops methodological ideas close to those of Jakobson's structural phonology (Jakobson and Halle [1956] 1971). In his "algebra of dichotomous systems" (1961a), Lazarsfeld worked out mathematically the methodology of multivariate analysis and of causal inference, but he certainly recognized that causal statements can be grounded on nonstatistical data. Thus, in his paper "Some Functions of Qualitative Analysis in Social Research" (1955i), he scrutinizes the way Lipset (1950) draws causal statements from comparative observations bearing on the Canadian provinces or on the English-speaking countries. *Stricto sensu,* no statistical analysis is possible with such populations, limited as they are to a very small number of units. Although Lazarsfeld has little to say about why such nonstatistical theories are convincing, he shows clearly that they can produce reliable causal statements. Here again, Lazarsfeld might have drawn upon examples from classical macrosociology. Tocqueville (1856), for instance, explained in a very convincing fashion why French agriculture was less developed than British at the end of the eighteenth century. But the important point is that, by contrast with those whom he sometimes called in private exchanges the "statistical zealots," Lazarsfeld was convinced that "qualitative" was not less important than "quantitative" analysis.

Finally, two other methodological innovations should be mentioned. The first, panel analysis, is too well known to need much discussion. The idea of panel analysis originated from Lazarsfeld's simple remark on the weaknesses of cross-sectional observations. For example, two surveys on voting intentions taken at two different times may give the impression that public opinion is stable. But the apparent stability may be the result of individual movements in opposite directions over time. The panel design contributed greatly to the effectiveness of Lazarsfeld's works in political sociology. Thus the classical analyses of the effectiveness of political campaigns on voting proposed in both *The People's Choice* and *Voting* were made possible by the panel design.

The second of the two developments was Lazarsfeld's idea of "contextual analysis." Lazarsfeld devised designs of observations that took into account the eventuality that, not only individual, but also contextual variables can explain observed behaviors, attitudes, or actions. Going back to the example drawn from Clausen, one interpretation of the correlation between poverty and mental disease makes the assumption that the main cause of mental disease is represented by variables characterizing the subject, another by variables characterizing the context. The influence of Lazarsfeld's contextual analysis is clear in works like Coleman's *The Adolescent Society* (1961).

Introducing contextual variables systematically into observation designs seemed to Lazarsfeld a very important move, not only methodologically, but also strategically. ESR was constantly accused of being a hybrid psychosociology rather than sociology proper. Lazarsfeld thought that through his contextual variables he could bring ESR closer to the mainstream sociological tradition, since contextual analysis made it possible to take into account nonindividual effects. *The Academic Mind* (1958c) is probably the empirical study where the fruitfulness of Lazarsfeld's contextual designs can be most clearly perceived. As was true of his other innovations, contextual analysis brought closer and even made complementary disciplines separated by traditional and institutional borders: psychology, social psychology, and sociology.

The Uses of Sociology

Lazarsfeld justified the work he did on Marienthal by saying that, while a victorious revolution needs economists, an unsuccessful social revolution needs psychologists. The ambiguity of his comment shows that he recognized both the importance of asking how the social sciences were to be put to use and the difficulty of answering that question. He saw clearly from the very beginning that the social sciences cannot generate applications as easily as physics or chemistry. The uses of the social sciences are more diffuse and diversified than those of the hard sciences, so that exploring, identifying, and listing them is a project in itself. In was a project that fascinated Lazarsfeld throughout his career. Indeed, as he acknowledged in private talks, potential applications of sociology were, beside methodology, his main interest.

Lazarsfeld recognized that sociology cannot serve political action directly. It can explore the basic mechanisms responsible for voting behavior. Surveys can try to explain why people vote or refrain from voting or why, how, to what extent, and under which conditions they are influenced or not by political campaigns. Surveys can also be used to predict the outcome of an election, but with a considerable chance of failure. This predictive function of survey research as it is practiced by pollsters has become dominant today. But Lazarsfeld himself had little interest in studies with a mere predictive use: Though they correspond to a strong demand, they bring little additional knowledge to our understanding of voting, Lazarsfeld's principal concern.

A "use" of the social sciences on which Lazarsfeld insisted repeat-edly was its critical function toward common sense. For example, according to common sense, the media have a strong mechanical in-fluence upon public opinion, structuring individual representations, leading people to buy the products they see advertised, and so on. But in his radio studies, Lazarsfeld showed that this influence was limited, that people tend to listen to what they perceive as familiar. Thus, middle-class listeners tend to appreciate the cultural products they have been initiated to during the years of their formal education, while lower-class people tend to attach little meaning to them. His studies on voting led him to the same conclusions: Political campaigns have little effect on those who are strongly involved in politics, because, in a half conscious way, they seldom expose themselves to opinions op-posed to their own. Furthermore, political campaigns have only a moderate influence on those who care little about politics. The family group holds more sway over its members, protecting them against outside influences. In the *Voting* sample (1954g), divergent political opinions between the members of families appeared only in 4 percent of the cases. *Personal Influence* (1955j) generalized this finding, show-ing as its title suggests, that personal interactions are much more effective in shaping decisions than the impersonal influence of the media.

Clearly, such findings might be considered disappointing by those who want to influence social actors in one way or another, as was true of the Viennese socialists of the thirties who where worried by the fact that the lower classes demonstrated little interest in the city's cultural programs. But if Lazarsfeld's findings are often negative from the point of view of political action, they are positive from a cognitive and possibly from a moral point of view. Is it after all a bad thing that people's tastes, choices, and preferences are not so easily manipu-lated? Is not one of the main interests of Lazarsfeld's studies on influ-ence to have shown that the mechanical theory of influence endorsed by common sense is far too simple?

Moreover, many opinions based on "common sense" prove invalid when examined through the lens of the social sciences. Our familiarity with all kinds of social phenomena convinces us that "we already know" the truth about many subjects. More generally, as social actors, we cannot help endorsing more or less fragile views on all kinds of things. Cognitive psychologists and sociologists have taught us that we often have many good reasons, beside the objectively valid ones, to believe in a variety of ungrounded ideas. So one might say that one of the main uses of the social sciences is to correct these distorted collective representations. This point was supported, more clearly perhaps than by Lazarsfeld, by one of his close friends—the French sociologist and social psychologist Jean Stoetzel. The primary use of the social sciences, suggested Stoetzel, is to correct the distortions normally produced by "collective memory" in Halbwachs's sense, or by "collective consciousness" in Durkheim's sense (Boudon 1992).

Lazarsfeld himself acknowledged the potential influence of the social sciences on what Flaubert called *idées reçues*. In his *Dictionnaire des idées reçues* (1911), Flaubert stressed the point that common sense tends to consider contradictory expectations, assumptions, or ideas as equally understandable or even true. The social sciences, argued Lazarsfeld, can help to determine which actually are true. Halbwachs (1930) had already made the same point, in his book *Les causes du suicide*. One could explain equally easily, he contended, that bachelors commit suicide *less* and that they commit suicide *more* frequently than married people. But as Durkheim (1897) showed, the former statement is true, while the latter is false.

Lazarsfeld foresaw many other uses for ESR. As he suggested in his important paper "The Historian and the Pollster" (1957a), ESR, with its new techniques for collecting data, would propose to historians an original source of information which would likely change their ways of thinking. Lazarsfeld maintained that if surveys had been known at the time of the French Revolution, our views on this crucial historical episode would probably be different. Futhermore, he was convinced that not only political history, but the history of family, as well as many other subjects would be greatly affected by the existence of survey data. In the work of today's historians, Lazarsfeld's prediction has started to be fulfilled: The influence of survey research on family studies is so strong that the history and sociology of family have merged into a single discipline.

According to Lazarsfeld's "Reflections on Business" (1959h), a comparable effect should be expected on the side of economics. As I have already mentioned, because of his background, Lazarsfeld was always skeptical about economic theory. He never grasped the importance of the stylized psychology used by economists as well as by historians and macrosociologists. This "conventional" psychology, to use Simmel's terminology (1907), was too incompatible with the psychology Lazarsfeld himself envisioned. Nevertheless, he believed that ESR could provide, if not an alternative, at least a complement to the traditional abstract psychological approach typical of economic theory.

Whether his predictions in this respect will also prove valid is not yet clear. According to some writers (e.g., McKenzie and Tullock 1975), a "new world of economics" that includes traditional sociological subjects is developing. This extension of the economic *imperium* goes against Lazarsfeld's argument. It remains to be seen, however, whether it will be as fruitful and lasting as its proponents claim. On the other hand, many economists have the impression that their traditional "conventional" psychology is of limited use in many *economic* problems, that its efficiency has been slowly exhausted. Some theories, like Simon's "satisficing theory" (1957) or the economic theories that take into account the cognitive dimension of decision processes, seem to acknowledge the shortcomings of the psychological style used by the neoclassical tradition. This trend, if it can be consolidated, seems to confirm Lazarsfeld's prediction.

The most reasonable assumption is that the two styles are probably important and complementary as far as economics and the other behavioral sciences are concerned: Lazarsfeld's style wil! certainly inspire future applications in applied economic research. Equally true, economists, like historians and macrosociologists, cannot dispense with the *a priori* models that they have traditionally used, even though they should, in a Lazarsfeldian fashion, become more critical of them. Clearly, these discussions raise fascinating epistemological problems. For this reason, it is a pity, claimed Lazarsfeld (1961b), that professional historians of science and philosophers, impressed as they are by the achievements of the hard sciences, pay so little attention to the social sciences.

I feel it necessary to add to these considerations a pessimistic note. Lazarsfeld's research style proposed a subtle combination of theory and observation. Unfortunately, what we observe today is the development of what Schumpeter (1954) would have called a "cameral" style. The production of raw data for its descriptive or predictive value seems to be the dominant activity in the social sciences. The legacy of *Voting* is represented largely by routinized opinion studies. As Luckmann (1991) has rightly complained, this cameral trend has invaded even the sociology of religion. While the main objectives of classical sociology were to explain the development of collective religious beliefs, contemporary sociologists of religion are often satisfied with answering questions of the type "Is the number of churchgoers of this particular denomination increasing or decreasing?" To take a more Lazarsfeldian example, market research has expanded tremendously, but one may wonder whether it still contributes to the understanding of action, as Lazarsfeld wished and insisted it should.

22   *Introduction*

Research Institutions

Because of the specific demands ESR makes upon its practitioners, Lazarsfeld came very early to the conclusion that empirical sociology could only be conducted in an original type of institution, in "research offices" or "bureaus of applied social research" like those he himself was to found three times—once in Vienna, twice in America. First of all, techniques like "surveys" are costly, and second, they can only be carried out by a team of researchers combining complementary abilities. Thus, ESR requires a particular organizational framework. It presupposes in academics a taste and competence for management, which neither traditional sociologists, nor experimental psychologists may possess. Empirical sociology also presupposes a more extended division of labor, where statisticians, interviewers, computer scientists, and so on, are associated with sociologists. With the development of ESR comes a new social role, which Lazarsfeld labeled the "managerial scholar." As in market research, the managerial scholar has to serve two masters and to display a variety of qualities, including a definite ability to negotiate. For this reason, observed Lazarsfeld, survey research centers took time to be established in Europe. (But we must also recall that, when Lazarsfeld arrived in the United States, the only research center in this country was the one led by Odum at the University of North Carolina.)

These problems have now been overcome to a large extent: ESR has been institutionalized in most places and coexists preacefully with other research styles. Lazarsfeld must therefore be credited not only with the development of a new research style, but also with the initiation of a new type of research organization. He spent much time trying to express and analyze, in a word, to "clarify" his own experience in order to make it transmissible to other contexts. For this reason, he devoted his presidential address to the American Sociological Association (1962b) to the sociology of sociology, dealing under this title with the problems raised by the institutionalization of social research. He was outspoken on this subject, trying throughout his career to find allies able to help him in his institutional enterprises (Pollak 1979).

The History of Empirical Sociology

I have already had occasion to mention Lazarsfeld's interest in the history of social research, a topic so organically related to his other intellectual interests that it needs only brief elaboration here.

Lazarsfeld (1961b) was of the opinion that the practices embodied in ESR had long existed as a trend in the past history of the social sciences and that he had himself integrated, systematized, completed, and finally institutionalized a number of ancient, if marginal, traditions. Some of these traditions had been lasting, others more ephemeral. Conring, Booth, Quetelet, and Le Play shared the idea that the systematic analysis of methodically collected data was an important dimension of social research. But many of these pioneers were interested more in the data themselves, in their informative, descriptive, and predictive dimension, than in using them for the purpose of understanding social action. The social sciences' main function was to provide information to help the decision makers, notably, the State (a vocable that is related etymologically to "statistics"). Others, like Durkheim and Tarde, though they too saw sociology as potentially "useful" socially, moved closer to Lazarsfeld's own conception of ESR. But they never conceived of building designs of observation or of collecting data to test specific assumptions. Some sociologists, like E. H. Sutherland, the American sociologist of crime (1937), became skeptical about the statistical data they had relied upon previously and turned to qualitative data. In contrast, the sociological pioneers of Chicago moved away from purely qualitative observations in the belief that standardized quantitative observations were a condition of objectivity and scientificity. On the side of the classical sociologists, Max Weber had seen the importance of empirical research and practiced it occasionally, but he considered this type of sociology marginal to his main intellectual interests. Quantitative analysis was only one episode in Durkheim's work, and Tarde never made any serious attempt to relate the theoretical models on human action which he developed, for example, in "La croyance et le désir" (1880) with statistical data. He explored them in an essentially descriptive fashion. On the whole, the field of empirical research had an anarchic past.

With ESR, Lazarsfeld believed he was "clarifying" the issues raised by this chaotic prehistory of empirical sociology, and by so doing, he would realize the potential of these heterogeneous traditions. He also hoped that this clarification would make ESR a permanent research style in sociology. Although he did not say it explicitly, he wanted not only to federate a number of traditions, but also to play the role of arbiter. He always insisted that quantitative and qualitative analyses should be combined: Analyze a contingency table, he advised, then go back to the deviant cases and use detailed interviews to see why they are atypical. Use statistical analysis when you can; be confident in quasi statistics when you can't.

Lazarsfeld felt strongly that by investigating and criticizing the prehistory of empirical sociology, he could consolidate the research style he himself advocated and eliminate the false discussions which had inhibited its development. Acknowledging the weaknesses of this pre-history, he also saw very clearly the strengths of the work done by Le Play, Quetelet, Lexis, or Durkheim. Beyond doubt, without his influence these pioneers would not be as widely read or commented upon as they are today. To use a musical comparison which Lazarsfeld himself might have endorsed, like a conductor who can make sensible the universality of a symphony, Lazarsfeld's readings of older socio-logical writers defined what was most seminal in their work.

In short, Lazarsfeld's interest in the history of empirical research closes a system of integrated intellectual interests: for methodology, for the uses of sociology, and for the institutionalization of ESR. His conviction of the importance of this critical-methodological reflection on the history of empirical sociology contributed to the development of this field, inspiring, for example, the works of Oberschall (1965) on German sociology and of Lécuyer (Lécuyer and Oberschall 1978) on French empirical social research.

Controversies

Like any innovator, Paul Lazarsfeld was confronted with objections both to his own work and to the ESR research style generally. His efforts to answer and meet them inspired, to a certain extent at least, some of his innovations. For this reason, it may be useful to outline some of the controversies raised by his work and by the research program he represents.

Very early, Blumer (1948) made the point that survey research is of little scientific interest because it deals with mere abstractions, that is, atomized individuals unrelated to any social context. Lazarsfeld always took such objections seriously, using them as a basis for "clari-fication" and further innovation. His answer to the type of objection Blumer raised was contextual analysis, a design of observation which, as we saw, proposes to characterize the individuals sampled in sur-veys, not only by personal variables such as age or number of years of formal education, but by variables characterizing their social con-text as well, for example, the proportion of churchgoers or the median income in the neighborhood, state, or country where they live.

Among the many criticisms he had to face, one in particular was repeated: The objection that statistical data are spurious, that statisti-cal analysis cannot lead to genuine causal statements, surfaced again and again. As I have indicated, it was formulated very early by Suther-

land (1937), reactivated by Douglas (1967), and by the ethnometho-
dologists and their followers in the sixties. The statistical data on
suicide used by Durkheim, contended Douglas, were spurious, so that
the causal statements drawn from them were themselves dubious. As
we have seen, to counter these arguments, Lazarsfeld developed the
idea of the "interchangeability of indices": Yes, the data may be spurious. But we can often have confidence in the existence of, say, a
positive correlation between two variables X and Y, even though we
may have serious doubts as to the way X and Y have been measured.
This was also Durkheim's diagnosis ([1897] 1960): Causal inference
is indeed difficult and one should be aware of the pitfalls one is exposed to on the way from correlational to causal statements; but in
many circumstances, the ambiguities can be eliminated. Halbwachs
(1930) made the same point. He was very critical of the causal interpretation Durkheim had presented of some of the correlations in his
Suicide. But these objections stimulated him to find ways of removing
the ambiguities. In so doing, he paved the way for Lazarsfeld's "multivariate analysis."

Another objection comes back in a mechanical fashion: People give
conventional answers to pollsters. True. But we know Lazarsfeld's
answer: Rather than throwing out the baby with the bathwater, culti-
vate the art of asking why.

It must also be recognized that many objections to Lazarsfeld's
work should be directed instead to the caricatures ESR has given birth
to. Merton (1949) proposed to call the confusion between means and
ends "ritualism." While, to Lazarsfeld himself, building typologies
was a means toward the understanding of human action, the "zealots"
of factor analysis or of the other methods of "data analysis" care little
about the reality, that is, the individual action, attitudes, and so forth,
behind the factors. Not infrequently, for example, sociologists of education who have found a correlation between orientation status and
level of education ignore the numerous deviant cases responsible for
the weakness of that correlation. In this way, statistical analysis serves
to legitimate a *feeling,* as Pareto would have said, rather than to
explain the reality of social action. This ideological use of statistical
analysis is as far as possible from Lazarsfeld's teachings. But it contributed to doubts about them.

Lazarsfeld's strength was also his main weakness: As I have mentioned, he failed to see that many analyses from classical macrosociology can be considered genuine scientific contributions in the sense
that they can be successfully submitted to the classical criteria more
or less implicitly used in the hard sciences to determine the validity

of a theory. Like theories developed by the hard sciences, analyses such as Tocqueville's explanation of American religiosity or Durkheim's explanation of magical beliefs are "generating models" (Boudon 1979; Pawson 1989), whose statements are logically or empirically acceptable and whose consequences are congruent with the relevant known facts. There is no reason to suggest, as Lazarsfeld did, that the "empirical" studies conducted by Weber were more scientific or more modern than the analyses of his sociology of religion.

As I suggested earlier, one reason Lazarsfeld probably did not see that many macrosociological analyses met his scientific ideals was that he rejected the "conventional psychology," the "abstract psychology" (Simmel 1907) used by macrosociologists, by historians, and in a more rigid fashion, by economists. He failed to see that, if Tocqueville or Weber are highly respected, this derives from the fact that for many puzzling phenomena they proposed explanations as valid and convincing as any scientific theory can be—though, to demonstrate their validity, an *explication de texte* is needed (Boudon 1990).

On the Selection

In making the selections for this volume, I have attempted to illustrate the diversity of Lazarsfeld's substantive, methodological, and organizational interests. This led me to exclude obviously important papers, for example, the autobiographical piece "An Episode in the History of Social Research," and others that are long, difficult to cut, and, moreover, accessible in previously published collections like Kendall's *The Varied Sociology of Paul Lazarsfeld* (1982).

The book is divided into three parts, corresponding to the three topics on which Lazarsfeld contributed most: ESR, methodology of social research, and history and sociology of social research. I have included in the first part five short articles illustrating the contributions of Lazarsfeld to the various substantive fields to which he devoted his energy: unemployment, audience research and mass communication, and voting behavior. Selections from the books on these fields, notably, *Personal Influence, The People's Choice,* and *Voting,* were also left aside, since they too are readily available. The second part provides an overview of Lazarsfeld's most significant methodological and technical innovations in sociology. It includes contributions belonging to the more epistemological aspects of Lazarsfeld's work as well. The last part covers papers on the history and sociology of social research which I found particularly insightful and important to the future of the social sciences. Needless to say, the texts included in this volume represent merely a tiny fraction of Lazarsfeld's output. I hope, however, this selection will help the reader to gain an accurate overview of his influential work.

References

Paul Lazarsfeld's works appear in a separate bibliography at the end of this book.

Barton, A. H. 1976. "Obituary Notice." In *Papers in Honor of P. F. Lazarsfeld*. New York: Columbia University.

Binet, A., and Simon, T. 1905. "Méthodes nouvelles pour le diagnostic du niveau intellectuel des anormaux." *L'Année Psychologique*.

Blumer, H. 1948. "Public Opinion and Public Opinion Polling." *American Sociological Review* 13:542–54.

Boudon, R. 1976. "In memoriam: Un marginal devenu un classique: P. Lazarsfeld." Article written on *Le Monde*'s request, printed in *Bulletin de la Société Française de Sociologie* 3, no. 8. Reprinted in *Sociologie,* edited by Van Meter. Paris: Larousse, 1992.

———. 1979. "Generating Models as a Research Strategy." In *Qualitative and Quantitative Social Research: Papers in Honor of P. F. Lazarsfeld,* edited by R. K. Merton, J. S. Coleman, and P. H. Rossi, pp. 51–64. New York: Free Press.

———. 1990. *L'art de se persuader.* Paris: Fayard. English edition forthcoming, Polity.

———. 1991a. "What Middle-Range Theories Are." *Contemporary Sociology* 20, no. 4: 519–22.

———. 1991b. "Weber's Notion of Rationality and the Theory of Rationality in Contemporary Social Sciences." In *Verstehen und Pragmatism,* edited by H. J. Helle, pp. 41ff. Frankfort: Peter Lang.

———. 1992. "Notice sur la vie et les travaux de Jean Stoetzel." *Discours de réception à l'Académie des Sciences Morales et Politiques,* February 18. Paris: Palais de l'Institut.

Clausen, J. A., and Kohn, M. L. 1954. "The Ecological Approach in Social Psychiatry." *American Journal of Sociology* 60: 140–49.

Coleman, J. S. 1961. *The Adolescent Society.* New York: Free Press.

———. 1972. "Paul Lazarsfeld's Work in Survey Research and Mathematical Sociology." In *Qualitative Analysis: Historical and Critical Essays,* pp. 395–409. Boston: Allyn and Bacon.

Douglas, J. 1967. *The Social Meanings of Suicide.* Princeton: Princeton University Press.

Durkheim, E. [1897] 1960. *Le suicide, étude sociologique.* Paris: PUF.

Flaubert, G. [1911] 1909–54. *Dictionnaire des idées reçues.* In *Oeuvres Complètes.* Paris. Published posthumously.

Gellner, E. 1987. "Zeno of Cracow or Revolution at Nemi or the Polish Revenge: A Drama in Three Acts." In *Culture, Identity, and Politics,* pp. 47–74. Cambridge: Cambridge University Press.

Girard, A. 1976. "Eloge de Paul F. Lazarsfeld." *Revue Française de Sociologie* 17, no. 3: 379–82.

Halbwachs, M. 1930. *Les causes du suicide*. Paris: Alcan.

Jakobson, R., and Halle, M. [1956] 1971. *Fundamentals of Language*. 2d ed. Paris: Mouton.

Kendall, P., ed. 1982. *The Varied Sociology of Paul F. Lazarsfeld*. New York: Columbia University Press.

Lécuyer, B. P., and Oberschall, A. R. 1978. "The Early History of Social Research." In *International Encyclopedia of Statistics*, pp. 1013–31. New York: Krower Mac-Millan.

Lipset, S. M. 1950. *Agrarian Socialism: The Cooperative Commonwealth Federation in Saskatchewan*. Berkeley: University of California Press.

Luckmann, T. 1991. *Die unsichtbare Religion*. Frankfort: Suhrkamp.

Lynd, R. S., and Lynd, H. 1929. *Middletown: A Study in American Culture*. New York: Harcourt and Brace.

McKenzie, R. T., and Tullock, G. 1975. *The New World of Economics: Exploration into the Human Experience*. London: Irwin.

Merton, R. K. [1949] 1961. "Continuities in the Theory of Social Structure and Anomie." In *Social Theory and Social Structure: Toward the Codification of Theory and Research*, pp. 161–94. Glencoe: Free Press.

Morgenstern, O., and Von Neumann, J. [1944] 1953. *Theory of Games and Economic Behavior*. Princeton: Princeton University Press.

Oberschall, A. R. 1965. *Empirical Social Research in Germany, 1848–1914*. Paris: Mouton; The Hague: Publications of the International Social Science Council.

Parsons, T. [1937] 1968. *The Structure of Social Action*. Glencoe: Free Press.

Pawson, R. 1989. *A Measure for Measures*. London: Routledge and Kegan Paul.

Pollak, M. 1979. "P. F. Lazarsfeld: Fondateur d'une multinationale scientifique." *Actes de la Recherche en Sciences Sociales* 25:45–59.

Schumpeter, J. [1954] 1972. *History of Economic Analysis*. London: Oxford University Press.

Simmel, G. 1907. *Die Probleme der Geschichtsphilosophie*. 3d ed. Leipzig: Duncker and Humblot.

Simon, H. A. 1957. *Models of Man: Social and Rational Mathematical Essays on Rational Human Behavior in a Social Setting*. New York: Wiley; London: Chapman and Hall.

Spearman, C. 1904. "General intelligence, Objectively Determined and Measured." *American Journal of Psychology* 15:201–93.

Sutherland, E. H. 1937. *Principles of Criminology*. Chicago: University of Chicago Press.

Tarde, G. 1880. "La croyance et le désir: Possibilité de leur mesure." *Revue Philosophique* 10: 150–264. Selected pages: "Belief and Desire," in *G. Tarde: On Communication and Social Influence*, edited and with an introduction by T. N. Clark (Chicago, University of Chicago Press, 1969), pp. 195–206; and *Essais et mélanges sociologiques* (Paris: Maloine, 1895), pp. 253–40, 264–75.

———. [1886] 1924. *La criminalité comparée*, 8th ed. Paris: Alcan.

Tocqueville, A. de [1835–40] 1952–70. *De la démocratie en Amérique*: In *Oeuvres Complètes*. Paris: Gallimard.

———. [1856] 1952–70. *L'ancien régime et la révolution*. In *Oeuvres Complètes*. Paris: Gallimard.

Thomas, W. I., and Znaniecki, F. 1918. *The Polish Peasant in Europe and America*. Boston: B. G. Badger.

Thurstone, L. L. 1947. *Multiple Factor Analysis.* Chicago: University of Chicago Press.

Zeisel, H. 1968. "L'école viennoise des recherches de motivation" *Revue Française de Sociologie* 9:3–12.

———. 1976–77. "In Memoriam: Paul Felix Lazarsfeld, 1901–1976." *Public Opinion Quarterly* 40, no. 4:556–57.

———. 1979. "The Vienna Years." In *Qualitative and Quantitative Social Research: Papers in Honor of P. F. Lazarsfeld,* edited by R. K. Merton, J. S. Coleman, and P. H. Rossi, pp. 10–22. New York: Free Press.

Zetterberg, H. 1954. *On Theory and Verification in Sociology.* Stockholm: Almquist and Wiksell; New York: Tressler Press. Reprinted in part in *The Language of Social Research,* edited by P. F. Lazarsfeld and M. Rosenberg. (Glencoe: Free Press, 1954), pp. 533–40.

I

SUBSTANTIVE SOCIAL RESEARCH

1

On Unemployment

Response to Deprivation

Our investigations in Marienthal began with visits to the homes of about one hundred families. The ostensible occasion was to ask them about their particular needs in connection with our proposed distribution of clothing. The observations and interviews recorded during these visits taught us much about the basic posture of the families. Whichever member of the family eventually came to collect the clothes was asked to tell us his life history, which was usually done willingly. These people were then observed in a variety of surroundings: at our courses and at political meetings we talked about them and with them, taking notes of everything as we went along. From these notes and from the special information obtained from meal records, time sheets, etc., detailed descriptions of each family emerged. Here are extracts from our files on two rather typical families.

Family 366: Husband, Wife, Five Children

5.0 consumer units altogether. Husband's unemployment relief: 49 schillings; wife's: 22.40 schillings every two weeks. Hence, total income per unit per day: 1.02 schillings. Have a garden allotment.

The apartment consists of one small room and a big kitchen with livingroom, nicely kept. Despite the lack of space everything is tidy. The children are clean and well cared for, the mother told us she

Reprinted with editorial adaptations from Marie Jahoda, Paul F. Lazarsfeld, and Hans Zeisel, *Marienthal: The Sociography of an Unemployed Community* (Chicago: Aldine Atherton, 1971), chap. 6, pp. 45–56. First published in 1933 as *Die Arbeitslosen von Marienthal: Ein Soziographischer Versuch über die Wirkungen langdauernder Arbeitslosigkeit* (Leipzig: Hirzel). There is some question as to when the Marienthal study first came out. Lazarsfeld himself stated that it was published in 1932 (1968c, p. 275). Marie Jahoda seems to confirm this when she notes in her essay honoring Lazarsfeld that the first edition of Marienthal "is now virtually unavailable as a result of the bookburnings episode in 1933" (in *Qualitative and Quantitative Social Research: Papers in Honor of Paul F. Lazarsfeld*, edited by R. K. Merton, J. S. Coleman, and P. H. Rossi (New York: Free Press, 1979), p. 4.

maintained and mended all their things herself. Nevertheless, the scarcity of clothing has already become acute. With regard to the clothing project, the mother asked whether she could get a coat for her fourteen-year-old son. They sold their radio a few months ago and stopped taking the paper because it was too expensive. The housework took a lot out of her, but sometimes her husband gave her a hand. The children too did their bit.

As to the husband, as long as he was at work he had been all right. He never put up with anything he did not like and always stood up for his rights. However, he had often been forced to change his place of work. He had been in the war, but that was by no means his worst time. In his leisure time he had been the leader of a band, an activity he pursued with all his heart. He still does this at times, but nowadays people just cannot afford to spend money on hearing music. He often used to go to concerts in Vienna. On Saturday evenings he went to the pub. Naturally, all this had now come to an end. He did not believe that things would ever get better in Marienthal. The government was to blame for the misery, therefore it was only fair for the government to support him. On the whole, he did not seem particularly dissatisfied. "One can get along like this as well. Bachelors are better off, they can emigrate. But with a family? . . . I would have liked to give the children an education, but as it is now we are glad we can still give them something to eat." The superintendent at the factory described the man as a particularly able worker.

The husband is a member of the Socialist Party though not much interested in politics. He likes to go for walks and often plays cards at the Workers' Club. His wife attended our pattern drawing course with great enthusiasm and did not miss a single lesson. She even mended her husband's suits. The packed lunch for her children of school age is not different on the day before the relief payment from the day after (bread and lard). One daughter who had taken various domestic jobs keeps coming back home because she feels happier here. The meal sheet shows that the family has meat (horse-meat goulash) once a week.

These records give some indications of the nature and extent of the reduction of wants: the family has given up their newspaper and radio; the husband does without trips to Vienna and visits to the pub: "One can get along like this as well." They economize above all on food and on the most basic clothing requirements. The higher education of the children, too, has to be sacrificed. At the price of all these restrictions the mother maintains the physical well-being of the children and an efficient level of housekeeping, which, for example, means a good packed lunch for the children every day.

Family 23: Husband, Wife, Three Children

Altogether 3.6 consumer units. Husband's unemployment relief: 47.40 schillings: wife's: 22.40 schillings every two weeks. Hence, income per unit per day: 1.38 schillings. Have a garden allotment.

The accommodations—big room, kitchen, anteroom—are well kept. The children are clean and well dressed. From the clothing project the wife wanted a jacket for her husband. She told us she could not go out to look for part-time work because the children were still too small. Her husband, she complained, does far too little to help her around the house. She does not believe that things will ever be different in Marienthal; she has no plans whatever. But they would get by somehow. Lunch was about to be served; it consisted of beans in gravy.

The husband wanted to become a butcher, but his father forbade it. Whereupon he declared that if he could not become a butcher he would not learn anything at all, and after leaving school went straight to the factory as an unskilled laborer. During the war he had been a prisoner in Russia. "I was better off there than anywhere." He could have stayed on "but after all, one belongs in one's own country." Since 1921 he had been living in Marienthal. His idea would have been to go back to Russia, but he was doing nothing about it. "We are still all right for the time being," he said.

As a child at home, the wife had been very unhappy. Her great desire had been to teach needlework, but that was out of the question. At seventeen she had her first child, which soon died. From then on she worked in the factory until it was shut down. She often quarrels with her husband because he does not bother about anything. It was not so bad before the unemployment years but now he was never at home. She so much wanted to go out once in a while. Sometimes she forced him to stay home and went off alone.

The husband spends most of his time at the Workers' Club or reading magazines and novels. He is always in a good mood and therefore very popular with everyone. He is often invited to parties at the pub because he is good fun. At home it is his wife who always has the last word, and she keeps demanding an exact account of how he spends his time. Once she remarked to us: "Somehow we will manage to keep alive; it can't finish us all off." This was very like the husband's statement, "Somehow we will manage to keep alive," an attitude of resigned composure that foreshadows the possibility of ever greater reductions of all their needs and demands. And as with everyone else in Marienthal, the major reduction cuts into the food budget.

On closer inspection, the various family records suggest a wide range of attitudes. The attitudes represented by the two families described above belong to the middle range, but one soon comes across deviations that call for more subtle differentiation. Let us begin with a divergence toward the positive side:

Family 141: Husband, Wife, Two Children

Altogether 3.0 consumer units. Husband's unemployment relief: 42.60 schillings, i.e., 1 schilling per unit per day. Have a garden allotment and keep rabbits.

The accommodations—one room, small bedroom, kitchen—are very well kept. The children are neatly dressed and give the impression of being well cared for. The wife apologized for not having cleaned up yet, although everything looked tidy enough. From the clothing project she wanted something for her nine-year-old boy. For lunch they had rabbit leftovers from Sunday.

Even in his apprentice years the husband had refused to be pushed around by the woman who employed him. During the war he was drafted. When he came up for promotion, he turned it down because he was a convinced pacifist. He had been taken prisoner in Italy and learned the language with great facility. After coming back to Marienthal he married a girl he had known at school. At the factory he soon became the chosen spokesman of his colleagues, and later head of the work council. He always held several different political posts. His idea had been to take a course in tailoring and open his own shop in Vienna. His son, too, is to learn to be a tailor. He is a passionate reader. He would have liked to emigrate to France, but his wife had been against it. Now he was glad that he had not gone, because his colleagues had bad luck there.

He thought the present situation quite bearable. His political job keeps him sufficiently busy because everyone comes asking for his advice, and at any rate they do not expect to starve to death quickly. Colleagues and superiors always held him in high regard. Even today he is still popular everywhere. His attitude is basically optimistic.

The wife brought the children repeatedly to the medical consultations and obeyed strictly all the doctor's orders. She also attended almost all other events in Marienthal. There were still a number of good clothes left which the husband himself altered if necessary.

Two things in particular are worth noting about this family record compared with the previous two: the meticulous care given to the household and the atmosphere of contentment that still emanates from the family. This is not a case of muddling through but still a rather purposeful existence. The husband finds the present situation tolerable, is optimistic, and has a number of plans for himself as well as for the education of his son. This family's orientation is toward the future.

The situation is different in the following families whose attitude diverged negatively from the average. This attitude can take two different forms. Family 363 is an example of the first:

Family 363: Husband, Wife, Four Children

Altogether 4.2 consumer units. Wife's unemployment relief has recently been withdrawn, allegedly because the husband should be able to find work on the land. Hence, income at present: nil (according to their statement). They keep rabbits.

The accommodations—a hut with one room, kitchen, and ante-room—are in a terrible state; very dirty and untidy. Children and parents have virtually nothing to wear. Mother and children are dirty; the entire household is slovenly. Unwearable shreds of clothing are littered around. The wife complains that the husband does not help at all and is merely a burden. From the clothing project she just wanted "something warm"—it did not matter for whom.

The wife had a hard adolescence; immediately after leaving school she started work in a factory. She came to Marienthal in 1925. Her marriage used to be better; now she is very unhappy. The husband is not entitled to unemployment relief because he had never worked regularly. Since unemployment began he has not bothered any longer about finding work and leaves everything to the wife. He often goes to the movies and "peddles" all her belongings in various deals, or else he spends his time gossiping and playing cards. The wife even has to chop the firewood herself.

"I couldn't care less now," she told us. "If I could hand the children over to the welfare people I would gladly do so."

The couple is known for its quarrelsomeness. The wife is not too popular. The husband, whom the war left an invalid, is not a bad

fellow, just incapable of doing anything. His wife is more intelligent
and takes advantage of this.

Here is a type of behavior quite different from that of any family
described so far. There is no longer any attempt to weigh different
needs against each other and establish a rank order of importance.
This family gives the impression of letting itself go completely; there
is nothing left to hold on to. The children and the home, usually the
last to fall into neglect, are in a bad state.

The next family represents a second type of negative deviation from
the average:

Family 467: Husband, Wife, Two Children

Altogether 3.0 consumer units. Husband's unemployment relief: 42
schillings, i.e., 1.0 schilling per unit per day. Have a garden allotment.

The wife was very nervous. When we visited her she immediately
started to cry and seemed terribly depressed. The accommodations—
one room, small bedroom, kitchen—are very clean and well kept. The
clothes of the whole family seemed to be clean and in good condition.
From the clothing project the husband wanted clothes for the children.
He said: "The most terrible thing is that one can't offer the children
anything at all." He was afraid they might become retarded.

The husband had always been very demanding in life, had wanted
to get on, and had been full of self-confidence and family pride. He
studied and worked and always asserted himself, so much so that
when the lay-offs began he was convinced that nothing could happen
to him. All during the first months he believed that a man of his ability
could not come to grief. During the first year of his unemployment,
he wrote 130 applications for jobs, all of which remained unanswered.
Now he is at the end of his tether. He told us that he spends half his
day in bed now in order to save breakfast and heating. He hardly
ever leaves the house. He is in utter despair: "It can't get better, only
worse." He hopes everything will collapse. "I could bear everything
if only the children could be spared."

There are still some good clothes around from former times, and
the wife is very concerned about the children, who are regularly sent
to a children's holiday home. The husband sits all day at home and
does nothing at all. He has hardly any more contacts with other
people.

The behavior of this family is characterized by a high degree of
orderliness. Despite their economic decline, a careful attempt is made

to run the household as well as possible. But this orderliness is, to an unusual extent, combined with expressions of despair. It is the vestige of an ordered life that distinguishes this family from the previous one; the mood of extreme depression distinguishes it from the main group.

We have presented, so far, four different attitudes. It is not always easy to separate them clearly; in particular, it is not easy to find appropriate names for them. It will be useful therefore, to restate once more the criteria that lead us to place a particular family in one category or another.

The most common basic attitude in Marienthal, the one most visible at first glance, is the one described in the first two family records. It is an attitude of drifting along, indifferently and without expectations, accepting a situation that cannot be changed. With it goes a relatively calm general mood, and even sporadically recurring moments of serenity and joy. But the future, even in the shape of plans, has no longer any place in the thought or even dreams of these families. All this seems to us best characterized by the word *resignation*. Perhaps this does not entirely tally with ordinary usage; normally the word does not convey the transitory picture of contentment which these families sometimes present. However, no other word seems to come so near to describing the reduced demands and the lack of expectations that characterize this attitude to life. In all these cases we found a fairly well-ordered household, and children who were well looked after. If we were to single out from this description the criteria which lead us to categorize a family as *resigned* and summarize them epigrammatically, we would say: no plans, no relation to the future, no hopes, extreme restriction of all needs beyond the bare necessities, yet at the same time maintenance of the household, care of the children, and an overall feeling of relative well-being.

This attitude must be distinguished from that exemplified by family 141: with that type of family one has the impression of greater activity. Their households are as well ordered as those in the *resigned* category, but their needs are less restricted, their horizon wider, their energy greater. Again, it was not easy to find an appropriate expression for this attitude. Eventually, we decided on the word *unbroken* and posited the following criteria for this attitude: maintenance of the household, care of the children, subjective well-being, activity, hopes and plans for the future, sustained vitality, and continued attempts to find employment.

The two remaining attitude groups can both be called *broken,* yet the difference between them is so great that we decided to treat each as a category by itself. The distinction goes to the area in which the state of collapse manifests itself. In family 363 it affected the running of the household, in family 467 it affected the mental outlook.

Let us first look at the latter category, whose outward mode of living is not much different from the resigned but unbroken homes. The difference lies in how they subjectively experience this reality. These people are in complete despair, and from this basic outlook the category receives its name. Like the *unbroken* or *resigned* families, they keep their households in order and look after their children. But we must add: despair, depression, hopelessness, a feeling of the futility of all efforts, and therefore no further attempts to find work or to ameliorate the situation; instead, constant comparisons of the present with a better past.

The fourth attitude, finally, differs from the others by the absence of an ordered household. Apathetic and indolent, these families let things take their course without making any attempt to salvage something from the collapse. We call this category *apathetic*. Its main characteristic is complete passivity, the absence of any effort. Home and children are dirty and neglected, the mental outlook is not desperate but simply indifferent. No plans are made, no hopes maintained. The household is in such disarray that it no longer satisfies even the most immediate needs; it becomes completely irrational. In this category we find the alcoholics of Marienthal. Family life begins to disintegrate; quarrels, begging, and stealing are some of the symptoms. Nobody plans for a more distant future, not even for the days and hours immediately ahead. The relief payment is always spent during the very first days without much thought as to what will happen during the rest of the two weeks.

One characteristic of three of the four categories is careful maintenance of the budget. From our conversations with the women, from the way they could remember all the relevant figures, we could tell that they were constantly preoccupied with working out how to spend the little money they had. This is why we were able to [make] some kind of survey of their budgets, although in most cases we could not persuade them to keep household accounts.

But it is equally significant that amid this strict economy we often came across traces of quite irrational spending. Sometimes these "splurges" are probably the first signs of disintegration, but sometimes they simply form the last links with the richer experiences of the past; it is not always possible to decide which. Here are some instances of surprising and seemingly irrational spending.

Flowers are growing on many of the garden allotments, although potatoes and other vegetables are vital; beds that could yield some

160 pounds of potatoes are filled instead with carnations, tulips, roses, bell flowers, pansies, and dahlias. When we asked why this was so, we were told: "One can't just live on food, one needs also something for the soul. It is so nice to have a vase of flowers at home."

A family whose claims to unemployment relief expired a year ago, who for lack of money had to give up, for instance, all sugar and only uses saccharine, whose children are totally neglected, one day bought a cardboard picture of Venice from a peddler, albeit for only 30 groschen.

Another family, living only on emergency assistance, spent good money on mourning clothes after someone in the family died. And a fifty-year-old woman suddenly decided to buy a pair of curling tongs on installments.

Such episodes are frequently bound up with frustrated love for the children. A twelve-year-old boy who, on the day before the biweekly payments appeared at school without even a bite of bread, was given on the following day a salami sandwich, two doughnuts, and a piece of chocolate.

The newspaper vendor who also sells picture books and calendars told us that the sale of picture books had by no means dropped as much as the sale of calendars. He had even gained some new women customers, who on a birthday or other festive occasion and following a sudden impulse, bought a picture book as a present for a child.

Perhaps the first and last examples are to be interpreted as a yearning for some remains of joy; some of the others are possibly symptoms of dissolution. At any rate, these examples should remind us that even the restricted modes of living in Marienthal have not yet reached complete uniformity. Nevertheless, the totality of life in Marienthal is correctly described by the patterns that characterize the four basic attitudes.

2

On Communication

Audience Research

The efforts to determine how many people read a magazine or how many listen to a radio program are historically linked with applied psychology. The first systematic readership survey was done by George Gallup when he was teaching psychology in Iowa and the first systematic work in radio measurement was carried out by two Ohio psychologists, Lumley and Stanton. Since then, more and more precise methods of measurement have been developed and a large mass of substantive results has been accumulated. It would be safe to say that there is now hardly an area of social behavior for which we have more copious and more exact information.[1]

It is worth while to reflect for a moment on the reasons why so much attention is given to a topic which does not seem of too great general importance. The explanation lies in the curious economic structure of the communications industry, which must serve two masters while other industries serve only one. If a soap manufacturer wants to make a profit he has to be sure that people buy his soap. If a broadcaster wants to make money he has to be sure that people listen to his programs, but he must also prove this fact to the soap manufacturer or the latter will not advertise over his station. Added to this is the fact that strong competition between the various media makes it doubly necessary to prove the size of the audience by a variety of very fine measurements. (In line with general practice this paper applies the term audience to radio, magazines, and newspapers, as well as to movies.)

Detailed consideration cannot be given here to problems of mea-

Reprinted with editorial adaptations from "Communication Research and the Social Psychologist," in *Current Trends in Social Psychology,* edited by W. Dennis, R. Lippitt, et al. (Pittsburgh: University of Pittsburgh Press, 1951), vol. 2, pp. 218–73 [233–48]. This essay took shape as a series of eight lectures given March 4 and 5, 1948, at the College of the University of Pittsburgh under the auspices of the Department of Psychology.

surement, but one case might serve to show the complexity of the field. The earliest measurement figures available for magazines were provided by the Audience Bureau of Circulation (ABC). The ABC is a co-operative venture which established complicated machinery to obtain reliable statistics on the number of copies each issue of a magazine sells. After some time it became apparent that mere circulation figures were not sufficient because one magazine was being read by a number of people. Ways were devised, therefore, to count the number of readers instead of the number of copies sold, and magazines were then grouped according to the number of readers they have per copy. But now the question arose of what a reader is. Is a person who just glances at a copy to be classed as a reader, or one who reads five items, or fifteen items, in an issue? It became necessary to find out which items and how many items in an issue people have read. This in turn led to further methodological difficulties. If a magazine, for instance, carried a serial story in several installments, how could one be sure that the people who were interviewed did not confuse one installment with another? Special "confusion tests" were developed to examine this factor of memory.

In this respect radio research had a special advantage. The memory factor could be eliminated by inserting a mechanical device in the radio set which would record the stations to which the radio was tuned. At the present time, magazine researchers are experimenting with chemicals by which one could measure the amount of time a magazine was open at a particular page and thereby exposed to light. There is, however, even a further difficulty which arises. It may be that people are more influenced by the advertising in a magazine if it is strongly identified with the magazine content. Therefore, one must discover the type of content and the balance of content which people prefer.

A similar development took place in research in the other mass media. It requires a two-term course to teach and discuss all the techniques of audience measurement. In the present discussion we shall be mainly interested in the findings which these audience surveys have brought about rather than in the technical problems of measurement. Efforts will be made to organize the research results around such generalizations as might be of interest to the social psychologist, or as might require his helpful interpretation or indicate new areas of research to him.

The criteria of classification of the audiences of the various media can be roughly divided into three parts. One is based on what is usually called *primary* characteristics, such as sex, age, education, and economic level. The second group might be called *psychological* characteristics, which are based on scores on personality tests, or attitudes on a variety of issues, and the like. Finally, people can be classified by their other *"communication habits"* and by this means we can compare, for instance, the reading habits of people with their listening habits.

Primary Characteristics of Various Audiences

One must distinguish between the printed media and the spectator media. Obviously the audience of the former need a certain amount of reading skill, but practically everyone can be part of a radio or movie audience. We would expect, therefore, to find rather sharp correlations between magazine reading and formal education. Varying somewhat according to the types of questions asked, it can be said that about two-thirds of the population read magazines with some regularity. The following table shows how this frequency varies among three educational levels.[2]

PROPORTION OF MAGAZINE READERS IN THREE EDUCATIONAL GROUPS AS REPORTED BY TWO STUDIES (NORC SURVEY AND MAGAZINE AUDIENCE BUREAU)

	NORC	MAB
College	86%	92%
High School	68	85
Less Than High School	43	48

Other studies have used more specific indices, such as the number and types of magazines read, with education always playing the expected dominant role.

When radio entered the scene, many educators took the optimistic view that this situation might be corrected with the new medium. All the people who, due to social circumstances, could not acquire much formal reading skill, would now quench their thirst for knowledge by listening to educational radio programs. This expectation was not fulfilled. All subsequent research studies have shown that listening to serious programs is also highly related to education. The following table is based on a survey in which people were asked to select their favorite radio programs from a long list. Taking public affairs discussions and classical music as the most typical representatives of serious programs, we can see here how the popularity of such fare increases with increased education. To indicate the reliability of these results, two national NORC samples taken at two different times are reported.

	Public Affairs		Classical Music	
	1945	1947	1945	1947
College	55%	63%	54%	54%
High School	40	43	32	27
Less Than High School	33	35	21	22

At least two lines of interpretation seem indicated. People with little formal education lack reading skill but they probably also do not have what might be called "conception skill"; they are not likely to be found in the audience for serious subject matter even if listening alone is required. In regard to classical music an added sociological element may be involved. In the so-called higher economic strata respect for good music and similar matter is imbued with prestige; there are pressures and rewards operating to make people listen to, and perhaps in the end to like, good music. The same is not true for the less educated low-income groups.

Obviously, this field is open for the social psychologist to develop more refined interpretations. Deviant cases would be one important avenue of further study. There are many people who do not follow the trend and in spite of little formal education are very much interested in serious radio programs. Only a very few beginnings in studying these exceptions have been made thus far and a detailed examination would be very desirable.

This matter is of considerable cultural importance. Documentary films and serious radio programs could do a great deal to raise the cultural level of a country if people could become more interested in them. But we must determine how we can overcome the resistance of just those groups which are most recalcitrant and which the educators most want to reach. We cannot do like the early Tudor king who, wanting his subjects to read one of his theoretical tracts, made arrangements with the Catholic Church to grant indulgences to the readers. Today psychological research must somehow deal with the problem of reaching the lower educated strata through the use of the new forms of mass education which the spectator media have developed.

While the relation between education and communication habits is probably more significant socially, the role of age is statistically more spectacular. Wherever it is possible to classify an item as light entertainment, studies show that its audience will be heavily drawn from the younger age groups. The following table provides two examples of age differentials in audiences of such light fare. The first two columns give the proportion in each age group which chooses popular music as one of its favorite types of radio program. The third column represents the proportion claiming at least once-a-week movie attendance. The data are from the two NORC surveys mentioned above.

PROPORTION OF PEOPLE FOR WHOM POPULAR MUSIC IS A FAVORITE RADIO
PROGRAM AND WHO GO TO THE MOVIES AT LEAST ONCE A WEEK

Age	Popular Music		Movie Attendance	
	1945	1947	1945	1947
21–29	72%	62%	48%	39%
30–39	50	52	28	25
40–49	41	47	27	21
50+	22	26	13	23

It is probable that something akin to "vitality" plays a part in the younger age group's preference for popular music. When it comes to movies, another factor—that of the generally different type of social life indulged in by different age groups—must be added.

Additional findings corroborate the age differential still further. All studies show a clear negative correlation between youth and interest in public affairs, young people being less concerned. The results of magazine research have not been compiled in a manner that makes for easy comparison, but again all the indications seem to be that, with increased age, interest tends to shift from lighter fiction to heavier nonfiction subject-matter.

Whatever the explanation of these differentials, we have here again an area where the results of communication research can be of concrete value to the social psychologist. There are few data available to him as highly related to age as these, and his investigation of various age-phases might be greatly enhanced by their incorporation.

A third primary characteristic, the difference between men and women, is also of significance. In the case of all media, women show considerably less interest in public affairs. Women in the main read fiction in magazines while men are much more inclined to read nonfictional material. Women, of course, also provide the vast majority of the daytime radio audience. As a result, radio during the day has developed a large supply of programs especially addressed to women, such as daytime serials, woman commentators, and home economics programs. It is interesting to speculate on the possibility that daytime radio tends to reinforce the difference in the interests of men and women which the social and economic structure of our society has developed.[3-7]

One further primary characteristic has been studied in considerable detail, the difference between urban and rural dwellers. For many years, Professor Wahn of Manhattan College, Kansas, and Professor Summers of Ohio State University have made periodic surveys in a number of Midwestern states in which they compare radio listening habits of farmers and urbanites. Unfortunately the results have not been summarized for general publication but the authors' reports are available to students especially interested in this aspect of the problem.

Personality Characteristics

On several occasions efforts have been made to determine the relation of personality characteristics to communication patterns, and this again is an area capable of great expansion by the psychologist. The study of daytime serial audiences is an example of the interesting beginning that has been made.[8] About half of the women at home during the day are avid fans of these descriptions of people in everyday life eternally getting into trouble, getting out of trouble, and immediately getting into trouble again. The other half of the available female audience dislike these programs as much as their friends are absorbed by them. Great efforts have been made to discover what psychological differences exist between those who do and those who do not listen to the serials. Are the fans more introverted and therefore more likely to live in a world of fantasy than of fact? Are they much more frustrated, more dissatisfied with their life? Are they less attractive and therefore more isolated socially? At one time or another every conceivable personality test has been applied to these two types of women. The results so far have been disappointing, but this does not mean that eventually a valid psychological explanation will not be found.

A similar effort was made at the time when the Orson Welles' broadcast on the invasion from Mars drove thousands of people into panic and flight from their homes.[9] Listeners who became frightened were compared with listeners who had the presence of mind to check and who found that the story of the invasion was merely a dramatic play. Thematic apperception tests were given to the two groups of

listeners following the hypothesis that the degree of general excitabil-
ity would be related to the two types of reaction. Again the results
were negative, but again it is not a closed chapter.

Nearest to a finding of passable caliber emerged from a comparison
of women who do and do not listen to the radio while at home in the
morning. In one study the women who did not listen while they did
their housework stated quite definitely that "it is difficult to do two
things at one time," revealing that they had so-called "one-track
minds." Obviously it requires further investigation to state clearly
what the psychological characteristics of such mentalities are.

In general, there seems to be practically no correlation between
personality characteristics and communication habits, and it is necessary to speculate on this fact. It might well be that the notion of
"interest" is less of a psychological category than we usually assume.
Perhaps what a person is interested in does not depend on his personality but on his position in the social system. People are interested in
the things which the groups to which they belong believe to be worth
while. Group stratification in our society is along economic, educational, sex, and age lines; so perhaps it is not surprising that these
primary characteristics are related to a greater degree to communication habits than are personality traits.

There are additional factors which help explain this low relationship of communication habits and personality traits. In all the fields
that have been touched by communications research the self-selection
of audiences plays a considerable role. People with political convictions read the newspapers that correspond to their opinions. People
with hobbies read the sections of the newspaper which report on these
hobbies most fully. This seemingly trivial observation becomes more
interesting as we add to it certain corollary findings which can be
gleaned from a variety of studies. It has been found, for instance, that
people are inclined to read the same news items in newspapers which
they have already heard discussed on the radio. In general, they do
not look for information on new topics in magazines but for more
information on topics with which they are already acquainted. When
a magazine or radio program occasionally has the purpose of telling
of the contributions of a specific minority to American culture, a large
proportion of the audience usually consists of the minority which is
being praised. The audience to which the content is being directed
and which presumably needs conversion is largely missing.[10]

If we accept the overwhelming evidence of the self-selectiveness
and circular reinforcement of audiences we may go a step further to
indicate an important element in this selection. In the further examina-

tion of such data the student is struck by a strong projective factor in audience behavior. When people are asked to name their favorite movie stars, the majority of men mention actors and the majority of women select actresses. Detailed studies of the readers of magazine stories have shown a distinct conformity between the content of the story and the structure of the audience. If the story is set in a small town more people coming from small towns will read it. The average age of readers varies markedly and is parallel to the age of the hero. Pictures of men in printed media are more often noticed by men, while women are more likely to look at pictures of women.

In general, then, people look not for new experiences in the mass media but for a repetition and an elaboration of their old experiences into which they can more easily project themselves. If we assume then that the types of experience they have had are determined more by their social roles and context rather than by their psychological traits, it is not surprising that we find primary characteristics so dominant in the correlations which communications research has unearthed.

It should be noticed, however, that this general consideration calls for refinement by the social psychologist. For one thing not even these correlations are very high and the exceptions deserve a great deal of consideration. It would not be difficult to pick out people who prefer subject matter which complements rather than projects their own experiences. How do such supplementary interests develop, and in what type of people do they occur? There are numerous people who lack formal education, who live in very uninspiring environments, and who still are awakened through some medium of mass communication to develop strong educational interests of their own. A detailed study of the exceptions to all the findings reported here, if guided by available knowledge and general theoretical consideration, should greatly advance the field which the communications researchers have recently opened up.

In the second place, the problem has not been solved when we say that the social role rather than the psychological characteristics of individuals determines their communication habits. This is an oversimplification of the matter, since the fact remains that individuals partly select their social roles. The interaction between what we have distinguished as primary and psychological characteristics is another part of the field where the social psychologist could be of help.

Interrelation between Various Kinds of Audience Behavior

It is not surprising that people who do not read magazines also do not read books, for reading skill is required in both activities. But even if education and similar factors are kept constant, many marked relationships remain. A list of examples would read as follows:

> People who listen to news commentators on the radio are also more likely to read news magazines and, in smaller towns, to subscribe to the Sunday edition of metropolitan newspapers.
>
> People who read the more serious type of magazine are also more likely to listen to the more serious type of radio program.
>
> Women who listen a great deal to the radio during the day also listen more during the evening.
>
> Women who are interested in the "true fiction" type of magazine are also more interested in daytime serials and prefer the romantic type of movies.
>
> People who never go to the movies at all are also likely to listen less to the radio.
>
> If a book has been turned into a movie the people who have read the book are more likely to see the movie and vice versa.

Some of these findings might sound obvious, but a rather important generalization can be derived from them. On mere speculative grounds one might assume that the mass media have to compete for audiences. If a person listens continuously to radio news his interest might be satisfied and he would not be available as a reader of a news magazine. But as an over-all fact, the opposite seems to prevail. One medium benefits by the interests which another medium stimulates. This mutually compensatory character of the mass media has a number of interesting social implications which have occasionally been discussed in the literature.[11]

From a psychological point of view the examples just given suggest strongly the application of factor analysis to communication behavior. A few preliminary studies make it appear quite likely that a number of basic factors could be found. One is likely to be a rather general element related to whether a person is more interested in individualized activities or more inclined to matters requiring mass participation. Another is the factor of general "seriousness," which determines whether a person is mainly interested in fiction material or is inclined to read and listen to such things as public affairs, popular science, biography, and so on. In radio there seems to be the tendency for those who are interested in music not to be interested in verbal programs, and vice versa. All this, however, is still very much a matter of speculation, because unfortunately little work has yet been done.[12]

One might, in this context, include also the relation between supply and demand in the mass media. It is by no means true that people have definite desires and pick out what they "need" from the available supply of programs, magazines, and so on. It seems rather that the supply itself *creates* the demand. There exist interesting findings, for instance, on the importance of availability of the communication in determining the size of its audience. In one study, Waples ascertained what books students were interested in and then put the less desired ones within easy reach in the dormitory, while the books which the students had designated as more attractive were placed at some distance. In general, the students tended to read the books which were easily available.[13]

Similar observations have been made by broadcasters. Every radio program has a certain "rating" indicating the proportion of radio sets that are tuned into it. A similar rating can be derived for a certain time spot: the proportion of radio sets which are tuned in at a given hour of the day. In a stable radio schedule it is of course not possible to unravel what part in a specific rating is played by the attraction of the program as against the role of daily listening habits. But sometimes a program is transferred to another time and then the change in rating can be used to weigh the importance of the two factors. The general finding is that on the average the time spot is more important than the content of the program itself, although there are some notable exceptions. Social psychologists might find such data worthy of their more careful attention.

Altogether, in fact, social psychologists might find it worth while to give more attention to the statistical data which the radio industry can offer in this respect. It is possible, for instance, to take a certain program type such as the quiz program and count the number of hours weekly such programs are offered. We also know the approximate number of people who listen to them. By a time-series analysis one could study how change in supply and change in extent of listening are related. In some preliminary calculations, Rashevsky has come to expect a certain regularity of changes in supply and demand which seems to be justified by the facts.[14]

The whole topic is of special importance for one who is interested in using the mass media for mass education. The argument against more serious movies and broadcasts is usually that people don't want them. The counterargument is that if more of them were available more people would develop an interest in them. In England there is more listening to serious programs than in America. Is this due to a national difference or to the fact that the British broadcasting system provides serious programs more systematically? If the latter is the case, then an important social question can be raised. Could we get in this country a more serious level of listening if the broadcasters considered "raising the level of taste" one of their responsibilities? The social scientist could provide important data by systematic experimentation.

It was mentioned before that lower educated people do not like to listen to serious programs even if all efforts are made by dramatizations and other techniques to make them easily understandable. Suppose under some pretext we were to pay lower educated subjects to listen to a list of such programs for three months. After this experimental period was over, we could watch to see how many would keep on listening to some of these programs of their own free will. If after overcoming their initial resistance, the people who need radio education most would really acquire a taste for it, an important argument would be made in favor of those who desire a more serious program schedule.

Notes

1. Blankenship, A. B. (editor). *How to Conduct Consumer and Opinion Research.* New York: Harper & Brothers, 1946.

2. Lazarsfeld, P. F. and Field, H. *The People Look at Radio.* Chapel Hill: University of North Carolina Press, 1946.

3. Anonymous. The continuing study of newspaper reading. The Advertising Research Foundation, 1945.

4. Anonymous. Continuing study of magazine audiences. *Life,* Reports, 6 and 8.

5. Beville, H. M., Jr. The ABCD's of Radio Audiences. *Public Opinion Quarterly,* 4, 1940, 4: 195–206.

6. Lazarsfeld, P. F. Audience research in the movie field. *The Annals of the American Academy of Political and Social Science,* 1947.

7. Lazarsfeld, P. F. and Wyant, R. Magazines in 90 cities: who reads what. *Public Opinion Quarterly,* 1937, 4: 29–41.

8. Herzog, H. Psychological gratification in daytime listening, Newcomb, Hartley, and others (editors). *Readings in Social Psychology.* New York: Henry Holt, 1947.

9. Cantril, H., Gaudet, H., and Herzog, H. *Invasion from Mars.* Princeton: Princeton University Press, 1940.

10. Lazarsfeld, P. F. *Radio and the Printed Page.* New York: Duell, Sloan & Pearce, 1940.

11. Beville, H. M., Jr. The challenge of the new media—television, F. M., and facsimile. *Journalism Quarterly,* 1948, 25: 3–11.

12. Robinson, W. S. Preliminary report on factors in radio listening. *Journal of Applied Psychology,* 1939, 23.

13. Waples, D. and Tyler, R. W. *What People Want to Read About: A Study of Group Interests and a Survey of Problems in Adult Reading.* Chicago: American Library Association and the University of Chicago Press.

14. Rashevsky, N. *Mathematical Theory of Human Relations.* Mathematical Biophysics Monograph No. 3, Principia Press, Bloomington, Indiana.

3

On Consumer Behavior

The Analysis of Consumer Actions

The Need for a Systematic Approach

The techniques of research may be divided into two broad classes: we shall call them "master techniques" and "servant techniques." The master techniques are those used in planning and organizing research, in controlling it, in interpreting the findings. The servant techniques are employed in the actual operations of digging up facts and assembling them.

As one looks over the market research field the question arises whether the master techniques and the servant techniques have received their respective dues. It is our strong suspicion that attention has focussed disproportionately upon the servant techniques—upon the details of gathering and tabulating bits of information. Certainly these details are crucially important. The formulation of master techniques may prove even more important. The latter go far toward determining the nature of the servant techniques to be employed; they supply the standards for judging how well the subordinate tools are functioning; they provide the rational framework within which the research materials are given orientation and meaning.

There is little doubt what the servant techniques of market research include: procedures for constructing questionnaires, conducting interviews, choosing statistical samples, tabulating inquiries, extrapolating from trend curves, formulating buying power indexes, and so on. These matters have been extensively and ably discussed in a number of places. Certain special problems of these servant techniques we shall consider later. For the moment, however, we shall direct our attention to the master techniques.

Reprinted from Arthur Kornhauser and Paul F. Lazarsfeld, "The Analysis of Consumer Actions," in *The Language of Social Research,* edited by Paul F. Lazarsfeld and Morris Rosenberg (Glencoe: Free Press, 1955), pp. 392–404. First published in 1935 as "The Techniques of Market Research from the Standpoint of a Psychologist," *Institute of Management* 16:3–15, 19–21.

First of all, what are they? The master techniques of the engineer are his mathematical and physical principles, his procedures for testing and experimentation, his professional engineering knowledge as a whole. The master techniques of the physician lie in the fields of physiology, bacteriology, and pathology. And what of the market researcher? What for him corresponds to the scientific equipment of the engineer or the doctor? Our answer—and we shall try to support it in the following pages—is knowledge of psychology—especially the psychological analysis of action.

We recognize fully the present limitations of psychological knowledge. We are not able to offer it as an adequate answer to the market research man's prayers. All that we are suggesting is: first, that market research needs general, orienting, intellectual techniques, even more at the present time than it requires everyday digging tools; and second, that these larger techniques are supplied in considerable part, though not at all exclusively, by psychology. *We suggest simply that a systematic view of how people's market behavior is motivated, how buying decisions are arrived at, constitutes a valuable aid in finding one's way around midst the thousand and one questions of specific procedures and interpretations in market research.*

This need for a psychological view grows out of the very nature of market research. For that research is aimed predominantly at *knowledge by means of which to forecast and control consumer behavior.* It is a matter of ascertaining sales opportunities in order that these opportunities may be utilized and developed on the basis of the facts. Sales opportunities exist—or fail to exist—in people's minds. Hence the task is essentially psychological. It is a matter of gaining detailed understanding of specific human reactions.

There is, to be sure, another type of market research. It makes use of census data, descriptions of what people buy, and purely statistical predictions based on past buying. These methods assume that people will continue to buy as they have bought, or that they will continue to change in the directions in which they have been moving. The techniques of these statistical predictions lie mainly outside the scope of this paper, though, even in these studies, the collection of data and their classification frequently present problems that are psychologically challenging.

Most market research goes beyond purely statistical predictions. It seeks underlying explanations or interpretations. For guidance in these studies psychological master techniques appear indispensable. Systematic explanatory concepts should serve, here, to help market inquiries avoid fragmentary and distorted market pictures. They should encourage continuing research which goes beyond the first partial and trivial answers, too often accepted as though they were grand final conclusions.

Clearly the point of view here suggested is in sharp contrast to that which insists on the exclusive use of objective data; only the facts of buying behavior! But what does one do with the facts? How does one know what facts are worth gathering? How tell what further types of evidence to seek? How fit the picture together? How interpret? How put meaning into the material? Questions like these point unmistakably to the need that is here emphasized.

We turn, then, to consider what the psychologist can offer toward the filling of that need.

An Action Schema

What we offer is an analysis of action—an analysis of how the individual's market behavior is determined.

Any bit of action is determined on the one hand by the total make-up of the person at the moment, and on the other hand by the total situation in which he finds himself. This relationship is represented in Figure 1. The action is a joint product of factors in the individual and factors in the situation. Explanations must always include both the objective and the subjective, and these are always in inseparable interrelationship. Hunger and available food are equally indispensable causes of eating. Likewise the advertisement which attracts one's attention and the subjective interest, attitude, or habit, which produces the attentive response.

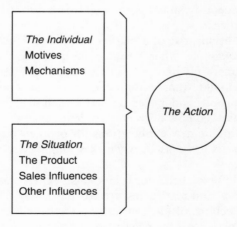

Figure 1

What a person *is* at any moment governs what he *does in the given circumstances*. What he "is," on the side of action possibility, comprises "motives" and "mechanisms." Hunger or a desire for a new red necktie are motives; the ability to walk, used in entering a restaurant, say, or the mental equipment used in reading an advertisement or in recalling one's lack of funds, are mechanisms. These mechanisms, it should be noticed, are not independent of the motives, but are directed by them. Motives and mechanisms are different aspects of the same total individual make-up which determines action at any moment.

By "motives" we mean to refer to the set of inner guiding processes which determine the movement of behavior toward ends or goals. The processes may be conscious or unconscious. They consist of some condition of tension or disequilibrium within the person, with the ensuing conduct serving to relieve the tension or to reestablish equilibrium. In mental terms this means that we have cravings, desires, wishes which, once they are aroused, insistently demand gratification.

The use of motives in explaining conduct is aided by having a working classification of these motives. Classifications have been offered by many psychologists, and while they differ among themselves, a considerable amount of agreement remains. Any reasonably carefully drawn list of motive categories is useful practically. It calls attention to the varied impulses that lead to a given type of action and thus indicates a range of possible explanations to be investigated. By thoughtfully running through the classification, one finds his mind directed to reasons for action which, although they had not occurred to him spontaneously, now appear well worth testing by the collection of further evidence.

We recall the surprise of a market research executive in the motor car field, for example, when he came upon the motive category, "desire to be alone." *He* had not felt this urge, and hence the thought that persons might want automobiles partly as a means of getting away from people had never occurred to him. Similarly we have repeatedly observed how university students, even those quite mature, are aided in finding new explanations for people's buying as they do, and new appeals to be used, when they employ a systematic motive classification.

Our actual buying behavior is largely an expression of *specific attitudes,* that is action-tendencies toward particular objects, reflecting the varied directions of motivation as these have been molded in the courses of experience. One's negative attitude toward a certain store, for example, may be an expression of injured pride occasioned by a domineering salesman. The attitude, in turn, leads one to avoid the store, to criticize it, perhaps to praise the leading competitor, and to concentrate one's buying there. Business affairs are conducted in a world of these attitudes. They are the form in which motives immediately enter into people's conduct and speech. They directly determine market behavior. The attitudes that lead to buying hence lie at the very heart of market research problems.

But "mechanisms," too, play an important role. An analysis of action must include more than motives alone. The motives operate in a way that is determined by other structures and processes as well. All these other processes may be lumped together under the name "mechanisms." Thus one division of mechanisms comprises the sensory capacities which determine what we can and cannot see or hear or taste. The halitosis "psychosis," for example, is no more dependent upon the desire for cleanliness or fears for our social acceptability than upon the fact of olfactory adaptation which prevents our being aware of our own breath because of continued exposure to it. Motor or muscular capacities of all sorts, and intellectual powers and limitations, are further important mechanisms which settle the course of conduct. Suffice it, by way of illustration, to mention the strenuous efforts to adapt motor cars and household conveniences to the natural physical abilities of people; and the deep interest of the advertising profession in questions of literacy, memory, and intelligence levels of consumers. Under mechanisms, too, belongs all our knowledge—knowledge of products, brands, prices; knowledge of how to judge merchandise; knowledge of the number of dollars in our pocket and the number of creditors on our heels; knowledge of the consequences of our purchase; and so on indefinitely.

We may note, in passing, how clear the motive-mechanism classification makes the distinction, so often overlooked, between *familiarity* with a brand name (a matter of knowledge—a mechanism) and *attitude toward the brand* (a motive). Thus a recent inquiry into this relation revealed such discrepancies as the following: Toothpaste A, while most familiar to 16 per cent of the women tested (the brand they first thought of) received only 8 per cent of top rankings when these women expressed their attitudes toward the several brands. Toothpaste B, in contrast, was first thought of by only 5 per cent but was most favorably rated by 11 per cent. Similarly one brand of toilet soap had percentages of 12 and 26 for familiarity and preference respectively, while another had corresponding percentages of 23 and 15. It is, of course, necessary to go back of such figures to find their meaning and their significance for future sales of the products. But even these gross findings do illustrate clearly the importance of measuring *both* knowledge and attitudes—both mechanisms and motives.

So much for a first sketch of the factors in the *individual,* which explain action. A word, now, about the *situation.* People's buying is governed by the influences playing upon them from outside no less than it is by their inner dispositions. These external factors may be thought of as centering in the product itself, and spreading from that center to a vast range of other influences more and more remote. Next to the attributes of the product, the influences most significant for purchase are the selling methods, advertising, store, and generally, conditions surrounding the sale. Beyond these influences lies the whole world—though obviously certain parts of the world are more closely related to people's buying behavior than other parts, and hence are more valuable to investigate. To mention only one illustration, investigation of the part played by advice of friends is often of utmost importance.

In general, then, one proceeds in his analysis of any bit of action by analyzing those motives and mechanisms that appear significant, and also by studying the outside conditions which appear most clearly related to those inner dispositions. Explanations are found by working back and forth between individual dispositions and external influences. The behavior of the moment is always governed by both.

The Importance of the Time-Line

The preceding analysis of action deals only with the *immediate* explanatory factors, with the *present* determinants of buying behavior. But the actual purchase is the end-point of a long-continued process. Back of this final response lies the *history* of the desires and attitudes which now dominate conduct. The task becomes that of accounting for the familiarity with the product and for the specific desires that eventually lead to the purchase. In market research, these earlier preparatory stages are no less significant than the last. Useful analysis must cover the temporal course of the act, not merely a single cross-section.

Figure 2 offers a schematic representation of this developmental or biographic analysis of action. It calls attention to two essential facts: The first is that present action can be understood only by reference to what went before; the complete buying act must be seen in a sequence of stages along an extended time-line. The second point is that each stage in the growth of the readiness to buy is itself a bit of response determined jointly by the person as he *then* is and by the then existing influences. The relationship pictured in Figure 1, in other words, repeats itself over and over again in the sequence constituting the complete action. At each successive stage along the time-line, however, we are dealing with a changed person, different by reason of what has occurred at preceding stages and also, of course, we have new influences that have come into operation to affect the on-going action.

In Figure 2, we begin with the individual I_1, as he is, say, at the time he first has his attention called to X-toothpaste or Y-automobile. He is already an extremely complex combination of motives and mechanisms—a man with deep-seated desires and prejudices, stores of information and misinformation, specific, felt needs for having an up-to-date car, for saving money, and so on. In a particular situation S_1, now, this man encounters some influence, perhaps an advertising appeal, which stops him and elicits the response A_1. His response is not an immediate purchase; it is a favorable feeling toward Y make of car or a belief that X dentifrice will protect his teeth. This A_1 response is always a joint effect of I_1 and S_1, and it leaves the individual a changed person. He is now no longer I_1 but he has become I_2, a person familiar with and favorably inclined toward X or Y.

This changed person I_2 some time later (it may be minutes or weeks) hears a friend comment enthusiastically about the product (S_2). This then is the second significant step: the I_2 and S_2 combination results in a further state of belief and acceptance. It is to be noted that the S_2 situation (friend's remarks) might have fallen on deaf ears if A_1 had not previously occurred. The sequence and interrelationship of occurrences along the time-line are crucially important.

The further altered person I_3 now encounters other influences. They may be akin to those already illustrated or it may be merely that the individual yields to a leisurely thought-encouraging situation S_3, where he deliberates about the new car or the dentifrice and definitely decides to buy (the decision is A_3). The final purchase occurs, then, when the person (now I_4) with an attitude of readiness to purchase (A_p) finds himself in a situation S_4 containing the precipitating influence to induce the purchase (I_{np}).

This longitudinal analysis of action may begin at stages near to, or remote from, the final purchase. Practically, it is wise to take as a starting point for inquiry the stage where the want and the means to its gratification are first clearly conscious. Sometimes, as in the above example, this means beginning with a particular advertising or sales influence; at other times, with the influence of friends or family, or an outsider's chance remark; in still other cases, the initial condition arises in the course of one's own observations and activities. Whatever

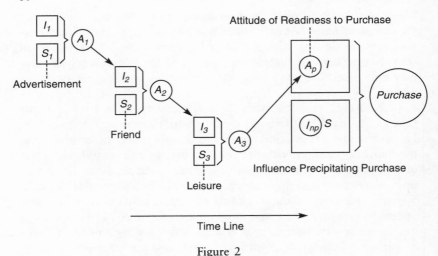

Figure 2

the starting point, however, a complex background already exists in the make-up of the person—itself a summary of vast ranges of preceding experiences. It is necessary, consequently, to begin at the point chosen, with whatever understanding of the then-existent individual one may possess or discover, and to proceed by tracing the most significant steps leading from that point to the final buying act.

In dealing with the market behavior of people in general, or with large sections of the population, our understanding of the individuals whose buying acts are to be traced comes from our organized knowledge about human nature—knowledge of the motives and mechanisms earlier discussed. Beginning with this psychological background, the problem is to analyze the steps by which people move to the attitudes and buying responses in which the interest of a particular investigation centers. At each stage, the analysis corresponds to that described in the preceding section and represented in Figure 1.

The Role of Interpretation

The procedure to be followed under the proposed pattern of inquiry is guided by two additional principles. The first of these may be called the *principle of differential explanation*. It calls attention to the fact that a market research study is not interested in *complete* explanations, in accounting for *all* aspects of buying behavior. It is always a matter of explaining particular features of what people do, as contrasted with certain alternative possibilities. Otherwise the inquiry would be literally endless. The principle, then, stated most bluntly is: *Specify precisely what is to be explained for present practical purposes.* This will mean specifying why, in the course of action, this alternative occurs rather than that. With respect to even very simple buying behavior, a large number of *different* explanation-seeking questions can be asked. Much muddled work arises from failure to keep the several questions separate.

Thus in the simple matter of soap-buying, the inquiry may aim at learning any one or all the following things about *this* purchase (and there are still numerous other causal questions still unmentioned): Beginning far back on the time-line, such questions as

(a) Why the consumer buys soap at all
(b) Why she likes soap of a particular color, odor, hardness, etc.
(c) Why she believes all soaps are equally good

Somewhat nearer the purchase, and more concretely

(d) Why she buys soap of the X-type and price
(e) Why she buys X-soap specifically
(f) Why she buys one cake instead of several
(g) Why she buys at this particular time
(h) Why she buys at this particular place
(i) Why she buys as she does now (this month or this year) as contrasted with other months or years
(j) Why *she* buys (i.e., why this kind of person rather than others, different as to sex, age, location, economic class, etc.)

If the investigation seeks explanations for several of these facts, it is none the less essential that they be definitely thought out separately, so that each portion of the inquiry will be clear about what it is trying to explain. If we are investigating the buying of Ford automobiles, one part of the study deals with reasons for purchasing low-priced cars; a quite different set of questions and tabulations is needed to ascertain why people buy Fords instead of Chevrolets; still other lines of inquiry must be pursued if we wish to learn why Fords are bought in preference to used cars, or why *any* car is bought, or why the Fords are bought at the times and places they are. Research results which seek to explain buying actions without clear specification of what part or aspect of the action is to be explained are foredoomed to confusion. If the "why" questions are to be clear, one must see the varied alternatives to the behavior studied; the specific alternative actions must be held in mind in planning the study. This is the first of the two guiding principles.

The other principle has to do with *the use of tentative interpretations*. It stresses the role of hypotheses, suggested explanations, psychological theories and bits of psychological insight in guiding market investigations. Explanations are never mere tabulations of observations; we never get useful explanations merely by "collecting the facts." Interpretations are indispensable in addition—interpretations in terms of the motives and the mental mechanisms which determine conduct in given situations. The practical spadework of market inquiry and analysis must be preceded and guided by hypotheses, by understanding of *probable* explanations of the specific features of conduct in question. The second principle, then, may be epitomized to read: *Use tentative interpretations in planning the inquiry and let the collection and analysis of data aim at checking upon and modifying these preliminary views.*

The interpretations are attempts at psychological understanding; they seek to find the *meaning* of the facts collected. Two broad classes of interpretations may be distinguished. The first is concerned with the dynamics of action, with explaining the causal sequences in buying behavior. This sort of interpretation falls into the pattern already sketched, but it requires detailed and specific applications within that general framework. The second type of interpretation attempts to account for similarities and differences in behavior among groups, and to understand the factors related to these similarities and differences. The nature of both classes of interpretation and their interconnection may be seen from a few illustrations.

The various categories in a classification of motives provide valuable, though too general, interpretations of the first class. These are supplemented by the more revealing interpretations having to do with specific attitudes and with the unconscious and indirect operation of hidden motivations. The motivation hypotheses range from the most ordinary to the most subtle and unusual. Research into the purchase of a particular brand of soap may be guided in part by simple notions that the soap is bought because of people's preference for its odor, shape, or price. One may inquire, too, how far purchases are affected by women's belief that the soap either injures or improves their health, beauty, or social acceptability. Less obviously, it may be that the soap is regarded as especially "masculine" or "feminine"; or it may carry vague memories of hospitals and sick-rooms; or its name may arouse half-conscious national loyalties or antipathies.

In addition to interpretations which turn upon features of motivation, there are others which have to do primarily with "mechanisms"—though the two are always intertwined. For example, one may wisely guess, on the basis of psychological knowledge, that an advertising campaign is pitched at too high an intellectual level, that a peculiarly shaped bottle is too inconvenient to handle or a carton too difficult to open. A psychologist using the type of procedure here suggested would almost certainly have seen the *problem* of opening cigarette packages wrapped in cellophane—*before* the package was on the market.

All such suggestions of course are *hypotheses;* they are guesses to be checked upon. Evidence is collected to show the truth or falsity of each. But unless one has these—and many additional—possible interpretations in mind, there is little likelihood that he will discover significant evidence at all. The more plausible and comprehensive the preliminary interpretations, the greater the probability of arriving at a sound, practically useful, understanding of the buying in question.

The other type of interpretation centers in statistical tabulations and comparisons. The aim is still to understand the actions of people in the market, but often it is necessary to divide the people into groups according to age, sex, buying power, intelligence, personality peculiarities, or what not, in order to reach a sound interpretation of the buying behavior under investigation. Frequently, too, the buying is associated with other observable facts; it occurs among people in certain localities, at certain seasons, after exposure to certain types of advertising, after previous use of the same product, and so on. Hence the market investigator requires guiding interpretations with respect to kinds of people and the measurable characteristics related to their conduct quite as much as he needs interpretations of the first type.

A first illustration pertains to age in relation to milk-drinking among adults. Tentative interpretations suggested that habit differences between different age groups and between groups differing in education might well cause differences in milk consumption. A simple analysis showed that remarkable differences do exist in milk consumption between groups with different levels of schooling. Among college educated people, more than 70 per cent drink milk; among people who have attended only grade school, less than 50 per cent; high school graduates lie in between. In another part of the study it was shown that milk consumption decreases markedly with age. However, and this is the significant use of interpretation in the case, there is in America today a clear correlation between age and education among adults. Amount of schooling has rapidly increased during recent decades. Hence, when the persons interviewed are divided into age groups, the younger ones will have the better schooling; conversely, if the sample is grouped according to schooling, the better educated are younger on the average. Hence an adequate interpretation demanded a further analysis of age and schooling to see which was primary. It turned out that the apparent influence of education was completely accounted for by the age difference. A special check made sure that it was really the age and not the educational difference which mattered. In a selected sub-sample with constant average age for all three educational groups, the educational differences in milk consumption disappeared.

Another illustration of statistical interpretation may be taken from the same study. It was found that persons who had been forced by their parents to drink milk against their will are more frequent among non-drinkers than among milk drinkers. The off-hand interpretation might be that coercion in childhood leads to distaste for milk as adults. But the alternative hypothesis is equally plausible, that since all parents believe in milk drinking, those whose children dislike it have to force them to drink it. Additional information is needed in this instance before one or another interpretation can be accepted. One might seek evidence, for example, concerning children who disliked milk but who were not coerced into drinking it or who were influenced by more subtle methods; likewise cases of children who liked milk but who were coerced to drink more.

At all events, whatever the limitations in a particular instance like this last, the necessity is constantly present to find meaning in the results as far as feasible, and to see where further data are needed. Giving "merely the facts" usually means giving an assortment of observations, more or less relevant as the case may be, together with trivial, vague, or incorrect interpretations instead of sound ones, which have been critically considered and based on careful psychological analysis.

The essential outlines of a "master technique" have now been sketched. The collection of market research data and the analysis of results are to be carried on within the broad framework provided by a psychological analysis of action. Within that framework it is further necessary that the inquiry be directed to specific limited aspects of the action—the choice to be dictated by the practical purposes that are paramount. The particular points of action to be investigated are most clearly defined by seeing *with what alternatives* they may be contrasted. The search is for causes why people act *this* way and in response to *this* type of influence rather than in *different* ways and in response to *different* influences. The research into these differential explanatory factors within the whole pattern of action is, finally, directed by tentative interpretations; it aims to collect evidence which will suggest more definite and specific psychological hypotheses about the phases of activity in question and which will then support or deny the validity of these interpretations.

The actual collection of information presents no end of additional problems of technique, even when the investigation is directed by the above guide-posts. The problems are ones of detail—albeit most important detail. Questionnaire and interview procedures, methods of direct observation, experimentation, attitude rating devices—all are utilized in the spade-work of research. The "master techniques" tell *where* to dig and what to dig *for;* they do not prescribe the exact tools or digging methods.

Here let it be stressed, however, that in whatever specific ways the evidence is secured, the investigator always has the problem of seeing the picture *whole.* Only thus can he know what parts or aspects of the market behavior deserve attention and what parts may be omitted. In planning the research, it is his job to canvass the entire range of external influences and of dispositions in people that may plausibly appear to play a significant part in the activity studied. Singly and separately, the various motives, mechanisms, and external influences to be weighed are obvious enough. But it is the open-minded, comprehensive, attention to *all* of them that is easily neglected. A psychological approach stresses the appreciation of the complete picture, where each separate influence can be assigned its proper place. The psychological analysis guards against over-simple, misleading emphasis on this or that factor, and against the neglect of other factors which may prove more important.

We can imagine that by this time the reader is saying to himself: Nonsense! The plan is far too elaborate. We can't ask the consumer to give us his life history in order to find out why he buys soap. We can't ask him a hundred questions. The answer is: You don't need to. We assume you will not. Then *why,* you ask impatiently, all this talk about what should be covered? And the answer is: The explorer must know far more of the country than the spot where he pitches his tent. You may survey tentatively scores and scores of points that might be inquired into—and you may end with an interview schedule of five questions. But those five questions will be vastly different from the ordinary ones. You will have explored and decided the *best* spot to pitch camp; not guessed. You will have determined what is worth asking and to what questions it is reasonable to expect usable answers. By analyzing the *whole* act, one sees what part is significant for his present purpose. He has a map by means of which to locate his present position. Only thus can he judge the meaning of his observations—and decide upon practical next steps.

Some Specific Applications

The next problem to which we wish to apply our theoretical approach has to do with the statistical analysis of interview and questionnaire responses. This field has been much neglected in theoretical discussions, in spite of its great practical importance. With any interview questions other than the simplest and most formal, a great variety of answers will be received. We take, for example, 200 questionnaires which contain the question, "What are the essential features of good oil?" and we find that 167 different comments are recorded. These comments have a certain direct value for the copy writer; he is to a certain degree justified in assuming that the language in which the consumers speak will be the language in which they can most easily be spoken to. But when it comes to drawing general conclusions from these varied answers, the necessity arises for grouping them. This involves the process of coding.

We shall not take time to deal with the astonishing mistakes in coding which occur in many studies. To cite only one illustration: The class *"bought for a member of the family"* is made to include, in one study, both the food asked for by the father and the food the mother judged might be good for the baby. The market significance of the cases is altogether different, though both are covered by the word "for." Many such examples could be given. But even leaving aside actual mistakes, we all have seen tables containing long lists of words with following frequency figures, with which no one really knows what to do. The psychologist has this advice to give: Group the data in such a way that they reflect the structure of the concrete act of purchase to which they pertain, and thus prepare them for the final job of interpretation.

Let us take as a first example the oil questionnaire mentioned above. In going through the comments we find such words as, "clear color," "not too thin," and others like "should be durable," "won't carbonize." These words can at once be referred, in our chart of the buying act, to the two groups of factors—motives and mechanisms. Apparently the second group of words like "should be durable" pertain to what we want the oil to do for us; the first group pertains to how we recognize its qualities. The *effects* of the oil correspond to our purposes or motives; the *features* of the oil correspond to our ways of judging its suitability. It is found that 75 per cent of the answers refer to effects, 25 per cent to features. Now we take the answers of the same 200 people given to the same question but pertaining to gasoline. Here 90 per cent speak about effects and 10 per cent about features. Thus we at once detect an interesting difference in the way people buy oil and gasoline though further data are needed for a detailed interpretation.

Before attempting a more general formulation we give another example. Women are asked why they bought their last dress in the store they did. Some say, "because the merchandise is good there," or "because I had agreeable experiences with the salesgirls"; others refer to an "advertisement," to "convenient location," or to "a special sale." Again we are reminded of a distinction in our basic scheme— the division of the situation into influences arising from the product (in this case the store) and other influences. We now group the reasons, according to that distinction, into "characteristics of the store" and "additional influences." The fact that, among 700 women, 41 per cent give responses of the first class and 59 per cent give responses of the second class is not yet important. But now we select two groups of 200 women each who patronize two different stores and find the following differences:

	Characteristics of the Store	Additional Influences
Store B	39	61
Store C	60	40

Here our grouping reveals a very significant difference in the standing of these two stores. Store "C" stands apparently much more on its direct merits than does Store "B."

A final example leads us to the most fundamental distinction we have made in our scheme. Women are asked what made them decide to send their laundry out of the house instead of washing it at home as they had done in the past. Typical answers are, "the baby was ill," "unexpected guests came," "wanted to have more time for myself." We realize that the last answer is of the character of a motive, the first two of the character of influences, in the sense of our chart. Altogether we find in this study 81 per cent of influences and 19 per cent of motives mentioned as answers to the question regarding the decision to send the laundry out. Therewith the ground is laid for a tentative interpretation to the effect that this special group of women is still reconciled to the idea of doing laundry at home, and that it requires unusual situations to cause them to change the habit.

Now a more general formulation can be made of the consequences of our analysis of action for the statistical handling of responses. *It seems to be advisable to group answers parallel to the general structure of the act.* The main distinctions given in our charts can be followed in such a grouping: individual dispositions versus influences (the laundry case), motives versus mechanisms (the oil case), the product versus other influences (the stores). By such a grouping we prepare the way for interpretations since the results are thus formulated in terms of the action which the study aims to understand as a basis for later control of that action.

We shall call this entire proceeding "complementary grouping." Complementary grouping means, then, to combine a great number of comments into a few groups corresponding to the main elements of the "act of purchase" in our chart. Our material might pertain to a general decision, as for instance, the laundry example did. It might pertain to the selection of a special outfit, as in the department store example. These two examples would be located on very different parts of our "time line"—the general decision much earlier than the special selection of an outfit. But, even for two such different phases of a purchase we use the same scheme of joint determination by individual and situation, and the main elements we have singled out therein.

In addition to the *complementary grouping* there is another which we shall call the *supplementary grouping*. This grouping pertains to subdivisions within some one heading in our analysis of the purchase. The sales influences, for instance, might be grouped into "newspaper advertisement," "magazine advertisement," etc. The specific motives which the gasoline has to satisfy might be grouped into "desire for quick pick-up," "desire for long mileage (i.e., economy)," etc. Many criticisms against the statistical treatment of consumers' comments are connected with confusions of complementary and supplementary groupings. The supplementary groupings are only sensible as partial breakdowns of the main complementary groups.

The results which appear in supplementary groups can apparently be used immediately; we can derive from them, with the usual caution necessary in all use of statistical results, the relative importance of different media, the relative importance of different appeals, and so on. The complementary groupings cannot be used so directly, because we always have to take into account that they result from different interpretations our respondents gave to our questions. The complementary groups are valuable, however, in such directions as indicating how explicitly (a) features of the product, and (b) sales influences, have been recognized by consumers, and how influential each of these has been; how far the buying is impulsive or emotionally motivated rather than being careful, deliberate, and informed; how far the buying occurs as a natural expression of desires and how far it is due to special causes in the external situation. Both forms of grouping are useful; it is only their confusion that is disastrous.

4

On Voting

Political Perception

The Candidates' Stand on the Issues

The modern political party in a town like Elmira has an effective existence more in the minds of the partisans than in the local community's formal political organizations. . . . This existence is primarily expressed through differences in attitudes toward political issues of the day.

But this is not the only way in which the partisans differentiate themselves. There is also the fact of political perception—how the voter *sees* events in the political world. Specifically, we are concerned here with how voters in 1948 saw the issues of the campaign and what difference that made in their political behavior.

Now this is not simply a nice psychological problem with little relevance for the political situation. The process of political perception can operate to increase cleavage or consensus within the community. It undoubtedly contributes directly to a "real" definition of the differences between the parties, in terms of what might be called their "political norms."

For political beliefs and perceptions have a strongly "normative" quality. They not only state that "this is the way things are," but they also imply that "this is their customary or normal state" and therefore what they "ought" to be. The parties are not only what their leaders do or say; the parties are also what their followers believe they are, expect them to be, and therefore think they should be.

Once again we encounter a brief glimpse of the spiral of cause and effect that constitutes political history—in this case the history of political issues: What the parties do affects what the voters think they are and what the voters think they are affects what they subsequently

Reprinted with editorial adaptations from Bernard Berelson, Paul F. Lazarsfeld, and William N. McPhee, *Voting: A Study of Opinion Formation in a Presidential Campaign* (Chicago: University of Chicago Press, 1954; Phoenix Edition, 1966), chap. 10, pp. 215–33.

do. Out of this interaction between subjective perception and objective reality, mutually affecting one another over decades, emerges not only our definition but the reality of a political party's role. The popular image of "what Republicans (or Democrats) are like" helps to define and determine what they "really" are. Today's subjective unreality in the voters' minds affects tomorrow's objective reality in the political arena.

About thirty years ago an analyst of public opinion gained lasting distinction by elaborating the differences between "the world outside and the pictures in our heads." Walter Lippmann discussed what many theorists—philosophers, psychologists, sociologists, political scientists, anthropologists—have noted and documented before and since: subjective perception does not always reflect objective reality accurately. Selective perception—sampling the real world—must be taken into account. The mirror that the mind holds up to nature is often distorted in accordance with the subject's predispositions. The "trickle of messages from the outside is affected by the stored-up images, the preconceptions, and the prejudices which interpret, fill them out, and in their turn powerfully direct the play of our attention, and our vision itself. . . . In the individual person, the limited messages from outside, formed into a pattern of stereotypes, are identified with his own interests as he feels and conceives them."[1] Another student of public opinion put it similarly: "Each looks at, and looks for, the facts and reasons to which his attention points, perceiving little, if at all, those to which his mind is not directed. As a rule, men see what they look for, and observe the things they expect to see."[2]

The world of political reality, even as it involves a presidential campaign and election, is by no means simple or narrow. Nor is it crystal-clear. Over a period of six months, and intensively for six weeks, the electorate is subjected to a wide variety of campaign events. Even if all the political events were unambiguous, there would still be a problem of political perception; but, as it is, the campaign is composed (often deliberately) of ambiguous as well as clear elements.

Perception and Voting

Just how clear was the objective field to be perceived in 1948? Some propagandists, and some students of propaganda, believe that ambiguity often promotes effectiveness, since each subject is then free to define the matter in terms satisfactory to himself. While a sharply clear statement may win some friends by its very decisiveness, it may also lose some people for the same reason. Now Truman and Dewey had both been public figures for some time and had taken public stands on many political matters; yet their positions on the issues in the campaign were not equally clear.

In 1948 Truman took a more straightforward and more aggressive position on these issues than Dewey (Table 1). The latter spoke to a large extent on the need for unity, peace, and freedom, while Truman specified his position *for* price control and public housing and *against* the Taft-Hartley Law. And Truman used quite vigorous language in stating his position, whereas Dewey employed a more lofty rhetoric. Except perhaps for the Russian issue (which became involved with the spy and domestic Communist issue), there can be no question but that, objectively, Dewey's position was more amenable to misperception than Truman's.

And this is reflected in the extent of nonperception of the candidates' stands.[3] On the four issues the proportion of respondents who do not know the candidates' stands average about 10 per cent for Truman and about 25 per cent for Dewey. (This also reflects the fact that Truman's official position brought him before the public on such issues on numerous occasions; but a counterconsideration is that Dewey's position as governor of New York made him especially familiar to Elmirans.)

Perception and Party Preference

More importantly, the voter's perception of where the candidates stand on the issues is not uniformly affected by partisan preference— only selectively so (Fig. 1). It is not marked on the central issues of price control and the Taft-Hartley Law. Republicans and Democrats agree that Truman is for price control and against the Taft-Hartley Law and that Dewey is for the Taft-Hartley Law and against price control (although on this last there is by no means a clear perception of where Dewey stood). On public housing (and, as we saw earlier, on the Russian problem) the difference between the parties was greater.

Why should the partisans agree in perception on some issues and disagree on others? For one thing, of course, perception varies with the ambiguity of the situation. The less ambiguous the objective situation (e.g., Truman's position on price control), the less disagreement. But, for another, perception seems to vary with the degree of controversiality of the issues in the community. On price control and the Taft-Hartley Law the respondents with opinions divided about 60–40; on the other two issues (including firmness toward Russia), in Elmira the split is about 90–10. In the latter case, then, there is virtual agreement within the community—which means that one side of the issue is considered "right" and the other side "wrong." Hence there

TABLE 1. POSITIONS TAKEN BY DEWEY AND TRUMAN ON FOUR ISSUES DURING THE
CAMPAIGN

	Dewey	Truman
Price control	Causes of high prices were war, foreign aid, the administration's discouragement of production, governmental mismanagement Remedies: cut government spending, reduce national debt, increase production No reference to imposition of controls Only one major reference	Republicans would not act against inflation in Eightieth Congress or special session; they rejected the administration's program Called for price controls or anti-inflation measures on several occasions
Taft-Hartley Law	Referred to it as "Labor-Management Relations Act of 1947," never as "Taft-Hartley Law" Made abstract remarks about "labor's freedoms" which would be "zealously guarded and extended" Approved the law in general ("will not retreat from advances made") but left door open for improvements ("where laws affecting labor can be made a better instrument for labor relations . . .")	Made the "shameful" and "vicious" law a major issue; recalled that Republicans passed it over his veto: "It ought to be repealed" Took this position in at least ten major campaign speeches during October
Policy toward U.S.S.R.	Took a strong anti-communism position; linked communism to administration Made this a major issue in about seven campaign speeches	Took an anti-communist position; major references twice
Public housing	Only minor references to need for more housing (Republican platform called for housing financed by private enterprise, with federal "encouragement" when private industry and local government were unable to fill need)	Republicans "killed" Taft-Ellender-Wagner Bill Called for public housing sponsored by government in at least ten major campaign speeches

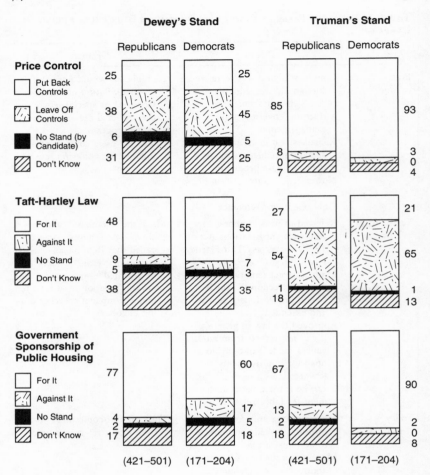

Figure 1. Party preferences does not particularly affect the voters' perception of where the candidates stand on some campaign issues.

is, so to speak, a standard to guide misperception—and each side pulls its own candidate toward the "correct position" and pushes the opponent away from it. On the two central issues, however, the controversy is too visible to allow a designation of "rightness" for one or the other side, and as a result there is less motive for or gain in misperception. If the voter gets nothing for his misperception (e.g., being "right"), there is less reason for him to engage in it. Deviation or misperception requires a certain degree of ambiguity in the objective situation being perceived, but it also requires a psychic indulgence for the misperceiver. Where this opportunity is not present, perception is likely to be more accurate.

Perception and Own Stand

This suggests that perception of the candidates' stands on issues may be affected by the respondents' own stands on them. The voters can thus manage to increase the consistency within their own political position, or at least the apparent consistency. And this is clearly the case. In almost every instance respondents perceive their candidate's stand on these issues as similar to their own and the opponent's stand as dissimilar—whatever their own position (Fig. 2). For example, those Republicans who favor price control perceive Dewey as favoring price control (70 per cent), and few who oppose price control perceive Dewey as favoring controls (14 per cent). And the Republicans who are against controls perceive Truman as favoring them somewhat more than the Republicans who are for them. As with their perception of group support, so with their perception of the issues: the partisans manage to "pull" their own candidate and "push" the opposing candidate with considerable consistency. Overlaying the base of objective observation is the distortion effect—distortion in harmony with political predispositions. As Schumpeter says, "Information and arguments in political matters will 'register' only if they link up with the citizen's preconceived ideas."[4]

At the same time, some voters maintain or increase their perceptual defense on political issues by refusing to acknowledge differences with one's own candidate or similarities to the opposition candidate. Such denial of reality, a defense utilized against uncongenial aspects of the environment, is well documented by case studies and laboratory experiments in the psychological literature of neurosis. Here we have evidence on its operation in the midst of a political campaign where motivation is less strong.

Take the two major issues of price control and the Taft-Hartley Law, on which the candidates took relatively clear positions. Objectively, an observer would say that Truman was for and Dewey against price control and that Truman was against and Dewey for the Taft-Hartley Law. Yet, when our respondents are asked where the candidates stand, a certain proportion of them do not know or profess not to know. But—and this is the point—the "Don't knows" are more frequent among partisans who themselves take a different position

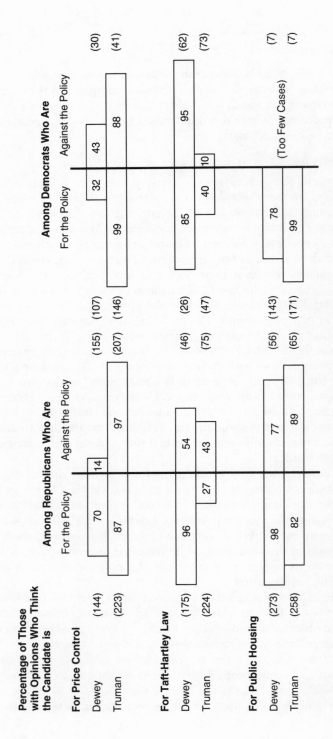

Figure 2. The voters' own stands on the issues affect their perception of the candidates' stands. *Note:* For simplification and clarity, the "No stand" and "Don't know" responses have been omitted from this chart. The omission does not affect the point of the data.

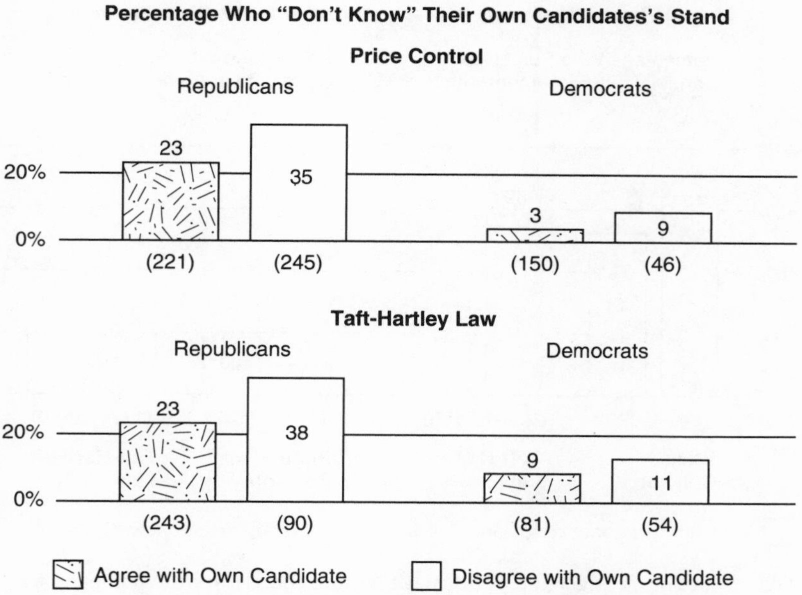

Percentage Who "Don't Know" Their Own Candidates's Stand

Price Control

Republicans   Democrats

23			
20%	35		
0%		3	9
(221)	(245)	(150)	(46)

Taft-Hartley Law

Republicans   Democrats

23			
20%	38		
0%		9	11
(243)	(90)	(81)	(54)

Agree with Own Candidate   Disagree with Own Candidate

Figure 3. Partisans tend not to perceive differences with their own candidate or similarities to the opposition candidate.

from their own candidate or the same position as the opponent (Fig. 3).

Perception and Strength of Feeling

This tendency to "misperceive" issues in a favorable direction does not operate in a uniform fashion within the electorate. The degree of affect attached to the election, in the form of intensity upon one's vote intention, also influences perception. Those voters who feel strongly about their vote intention perceive political issues differently from those who do not feel so strongly about the matter (Fig. 4). With remarkable consistency within each party, the intensely involved "pull" their own candidate and "push" the opponent more than the less involved. (Incidentally, it is probably not too much to suggest that this "pull" and "push" are equivalent to the psychological defense mechanisms of generalization and exclusion.)

For example, when objectively they are *not* in agreement with their own party, *strong* Republicans and Democrats perceive their candidate's stand on the issues as more in harmony with their own stand than do weak Republicans and Democrats in the same situation. But,

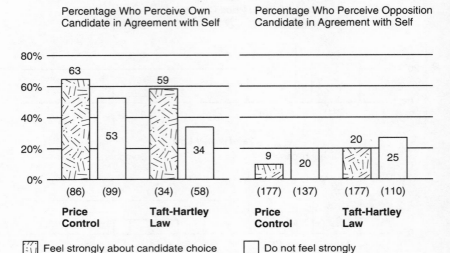

Figure 4. The stronger the political affiliation, the greater the tendency to perceive political issues favorably to one's self. *Note:* Analogous results are obtained for the housing and "firmer with Russia" issues. This same tendency appears in the case of perception of the support given the candidates by various socioeconomic and ethnic groups. In almost every case strong partisans "pull" approved groups more than weak partisans.

by no means is this a general tendency to see everyone in agreement with themselves. When they objectively disagree with the *opposition* candidate, the strong partisans are quickest to perceive that disagreement. The stronger the partisanship, the *greater* the (mis)perception of agreement with one's own side and the *less* the (mis)perception of agreement with the opposition. Presumably, misperception makes for partisanship, and the reverse. Thus, the people strongest for a candidate—the ones most interested in and active for his election, the ones who make up the core of the party support—are the ones who take the least equivocal position on what their party stands for. And, at the same time, those who favor the party position as they see it are more likely to support the candidate strongly.

In the course of the campaign, then, strength of party support influences the perception of political issues. The more intensely one holds a vote position, the more likely he is to see the political environment as favorable to himself, as conforming to his own beliefs. He is less likely to perceive uncongenial and contradictory events or points of view and hence presumably less likely to revise his own original position. In this manner perception can play a major role in the spiraling effect of political reinforcement.

Necessarily, such partisanly motivated perception increases the recognized or believed differences between the parties. Strong Republicans and Democrats are farther apart in perception of political issues than weak Republicans and Democrats; they disagree more sharply in their perception of campaign events. Among the strongly partisan, then, the process of perception operates to make the opponent into more of an "enemy" and thus to magnify the potential for political cleavage.

But all this should not be taken to exaggerate the effect of perception (or issues). Regardless of their perception of the issues, important social groups still follow their own voting tradition.[5] An index of agreement was constructed between the position of each respondent and the position he perceived each candidate to be taking. Here again Catholics vote more strongly Democratic regardless of the degree of their ideological agreement with Truman or Dewey (Fig. 5). But why does agreement with Dewey make more difference for Catholics, and agreement with Truman for Protestants?

Now when these two indexes of agreement are combined into one, this curious effect of perceived agreement sharpens. If Protestants and Catholics agree with "their own group's" candidate and disagree with the opponent, then the vote is overwhelmingly for one's own candidate; and, if the situation is reversed, so is the vote—though not so strongly (see Fig. 6). But what of those people who agree with both candidates, as perceived, or with neither? The answer is that voters who *disagree* with both candidates' stands on the issues, as they perceive them, end by supporting their group's "proper" candidate (more strongly than those who agree with both). If they disagree with both candidates, they seem to have no alternative. So they remain loyal, "at home." If they *agree* with both, however, they are more likely to try the other side. When the grass is green in *both* yards, it seems a little greener in the other fellow's!

Accuracy of Perception

The question of "correct" and "incorrect" perception has been implicit in our discussion thus far, since differentiation in perception requires a degree of misperception on the part of some perceivers (assuming a definition of objective reality). But the question has not been given explicit consideration. Without retracing our steps, let us now summarize from this vantage point.

Percentage Republican of Two-Party Vote

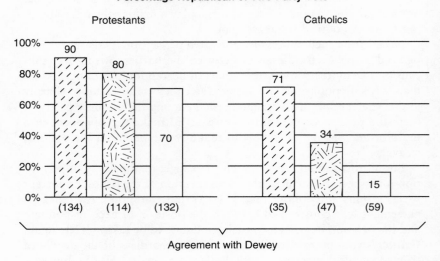

Agreement with Dewey

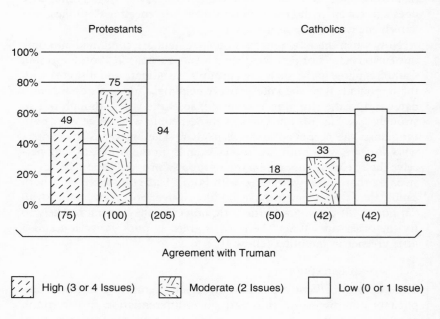

Agreement with Truman

High (3 or 4 Issues)   Moderate (2 Issues)   Low (0 or 1 Issue)

Figure 5. Social differences in voting remain regardless of perceived agreement with candidates.

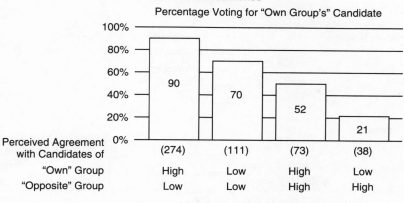

Protestants and Catholics

Percentage Voting for "Own Group's" Candidate

90	70	52	21
(274)	(111)	(73)	(38)
High	Low	High	Low
Low	Low	High	High

Perceived Agreement with Candidates of "Own" Group / "Opposite" Group

Figure 6

Analysis of the perception that occurs during a presidential campaign requires a definition of what is "correct" perception. In the case of political issues, perceiving the candidates' stands as they predominantly appear in the campaign speeches should serve. Since some stands are ambiguous, or at least contain an element of propagandistic vagueness, we use here two stands of Truman and Dewey that are reasonably straightforward and clear—those on the Taft-Hartley Law (with Truman against and Dewey for) and on price control (with Truman for and Dewey against). The index of correct perception on the issues is based upon the number of correct responses given out of the four possible.

In the first place, the amount of correct perception in the community is limited. Only 16 per cent of the respondents know the correct stands of both candidates on both issues, and another 21 per cent know them on three of the four. Over a third of the respondents know only one stand correctly or none at all. And these are crucial issues in the campaign, much discussed in the communication media. Thus, a good deal less than half the political perception in the community is reasonably accurate, by such definitions.[6]

But any such arbitrary measure is less useful for its absolute than for its relative value. Who are the people more and less likely to perceive political issues correctly? For example, what of attention to the campaign in the press and radio? Do the people who read and listen about politics more than others perceive more correctly, or does selection perception get in the way? It seems that communication exposure clarifies perception probably more than any other factor

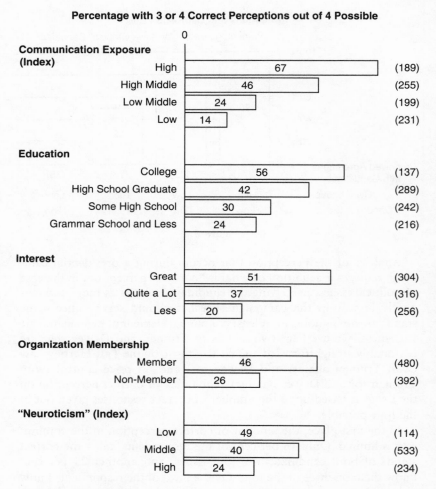

Percentage with 3 or 4 Correct Perceptions out of 4 Possible

Figure 7. Several characteristics are associated with accurate perception of the candidates' stands on issues. *Note:* Each of these characteristics works independently of the others.

(Fig. 7). This is an important consideration: the more reading and listening people do on campaign matters, the more likely they are to come to recognize the positions the candidates take on major issues. It is as though the weight of the media is sufficient to "impose" a certain amount of correct perception, regardless of the barrier presented by the voter's party preference (and despite the fact that those who do most of the reading and listening also feel most strongly for

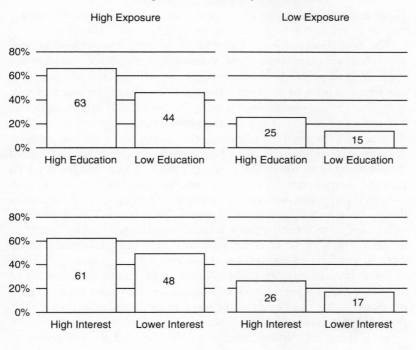

Percentage with 3 or 4 Perceptions Correct

Figure 8

their candidate and are hence more amenable to selective perception). The more that people are *exposed* to political material, the more gets through.

Other characteristics also make for accurate perception. The intellectual training received in the classroom enables the voter to make clearer discriminations in the political arena. And, despite greater affect toward campaign affairs, the interested people manage to maintain a clearer view of the issues (see Fig. 8). In addition, accuracy of perception is a function of cross-pressures. Voters cross-pressured on class and religion are less accurate than those not so cross-pressured (34 per cent high to 41 per cent); and voters cross-pressured (inconsistent) on price control and Taft-Hartley are less accurate than those not so cross-pressured (42 to 65 per cent). But, of all these factors, the strongest is communication exposure. It is more effectively related to accurate perception of where the candidates stand than either education or interest. Reading and listening must make a difference.

Inferences: Psychological and Political

What are the implications of this perceptual situation? Broadly speaking, there are two sets of conclusions which can be drawn.

The first deals with the psychology of political perception. For perceptual selection must serve a definite psychological function for the individual voter. As in other spheres of activity, so in the political: one function must be to avoid potential stress. The voter must do this, even though unconsciously, by using his perceptual opportunities as a defense or protection against the complexities, contradictions, and problems of the campaign. Indeed, the extent and nature of misperception suggests that the voter may even be aware of the attitudinal cross-pressures to which the campaign subjects him and from which he gains escape through perceptual processes. For the greater his affect toward the election (in terms of strength of feeling toward the candidates), the greater the degree of psychic protection. The voter tends to oversee or to invent what is favorable to himself and to distort or to deny much of what is unfavorable. This must leave him fewer internal conflicts to resolve—with, so to speak, a favorable balance of perception. In any event, the voters manage to use the materials of politics, even of a presidential campaign, for their own psychological protection—for the avoidance of some inconsistencies in their beliefs that otherwise would be manifest.

Then there are certain political implications of the patterning of perception. First, there are in a sense two political campaigns. One is the objective campaign that is carried on in the "real" world, and the other is the campaign that exists in the voter's mind, that is, the "real" campaign as perceived. There is no one-to-one correspondence between them. Given the chance, some voters transform the objective campaign into a subjective one more satisfying to them. The campaign waged by the candidates—even when deliberately unambiguous—is not the one perceived by all the voters, but this does not make it any less "real" for the voters themselves. "If men define situations as real, they are real in their consequences."

Second, there is the meaning of perception for rational political judgment. Here its role must make the voter's political judgment *seem* more rational to him because it maximizes agreement with his own side and maximizes disagreement with the opposition. In other words, perception often operates to make the differences between the parties *appear* greater than they actually may be—and thus to make the voter's decision *appear* more rational (in one sense) than it actually is. In this way, paradoxical though it may seem, misperception contributes to a seeming "rationality" in politics.

Third, perception must reduce or even eliminate certain political cross-pressures before they come to the level of visibility—before they start pressing. If the voter finds himself holding opinions championed by opposing parties, it has been thought that he could do one of two things: remain in this "inconsistent" position (which is, of course, altogether legitimate) or remove the "inconsistency" by changing one opinion to fit the other. But he has another out: he can perceptually select, out of the somewhat ambiguous propaganda of the campaign, those political cues which remove the problem by defining it away. He can "see" that the candidates do not disagree on the issue at hand or that his candidate really agrees with him or that the opponent really disagrees or that he cannot tell where his candidate stands. Just as the process may reduce the voter's level of psychological tension, so may it reduce his political inconsistency.

Finally, this serves to introduce the major political implications of our perceptual material—its implications for the problem of cleavage and consensus in the democratic community. The over-all effect of political perception is to increase the amount of political consensus *within* the parties and to increase the amount of political cleavage *between* the parties—once again, homogeneity within and polarization between. Both are achieved by something like the mechanisms of generalization, exclusion, and denial—through the perceptual enlargement of the area of agreement with one's own candidate (generalization); through the misperceived rejection of the opponent's position (exclusion); and through the professed lack of knowledge of one's candidate's stand where disagreement is likely (denial).

Let us close this chapter by comparing it briefly with the chapter on the perception of groups.[7] In each case the perceptions are likely to help voters to maintain their own position, without being too much concerned by contradiction. In the social case it is harmony with people; in the present case it is a harmony with ideas. With groups the matter was fairly simple: each respondent is surrounded by a primary group in which the large majority thinks like himself. No wonder, then, that he infers that "everyone" will vote as he does. (Of course, this tendency is tempered by a strong sense of reality; misperception is only superimposed upon it.) In the case of the candidates' stand, the voter gets his information from reading, listening, and discussion. This is subject to *selective* gathering of information, forgetting of disturbing elements, reinterpretation of what the candidate "really" means—all mechanisms familiar in social psychology. Probably, even, social selection reinforces the selective collection of information, as a result of discussion between like-minded people.

In a way, both phenomena can be subsumed under one heading. Voters cannot have contact with the whole world of people and ideas; they must *sample* them. And the sampling is biased. People pick the people and the ideas to suit their personal equilibrium and then project that sample upon the universe. First, selective perception, then misperception, then the strengthening of opinion, and then, in turn, more selective perception. Fortunately, there are realities, competing concerns, and corrosion of existing beliefs that, under normal circumstances, do not permit this process to get far out of bounds.

In sum, then, the actual operation of political perception during a presidential campaign decreases tension in the individual and increases tension in the community—one might almost say, *by* increasing tension in the community. The voters, each in the solitude of his own mind, wish to see the campaign in a favorable way, and they use their perception of where the candidates stand to this end. "Democracy in its original form never seriously faced the problem which arises because the pictures inside people's heads do not automatically correspond with the world outside."[8]

Summary

Perception and Voting

1. Party preference does not particularly affect the voter's perception of where the candidates stand on the issues.

2. The less ambiguous the objective situation, the more agreement in perception between the two sides.

3. Partisans tend to perceive the candidate's stand on the issues as favorable to their own stand. (1) They perceive their candidate's stand as similar to their own and the opponent's stand as dissimilar. (2) They tend *not* to perceive differences with their own candidate or similarities to the opposition candidate.

4. Voters who feel strongly about their choice are more likely to misperceive the candidates' stands on the issues as favorable to their own positions.

5. Social differences in voting are largely maintained regardless of perceived agreement with the candidates.

6. Voters who disagree with both candidates' stands, as perceived, support their own candidate more strongly than those who agree with both.

Accuracy of Perception

7. Only about one-third of the voters are highly accurate in their perception of where the candidates stand on the issues.

8. Accuracy of perception is affected by communication exposure, education, interest, and cross-pressures—with communication exposure probably the strongest influence.

Notes

1. Walter Lippmann, *Public Opinion* [New York: MacMillan Company, 1922], p. 21.

2. A. Lawrence Lowell, *Public Opinion in War and Peace* [Cambridge, Mass.: Harvard University Press, 1923], p. 22.

3. The questions followed this form: "From what you know, is Truman (Dewey) for the Taft-Hartley Law or against it?" The respondent could say "Don't know" or state that the candidate had not taken any stand on the issue. The perception questions were asked in August, before the campaign proper; replies may have been different in October.

4. Joseph Schumpeter, *Capitalism, Socialism, and Democracy* [New York: Harper and Brothers, 1962], p. 263.

5. Nor was perception related to *changes* in voting. We hypothesized that voters might maintain stability by means of misperception, but there were no differences in the data on voting changes subsequent to the asking of perception questions. If perception questions had been repeated, then one would expect perception to adjust to vote more often than the reverse.

6. To repeat: these figures apply to the early campaign period of August. Similar data for October, at the end of the campaign, would almost certainly raise these estimates.

7. Editor's note: see chapter 5 in B. Berelson, Paul F. Lazarsfeld, and W. N. McPhee, *Voting* (Chicago: University of Chicago Press, 1954).

8. Walter Lippmann, *Public Opinion*, p. 21.

5

On the Academic Mind

Social Scientists and Recent Threats to Academic Freedom

Introduction

In the spring of 1955, 2,451 social scientists in 165 colleges were subjects for a rather lengthy interview. The purpose of the study was to learn their reaction to what, in the study, is called the "difficult years." By this term we mean the period of accusations and investigations concomitant to the security problems of the cold war and symbolized by the activities of the late Senator from Wisconsin.

The origin of the study was a debate which had been going on for a while among prominent educators. Some claimed that professors had become afraid to teach and that the effect of the difficult years on higher education in this country was formidable; others felt that it was a passing episode, not much different from what happened after the first world war. The Fund for the Republic sponsored a study to find out how much apprehension existed among teachers. After some discussion, it was decided to devote the available budget to a large number of interviews in a specific group of teachers, rather than to spread them thin over all disciplines and all levels. What was loosely called a social scientist includes sociologists, economists, historians, political scientists, social psychologists, geographers, and anthropologists. The sampling was done in two steps. First a stratified sample of all 900 accredited colleges was drawn, including teachers colleges but excluding business schools. Within each of the colleges a probability sample taken from the faculty lists was set up. The number of refusals on the college as well as on the individual level was very small.

The first tool developed was a so-called index of apprehension. The respondents were given a list of about twenty situations developed in

Reprinted with editorial adaptations from Paul F. Lazarsfeld and Wagner Thielens, Jr., "Social Scientists and Recent Threats to Academic Freedom," *Social Problems* 5, nos. 1–4 (1957): 244–66 [244–45, 255–66].

an elaborate set of pretests. They were asked whether in recent years they were specially worried about community gossip and misrepresentation by students; whether they had toned down their writings or changed their reading lists in order to avoid political difficulties; whether they had become more cagey in their personal relations with colleagues and students, etc. The professors were classified according to the number of such symptoms of apprehension they reported. This kind of an index is subject to the usual limitations inherent in any attitude test. Our main report discusses its foundation in great detail.[1] In the present context only one specific aspect of the approach is relevant. The apprehension index was clarified by a large number of cross-tabulations against other information available from the interviews. The main finding is that the apprehension so measured really consists of three elements: (a) fear for one's job security (b) general concern about the state of academic freedom and (c) defiant resistance to the prevailing attacks. In future psychologically-oriented studies it will certainly be desirable to separate the three elements. For the purpose of the present study it seemed more realistic to treat this attitude syndrome as a single variable.

Once the basic classification had been achieved the next task was to find out the factors which determine variations in the extent of apprehension. As usual, a large number of correlations was available. After they had been carefully studied it became possible to organize the material around two pivotal variables, one pertaining to the professor himself, and one to the college in which he teaches. A pivotal variable, in general, has the following characteristics: it is relatively highly correlated with the main criterion, to-wit, apprehension; it is also well correlated with other items, which in turn are associated with the criterion; and, most of all, the substantive meaning of the pivotal characteristic is such that it makes a larger number of the findings understandable in the light of other sociological and psychological knowledge, as well as of common sense. The pivotal variable pertaining to the college is its quality; we shall return to it at the conclusion of this paper. The pivotal characterization of the professor will be called, hereafter, his permissiveness. The nature and role of permissiveness is the main topic of the following pages.

In an initial chapter of the main report a large amount of general information on the social scientists is reported. In addition to the usual demographic characteristics, two findings stand out. For one, our respondents have what one might call a strong inferiority feeling. By a series of questions it was gauged how they think various community leaders would rate the professorial job as compared to occupations like, for instance, lawyer or bank manager. The large majority of our respondents feel that congressmen and businessmen would give the professor a very low prestige rating. The second finding pertains to the political vote of the social scientists: it is strongly on the side of the Democratic party, the traditional home of American minorities. In a somewhat exaggerated sense, one could say that our respondents think of themselves as a discriminated-against minority.

But all this background material didn't seem to fully account for the role these social scientists played and the reaction they had during the difficult years. Step by step the notion of permissiveness forced itself upon us, until it turned out that it has considerable relevance beyond the immediate purpose of the study. It seems worthwhile, therefore, to bring it to the attention of readers who have general interest in the sociology of the academic profession. This paper is essentially a chapter of our forthcoming report. But in a final section we will summarize some findings from other chapters which show the implications of the data we present here and explain why, in our opinion, they signal a rather crucial social problem for American higher education.

[· · ·]

Permissiveness and Dissent

We now return to an issue which we raised earlier and which is important if one wants to clearly understand the nature of a pivotal characteristic. The classification along the permissive-conservative axis was based on a few questions, mainly concerned with what should or should not be allowed on the campus. We set out to show that the index so formed was well related to the more general educational philosophy of our respondents. Now we shall see that it is also indicative of what one might call a general political outlook. What evidence do we have on this point? Firstly, the answers to a general question about teachers' political views are given in Table 1. The distribution of replies, incidentally, is interesting by itself. From the meaning of an average one would expect to find that an equal number

TABLE 1. ON POLITICAL MATTERS DO YOU FEEL THAT YOU ARE MORE LIBERAL OR MORE CONSERVATIVE THAN THE OTHER MEMBERS OF YOUR FACULTY?

More liberal	39%
Same	39%
More conservative	12%
Doesn't know	10%
	100%

TABLE 2. INDICATIONS THAT DISSENT IS RELATED TO PERMISSIVENESS

	Highly Permissive	Quite Permissive	Somewhat Permissive	Somewhat Conservative	Clearly Conservative
Percentage of Democrats in 1952 two-party vote	91	78	62	53	31
Percentage reading at least one of three liberal magazines	62	57	44	29	13
Percentage showing high interest in civil liberties matters	70	64	51	46	42

of teachers consider themselves more liberal and more conservative; actually there seems to be a premium on thinking of oneself as more liberal—we will come back to this point later. In the present context what matters is the fact that of the highly permissive respondents 57% consider themselves politically more liberal, while among the clearly conservative ones, only 20% classify themselves this way. On the two extremes, then, our respondents deviate by about 20% up and down from the average; the middle group has about the same proportion of "more liberal" teachers as the whole sample. But we have much more detailed and stronger evidence on how closely our index is related to other indicators of the respondents' general ideological position.

As discussed earlier, a vote for the Democratic Party may have a symbolic meaning of protest. By and large, in the last few decades the Democratic Party was also considered the proponent of economic and social innovation. No wonder, then, that we find a sharp interrelation between permissiveness and Democratic vote, as shown in the top row of Table 2.

It could be countered that our respondents are mistaken and that the "New Republicanism" is more deserving of the support of intellectuals concerned with improvements in the government and social system. But what matters in the present context is whether permissiveness implies a concern with social criticism and social change. This can be seen again from the second line of Table 2. There we present data on magazine reading. For each group the proportion of teachers is given who read one of the three liberal magazines: *The Reporter, The New*

TABLE 3.

	Highly Permissive	Quite Permissive	Somewhat Permissive	Somewhat Conservative	Clearly Conservative
Percentages who:					
Welcome teacher's oath	3	7	14	27	52
Stress faculty rights	80	73	64	54	46
Are members of AAUP	58	55	54	40	34

Republic, and *The Nation.* Again the result is clear-cut: the more permissive a social scientist, the more likely he is to read at least one of the three magazines. Finally, we know how often our respondents discuss civil liberties cases with friends and read news items on such matters. The proportion of teachers giving affirmative answers to at least one of the two matters is reported in the third line of Table 2.

A last set of data will round out the picture. We asked our respondents two questions, which while related to college matters, imply general principles. One of these questions pertained to the teacher's oath. In some colleges an oath was required and there the professors were asked whether they welcomed signing it. In the other colleges the question was put on a hypothetical basis: If an oath were required, would they refuse, sign with reluctance, or welcome the opportunity. The first line of Table 3 shows how sharply our five classes of social scientists differ on this point. Only three per cent of the very permissive ones would welcome an oath, but 52% of the very conservative ones provide this response.

Our other pertinent questionnaire item has to do with the problem of public relations, which has often been commented upon by students of the American college scene. Robert Hutchins calls concern with public relations the main motive driving trustees toward conformity. We wanted to know how social scientists feel about the matter, and this is the way we worded the inquiry (Table 4).

The second line of Table 3 shows that 80% of the highly permissive professors would give priority to faculty rights but only 46% of the clearly conservative. The permissive teacher then is strongly opposed to the oath, and if he has to make a decision between the public relations problems of his college and the interest of his profession, he is inclined to hold out rather for the latter. He is relatively more

TABLE 4.

If you had to make a choice, in a case in which a member of the faculty is accused of being subversive or of engaging in un-American activities, which do you think it most important for the college administration to protect—the reputation of the college or the rights of the faculty members?	
The reputation of the college	11%
Both	15%
The rights of the faculty members	65%
No answer	9%

oriented toward his professional group at large than toward the specific college at which he works. We could call him more union-minded and it wouldn't be only a metaphorical use of the term. There is a tendency for more permissive teachers to be more often members of the American Association of University Professors, which can be seen from the third line of Table 3. Thus while the permissiveness end of our index doesn't mean extreme radicalism it does indicate a strong element of dissent from things as they are and a feeling that solidarity with one's professional group is important.

We have now considerably clarified this pivotal concept, but especially the findings of Table 3 suggest that, before we turn to the role of permissiveness in the broader context of our study, we raise one more question: Is it a matter of purely personal taste or a relevant aspect of the whole professional life of a college teacher?

The Professional Relevance of Permissiveness

Social scientists could be tolerant of other people's opinions; they could have a searching attitude regarding the current state of society and feel that their teaching should imbue their students with a similar spirit. Yet this might be a private state of mind—like, for instance the preference for a certain type of music or of food—without characterizing the profession as a whole. For an attitude to be relevant in this larger sense, we should expect to find that the leaders of the profession display it prominently, that prestige is attached to it, that it forms part of the cement of friendship groups, and that the average member would hesitate to deviate from the general norm. In a sense we have already assumed that much of this is true. In a chapter of our larger study we reported that many teachers find themselves under cross pressure between the more conservative mood of the larger community and the more permissive atmosphere on the campus. This suggests that permissiveness is a relevant characteristic of campus life.

Only a special study could give conclusive evidence on this point. Our data, however, make it quite plausible. First of all, we can demonstrate that the permissive teachers are more likely to achieve professional distinction. In the course of the study we developed a measure of professional achievement through an index of productivity; while this measure is mainly based on publications, we were able to show that it is broadly indicative of academic merit. Now, Table 5 demonstrates how the proportion of productive scholars goes up as we move from the very conservative to the very permissive respondents. It should be remembered that by its very nature our index of productivity goes up with age. Permissiveness, however, has the opposite tendency; younger people are much more likely to be permissive. It is therefore necessary to study the relation between permissiveness and productivity separately for different age groups. This is done in Table 5. For each age level (represented by a row), the proportion of productive social scientists is highest in the highly permissive group and goes down continuously to the clearly conservative.[2] It is not essential to unravel the causal nexus implied in Table 5. Partly, permissive social scientists are more integrated in their profession and can therefore devote themselves more successfully to their academic work. At the same time, expressing permissive viewpoints might facilitate getting well known, having, therefore, easier access to publishers, and so on. By a relevant characteristic we mean such an overall effect resulting from many interactions. A similar terminal outcome can be sensed in another finding.

One of our items asked how respondents felt about personal relations within the faculty. If permissiveness is a relevant characteristic on the campus, then we should find that where a group of colleagues have similar attitudes—either permissive or conservative—the cohesion between the members should be greater than in a faculty which is split on the matter. For an irrelevant characteristic this would not hold true: the good relations between social scientists are probably relatively unaffected by their feelings about baseball or food. To make an appropriate test, we restricted ourselves here to the 77 schools for which we have enough interviews for the computing of rates to make sense.[3] By determining the proportion of permissive professors for each of these schools, we may classify the colleges themselves according to the spread of permissiveness on the faculty. In somewhat loose language, we can then speak of permissive institutions and conservative ones, as distinguished from those where the faculty is divided. Table 6 corroborates our expectation. In permissive as well as in conservative colleges the proportion of respondents who consider

TABLE 5. THE PROPORTION OF PRODUCTIVE PROFESSORS WITHIN GROUPS AT THE VARIOUS LEVELS OF PERMISSIVENESS

Age	Highly Permissive	Quite Permissive	Somewhat Permissive	Somewhat Conservative	Clearly Conservative
40 years or younger	34	32	26	24	18
41–50	65	63	59	51	41
51 years or older	73	73	66	56	52

TABLE 6. SATISFACTION WITH FACULTY RELATIONS IN COLLEGE CLASSIFIED BY DEGREE OF AGREEMENT ON PERMISSIVENESS

	Permissiveness of the Faculty			
	Mainly Permissive	Divided, Majority Permissive	Divided, Majority Conservative	Mainly Conservative
Proportion of respondents who are highly satisfied with faculty relations	43	32	31	48
No. of professors	631	664	362	197
No. of colleges	21	27	18	11

their relations with colleagues unusually good is higher than in the two middle groups, which are more divided.

Several studies have shown that the sharing of beliefs *which are relevant to a group* facilitates friendships among the group and that, inversely, close personal contacts lead to a similarity of relevant attitudes. If this general finding is accepted, then Table 6 with its intimation that faculties divided on permissiveness are likely to be socially less satisfied as well, supports the relevance of conservatism and permissiveness for social scientists.

Now that we have somewhat clarified the meaning of permissiveness, its frequent occurrence among social scientists, and its relevance for their work, time may be taken out for speculations: What makes these teachers permissive?

The Professorial Mind

We can think of several reasons why there is a natural selection of permissive persons in the recruitment of professors. For a young man coming from a business background, an academic career involves a break in tradition. The business community has an understandable affinity with the conservative credo, with its belief in the value of tradition and authority, its corresponding distrust of people who critically scrutinize institutions like religion and the family, and its belief in the social advantages of private property and the disadvantages of too much state interference in economic affairs. Take, now, a son or daughter who for some reason—be it rebellion from parents or intellectual curiosity—has begun to question these values; he or she will look for new ones, and be more hospitable to unorthodox possibilities. In our terminology, such an individual will be permissive.

If the prospective teacher comes from a professional background he is likely to have grown up in an atmosphere of permissive ideas and—barring special circumstances—will carry them into his own academic work.

Once he is on the campus, socio-economic circumstances also militate against a conservative affirmation by the academic man. College professors are among the lowest paid of all professions requiring comparable training. This might not be decisive if the lack of economic advantages were counter-balanced by considerable prestige, as is true for certain ecclesiastic and judicial positions in America and for the university professor in Europe. But such is not the case with college teachers in this country. We know that our respondents believe their occupation is not highly esteemed in the community; the higher the professional status of a professor, in fact, the more strongly he feels that his prestige is low in the outside world. The reasons are not difficult to trace. An important factor is the organization of education in America. The American college is a strange combination of an extended high school and the beginning of a truly academic training center. One hundred fifty thousand college professors staff these schools. Many of them may not deserve special prestige. But the elite among them, who properly compare themselves with the small number of university professors in other countries, find that they have in no way comparable prestige and influence because, for the general public, they are indistinguishable from the large mass of all other college teachers.[4] One might answer that the American professor could derive his self-respect from the prestige he has within his own profession and could forget about what the community thinks of him. Leaving aside the psychological unrealism of such an idea, the very size of the American professoriate makes it improbable. In a small professional group there can be a high degree of social acoustics. What a man says will be quickly appraised by the others and such appraisal could matter very much. But in a large profession it takes a long time before a single voice is heard, and the lack of an echo deprives the single individual of another means of psychological support. Small economic returns, little prestige on the outside, and scarce means of mutual prestige reinforcement—little wonder that the very position of the professor in the American social structure is not likely to make him feel that everything in it is unquestionably for the best.

What has been said so far is true in general for the academic world. The social scientist faces an additional situation deriving from the nature of his work, which is likely to strengthen a basically permissive attitude. A great discovery of anthropology was that there are social systems completely different from ours and yet viable. A major contribution of historians is the idea that in other periods the modes of thinking and the forms of social relations were different than ours, and require reconstruction for contemporary understanding. The intellectual task involved in these and many similar endeavors of the social scientist is contingent on his ability to visualize a state of human affairs radically different from that of today. While it is true that the social scientist is subject to the same laws of evidence as are his colleagues in all other divisions of knowledge, for him ultimate scholarly accomplishment must depend upon a kind of imagination which has initially to be akin to criticism and therefore is not consonant with the intellectual mood of the conservative.

Occupational self-selection, then, certain features of the American social structure, and the very task of the social scientist make permissive tendencies probable to begin with. Once these conditions and functional consequences have come into play, an additional process sets in. Any group which inclines to a professional ethos, be it medical doctors or businessmen or civil servants, will tend to reinforce it by mutual interaction. It is naive to believe that there is a conspiracy by which faculties exclude from appointment candidates with a conservative mind. The mere balance of power, which in most colleges is on the side of the trustees and the administration, would preclude such a possibility in the long run. What actually is likely to happen is this. Many people drift into occupational pursuits without any clear ideological commitment. They could develop either the conservative or the permissive tendencies in their thinking and their personality. But two factors crystallize and reinforce the nonconservative component. For one, they see that professional success goes more often to permissive seniors. Furthermore, once permissive colleagues are in the majority, even a slight numerical differential may build up to a considerable effect on the uncommitted man. By mere chance he is likely to find friendships among the less conservative; the result will be a slow atrophy of conservative potentialities unless they were very strong to begin with. This is a process to which we have referred before: the development of norms by mutual interaction. And it applies to faculties as well as to any other group.[5]

Irrespective then of one's own predilection, one has to accept it as a "fact of nature" that among social scientists in 20th Century America permissiveness characterizes the prevailing climate of opinion. Our speculative digression has tried to explain this in terms of the experience of the typical academician. But we also probably face here a trend which considerably over-reaches individual experience. The historian Carl Becker is one of those who might see in our data corroboration of a much broader development:[6]

> Until recently the chief function of the sophisticated, the priests and scribes, has been to stabilize custom and validate social authority by perpetuating the tradition and interpreting it in a manner conformable to the understanding of common men. During the last three hundred years . . . there has emerged a new class of learned men, successors to the priests and scribes, whose function is to increase rather than to preserve knowledge, to undermine rather than to stabilize custom and social authority.

This is to say that a permissive professoriate, or an equivalent in some other part of the social fabric, is needed now to help society adjust to novel conditions while discarding out-moded patterns. It is thus the function of the social scientist to be sensitive to innovation in society to be permissive in the full sense of our analysis.

As usual, when one meets such a situation one question has to be raised. Why doesn't the system veer into extremes? Why aren't all social scientists violent radicals? The general answer is obvious. Checks and balances in the form of trustees and administrators make such an outcome unlikely; and personality types inclined toward radical action would, in general, not be prone to choose class-room teaching as an occupation. A cross-sectional study like ours does not permit tracing out these kinds of ramifications. It happens, however, that we have a few data which shed some light on the restraining factors in the situation.

One of them returns to the distinction between generalized and local sources of gratification. We have already pointed out that the permissive teachers are more oriented toward the profession at large and the conservative social scientist more toward the local college institution.[7] It seems that an inverse relationship also holds true: the profession at large is more likely to reward the permissive professor than is the local institution, including its own faculty. We asked each professor whether he had been a member of a college committee which was entrusted with some administrative function and whether he was or had been a department head. It is not the most permissive group which has had these local honors. This is true in spite of the fact that, as we know, the most permissive social scientists furnish the largest proportion of highly productive scholars and the largest proportion of men and women called in as consultants by business firms. We are inclined to interpret this finding in the following way: When a faculty wants to see its interests represented on a committee, it is not inclined to pick the man with the greatest professional prestige, but the one who is likely to be most successful in negotiations with the constituted authority. The natural choice is a middle-of-the-roader, and it is indeed among them that we find the highest proportion of such representatives. In the case of a departmental chairman, this tendency would be even stronger, because very often they are not selected by the teachers but appointed by the administration. It is often claimed that academicians recoil from administrative assignments and committee positions. Still, these involve a certain amount of honor which is undoubtedly attractive to many persons. If the local honors are going to somewhat more conservative professors, then here we have one countervailing force which would set limits on the reward connected with permissiveness in the academic community.

A second such restricting factor is age. By and large in a more or less conservative community people tend to grow more conservative with age. We have already seen that this is also true for our social scientists: the proportion of permissives is largest in the youngest age group. There are several indications that this is not the result of temporary political circumstances. The depression generation has now reached well past the age of forty and they are more conservative than the most recent recruits to the profession. It also happens that our geographers who are much less permissive to begin with don't show a decline of permissiveness with age. What actually seems to happen is that age exercises a dampening effect on the innovating spirit with which younger people enter the social sciences. The equilibrium is maintained because each generation brings its own momentum into the system, replacing an older generation[8] who have become less permissive.

In spite of all these qualifications our data leave no doubt that permissiveness is among the prevailing norms in the social science profession. As such, it has all the prerequisites of a pivotal characteristic. And we can now use it to summarize some of our major findings.

Permissiveness and Apprehension

From all that has been said so far one result is almost a foregone conclusion: the more permissive a social scientist, the more apprehensive will he be. For a succinct picture, Table 7 gives a condensed cross-tabulation of the two indices.

In some respects this table corroborates previous findings. If apprehensive people are more permissive, this means that many teachers are not subdued by their apprehension. They are willing to go on record that unorthodox colleagues and students should not be interfered with. Also, the relationship reminds us of a common element in both attitudes: being permissive means looking at the contemporary scene with more critical eyes, and apprehension, it will be remembered, has a marked component of alertness to civil liberties. A third link between the two positions deserves more careful documentation.

Our data show that it was the permissive teacher who bore the brunt of the attacks on colleges during the difficult years. At three points in our questionnaire respondents had the opportunity to tell whether they themselves had come under fire. They were asked whether their own academic freedom had been threatened, whether they had ever been reported unfavorably to higher authorities, and whether they had felt pressures to conform to the prevailing climate of opinion. Table 8 shows that on each of the three matters permissive teachers much more frequently report unpleasant episodes.

This result cannot be taken lightly. We have seen that the permissive social scientist is most representative of his profession. He furnishes much of the academic leadership; his way of thinking is in

TABLE 7. THE RELATION BETWEEN PERMISSIVENESS AND APPREHENSION*

	Apprehension Score			
	0	1 and 2	3 to 6	Total
Level of Permissiveness				
Clearly permissive	241	444	363	1048
Somewhat permissive	207	311	179	697
Conservative	294	299	113	706
	742	1054	655	2451

*For further details, see the bottom line of Table 9.

TABLE 8. PROPORTION OF RESPONDENTS ON VARIOUS LEVELS OF PERMISSIVENESS
WHO HAD UNPLEASANT EXPERIENCES

	Highly Permissive	Quite Permissive	Somewhat Permissive	Somewhat Conservative	Clearly Conservative
Percentages who:					
Reported own academic freedom threatened	32	24	19	14	7
Were reported to higher authorities	21	19	16	14	7
Felt pressure to conform politically	30	23	19	17	7

TABLE 9. PROPORTION OF APPREHENSIVE RESPONDENTS IN SUBGROUPS CLASSIFIED
BY 1952 VOTE AND LEVEL OF PERMISSIVENESS*

	Highly Permissive	Quite Permissive	Somewhat Permissive	Somewhat Conservative	Clearly Conservative
Percent apprehensive among:					
Republicans	48	32	33	24	22
Democrats	62	54	50	49	32
Total sample	61	50	44	37	25

*For purposes of this table a respondent is considered apprehensive who reveals 2 or more out of a possible 6 "symptoms" of apprehension.

harmony with the intellectual tasks entrusted to him; his educational philosophy is relatively more consistent. It is not surprising that being under attack makes him more apprehensive. But the attacks themselves now appear in a new light. They are not only directed against single individuals: they might endanger the very nature and quality of social science teaching. This point decidedly deserves our further attention. But first, one other aspect of the situation needs to be discussed: the role of party politics.

In Table 9 we report the relation between permissiveness and apprehension separately for Republicans and Democrats. If we compare the proportion of apprehensive respondents among the two groups of voters, we find that Democrats are considerably more apprehensive than Republicans on each level of permissiveness. It seems likely that professors in both political camps looked at the attacks during the difficult years as to some degree party inspired. Irrespective of their own attitudes and the extent to which they might therefore be subject to attacks, the Democrats felt considerably more endangered than the Republicans.[9]

If our interpretation of this finding is correct, it harks back to a problem serious for any popular government. One function of parties is to crystallize issues and thus to mediate between the interest of various sectors of the nation. But sometimes the process gets reversed. There are issues of national concern on which no genuine disagreement among the general population is possible. And still, such issues are sometimes seized upon by parties and thus become sources of division from which it is difficult to find a rational base for compromise. Foreign policy has most often provided pertinent examples in the United States as well as in other Western democracies. We seem to have here a similar case. Basically all Americans will agree on both the need for national security and for civil liberties. Nevertheless, even as sophisticated a group as the teachers in our study ends up by experiencing the problems involved as party issues. It might very well be that men of good will are not fully aware of this fact and that a finding like Table 9, if better known, could have a salutary effect.

We return to the major issue, the fact that attacks on permissive professors are at the same time directed against the more distinguished and representative sector of the professoriate. Many readers might feel that this is not serious. Even if a few good social scientists were endangered, there were undoubtedly many equally good ones who remained safe because they were less permissive. Besides, the argument might run, the conservative sector of the professoriate should be strengthened anyhow. Thus the whole problem would be reduced to a matter of individual human rights, serious enough in itself but not affecting American colleges at large. But the matter is not that simple. It is at this point that our second pivotal variable enters: the quality of the college.

The Role of the College

Offhand, it seems very difficult to classify colleges by their quality. And yet for the purpose of statistical comparison, the matter isn't as complicated as it seems. In the course of the study we developed an index of college quality based on a few available items of information: proportion of Ph.D.'s on the faculty, number of library books per student, proportion of graduates who were successful in post-graduate work, etc. The index so formed permitted the classification of colleges into four quality groups. In three ways it was possible to get reassurance on this classification. For 45 colleges we had additional information from the College Entrance Examination Board. For these schools we knew the ratio of applicants to admissions, the scholastic test level of the admitted students and the distances from which they came. In other words, we had information on the demand for the college, and the correlation with our quality rating based on objective characteristics was very high indeed.

Furthermore, we had corroboration from the data in our own survey. In the high quality colleges 66% of our respondents had a high productivity score, while in the low quality group, only 26% of highly productive scholars were in our sample of social scientists. Finally, we submitted our classification of colleges to a number of experts in the field, and their impressions agreed most closely with our statistical ranking. Thus pending a detailed discussion in our main report, the reader of this paper can accept our classification with confidence. He will then appreciate the importance of Table 10.

The table shows that the high quality colleges have almost three times as many clearly permissive social scientists as the colleges in the low quality class. The reason for this is rather obvious from our previous discussion. In the profession at large, the more productive men and women are more permissive; an administration therefore which wants a good faculty has little choice but to accept a considerable proportion of permissive faculty members, irrespective of its own ideology. Actually, as we show in another part of the main report, the trustees and administrators of the high quality colleges are themselves more permissive in terms of academic freedom granted to their faculties.

The social implications of the findings are very great. A chapter of our main report, following the one reported in this paper, shows that high quality colleges were much more frequently attacked during the

TABLE 10. DISTRIBUTION OF PROFESSORS' PERMISSIVENESS IN SCHOOLS OF VARIOUS QUALITY RATINGS

Attitude of Professor	Quality Rating of School			
	High	Medium High	Medium Low	Low
Clearly permissive	58%	44%	27%	22%
Somewhat permissive	30	33	24	19
Conservative	12	23	49	59
	100	100	100	100

difficult years. This result in turn derives from their having a more permissive faculty. But the fact remains that the brunt of the accusations and attacks were directed against the top-level colleges. The difficult years were thus a danger to American higher education as an institution and not only to the civil rights of the individual professor.

This is shown in those parts of our main study which describe in detail the incidents which occurred in the various colleges and the consequences. In our 165 schools we were able to trace approximately 1,000 episodes, ranging from congressional investigations to attacks by a local newspaper. We did not find a break down of morale, because there was considerable solidarity among teachers which strengthened the element of defiance in each individual's apprehension. But what the study found was a beginning corrosion of morale. One out of five professors had probably become more cagey in his research and in his writings. Many more had experienced a deterioration in his relations with students and colleagues. Most frequent and affecting more than half of our respondents, was a withdrawal from the larger community. Teachers refused to give speeches to local organizations and avoided writing in general magazines on controversial issues. Many refrained from participation in conventional party politics. This had a two-fold disadvantage: The local community lost valuable talents; in turn, the professor lost the opportunity to test his thinking on the realistic stage of public life.

The description and analyses of these incidents fill about one-third of our main report. However, important it might be to show the impact of the difficult years, it isn't the main service which a social research study like ours can render. In the long run, what contributes most is the development of basic variables which can serve to analyze a variety of historical situations. The three outstanding ones in our effort were the index of apprehension, the index of college quality, and the index of a teacher's permissiveness. The present paper concentrated on the last of the three, but it is hoped that it gives a general idea of the procedures employed, the results obtained, and the social implications derived.

Notes

1. Lazarsfeld, Paul F., and Wagner Thielens, Jr., *The Academic Mind* (Glencoe, Ill.: Free Press, in press). [First published 1958.]

2. The relation between permissiveness and age is as follows:

	Highly Permissive	Quite Permissive	Somewhat Permissive	Somewhat Conservative	Clearly Conservative
40 years or younger	328	258	299	127	126
41–50	125	132	188	86	101
51 years or older	98	115	201	140	121

Without further data, it is difficult to interpret this relationship satisfactorily. It could be that increasing age makes people more conservative. But the finding might also be due to some process of selection which voluntarily or involuntarily eliminates the most permissive people from the academic field. For the purpose on hand, it should be clear that the figures just given form the base for the percent figures reported in Table 5.

3. At each of these schools at least 13 respondents were interviewed. This number (chosen a bit arbitrarily: 14 or 15, or perhaps 12, would have served) insures against too much weight being given the replies of any single respondent in forming an overall school rate.

4. At least one other comparison with Europe is worth mentioning. Here the teacher in the grade school, the one with whom every American has contact, is usually a woman. Especially in small towns, she does not have nearly the prestige of her male counterparts in European villages and towns.

5. The recurrent disagreements among the armed services provide an interesting parallel. Self-interest and selective perception would explain that the majority in the Army and Navy are often on different sides of a controversy. But the *extent* of in-group agreement on both sides can only be explained by a process of mutual reinforcement.

6. Becker, Carl, *Progress and Power* (Stanford: Stanford University Press, 1936).

7. In another part of the study it is shown that the attitude of conservative professors is more affected by academic freedom incidents in their own college, while the permissive professors know more about and are relatively more agitated by incidents which have aroused national attention. The parallel is clear to Merton's comparison between local or cosmopolitan community leaders.

8. We have another set of data which seems to indicate that the respondents of highest permissiveness are less favored by salary increases, but our information on this point is somewhat vague. The indications are strong enough to deserve further explorations wherever more precise data on salaries should be available.

9. The third line of Table 9 gives for the total sample a more detailed account of how apprehension rises with permissiveness. The relation is considerably stronger than was visible in the condensed form of Table 7.

II

METHODOLOGY OF SOCIAL RESEARCH

6

Observing

The Controversy over Detailed Interviews:
An Offer for Negotiation

If two people vigorously disagree on whether something is blue or green, the chances are that the object is composed of both colors and that for some reason the two contestants are either unable or unwilling to see more than the one. If in methodological discussions, competent workers assume vehemently opposite positions, it is generally a good time for someone to enter the scene and suggest that the parties are both right and wrong.

A recent issue of *Public Opinion Quarterly* (Summer, 1943) provides one of the many indications that such a situation has come about in the public opinion field. A representative of the Division of Program Surveys in the Department of Agriculture reports on large-scale research work, the core of which is an interviewing technique "intended to draw full intensive discussions" and using "various nondirective means of stimulating full discussion in the interviewing situation."[1] Preceding this report is an article by a well-known psychologist who dubs this technique "depth interview" and describes it in rather uncomplimentary terms. One of his conclusions is that "there is little or no evidence to support the tacit assumption that the so-called depth interview yields more valid responses from people than do other types."[2] For him, simple, "yes-no" questions, used judiciously, are sufficient.

The matter is important from more than a scientific point of view. Applied social research is a new venture. Only yesterday did the government begin large-scale studies in public opinion. The market and consumer studies which are now finding acceptance in many industries are likewise all of recent date. Managers in business as well as in public administration are faced with sharply contending factions among research professionals. Should they succumb to skepticism or

Reprinted from "The Controversy over Detailed Interviews: An Offer for Negotiation,"
Public Opinion Quarterly 8 (Spring 1944): 38–60.

discouragement and fail to give this new branch of the social sciences the opportunity to prove itself, then development might be seriously retarded. It therefore seems justified to present the problem to a larger public with an earnest effort toward impartiality.

Employing a neutral terminology, we shall allude to our subject as the "open-ended interview." The term serves to describe a crucial aspect of this type of interviewing—the fact that "open-ended interviews" do not set fixed answers in terms of which a respondent must reply. Eventually a more animated expression may be desirable. (To save space we shall abbreviate the term and refer to it hereafter as OI.) Rather than asking for a definition it would be better if the reader visualizes the situation in which an OI occurs. In the interview situation the interviewer by an appropriate introduction attempts to establish the best possible rapport between himself and the respondent because he is aware that he may have to interview the respondent an hour or longer. He then proceeds to ask one of the ten or fifteen questions which have been assigned to him by the central office. Sometimes the respondent himself immediately plunges into great detail, and the interviewer simply permits him to continue. If the first answer is brief, however, the interviewer is instructed to "probe." There are quite a number of devices for eliciting detailed, free response. Mere silence will sometimes induce the respondent to elaborate. Or, the interviewer may just repeat the respondent's own words with an appropriate inflection. Asking for examples will often prove helpful. Then again questions such as the following are used: "How did you happen to notice it? What makes you think so? How did you feel about it before? Do most of your friends have the same opinion?" The trained OI field worker has the goal of his inquiry clearly imprinted in his mind, but he adapts his inquiry to the concrete situation between the interviewee and himself.

If properly conducted, such an OI will result in a detailed document which covers the whole area under investigation, including the interviewer's observations of the respondent's reactions and background.

The OI is suggested by its proponents in opposition to what one might term the "straight poll question." The latter gives the respondent the occasion to answer only "Yes," "No," "Don't know," or to make a choice among a small number of listed possible answers. Between these two extremes there are, of course, several steps. Actually there is hardly a poll where there is not some freedom left for the respondent to express himself in his own way. It is not necessary here to discuss where the straight poll question ends and the OI begins. For all practical purposes the distinction is clear enough.

A rather thorough survey of published and unpublished studies based on the OI technique was made for the purpose of this paper. It is necessary to describe and classify these in some detail because many current misunderstandings come from an insufficient distinction among the different functions of the OI; if people disagree on its usefulness, they very often do not have the same functions in mind. It is the plan of this paper to present the main uses of the OI at their very best and to stress the advantages which are generally singled out by the advocates of this technique. Then we shall select a specific criterion for evaluation and summarize pertinent criticism. It is hoped that as a result we shall end up with a balanced view on the subject.

The Six Main Functions of the OI Technique

1. *Clarifying the meaning of a respondent's answer.* Before asking him whether war profits should be limited, we have to find out what the respondent thinks the word "profit" means. Some people talk of the total income of a company as profit, others believe it is the difference between wholesale and retail prices, still others are of the opinion that war profits are the difference between pre-war and war earnings. By discussing the general subject matter with him we are very likely to obtain a fairly clear picture of what would be equivalent to his *private definition* of these terms. One frequently underestimates the number of terms which seem obvious to the interviewer but which are ambiguous or even unknown to the lower educated section of the population.

In other cases it is not so much the meaning of words as the *implication of an opinion* which has to be clarified. If a respondent is in favor of reducing taxes, does he know that as a result many government services will have to be reduced? If he is in favor of free speech, does he realize that such freedom must also pertain to people who may express opinions that are very distasteful to him?

If respondents are asked to voice their thoughts on a course of action, it is important to know against what *alternative possibilities* they had weighed their choice. A respondent is for the continuation of the Dies Committee: has he weighed that against the possibility that the Department of Justice can adequately handle the problem of subversive activities, or did he feel that if the Dies Committee does not do so, no one else will? Another respondent is for government regulation of business: does he prefer this to completely free enterprise, or has he considered the different ways by which an individual business man can be regulated through his own trade organizations?

Finally, the OI permits a respondent to clarify his opinion by introducing *qualifications*. He is in favor of rationing if it is administered fairly for everyone. He is in favor of married women getting defense jobs if it has been made sure that there are no unemployed men left. The respondent might not volunteer such qualifications if the interview is a too hurried one.

2. *Singling out the decisive aspects of an opinion.* If we deal with attitudes toward rather complex objects, we often want to know the *decisive aspects* by which a respondent is guided. Take the opinion on *candidates* for public office. At this moment, for example, the Republicans in some mid-western states prefer Dewey to Willkie as Presidential nominee. What does Dewey stand for in the eyes of these people? Party loyalty? Isolationism? Administrative ability? Gang-busting? Here again the OI would proceed in characteristic fashion. What has the respondent heard about the two candidates? What does he think would happen if Dewey were to become President? And so on. In the end we should be able to distinguish groups for which Dewey means quite different things, and fruitful statistical comparisons on a number of social characteristics could be carried through.

Similar possibilities can come up when people are called upon to judge *concrete situations*. They do or do not like the working conditions in their plants. If the answer is in the negative, what features do they especially dislike? In order to get a reasonable idea of people's complaints a rather detailed discussion is necessary; the OI is a good device for this purpose. Other examples of such procedure can easily be found: to what does the respondent attribute rising prices? Or the increase in juvenile delinquency?

Here belong also some recent efforts in the field of *communications* research. People like or dislike a film or a radio program. Through detailed discussions it is possible to bring out quite clearly which elements in the production make for the audience's reaction.[3]

The singling out of decisive aspects also pertains to *issues*. If respondents are against sending lend-lease supplies to Russia, it is important to know what about such a policy they dislike. Do they disapprove of Russian communism, or do they think that the Russians do not need the supplies, or do they feel that other parts of the world war panorama are more important? Here, again, the OI would not only ask for an opinion on the basic issues but would probe the respondents for further details.

Very often the decisive aspects of a candidate, a situation, a document or an issue will be elicited by starting a discussion with the words: "Why do you think so?" Or, "Why do you prefer . . . ?" But hardly ever will one such question give all the necessary information.

If people prefer Dewey as the Republican nominee and are asked why they do so, they will very often say, "Because he is the better man," or, "Because a friend feels the same way." Then the interviewer must keep in mind the fact that he is looking for decisive features and must keep on asking questions. For instance: "What makes him a better man?" Or, "Why do you think your friend favors him?"[4]

3. *What has influenced an opinion.* If people approve of an issue or vote for a candidate (or buy a product), it is useful to divide the determining factors of such action into three main groups: the *decisive features* of the object in question, which account for its being chosen; the *predispositions* of the respondents, which make them act one way or another; and the *influences which are brought to bear upon them*, especially those which mediate between them and the object of their choice.[5] The use of the OI to investigate the first group has just been discussed. The quest for predispositions (attitude, motives) will be dealt with under points four and five. We now consider the use of the OI in the search for *influences*.

The typical research situation here is one wherein we try to assess the importance of a certain event. Let us turn, for example, to people who bought bonds after listening to Kate Smith or who started storing potatoes after a government campaign to this effect had been started or who improved their production records after a system of music-while-you-work had been introduced in a plant. A well-conducted OI should provide enough information so that the causal role of the exposure can be appraised. The rules for such interviews have been rather well worked out.[6]

If the respondent claims that the specific speech had an effect on him, a sort of cross-examination is necessary along the following lines: Wasn't he ready to perform the final act before he heard the speech? Didn't something else happen after the speech which is a more likely explanation for his action? If the respondent denies being affected by the speech, then the whole interview has to be conducted as if the purpose were to break down this contention: Why didn't the respondent act before he heard the speech? Did he have any other sources of information? In other words, the technique consists of checking up on whether, according to logical and psychological commonsense, the respondent would have acted otherwise than he did if he had not heard the speech or read the pamphlet. Obviously it is not possible to anticipate all the questions which have to be asked in order to bring to light the elements preceding the final act and surrounding the influence under investigation. The task of the OI is to draw out those factors so sharply that the reader of the interview can form a judgment as to whether any causal role of the influence should be assumed or not.

This technique of unearthing influences by OIs is especially pertinent to advertising problems because of the insistent use of the same "stimuli" in radio programs or magazine campaigns. With the Government turning to "campaigns" to influence the consumption or saving habits of the citizenry, however, it would deserve more attention from students of public opinion. During election campaigns similar problems come up, particularly if an effort is made to study those people who at the beginning of the campaign had not yet formulated opinions.

4. *Determining complex attitude patterns*. A fourth group of applications comes into play when we turn to the *classification of rather complex attitude patterns*. If we want to ascertain how active people are in their war participation or how disturbed they are by current food shortages, the OI actually discusses such subject matters with the respondents, getting their recent experiences and reactions. The purpose is to make an adequate classification of the material so obtained. Further assumptions come easily to mind. People can be classified according to how satisfied they are with local handling of the draft situation, according to the ways they adjust to the lack of gasoline, according to their satisfaction or dissatisfaction with the amount of information they get on the war, etc. This procedure is singularly characteristic of Rensis Likert's work in the Department of Agriculture.[7]

If it is used to assess the extent to which respondents are concerned with a certain problem and how intensely they feel about it, this approach assumes special importance. Two respondents might give the same answer to a simple opinion poll question. For the one, however, it is an important issue on which he has spent much thought, whereas the other may have formed his opinion spontaneously as the poll investigator asked him about it. The possible perfunctory nature of replies to public opinion polls has been the object of much criticism. Those who feel strongly in favor of the OI emphasize that right at this point such a danger is obviated—the danger that poll results will be misleading because they do not take into account intensity of feeling or amount of concern.

This role of the OI does not necessarily terminate with a one-dimensional rating scale of, say, intensity of feeling. The OI is suitable for more complex ratings as well. In a study of people's reactions to changes in food habits, sponsored by the National Research Council, the interviewers were instructed to "watch carefully for all offhand comments to one of the following frames of reference: Money, Health, Taste, Status."[8] The procedure was to talk with people about current food shortages, the adjustments they had made, and the points at which they experienced difficulties. From their discussion it was possible to classify them into four groups according to which of the four contexts they spontaneously stressed. The study found, for example, that high-income groups refer to health twice as often as money, whereas in low-income groups money is the frame of reference three times more frequently than is health.

Finally we have what is known as the "gratification study." In an analysis of the gratification people get from the Professor Quiz programs, for example, a variety of appeals could be distinguished. Some listeners are very much intrigued by the competitive element of the contest; others like to test their own knowledge; still others hope to learn something from the questions posed on the program.[9] We could not expect the untrained respondent to explain clearly the psychological complexities of his interest or his reaction. It is not even likely that he would classify himself accurately if we let him choose among different possibilities. Again the OI is needed to provide the necessary information for the trained analyst. Its practical use lies in the following direction: If we know what attitudes are statistically dominant we can either strengthen the "appeal" elements in the program which are likely to get an enlarged audience; or we can try to change these attitudes if, for some ulterior reason, we consider the prevailing distribution unsatisfactory.

Such studies have also been made in the public opinion field; for example, in analyzing the gratification people get out of writing letters to senators.[10]

5. *Motivational interpretations.* Ratings, attitude types, and gratification lists are only the beginning of a conceptual line which ends in studies based on *broad motivational interpretations.* We cannot hope here to present systematically the ways in which psychologists distinguish between the different kinds of "drives" according to their range, depth, or the specificity of their relations to the world of objects.[11] The picture would not be complete, nevertheless, if we were to omit a mention of the use of the OI technique for the purpose of understanding people's reactions in such broad conceptual contexts.

The OI collects a variety of impressions, experiences, and sidelines which the respondent offers when he is asked to discuss a given topic. The man who does the study then makes a kind of psychological construction. He creates a picture of some basic motivation of which all these details are, so to speak, manifestations.

Consider an example. In studying certain groups of unemployed one makes a variety of observations: they walk slowly, they lose interest in public affairs, do not keep track of their time, express opinions only with hesitation, stop looking for jobs—in short, they can best be understood as discouraged, resigned beings whose psychological living space has been severely contracted. On the basis of this conceptualization we would not expect them, e.g., to join revolutionary movements which require initiative. If, on the other hand, we are interested in retaining whatever morale they do have left, we would reject the idea of a straight dole in favor of work relief which would keep them psychologically "on the go."

There is only a rather short step from this example to the kind of OI studies which we want to discuss. For a number of reasons most of them have been done in the field of advertising.

People who talk about their shoe purchases often mention how embarrassing it is to expose one's feet in stockings, how one is virtually a prisoner in the hands of the salesman, etc. They are also likely to point out that such-and-such a salesman was friendly, or that they do like stores where the customers are not seated too near each other. The study director finally forms the hypothesis that the shoe-buying situation is one likely to evoke a feeling of inferiority. To alleviate this feeling and thus lead to a larger and more satisfied patronage, a number of obvious suggestions can be made for the training of salesmen and the arrangement of the store.

Finally, take a series of OI's where women say that they like fruits in glass jars because then they can see the product and also because they feel there is greater danger of food spoiling in tin cans. The conclusion is not that lots of fruits in glass jars should be shown. A motivational interpretation which takes all the pertinent remarks in the OI's into consideration will rather proceed as follows. Glass jars have something reassuring about them, whereas tin cans have a slight connotation of a dungeon in which the food and even oneself is jailed. The appropriate advertising for glass jars, therefore, would show them among flowers, in rays of sunshine, to stress the exhilarating elements in the whole complex. Visibility would then be only one of these elements.

To discuss this use of OI's in a short space is impossible, especially since its logic has not yet been thought through very well. The social scientist who tries to clarify such analysis faces a conflict between two goals to which he is equally devoted. On the one hand, these interpretations serve to integrate a host of details as well as make us aware of new ones which we might otherwise overlook; often they are very brilliant. On the other hand, they violate our need for verification because by their very nature they can never be proved but only made plausible. It is no coincidence that in the two examples given above we have added to each interpretation some practical advice derived from it. What such motivational analysis does is to see past experiences as parts of some psychological drive which can be reactivated by related material, be it propaganda or institutional devices.[12]

6. *Clarifying statistical relationships.* In the five areas outlined so far the OI was the point of departure for all subsequent analysis. Now finally we have to deal with studies where statistical results are available and where the OI serves to *interpret and refine statistical inter-relationships.* The procedure could be called the analysis of deviate cases.

When, for instance, the panic was studied which followed the famous broadcast on the "Invasion From Mars," it was found that people on a lower educational level were most likely to believe in the occurrence of the great catastrophe.[13] Yet some lower-educated people were not frightened at all. When these deviate cases were subject to an OI, many turned out to be mechanics or people who had mechanical hobbies; they were accustomed to checking up on things, a habit the "regular" people had acquired by a successful formal education. On the other hand, quite a number of well-educated people were frightened. When an OI was made with them, the following was sometimes found: During the broadcast they had been in special social situations where it was not clear who should take the initiative of checking up; the lack of social structure impeded purposeful action, and everyone got panicky.

Another example can be taken from unemployment studies. In general it is found that the more amicable the relations in a family prior to the depression, the more firmly would the family stand the impact of unemployment. Again we can inspect deviate cases. A couple fights constantly before the depression, but after the husband becomes unemployed, they get along better. A detailed interview reveals the probability that here the husband wanted to be submissive and the wife dominant, but folkways prevented them from accepting this inverse role. Unemployment, then, enforces a social situation here which is psychologically adequate. Or, a good marriage breaks down surprisingly quickly as a result of the husband's unemployment. A specification of the case shows that the man's sexual habits are rather vulnerable and become disorganized under the blow of the loss of his job.[14]

The general pattern of these studies proceeds from an empirical correlation which is usually not very high. We take cases which do not follow the majority pattern and try to gain an impression or to account for their irregularity. The political scientist is used to such procedure.[15] He knows, for instance, that the more poor people and Catholics live in a given precinct of a big city, the more Democratic votes he can expect. But here is a precinct which qualifies on both scores, and still it went Republican. What accounts for this deviation? Is the Democratic machine inefficient? Has a special local grievance developed? Was there a recent influx of people with different political traditions? This is quite analogous to what we are trying to do when we are faced with individual cases which went statistically out of line. With the help of the OI we try to discover new factors which, if properly introduced, would improve our multiple correlation.

Usually the matter is put by saying that detailed case studies help us to understand an empirical correlation. This is quite all right as far as the psychology of the investigator goes. It would be more correct, however, to say that the OI helps to develop hypotheses as to the conditions under which you would expect our first correlation to become higher. If it were our task to formulate in general terms why the OI is so helpful to the better understanding of an attitude, our starting point would actually be here. We would have to make quite clear that the insight gained by a qualitative approach is nothing else than a hypothetical relation between a number of factors. But that would go beyond the purpose of this section, in which we intended to give no more than a vivid picture of the actual research experiences out of which the OI technique has grown. It is to the controversial aspect of the problem that we now turn.

The Issue Becomes a Problem

The six areas just outlined could be looked at in two ways. For one, they represent desirable goals for public opinion research. We need more detailed knowledge as to what the answers of our respondents mean, on what specific points their opinions are based, in what larger motivational contexts they belong, etc. At the same time, the different applications of the OI also imply criticism to the effect that one straight poll question will hardly ever reach any of these goals successfully.

One can agree with this criticism without concluding that the OI technique is the only remedy. If this paper were written for a psychological journal, for instance, the course of our discussion from here on would be prescribed. We should have to compare results obtained by straight poll questions with those collected by OI's and decide which are preferable according to some adequate criteria. The present analysis, however, falls under the heading of "Research Policy." The research administrator has to make decisions as to the most desirable procedures long before we have provided all the necessary data on the comparative merits of different research methods.

What line of argument would one take in such a situation? No one can close his eyes to the shortcomings of many of the current opinion-poll practices. Having begun with the simple problem of predicting elections, they use, very often, a greatly oversimplified approach for the gauging of attitudes toward complex issues. We shall also agree that a well-conducted OI gives us a fascinating wealth of information on the attitude of a single respondent. When it comes to the statistical analysis of many OI's, the matter is already not so simple. It is in the nature of this technique that just the most valuable details of one OI become difficult to compare with the answers obtained in another interview. It can safely be said that the proponents of the OI technique have made much more progress in the conduct of the interviews than in their statistical analysis.

But even if the OI technique were not to have methodological troubles of its own, it would still be open to one very serious objection. It is necessarily an expensive and slow procedure and, as a result, studies which are made for practical purposes will always be based on a small number of cases. It is inconceivable at this moment that an agency would have the resources or the time to make many thousands of OI's on the subject. This is a decisive drawback. True, a surprisingly small number of cases is needed for a fairly correct estimate of how many Republicans there are in a community or how many people save their fat and grease. But do we want to stop here? Don't we want to know in which social groups some of those activities are more frequent than in others? Aren't we trying to account for the reasons why some people do a thing and others do not? And how can this be done except by careful cross-tabulation of one part of our data against other parts? And for this, a much larger number of cases is needed.

In other words, the OI technique, even if it were perfect in itself, places us in a dilemma. By laying all the stress on the detailed description of the single respondent's attitude, it forces us into relatively small numbers of interviews. This in turn handicaps another important progress in public opinion research: the progress which consists of comparing carefully the distribution of opinions in different subgroups of the population and relating a given opinion to the personal characteristics and to other attitudes of the respondent.

From the standpoint of research policy, therefore, which is the standpoint taken in this paper, the whole problem comes to this. Is there not some way to use all the good ideas which the proponents of the OI technique have and still to develop methods which are more objective, more manageable on a mass basis—which, in short, give us sufficient material to do a thorough analysis of the factors which make for a given distribution of public opinion?

Under these aspects we shall go once more through the six areas discussed above. In each case we shall look for procedures which combine the administrative advantages of the straight poll questions with the psychological advantages of the OI. Quite frankly we want to "eat our cake and have it, too." All folklore notwithstanding, research progress consists in the art of doing things which at first seem incompatible. As we proceed, it will turn out that these compromise techniques do not make the OI superfluous but give it a new and, as we feel, more valuable place in the whole scheme of public opinion research.

To bring out more clearly our trend of thought, we begin with a little scheme. To the left we have our six areas; to the right we have short names for the procedures which would overcome some of the shortcomings of the straight poll question and still be more formalized and manageable on a mass basis than the OI.

Current Applications of the OI Techniques	Possible Objective Alternatives for the OI
1. Clarifying the meaning of a respondent's answer	1. Interlocking system of poll questions
2. Singling out the decisive aspects of an opinion	2. Check lists
3. Discerning influences	3. None
4. Determining complex attitude patterns	4. Scales and typologies
5. Interpreting motivation	5. Projective tests
6. Clarifying statistical relationships	6. None

It is to the short description and evaluation of the right side of the scheme that we now turn.

1. *Clarifying meaning by the use of interlocking poll questions.* In the first area we dealt with the clarification of the respondent's opinion. Did he know the significance of what he was talking about? In the course of an OI, by making the respondent elaborate in more detail, we will find out. But after all, the number of possible variations is not so great; it is often possible to get by explicit questions all

the material we can use for comparative analysis of many interview returns.

Consider the following two cases. Studenski has pointed out that when people are asked whether they want lower taxes, most of them will say "yes."[16] After having asked this general question, however, he then asked a series of specific questions on whether the government should discontinue relief, work projects, expenses for national defense, expenses for schools, police, etc. Respondents who wanted taxes reduced but services maintained had obviously, to say the least, an inconsistent attitude toward the problem.[17] In a different context, Kornhauser has pointed out the shortcomings of the question: Should Congress pass a law forbidding strikes in war industries or should war workers have the right to go on strike? Obviously there are other devices, such as an improved arbitration system or the endowment of union leaders with some semi-public power to keep their members from striking. By offering a whole set of such alternatives it is undoubtedly possible to get a much clearer picture of the respondent's real attitude.

In this and many similar examples the technique used consists of an *interlocking system of poll questions,* each of which is very simple but which through proper cross-tabulation permits the separation of respondents according to the extent to which they see the implications of their opinion

Although we cannot go into details here, we have studied dozens of pertinent cases and are satisfied that for any given topic it is always possible to find an appropriate system for interlocking questions. The right procedure consists of beginning the study with a considerable number of very detailed OI's. These should come from different parts of the country and should serve to develop the structure of the problem. Experience shows that after one to three hundred such reports have been studied, very few new factors come up. At this point we can begin to develop a set of specific questions centering around the main attitude and bringing out its implications and qualifications. There is no reason why we should not ask specifically (by the use of ordinary poll questions) what knowledge and experience the respondent has in this field; what his opinions are in related fields; whether he does or does not expect certain things to happen; whether he has ever thought of the problem, or whether he cannot make up his mind about it, and so on.

Here we come across a very characteristic relationship between the OI and more formalized methods in opinion research. The OI serves as a source of observation and of ideas from which sets of precise poll questions can be derived which will be more manageable in the field and more susceptible to statistical analysis. On one occasion the useful suggestion was made that the special job of *converter* should be developed: that people should specialize in studying OI's and seeing how they could be converted into systems of interlocking questions.

So far not enough thought has been spent on making this conversion procedure an explicit research operation for which standard examples and rules should be developed. Once this is done, it will probably turn out that in the area under discussion here the OI, although much preferable to isolated straight poll questions, is not so good as a well-structured set of straight poll questions. The proponents of the OI technique at this point usually see only the justified goal and the shortcomings of current public opinion polls. They have seldom the occasion to see in their own studies the hundreds of OI's which either do not yield really useful information or are so unique that if they are submitted to a comparative analysis, all the details which make them invaluable as a first phase of an investigation are lost when the final report is reached.

Sometimes when we want to clarify the meaning of an answer, especially in regard to qualifications, check lists can be considered an appropriate procedure. Since, however, check lists are more frequently indicated when it comes to the assessment of decisive features, they will be discussed under the next heading.

2. *Using check lists to get at the decisive aspects of an opinion.* If we want to know what people like about a candidate or what bothers them about the present rationing system, we can make a list of the probable answers and ask the respondents which answer fits their case.

The advantages and disadvantages of *check lists* have been repeatedly discussed. The minimum requirement is that they contain an exhaustive list of all the possibilities, for it is known that items not mentioned in a check list are less likely to be mentioned by the respondents. But even a good check list has certain dangers. If people are asked what wish they would make if they had a magic ring, they seldom mention "being very bright," because they do not think of intelligence as something that can be wished for. If, however, they get a check list of possible wishes which includes "intelligence," they are more likely to pick it. The less concrete the topic is, the more will the check list influence the answers.

As long as all this is not better explored by comparing the results from large-scale check lists and from the classifications of free answers, it is not possible to make a valid decision. Yet with the help of a careful analysis of OI's it seems logical to assume that exhaustive check lists can be safely constructed—ones which would be as safe as the results of open-ended interviewing. For complex topics the cautious research student will, of course, be hesitant to rely too easily on check lists. When in doubt he will prefer to rely on OI's recorded by conscientious interviewers and classified by sensitive analysts for the study of decisive features.

In studying the decisive aspects of opinion there are cases where the more formalized alternative for the OI would not be a check list, but a system of interlocking questions. This is especially true in dealing with opinions on policy issues. Suppose people have expressed themselves on the idea of married women working in war industry and are opposed to it. The open-ended question, "Why do you feel this way?" brings out a variety of comments which show that people look at the matter from a number of aspects: some feel that it is bad for the home if women stay out too much; others feel that women are not equipped for factory work or that working conditions are not adequate for them; still others do not want women to compete with men for jobs. Here are four features of the whole problem on which respondents could be asked their opinions explicitly. Do you feel that women are equipped for war jobs? Do you feel that they are a competitive danger for men? Etc. By cross-tabulating the answers to the sub-issues against the main issue of women in war work, one probably would get a better idea of the general attitude pattern than if the "reasons" were directly tabulated.

Again the OI is indispensable in preliminary studies to give one an idea as to what aspects should be considered. If, however, a large number of interviews is to be collected, the interlocking system of questions might be preferable, especially if great effort is made to get an appropriate conversion of preliminary OI's into a system of more precise questions.

3. *Are there other ways of studying what has influenced opinion?* Whether it is possible to discern influences which are exercised upon people is a controversial question. In more extreme cases such decisions are obviously possible or impossible. If a child goes down to the grocer's "because my mother sent me down," we should consider such a statement as equivalent to a controlled experiment. Putting it rather exaggeratedly: if we set up two groups of well-matched children and had the mothers of the children in one group tell them to go to the grocer's, we should certainly expect to find more children from the "experimental" than from the control group at the grocer's. On the other hand, if a person has committed a crime and we ask

him whether that is due to the fact that his parents immigrated to this country, we shall consider whatever he says not very reliable. The command of the mother is much more "discernible" as an influence than the whole background of family life.[18]

Fortunately, in public opinion research we are mostly interested in rather "discernible" influences. Whether people began to salvage paper under the influence of a government campaign or whether a specific pamphlet made them contribute blood to the Red Cross can be discovered fairly well by direct interviewing. For such studies the OI appears to be an important research tool. Thus, it becomes even more urgent to make its use as expert as possible. Sometimes it is not used wisely. Studies of the following kind have been circulated. People who began to can fruit were asked why they did so. Sixty per cent said "because of the campaign," 15% "because it is necessary for the war effort." Here is obviously a meaningless result—for OI or otherwise. Many of the 15% may have learned from the campaign that private canning was a patriotic duty. However, the interviewer was too easily satisfied with the first answer which came to the mind of the respondent instead of asking "Where did you learn that canning is important for the war effort?"[19]

We do not wish to discuss here under what conditions controlled experiments are possible and justified. Just for the record, we might add that the result of a controlled experiment does not necessarily indicate correctly the effectiveness of a real campaign. In a controlled experiment we expose some of the people artificially and may then find that they are strongly influenced by the campaign material. In real life people select themselves for exposure. It might well be that mainly those who are not affected by a radio speech are willing to listen to it. This is, for instance, one of the problems in educational broadcasting, where there is a wide difference between experimental and actual success of programs.

4. *Scales and typologies for the analysis of attitude patterns.* When it comes to the objective correlates for the use of the OI in the classification of complex attitude patterns, we find ourselves in a peculiar situation. The topic has been a favorite one for social-research students; we have discussed "case studies" versus quantitative methods for a decade.[20] An appropriate instance comes from the study which this writer made during the presidential election of 1940. The task was to appraise how interested people were in the election. Had we used the OI technique, the interviewer would have talked with the respondent and by taking down what he said, by observing his participation in the discussion, he would have formed an opinion on his

interest and then noted it in the form of a rating. Instead we asked the respondent three questions: whether he had tried to convince someone of his political ideas; whether he had done anything for the success of his candidate; and whether he was very anxious to see his candidate elected. Each respondent got a definite score according to how he answered the three questions.[21]

But how does such an objective scale compare with the impressionistic ratings obtained from an OI? The problems involved can best be explained by an example.

If in everyday life we call another person timid, we do so because of the way he walks or because of his hesitant speech and sometimes because of cues of which we are not precisely aware ourselves. In each case we use whatever cues the situation offers; they might be quite different from one case to the next. A "timidity rating," on the other hand, would provide us with a list of items on which an interviewer would have to get an observation for every case, if necessary by asking a direct question. The more timidity characteristics on this list applied to the respondents, the higher would be his timidity score. Using such a scale, the interviewer could not make use of incidental observations if they were not included in the list, even if in a special case he had a strong conviction that the respondent was much more timid than his scale value indicated.

All this can be directly applied to our problem. A good OI reproduces the full vividness of an actual observation; but if nothing characteristic happens in the interview situation or if the interviewer misses cues, then we have little on which to base our final classification. With the scale we can count on a definite amount of data, but some of them might be rather artificial and often we must forego valuable observations within our reach. *Thus, a scale because of its rigidity will hardly be as good as an OI under its best conditions but can hardly let us down as much as an OI sometimes does.*

Sometimes we classify material not in a one-dimensional order but according to *types* of attitudes, types of interest, or types of gratification. The objective tools for this purpose do not present problems which go beyond what we have said about the use of scales. Suppose, for instance, we want to classify people into three groups, according to whether they look at postwar problems mainly from a domestic-economic, a foreign affairs–peace, or a civil liberties–justice point of view. We would set up a number of questions and classify people according to the pattern of the answers they give. The standard example for such procedures can be found in Allport and Vernon's Study of Values Test.[22] These psychologists took as a starting point Spranger's well-known personality types. People are characterized according to the values they are most concerned with: power, money, religion, beauty, wisdom, or personal contacts. In order to get to a formalized classification, the test asks people, for instance, what they look for first when they enter a living-room, what historical person they would be most interested in meeting, and so on. A respondent who looks at the books in the room first and who would like most to meet Einstein, etc., would be classified as an intellectual type.

In deciding whether such objective tests or an impressionistic classification based on an OI is preferable, one should keep in mind the fact that it is difficult to develop good test questions of this kind. Impressionistic classifications, even if they have methodological disadvantages, are more easily made in a *new* situation. One practical solution, therefore, might be to use OI's whenever a problem comes up only once. If we deal with recurring problems such as, for instance, people's eagerness to help in the war effort or their attitude toward our allies or toward government regulation of business, more explicit and standardized criteria for classification might be desirable.

There is also the possibility of trying a combination of both approaches. Taking once more the example of interest in the election, the interviewer might first ask standard questions of the type mentioned above; then he might continue the discussion and note any additional observations which might suggest a correction of the rigid score. Such procedures are often used when it comes to classifying people according to socio-economic status. It seems useful to classify people first according to the rental area of the city in which they live. Then, after the interviewer has talked with the respondent, seen how he dresses and how his living-room looks, he might make an impressionistic correction of the original score.

5. *Is there an easy way to get at motivation?* When we discussed broad motivational interpretations, we stressed all the hazards involved in this method. Correspondingly, it is very difficult to find an objective or formalized method for such an approach. *Projective tests* come nearest to it. The general idea of these tests is that people are presented with unstructured material. Here is a crying girl; other children are asked to guess why she is crying. Or, an inkblot is shown to some people, as in the Rorschach test, and they are asked to state what form it signifies to them. It is then assumed that the way people interpret such material, which has no definite meaning of its own, is indicative of what the people themselves are concerned with.[23]

Applications to a public-opinion problem can only be invented because, to our knowledge, such studies have never been tried. If one wants to test people's attitudes toward public administration, one might, for instance, tell a short story of a successful public official who was suddenly dismissed. What was the reason? Was he found to be corrupt? Or was he the victim of a political intrigue? Or didn't he agree with the government's policy?

After Pearl Harbor, when so many people were concerned about the weakness of the American Navy, it would not have been easy to ask direct questions on this subject; few people would have cared to give an unpatriotic answer. One might, however, have shown them a series of pictures of battleships varying in degree of technical perfection. Which, in the opinion of the respondent, is an American and which a Japanese battleship? The proportion of people picking out the poor ship as an American model might have been a good index of the extent of concern about American armaments.

The psychological assumptions involved in a projective test have yet to be studied exhaustively. The answers are usually quite difficult to classify, and much depends upon the interpretation of the analyst. In the future such techniques may provide a very important tool for public opinion research. For the moment it can hardly be claimed that they are much better formalized than a good OI. If, therefore, one is interested in broad motivational interpretations, a well-conducted OI is probably still the best source for material.

6. *The meaning of statistical relationships.* Nothing has to be added to our discussion of the analysis of deviate cases in the preceding section. Here the OI is in its most legitimate place.

Some Conclusions

If we now summarize briefly this critical survey of the OI technique, we can make a number of points as to its position in the general scheme of public opinion research.

We saw that the problem is not new. Since the beginning of social research, students have tried to combine the value of detailed qualitative applications with the advantages of more formalized techniques which could be managed on a mass basis.

We saw, furthermore, that a line along which such an integration could come about emerges. The OI is indispensable at the beginning of any study where it classifies the structure of a problem in all its details. It is also invaluable at the end of a study for anyone who is not satisfied with the mere recording of the low correlations we usually obtain. Good research consists in weaving back and forth between OI's and the more cut-and-dried procedures.

The *conversion* of OI's into sets of specific poll questions has shown up a new skill in our field and one which has found much too little attention.

The stress on this problem of conversion has revealed a weakness on both sides of the controversy. The proponents of the OI have successfully denounced the shortcomings of single straight poll questions, but by stressing so strongly the informality of the OI they have driven the poll managers to a defensive position, which is delaying the whole progress of opinion research. Field staffs are not equipped to make difficult decisions in the course of the interview. However, the idea of *interconnected question sets* converted from preceding OI's shifts the weight of the problem from the field staffs to the central office. The attack should be directed against the directors of polls, who do not take the time and the effort to structuralize the problem and to devise the interlocking question structure which any well-trained field staff should be able to handle.

Concerning the classification of complex attitude patterns, another point can be made. Public opinion research has grown so quickly that much of the work is handled by people who do not know the history of social research in the last thirty years. Much valuable thinking and experimenting done in universities long before election results were predicted is immediately applicable to this new field. The construction of scales and the whole tradition of attitude measurement has developed its own logic, which can be profitably applied to the present controversy.

The same efforts have also opened up a considerable number of problems which have not yet been solved at all. The value of check lists, the use of projective tests, and the question of whether simple propaganda influences can be discerned by direct interview are characteristic examples. At all these points patient and painstaking work is needed. The solution of these problems will only be retarded if we let research administrators believe that they face different schools of research, whereas they deal only with different guesses as to what the final answers to these problems will be.

The hope might be expressed that this paper will not be regarded as an attempted judgment in the OI controversy. It tries to show that the problem consists of many different parts. For some problems the OI is indispenable; for others it is definitely wasteful. Often we do not really know the right answer. In these last cases the prudent administrator will do best to look for the *combination of method* best adapted to the specific research task on hand.

Notes

1. Hans E. Skott, "Attitude Research in the Department of Agriculture," *Public Opinion Quarterly*, 1943, 7, 280–292.
2. Henry C. Link, "An Experiment in Depth Interviewing," *Public Opinion Quarterly*, 1943, 7, 267–279.
3. P. F. Lazarsfeld and R. K. Merton, "Studies in Radio and Film Propaganda," *Transactions of the New York Academy of Sciences*, Series II, 1943, 6, No. 2, 58–79.
4. It should be emphasized that the question "why" is useful also for the other purposes which will be discussed in the remaining four points. This is easily understood if one considers that the word has hardly any meaning in itself. It is about equivalent to saying that the respondent should talk some more. "Why" is a good start, but it seldom leads to a constructive end if it is not followed by specific questions directed toward what the interviewer really wants to know.
5. Paul Lazarsfeld, "The Art of Asking Why," *National Marketing Review*, 1, 1935, 32–43.
6. Paul Lazarsfeld, "Evaluating the Effectiveness of Advertising by Direct Interviews," *Journal of Consulting Psychology*, July-August, 1941.
7. Lickert's work is mainly done for Government agencies and therefore cannot be quoted at the present time. The present paper owes much to discussions with him and some of his associates, especially Bill Gold.
8. Kurt Lewin, "Forces Behind Food Habits and Methods of Change," *The Problem of Changing Food Habits,* Bulletin of the National Research Council, Number 108, October 1943.
9. Herta Herzog, "On Borrowed Experience," *Studies in Philosophy and Social Science,* 1941.
10. R. Wyant and H. Herzog, "Voting Via the Senate Mailbag," *Public Opinion Quarterly*, 1941, 5, 590–624.
11. Gordon W. Allport, "Attitudes," *Handbook of Social Psychology* (ed. C. Murchison), Worcester: Clark University Press, 1935, 798–844.
12. Rhoda Metraux, "Qualitative Attitude Analysis—A Technique for the Study of Verbal Behavior," *The Problem of Changing Food Habits,* Bulletin of the National Research Council, No. 108, October 1943.
13. Hadley Cantril, Herta Herzog, and Hazel Gaudet, *Invasion from Mars.* Princeton: Princeton University Press, 1939.
14. Mirra Komarovsky, *The Unemployed Man and His Family.* New York: Institute of Social Research, 1940.
15. Harold F. Gosnell, *Getting out the Vote.* Chicago: University of Chicago Press, 1927.
16. Paul Studenski, "How Polls Can Mislead," *Harpers Magazine,* December 1939.
17. This is the technique which Henry Link used in a more recent study ("An Experiment in Depth Interviewing," *Public Opinion Quarterly*, 1943, 7, 267–279). He first obtained a broad commitment on world participation for the post-war period from his respondents; then he asked a series of definite questions: for the sake of America's participation in world affairs, what would people be willing to accept? A standing army? Higher taxes? A lower standard of living? Etc. As a device to clarify the implications of people's opinions this is an appropriate procedure, but it is very confusing if it is suggested as a substitute for or even an improvement on the OI in all areas. It is precisely the purpose of the present paper to provide a general scheme, so that in

discussing "depth interviews" *each participant can point to the specific sector of the entire field he has in mind.*

18. E. Smith and E. Suchman, "Do People Know Why They Buy?" *Journal of Applied Psychology,* 1940, 24, 673–684.

19. We find here a mistake which corresponds to the objection we voiced above against Henry Link's paper. Because he used interlocking questions in one area, he thought that he had shown the uselessness of the OI technique in all other areas. Many of the proponents of the OI, on the other hand, do careful interviewing for the description of attitudes; but when it comes to the discerning of influences, they do bad interviewing and subject their returns to poor classification.

20. Paul Wallin, *Case Study Methods in the Prediction of Personal Adjustment* (ed., Paul Horst). New York: Social Science Research Council, 1941.

21. If such an interest score was used, it was found that for men the correlation between interest and voting was .20, whereas for women it was .50. Women, if they are not interested, do not vote. Men vote even if they are not interested, probably because they are more subject to social pressure. For a general theory of this score procedure see P. Lazarsfeld and W. Robinson, "Quantification of Case Studies," *Journal of Applied Psychology,* 1940, 24, 831–837.

22. Forms of the Allport-Vernon Value Test are distributed by the Psychological Corporation of New York.

23. P. Symonds and W. Samuel, "Projective Methods in the Study of Personality" (Chap. VI of *Psychological Tests and Their Uses*), *Review of Educational Research,* 1941, 11, 80–93.

Problems of Survey Analysis

In many ways the analysis of survey results can be described as the clarification of relationships between two or more variables.

There can be little doubt that we are interested primarily in relationships, rather than in the description of single variables. It may be an interesting fact that x per cent of a sample subscribed to a particular opinion or reported certain activities. But inferences of practical or theoretical significance usually emerge only from a study of the demographic characteristics, the previous experiences or attitudes to which the opinions and activities are related.

The clarification of these statistical relationships proceeds in two directions. In the first place, we want to determine how legitimate it

Reprinted from Patricia L. Kendall and Paul F. Lazarsfeld. "Problems of Survey Analysis," in *Public Opinion and Propaganda,* edited by Daniel Katz and Dorwin Cartwright et al. (New York: Holt and Company, 1960), pp. 718–28. Abridged version from *Continuities in Social Research: Studies in the Scope and Method of "The American Soldier,"* edited by Robert K. Merton and Paul F. Lazarsfeld (Glencoe: Free Press, 1950), pp. 133—96 [135–65].

is to draw inferences of cause and effect. Secondly, we want to examine the process through which the assumed cause is related to its effect. Both types of clarification involve a logic and a series of analytical procedures of their own. Part I of this paper is devoted to spelling these out.

Section I—Approximations of Survey Results to Controlled Experimentation

Even when not explicitly stated, the presentation of a relationship between two variables suggests a causal connection between them. We do not report that combat veterans are more dissatisfied than non-veterans with certain Army policies without implying that somehow the experience of combat changes the perspectives and attitudes of soldiers.

The scientific model designed to study cause-and-effect relationships of this sort is the *controlled experiment,* in which the responses of an experimental group, exposed to the crucial stimulus, are compared with those of an exactly equivalent control group, from which the stimulus has been withheld. The difficulties of carrying out such experiments in the social sciences are well known. It is important, therefore, to consider the kinds of approximations provided by survey materials.

Sub-group Comparisons

The type of approximation most often used in survey analysis involves a comparison of the frequency with which groups *characterized in different ways* express a certain attitude or indicate a particular behavior. Thus in *The American Soldier* we find that:

> There was a marked relationship between job satisfaction and chance to choose one's Army job. Those who asked for and got their Army jobs were much more satisfied than those who did not get the jobs they asked for, or who did not get a chance to ask. (I, Chap. VII, Chart II and Table I.) There was a relationship between the theater in which the soldier served and his personal adjustment. For example, men stationed overseas reported themselves in less good spirits than did men stationed in the United States. (I, 155–189. See especially Table I.)[1]

In the first example it is the experience of having asked for and obtained the job they wanted which distinguished soldiers in the "experimental" group from those in the "control" group. In the second case the distinction is in terms of the soldier's location. To what extent can we attribute differences in job satisfaction, on the one hand, and different levels of personal adjustment, on the other hand, to these "stimuli"?

There are two main difficulties in equating the simple cross-tabulations of survey materials to real experimentation. One of these is the danger that spurious factors are present in the relationship. The second is the difficulty of establishing clearly the time sequence of the variables involved.

Spurious Factors

To illustrate the problem of spurious factors, let us consider the relationship between theater of service and answers to the question, "In general, how would you say that you feel most of the time, in good spirits or in low spirits?" We recall that men stationed overseas reported themselves in less good spirits than did men stationed in the United States who had not yet been overseas. One possibility which occurs to us is that length of service might operate as a spurious factor in this relationship. It might be that men stationed overseas had, on the average, served for longer periods of time, and that men with records of long service had lower morale. If this were the case, we would not be justified in saying that personal esprit was determined by theater of service. Experimentally, this would express itself in the following way: two groups of soldiers, equated according to length of service, would show no differences in morale even when one group was shipped to an overseas theater.

In order to minimize the danger that spurious factors of this kind remain undetected, we employ analytical procedures which enable us to examine the relationship between the assumed cause and the assumed effect *when the influence of the possible spurious factor is eliminated.* We divide the sample into different groups according to length of service in the Army. Within each of the groups we examine the relationship between theater of service and personal esprit. In this way we are able to observe the original relationship when the possible spurious factor is "controlled" or "held constant."

Often it is not enough to introduce only one control. There are a number of other possible spurious factors in the relationship which we have considered. For example, the men overseas probably held higher rank and served in different branches of the Army. There might also have been educational differences between the two groups. All of these are factors which could have produced differences in the proportions saying that they were in "good spirits"; consequently, all of them must be controlled. For these reasons, it is necessary to carry

out the comparison between men stationed overseas and men stationed in the United States in a large number of subclasses. But this
leads to a problem. It is obvious that if we consider four controls,
each divided into three classes (if we controlled branch of service we
might divide our sample into Infantrymen, Air Corps men, and all
others), we would end up with 81 separate comparisons. As we extend
this process of controlling possible spurious factors, the number of
cases in any one subclass becomes very small.

To cope with this difficulty the author uses the following technique
throughout the volumes. First of all he divides his total sample (or
samples) into small homogeneous sub-groups, using the relevant control factors to achieve his stratification. Within each sub-class he then
makes the crucial comparison. He does not consider the size of the
differences, but only their direction. His final conclusion is based on
the *consistency* with which a specified relationship is found. In the
example which we have been considering, the relation between overseas service and good spirits, the analyst had available 138 small but
homogeneous sub-groups in which he could make his basic comparison. In 113 of these, men stationed overseas reported less good spirits
than men in the United States not yet overseas; in 23 of the sub-groups
the relationship was reversed; and in the remaining 2 there was no
difference in the proportion of overseas and United States soldiers
reporting themselves in good spirits. (I, 157, Table 1) Because the
crucial relationship persists in the large majority of homogeneous subclasses, the presumption that overseas service leads to a deterioration
in morale gains some credence. This technique, combining results
from many different but homogeneous sub-groups, is used at a number of points in *The American Soldier;* it is a procedure which deserves
careful study.

It is possible, then, to guard against spurious factors, and thereby
make our survey results approximate more closely those that would
be obtained through experimentation. But these results will always
remain approximations to, and never equivalents of, controlled experiments. We can never be sure that it is impossible to find another
factor, not included among our controls, which would disqualify the
main result. If we want to study the relationship between overseas
service and lowered morale through controlled experimentation, we
would proceed in the following way. Half of a group of soldiers,
selected at random, would be shipped overseas, while the other half
remained in the United States. After a lapse of time the morale of
both groups would be compared. If it turned out that the group ran-
domly selected for shipment overseas showed significantly lower spir-

its, we would have the necessary evidence that it was overseas service which brought about a decline in morale.

As long as we can only control factors after the fact, however, our findings are always open to doubts. If we study the relationship through a statistical analysis of survey materials, rather than by experimentation, we can, at best, control four or five factors. Let us assume that we consider length of service in the Army, rank, branch of service and education to be important factors. It might be that none of these is important, and that we overlook the really relevant spurious factor. Perhaps certain soldiers were less popular than others; their lack of popularity might be reflected in low spirits, and it might also mean that their officers were more likely to put them on lists for shipment overseas. In this case, both overseas service and low spirits are the result of personality differences, and there is no causal connection between them. . . .

In actual survey analysis, the control of spurious factors requires a constant weaving back and forth between speculations as to the possible factors and examination of the data when the influence of each factor has been eliminated. There is one particularly important result in *The American Soldier* which illustrates this process very well.

> The closer the contact of white with Negro soldiers, the greater the willingness of the whites to serve in mixed Negro-white companies. (I, 594, Chart XVII)

This relationship is one in which typically we might suspect that spurious factors are operating. Whenever we deal with a variable like "amount of contact" or "closeness of contact" we have a feeling that the persons who are found at various points along these continua made their way there voluntarily. That is, we suspect the presence of "self-selection" factors; those who have close contact with Negroes may do so because of initially favorable or "tolerant" attitudes. If this were the case, it would not surprise us to find that their attitudes following contacts with Negroes were also favorable.

The way in which the Army's "racial experiment" came about reduced the likelihood that these self-selective processes were at work. The Negro platoons were placed *at random* within Infantry companies needing replacements. While the Negro men had volunteered for combat service, men in the white companies were not consulted about their willingness to serve in mixed companies.

While the real-life situation seemed to meet those conditions required for controlled experimentation, the Research Branch sought additional checks. For example, the companies which had suffered the greatest casualties, and were therefore most likely to receive replacements, might have become more tolerant toward other men as a result of their combat experience. If this were the case, the men in mixed companies could be expected to have initially more favorable attitudes toward service with Negroes. In order to check this possibility, the Research Branch made use of a retrospective question: The soldiers in mixed companies were asked to recall how they had felt about serving with Negroes prior to the actual experience of doing so. The results indicated an even more *un*favorable attitude initially than was observed among men not serving in mixed companies.

Another possibility is that the persons in charge of assigning replacements put the Negro platoons in companies which they felt would receive them more favorably. There was undoubtedly some leeway in deciding which companies got which replacements, and the officers responsible for those decisions may not have distributed the troops at random. Again, if this were the case, we would conclude that the original relationship was a spurious one. Partial evidence that it was *not* the case is seen in the fact that there were as many Southerners serving in the mixed as in the unmixed companies.

The interweaving of speculations about possible spurious factors and actual analysis of the data emerges very clearly from this example. The original relationship was one which is typically suspect as being spurious. But the results were obtained in a situation which seemed to reproduce, in real life, the conditions required in controlled experimentation. There was more reason to believe, therefore, that the original relationship was a reasonable approximation of what might have been found through actual experimentation. But the analysts did not lose sight of the possibility that spurious factors were in operation. They introduced suitable controls and checks. Even though these did not destroy the original relationships we cannot say that the causal connection between contact with Negroes and favorable attitudes toward them has been demonstrated. The connection is more *probable* after the checks have been introduced than it was beforehand, but it is never quite certain.

The Time Order of Variables

Clearly to be distinguished from the problem of spurious factors is the second difficulty in approximation procedures. In order even to consider whether the statistical relationship between two variables is a causal one, the variables must stand in a determinate time relation, with the assumed cause *preceding* the assumed effect. (When we say that Variable A precedes Variable B in time, we mean that A was *acquired or developed* first.)

Often the time order between two variables is quite clear. If we relate formal educational level to rank in the Army, we can be quite sure that education precedes rank. Or, if we study the relation between civilian occupation and type of Army job, there is little doubt that Army job follows after civilian occupation in time.

There are some instances in which the same attribute is used as an index of different phenomena, so that its time order, rather than being fixed, is determined by the particular problem being considered. Suppose, for example, that we related each man's rank to the length of time which he had been in the Army. Now "length of time in the Army" can stand for a variety of different phenomena. We might consider it an index of the time when the soldier entered the Army; given this meaning, it would *antecede* promotion. We would then look at the relationship to see whether those who had entered the Army during early stages of the war were more likely to be promoted. But "length of time in the Army" can also indicate the amount of experience which the soldier has at the time he is interviewed. Looked at in this way, length of service is a characteristic which follows *after* the soldier has acquired his rank. We then ask whether those with particular ranks are more experienced than others.

Finally, there are some instances in which the time sequence of two or more variables is indeterminate. One such case is the relationship between attitudes toward one's officers and willingness for combat. (II, 126, Table 7) Which of these attitudes developed or was acquired first? Does a soldier reluctant to go into combat "rationalize" his feelings by saying that his officers are not good? Or does a soldier with favorable attitudes toward his officers develop a feeling of confidence which makes him willing for combat? Because of our inability to answer these questions, because we do not know and cannot know which of the attitudes developed first, we cannot discuss whether there is a causal connection between them. (As we shall see in the next section, panel techniques often enable one to circumvent these difficulties.)

It is very difficult to answer these questions of time sequence with the materials of only one survey. But it is possible that in some cases clues to the time order will be found. In *The American Soldier,* for example, the authors are interested in the relationship between marital status and rank. They found (I, 118–20, see especially Chart V) that married men were more likely to have higher rank, even when age and length of service in the Army were controlled. But which came first, marriage or promotion? Is it that married men are more likely to be promoted, or that promotion encourages the soldier to marry? With knowledge only of marital status and rank, very little can be said. But fortunately Research Branch analysts obtained one other bit of information which provided some clue to the time sequence: they knew whether the soldier had been married prior to his entrance into the Army or whether he had married after becoming a soldier. These data enabled them to make the following observations. They noted that there was very little relationship between rank and having been married prior to entering the Army. On the other hand, there was some relationship between rank and marriage taking place after in-duction. This leads them to suggest that "marriage was even more likely to be a *resultant* of promotion or of expected promotion than to be a factor *predisposing promotion.*" (I, 120, authors' italics.) The clue to the sequence of the variables was the fact that where the time order was known, one kind of relationship existed; where it was unknown, another relationship, suggesting another time sequence, prevailed.

Panel Techniques

While the data of one survey may sometimes suggest the time order of variables whose sequence is apparently indeterminate, they give us nothing more than clues to be checked by other means. So-called panel techniques provide the relatively best device for establishing a time sequence of two variables. In a panel study, the same respondents are interviewed at different time periods. In those cases where the respondent changes between successive interviews, it is possible to determine when a particular attitude or behavior pattern developed.

These techniques contribute many new analytical devices.[2] While it is not possible to discuss all of these here, references to one finding in *The American Soldier,* of substantive interest as well as method-ological value, may give a general idea. It was found that non-commissioned officers had more conformist attitudes toward Army discipline than did privates. This relationship could be explained in a variety of ways. The non-com might have a better understanding of the importance of discipline or he might endorse disciplinary measures in order to bolster his own position. It could also be, however, that a private with what one might call an authoritarian personality has a better chance of being promoted. One of the panel studies carried out by the Research Branch shows that this latter relationship is involved in the respondents according to their answers to a number of ques-

TABLE A Distribution of Conformity Scores among
Privates in November, 1943

	Number of Cases	Percentage of These Cases Promoted by March, 1944
Relatively high score	68	31
Medium score	138	28
Relatively low score	112	17

tions on discipline. Then a few months later they ascertained what proportion of the original respondents had become non-coms. Some of the findings are as follows. (See I, 265, Chart XI)

Through their analysis of these panel materials, the investigators were able to establish that privates who held conformist attitudes were more likely to be promoted during a subsequent six months period than were their relatively more rebellious barracks mates. As Table A shows, among those who had indicated a relatively high degree of conformity in the Fall of 1943, nearly one-third had been promoted by the following Spring, as compared with only one-sixth of the men who had originally received a low score on the conformity index.

Retrospective Questions

One of the main difficulties in a panel study is keeping the original sample intact. This is a problem even in studies of civilian populations: respondents move; some become ill and unable to participate further in the study; others become bored and refuse to participate. The enormity of these difficulties in studies of soldiers during a global war is obvious.

Because of these handicaps we sometimes use *retrospective questions* as a substitute for panel techniques. By asking the respondents to recall what their attitudes were at some earlier period (generally prior to a crucial experience whose effect we are trying to study), we attempt to reconstruct what would have been observed had there been a previous interview. We ask, "How did you feel about y before x took place?" We remember that the Research Branch used a question of this kind in checking the relationship between service in bi-racial companies and the willingness of whites to serve with Negroes. In addition to stating their present willingness to serve in mixed companies, the respondents were asked to recall what their attitudes had been before Negro platoons were put in their companies.

There are a number of grounds on which one might object to the use of retrospective questions as a substitute for panel techniques. First of all, it is difficult to know how accurate respondents are in their retrospection. Do they tend to remember selectively? Do they discount the extent to which they have actually changed their attitudes or habits? Secondly, there is the problem of specifying the exact time period to which the subjects should retrospect. "Before x took place" covers a wide time range.

Wherever possible, then, the accuracy of the retrospections should be checked. This was done in an interesting way at one point in *The American Soldier.* In investigating the effects of combat on the incidence of psychosomatic symptoms, the researchers used a number of different procedures. First of all, they cross-tabulated such variables as nearness to combat and length of time in combat with questions about psychosomatic symptoms. In one study of combat veterans, however, they included a retrospective question. In addition to asking, "Since you have been on active combat duty, are you ever bothered by (hand tremors, stomach disturbances, fainting spells, nightmares, shortness of breath, and pressure in the head)?" they also asked, "During your civilian and military life, but before you went on active combat duty, were you ever bothered by . . . ?" Comparison of the retrospective form of the question with the postcombat form reveals a marked increase in the proportion of men experiencing many anxiety symptoms. (II, 449, Table 17)

But how accurate were these retrospections? As a check, the analysts compared the pre-combat answers of the veterans with those given by Infantrymen in training in the United States. The close correspondence of the answers provided some assurance that the combat veterans did not distort their answers, either consciously or unconsciously, to any extent. (II, 448, Table 16)

These, then, are perhaps the major procedures through which the data obtained through surveys and utilized in secondary analyses can be made more nearly equivalent to experimental results.[3]

Section 2—Interpretation and Its Place in a General Scheme of Elaboration

Once we have satisfied ourselves that a particular statistical relationship is an adequate approximation of experimental results, we raise a somewhat different series of questions. We explore the relationship further, elaborating and clarifying it.

The general process of elaboration takes a variety of specific forms. It also can be described in quite formal terms. Before discussing either of these points, however, let us outline the general argument of one type of elaboration—interpretation. When we interpret a result we try to determine the process through which the assumed cause is related to what we take to be its effect. How did the result come about? What are the "links" between the two variables? Answers to these questions are provided in the interpretation of the result.

The General Argument of an Interpretation

The interpretation of a statistical relationship between two variables involves the introduction of further variables and an examination of the resulting interrelations between all of the factors.

To illustrate the steps which one goes through in interpreting a result, and to indicate the types of material which are required, we shall start with one relationship in *The American Soldier* for which an interpretation is suggested. On one index of personal commitment, "At the time you came into the Army did you think you should have been deferred?" the analysts found a positive correlation between education and favorable responses: the higher the education of the soldier, the more likely he was to say that he had volunteered or that he should not have been deferred. (I, 124, Table 3) This finding was somewhat surprising in view of the general tendency of better educated soldiers to be more critical of the Army. The authors interpret the results in terms of the concept of "relative deprivation," which they define in the following way:

> Becoming a soldier meant to many men a very real deprivation. But the felt sacrifice was greater for some than for others, *depending on their standards of comparison.* (I, 125, authors' italics.)

The analysts suggest that the lower educated soldiers, coming mainly from skilled labor occupations which accounted for many exemptions from service in the Army, compared their lot with that of their friends, many of whom had been deferred because of the importance of their jobs. On the other hand, "The great mass of professional, trade, and white-collar occupations were not deferable . . . The average high school graduate or college man was a clear-cut candidate for induction . . ." (I, 127) In other words, lower educated soldiers, coming from an environment in which deferments were relatively frequent, were more likely to experience their induction as a personal sacrifice than were the better educated soldiers, fewer of whose friends had received deferments.

How would one go about studying this interpretation? To simplify our discussion of the actual procedure, we should perhaps first restate the interpretative statement, so as to see the statistical relationships which it implies. It might read as follows:

> Better educated soldiers are more likely to accept their inductions, because better-educated soldiers come from an environment in which deferments are infrequent, and coming from an environment in which deferments are infrequent leads to more willing acceptance of induction.

When we rephrase the statement in this way, we note that one characteristic of any "complete" interpretation is that the interpretative variable, the "test factor" as it might be called, is related to each of the original variables. The Research Branch interpretation implies (a) that the test factor, relative frequency of deferment in the environment from which the individual soldier comes, is negatively related to education, and (b) that the same factor is also negatively related to the dependent variable in the original relationship, the soldier's acceptance of his induction into the Army.

But this characteristic is not the only one. If we extend our reformulation of the interpretative statement, we note another aspect of "complete" interpretations.

> If it is true that the relationship between education and attitudes toward one's own induction can be explained entirely by the frequency of deferments in one's civilian environment, then when soldiers are classified according to this test factor, when they are separated into different groups according to the frequency of deferments in the environments from which they come, there should no longer be any relationship between education and attitude toward induction.

Stated in somewhat more technical terms, we expect that when the population is stratified according to different values of the test factor, the partial relationship between the two original variables will vanish. If we can classify men according to whether or not they came from an environment in which deferments were frequent, we shall find, within any of the homogeneous groups thus obtained that there is no relationship between education and acceptance of induction. The well-educated soldiers who come from an environment in which deferments were common will be just as disgruntled about their inductions as are poorly educated men from similar backgrounds; the less well educated soldier from an environment in which there were few deferments will be as likely to accept his own induction as is the better educated man in the same kind of situation. In other words, if the partial relationships between education and attitudes toward induction disappeared when soldiers were classified according to the fre-

quency of deferments in their civilian environment, we would conclude that one's previous environment completely interpreted the
original relationship.

In order to test the interpretation, then, we need to know something about the rate of deferment in the civilian environment of each
man. This information, apparently not available in the Research
Branch study, might have been obtained from answers to a question
like, "Have some of your friends or acquaintances been deferred because they are in indispensable civilian occupations?" Let us assume,
for the sake of illustration, that such a question actually was asked,
and that about half of the soldiers answered "yes." The next step
would be to see whether this test factor actually is related to the
two original characteristics, education and attitude toward induction.
Again we must invent the two relationships if we want to end up with
the full scheme for testing interpretations. We shall assume, finally,
that, had information on this test factor been available, it would have
provided a complete interpretation of the original result. Then we
would have found a set of tables like those in Table B. The figures on
the left represent the original relationship, taken from actual data
reported in *The American Soldier*. (See I, 124, Table 3) The figures
on the right are italicized because they were invented for the sake of
our schematic illustration. On the left-hand side of the table, we find
a relationship between education and attitudes toward induction:
among the better educated men, the ratio of favorable to unfavorable
attitudes toward induction is more than 7 to 1, while among the less
well educated men, the ratio is less than 3 to 1. In the two partial
tables on the right side of the "equals" sign, however, there is no
relationship between the soldier's education and acceptance of his
induction: in each table, the ratio of favorable to unfavorable replies
on the attitude question is the same in both educational groups, even
though the ratio differs in the two tables. Other aspects of Table B
will be discussed in the following section.

If a particular test factor actually does interpret the relationship
between two variables, we shall find that the relations between all
three are characterized in the following ways:

    I. The test factor is related to the assumed causal variable in the original
       relationship.
   II. The test factor is also related to the assumed effect.
  III. When the sample is stratified according to the test factor the partial
       relationships between the original variables are smaller than the origi-
       nal relationship.

TABLE B

	High Education	Low Education	Total		High Education	Low Education	Total		High Education	Low Education	Total
					Friends or Acquaintances Deferred				No Friends or Acquaintances Deferred		
Volunteered or should not have been deferred	1556	1310	2866	=	210	939	1149	+	1346	371	1717
Should have been deferred	205	566	771		125	545	670		80	21	101
	1761	1876	8637		335	1484	1819		1426	392	1818

In interpretation the test factor lies *between x and y* in time, or, in other words, it follows *after x*. Only those factors which *precede x* in time, however, can be spurious factors. For the sake of convenience, we shall label these two time orders. A test factor which follows after x will be referred to as an *intervening variable,* while one which precedes x will be called an *antecedent variable.*

This difference is an important one, for, when it is not kept clearly in mind, we are apt to confuse the two types of elaboration despite their very different objectives. In the example of interpretation which we considered, the time relation of x and t is clear: there can be little doubt that an individual's formal education precedes in time the number of deferments among his friends and acquaintances. In other words, the test factor is an intervening variable. If the rate of deferment is a relevent test factor, its relevance is as an interpretative variable, providing a *link* between education and acceptance or rejection of one's induction. In contrast, when Research Branch analysts sought to make sure that the relationship between contact with Negroes and willingness to serve with them in mixed companies was not a spurious one, the factor which they introduced as a check—various measures of initially favorable attitude—was one which was clearly *antecedent* to the assumed cause.

We can thus distinguish three different types of elaboration.

I. *The M type* in which one is interested in noting whether the partial relationships become smaller than the original relationship. This can be further sub-divided according to the time relation of x and t.

A. *Interpretation* in which the test factor is an intervening variable.

B. *Explanation (or control for spurious factors)* in which the test factor is an antecedent variable.

The distinction between interpretation and explanation can be represented schematically in the following way:

Interpretation   Explanation

$$\swarrow t \searrow$$

$$x \rightarrow t \rightarrow y \qquad\qquad\qquad\qquad x \qquad y$$

II. *The P type* in which interest is focused on the relative size of the partial relationships in order to specify the circumstances under which the original relation is more or less pronounced. This type of elaboration will be called *specification*.

We are now in a position to review much of our preceding discussion. In the first section of our paper, we talked of the way in which we control for spurious factors. This, as we now see, is one type of a more general system of elaboration, that type which we have called explanation. In our earlier discussion, we talked quite loosely about spurious factors. The definition which we have arrived at in the course of our discussion is as follows: a spurious factor is an antecedent variable which, in the M type of elaboration, reduces the average of the partial relationships.

In the opening parts of the second section we turned to a kind of analysis which we have called interpretation. We based our discussion on an example suggested in *The American Soldier* and, using hypothetical figures, indicated the conditions to be met if the interpretation were to be a complete one.

What remains to be discussed, then, is the type of elaboration which we have labeled specification. While we have indicated briefly the questions which one attempts to answer through the specification of a result, we have not shown the kinds of findings which are obtained through this analysis.

Specification—The P Type of Elaboration

In the final type of elaboration which we shall consider here, we focus our attention on the relative size of the partial relationships. We want to see whether the original relationship is more pronounced in one sub-group than in the other, when the total sample is divided by the test factor. Thus, we try to specify the conditions of the original result.

Because the P type of elaboration is so different from the M type, it may be instructive to give a numerical example of what is meant by specification. In studying social mobility within the Army, the Research Branch found that there was a positive relationship between formal educational level and rank among enlisted men: the better educated the soldier, the more likely he was to have higher rank. (I, 249, Table 7) This relationship is presented in the following four-fold table:

TABLE C

| | Educational Level | |
Rank	High School Graduate or Better	Less Than High School Graduate
Non-Com.	61%	43%
Pvt., Pfc.	39	57
Total cases	3222	3152

146

Observing

If we use as a crude measure of the relationship between education and rank the difference .61 − .43 (which we can symbolize by "f"), the relationship here is .18.

But as is so frequently the case when one deals with relationships of this sort, it occurred to the analysts that the relationships might be more pronounced under varying conditions. The time at which one entered the Army, for example, might affect the correlation between education and rank. It might be that not even the better educated men had much chance to be promoted if they came into the Army at a late date, when tables of organization were pretty well fixed. Accordingly, length of time in the Army, indicating the time at which one had been inducted, was introduced as a test factor. The partial relationships thus obtained were then examined:

TABLE D

Rank	Have Served for Less Than 2 Years		Have Served for 2 Years or More	
	High School Graduate or Better	Less Than High School Graduate	High School Graduate or Better	Less Than High School Graduate
Non-Com.	23%	17%	74%	53%
Pvt., Pfc.	77	83	26	47
Totals	842	823	2380	2329
	f = .06		f = .21	

The f coefficients for these two partial tables are very different, indicating varying degrees of relationship between education and rank. Among late entrants into the Army, the better educated men had only slightly greater chances for promotion than did less well educated soldiers. Among those who had come into the Army at an earlier stage in the war, however, the better educated had considerably greater chances of being promoted. In other words, the relationship between education and rank is a conditional one, depending on the time at which the soldier entered the Army.

Most specific examples of statistical analysis will be described by one or more of these different kinds of elaboration. Either we try to "explain" the result, by showing that it is spurious, or we "interpret" it, or we "specify" it. In general, our analysis will follow a definite pattern. We start out with a simple association between two variables. Our first concern is whether or not the relationship is a spurious one; consequently our initial efforts of elaboration are usually of the explanatory type. Once we have gained some assurance that the original relationship is not a spurious one, we try to interpret the result or to specify it. We ask ourselves what variables might provide the links between the "cause" and the "effect," or what conditions might show the original relationship to be even more pronounced than we originally saw it to be. The elaboration of a particular result can go on almost indefinitely. We are limited only by our lack of ingenuity in thinking of factors by which to elaborate the result, by the absence of data to check the relevance of factors which we have thought of, or by the difficulties of dealing with a few cases as the process of elaboration is extended.

Notes

1. Editor's note: *The American Soldier,* vol. 1: *Adjustment during Army Life,* by Samuel A. Stouffer, Edward A. Suchman, et al.; vol. 2: *Combat and Its Aftermath,* by Samuel A. Stouffer, Arthur A. Lumsdaine, et al. (Princeton: Princeton University Press, 1949). The parenthetical references in this essay are all to this edition.
2. See Paul F. Lazarsfeld, "The Use of Panels in Social Research," *Proceedings of the American Philosophical Society,* 92 (1948), 405–410. The Bureau of Applied Social Research of Columbia University is currently working on a project to codify and evaluate these analytical devices.
3. In a recent article ("Some Observations on Study Design," *American Journal of Sociology,* LV, 1949–50, 355–361), Stouffer himself suggests a general scheme through which the interrelationships of controlled experiments, panel studies, surveys, and so on, can be shown. His paper is an elaboration of pp. 47–48 in the first volume of *The American Soldier.*

The Use of Panels in Social Research

The following remarks are designed to draw attention to a fairly recent development in social research. In its bare essentials, the type of study to be discussed consists of repeated interviews made with the same group of persons. The people participating as subjects in such studies are commonly known as panel members and the whole procedure has become widely known under the name of panel technique.

There are two main types of research problems to which the panel

Reprinted from "The Use of Panels in Social Research," *Proceedings of the American Philosophical Society* 92, no. 5 (1948):405–10. First read February 7, 1948, in the Symposium on Research Frontiers in Human Relations.

technique is likely to be applied. If the effect of some specific event
or series of events is to be studied, then we have the first type of
situation in which the panel technique may be used. In one such case,
a sample of voters in an Ohio county was kept under observation for
six months during the 1940 Presidential campaign, the purpose being
to study what effect the propaganda of the two parties had upon the
way people made up their minds.[1] In another case, the American
Association for the United Nations wanted to find out the best way
of getting Americans more interested in the progress of U.N. activities.
A sample of persons in a Midwest city of about 800,000 was interviewed about their attitudes towards the United Nations and the actions of the United States in foreign affairs. An intensive informational
campaign was conducted by this organization and after the campaign
was over the same sample was interviewed again.[2] In a similar way,
advertising agencies sometimes use panels to study the effectiveness
of their promotional efforts.[3]

The other main type of panel study is somewhat more difficult to
describe because no major findings are yet available in the literature.
In a society as complex and changing as our own, the individual is
continually placed in a situation where he must reconcile the different
and variant elements of his experience. A Quaker who is a convinced
pacifist sees the country endangered by an enemy. How will he resolve
the conflict between his pacifism and his patriotism? A convinced
Communist sees the Soviet Union making moves which he considers
imperialistic. How will he reconcile his party loyalty and his intellectual judgment on a specific political issue? But we don't need to remain in the area of big issues to look for problems of this kind. In
everyday life almost everyone is continuously under cross-pressures
of some kind. People belong to different social groups which may
have conflicting interests. The individual must make all sorts of
choices among his needs, desires, and situational demands, some of
which are relatively important, others relatively insignificant.

The study of people under cross pressures is one of the major
concerns of social science today. In going through recent social science
literature one often comes across statements of the following sort, "In
getting higher education the English Catholic must choose between
ethnic affiliation and religion; he generally chooses to study with his
Protestant ethnic fellows at McGill University. . . ."[4] The application
of the panel technique to problems of this sort allows a greater degree
of analytical precision. It would allow us to state, for example, the
proportion of English Catholics who go to McGill for their higher
education and the proportion who go to Catholic institutions, and to

compare intensively those who resolve the conflict between their ethnic affiliation and their religion in one way with those who resolve this conflict in another.

The understanding of what actually transpires in such situations will make for tremendous gains in the understanding of social change. The application of the panel technique to this area of social science interest will be one of its major contributions. By keeping sets of people under repeated observation, we can register the changes they make in their attitudes, affiliations, habits, and expectations. We can learn which of the various attitudes, affiliations, etc., are more basic and hence more constant and which are more superficial and changeable. We hope to determine, if elements change, which element in a psychological or social situation is the more dominant one controlling the changes in the other factors.

The outstanding example of such a study is that undertaken by Theodore Newcomb of the students of a "progressive" college attended by the daughters of well-to-do families. The faculty of this college was quite liberal but the background of the girls quite conservative. For four years the investigators observed the various ways in which one group of girls resolved this conflict.[5]

The reader who is somewhat acquainted with social science literature will at this point raise a justified question especially with reference to the first type of study. If we want to know the effect of a political campaign or a similar event, why do we have to reinterview the same people? Couldn't we interview one group of respondents before the event and a similar one after the event? By comparing the two, the argument runs, we would get a fairly good idea as to the influence which the event had. Numerous examples of this kind come to mind. Many of us have seen public opinion polls taken, for instance, before and after the President made a major public announcement. If people think better of him after the speech then we are sure the speech was a success. Poll data are available which show that the attitude of the average American to the Russians improved every time they were victorious in a battle during the war and slumped every time the Russians, after the war, made a move against one of their neighboring countries. This type of study is undoubtedly of very great value and is usually called a trend study.[6]

It is important to consider the differences between such trend studies and the panel technique. A considerable amount of additional information is obtained by reinterviewing the same people. The most important difference is our ability to single out in a panel study exactly who are the people who change. Once singled out, the changers can be subjected to more intensive study to determine the psychological and social-psychological elements which operated to produce the changes in question. A trend study may show us the net impact of events on opinion. A panel study can allow us to single out the individuals who changed their opinion in the course of the repeated interviewing, to probe for the psychological meaning of the event, and the role played by the various mass media of communication in the change. By interviewing the same people at least twice, we can answer questions such as the following: Are people more likely to change when they are very interested in an event and follow it in great detail; or when they are only slightly concerned and know of it only in a casual way? Some preliminary evidence seems to show that the latter is more likely to be the case. There are many proverbs which claim that men are more apt to shift than women and many others which claim the exact opposite. The panel technique permits us to say whether men or women are more likely to shift their opinions. Incidentally, the results so far do not seem to point to any sex differences.

The study of actual changes often leads to unexpected results. At the time that Senator Black was appointed a judge of the Supreme Court, he was accused of having been at one time a member of the Ku Klux Klan. It happens that there is some information available on who was affected by this allegation which suddenly threatened to change the image of a liberal into that of a reactionary. Although Senator Black received about the same amount of approval before and after the allegation, a kind of game of musical chairs took place. Jews and Catholics turned against him while about an equivalent number of Protestants were more in favor of his appointment than before the storm broke.[7]

The last example points to a second value of the panel technique. Trend studies often indicate that an event has not brought about any net change in opinion. But it might very well be that underneath this apparent constancy, there is a great amount of shifting of positions which can only be found out if the same people and their attitudes are traced over a period of time. At the beginning of the present 1948 presidential campaign, there is some indication of a new development in American politics. As long as Roosevelt was alive, there was a strong feeling in the population that the Democratic Party was the party of the common man whereas the Republicans represented more the interests of the wealthier sections of the population. There are indications that this appraisal of the two parties has changed somewhat and that voters, especially among the working class, are less sure than before which of the two parties represents their interests better.

Suppose that one further development takes place (for which there is no evidence but which we bring in to make our example more dramatic); some sections of the business community might feel that their interest in an active recovery program in Europe is better served by a Democratic administration. Then we might have at this moment an internal shift in the social stratification of the two parties which might go beyond any net change in both which polls or the election might show up. Such a social restratification of the major parties has taken place several times in the political history of this country. The historian looking back over this period many decades hence will not miss such a development. But if we want to know and understand it at the time it happens, we have to make studies of repeated interviews with the same people.

This is not the place to go further into detail on the comparison of panel and trend studies.[8] We shall turn rather to the other type of panel study in order to show briefly some of its considerably more complex technical aspects. The following table (table 1) exemplifies some of the technical difficulties. It is taken from a small group of people who were interviewed twice during a presidential election. Each respondent was asked two questions: How he intended to vote and whether he felt that the Republican candidate if elected would make a good President. Because both questions were each answered on two different occasions by each respondent we have four pieces of information about each member of the panel. Table 1 classifies these replies first according to whether they were obtained at the first interview or at the second. For each interview we can then sub-classify the respondents into four groups: those who wanted to vote Democratic and who were also personally opposed to the Republican candidate; those who wanted to vote Democratic but personally respected the opposing candidate; those with Republican vote intentions who, however, disapproved of their party's candidate; and those with Republican vote intentions who also approved of the candidate.

All the information which can be obtained from two questions and two interviews with the same respondents can be represented in the following type of table.

Let us first look at the last column. Most Democrats are against the person of the Republican candidate and most Republicans are for him. But 59 of the 266 respondents have a kind of personal attachment. Twenty-four Democrats think that the opposing candidate is

TABLE 1

First Interview	Second Interview				
	Dem. Ag.	Dem. For	Rep. Ag.	Reg. For	Total
Dem. Against	68	2	1	1	72
Dem. For	11	12	0	1	24
Rep. Against	1	0	23	11	35
Rep. For	2	1	3	129	135
Total	82	15	27	142	266

all right while 35 Republicans, although they intend to vote for their party, obviously wish that another candidate had been put up.

Now let us look at the bottom row of figures which come from the second interview. The number of people with such detached views has decreased. Obviously, what the campaign has done is to intensify partisan feeling. Only 15 Democrats now have a good word to say about the Republican candidate and only 27 Republicans have any doubts left about him.

But that is not all that we would like to know from this table. How do people reconcile their vote intention and their opinion on a specific issue? Do the Democrats who like the opposing candidate shift to him or do they remain Democrats and start to see him in a darker light? The answer is given in the second row of our table. There is only one case of the former, but 11 cases of the latter type. And it so happens that similar figures prevail for the Republicans. Let us look at the third row where we find the respondents who at the first interview intended to vote Republican but didn't like their candidate. One of them switched to the Democrats but 11 now feel better towards their candidate. In this one case there is no doubt that most people adjust their cross-pressures in a one-sided direction. If their party loyalties are in conflict with a specific opinion of their own they are rather more likely to maintain their party loyalties and change their opinion.

This is of course just one example from which no general conclusion should be drawn. But it shows the type of problem and the type of procedures which derive from the use of the panel technique. Just for the record it might be mentioned that the statistical analysis of tables like the preceding one is quite difficult and proper procedures are still in the process of development. It can easily be seen how many more problems would arise if we had more than two interviews and more than two questionnaire items to deal with.

Besides the difficulties in analysis discussed above, there is one other drawback of the panel technique. There is a danger that we may change our respondent's attitude by the very fact that we reinterview them repeatedly. In some cases the danger is obvious. Suppose, for example, we interview people during a vaccination campaign. If we repeatedly ask people whether they have been vaccinated, our interviewers will probably act as reminders and speed up the success of the campaign in our panel beyond the performance of the population at large. In this case, then, the results of our study will be quite misleading. It could of course happen that our interviewers antagonize the respondents and as a result they might be less likely to get vaccinated. In other cases the panel bias is not likely to be marked. If interest in an election is high and everyone talks about it, the fact that a respondent has been asked about his vote intentions is not going to influence him very much. In any case this is a matter for concrete study. We cannot tell in advance when bias is likely to exist or not.

Actually, a few such studies of bias have been made. The technique used is fairly simple. At the time the panel is picked out a second group of respondents known as a "control group" is set up as closely matched to the panel as possible. This second group, however, is not interviewed until the whole panel study nears its end. At the time the last interview is made with the panel, the control group is also interviewed. From a statistical point of view the two groups were originally alike and should therefore at the end of the study show the same distribution of attitudes were it not that the panel group was interviewed repeatedly. Whatever significant differences show up between the two groups can be attributed to the effect of the panel bias.

Two examples should give an idea of how much work there is still to be done in this direction. During a presidential campaign it was found that the distribution of opinions in the panel was no different than in the control group. But the panel made up its mind somewhat quicker. Under the impact of the repeated interviews the "Don't Knows" in the end were less numerous in the panel than in the control group. This is a very encouraging result. On the other hand it was found that if people were repeatedly interviewed about their newspaper reading habits the panel group was likely to do more newspaper reading than the control group. The reappearance of the interviewer obviously stimulated the reading interests of the panel members. There was some indication, however, that approximately from the third interview on this effect became less and less marked. It might very well be that if the panel had gone on longer, the panel bias would have disappeared in the end.

There are many operational problems involved in panel studies just

as in any other large-scale research operation. How can we get people
to participate in a panel and to stick to it? How do we substitute for
unavoidable losses? Is it sometimes possible to correspond with panel
members by mail rather than to make personal contacts? Should we
handle a panel as the American Senate is handled, always substituting
part of it by new members?

Finally, there are a number of serious statistical problems to be
dealt with. They all center around the concept of turnover. The following two tables exemplify the problem. They each represent one
question on which people have been interviewed twice.

TABLE 2

		2nd Interview		
		Yes	No	Totals
1st Interview	Yes	50	50	100
	No	50	850	900
Totals		100	900	1000

TABLE 3

		2nd Interview		
		Yes	No	Totals
1st Interview	Yes	400	100	500
	No	100	400	500
Totals		500	500	1000

In the first question (table 2) 100 people changed their minds one
way or another. On the second question (table 3) 200 people did so.
One might feel that the turnover on the second question is therefore
greater. But one must consider that many fewer people said "Yes" to
the first question at the time of the first interview. One therefore
cannot expect as many people to change as in the second case. It
might be more advisable to compute the turnover as percentage of
the people who said "Yes" both times. This would give a turnover of
200 per cent for the first and 50 per cent for the second table and
now we would have to say that the first question has the larger turn-

over. There are obviously still many other ways in which turnover can be described. What index we can use to describe best the turnover in such tables is a very vexing problem, especially because most all of the statistical treatment of panel data goes back to this one point. But this is not the place to deal with such technical matters at length. It is preferable to end up with some more general theoretical considerations which will show the place panel studies are likely to hold in the social sciences in the coming years.

Basically, what we do in a panel study is relate information obtained at one time to information obtained at a subsequent time. We are in the center of what has come to be called dynamic social research. We study changes and we want to explain these changes. We know who changed and we have information on people prior to their change. Explaining the change necessarily means to relate this previous information to the subsequent change. Everything will depend therefore upon how ingenious we are in deciding what information we should gather at different time periods. To exemplify the problem more clearly, let us assume that we are dealing with a panel of people who are about to move into a public housing project where Negroes and whites will live together.[9] If we center our attention on the whites then we know in advance that some of them will get along with their Negro fellow tenants and some will not. Some will improve their ability to get along with people of other races and some will not. What information should we collect from all these prospective tenants prior to the time they move into the housing project to help us explain what shifts in racial attitudes will take place?

We will obviously want to know their race attitudes prior to their entrance into the housing project. But it will also be important to know their *expectations*. It may turn out that the greater their initial uneasiness the more will they be pleasantly surprised by reality. On the other hand we know that some people have a hard time experiencing "reality," and if they enter a situation with apprehension they behave nervously and start trouble. Some sort of index of psychological flexibility is needed.

Pieces of information about the psychological predisposition of the respondents have been called *intervening variables* because they intervene, as it were, between the individual's reaction and the situation in which he is placed.[10] In the example given above, where a group of individuals are about to enter a public housing project, we have people who will be subject to the same external experience. They will, however, react differently. Between the external situation and the individual response there intervene certain psychological and social characteristics which channel the response in an individually characteristic fashion. Social psychologists in recent years have developed out of their experience many hypotheses as to which intervening variables are of importance. We talk of a person's *level of aspiration* or of a person's *expectations,* indicating that we consider that such information will be of value in interpreting how the individuals will react to the situations in which they are placed.

The important intervening variables have to be ascertained before expected changes take place. To follow through with the example given above, we should know as much as we can about the panel members before they move into the inter-racial housing project. Once they have been living there it is too late to look for such information, for we can never know then whether what we have found has not already been influenced by their new experience. This is, of course, exactly where the importance of the panel technique lies. We periodically study people's attitudes, expectations, and aspirations. We find out what has happened to them between interviews: what they read, with whom they talked, what external events impressed them, etc. Both the situational factors and the intervening variables change continuously. Our analysis would weave back and forth from these two series of data, expressing, in one case, reaction to the situation as a function of some psychological predisposition, and, in another, the psychological predisposition as a function of the changing situation. We would want to know how people's expectations affect the way they react to changes in their environment; and how the environment experienced changes their hopes and concerns.

On more than one occasion it has been said that one of the difficulties which impede the progress of social science is the fact that we cannot experiment with human beings in the same way that the agricultural station experiments with animals and plants. It should not be overlooked, however, that life itself is in a very real sense a continuous series of experiments. In the course of time, almost everything conceivable and sometimes things previously inconceivable happen to one group of persons or another. Although many of these events are, as yet, unpredictable, some events, fortunately for our purpose, occur with sufficient regularity or frequency so that if we know just what sort of persons will be subject to them, we can observe the various ways in which they will respond. Panel studies are conducted, usually, on the impact of events of a given predictable regularity such as voting in a presidential election, exposure to certain advertising, etc. If we find the right statistical technique we will be able to interrelate "stimulus, predisposition, and response" and with time and experience our hope is to understand, predict, and control human behavior more successfully.

The panel technique discussed here is an expensive and rather slow research operation. A social science, unfortunately, will not develop overnight, and, if we want to develop one, we will have to pay for it in time and money. We cannot prefer mere speculation because it comes to us quickly or simpler methods like cross-sectional polls and artificial laboratory experiments because they are cheap. The panel technique is just in its beginnings—we have just begun to explore some of the implications of its use—and most of its future development will require long and arduous work. Among the many lines along which the methods of the social sciences are developing, the panel technique seems to be one of the most promising for the future of a fuller understanding of human behavior.

Notes

1. Lazarsfeld, P. F., B. Berelson, and H. Gaudet, *The people's choice*, N.Y., Duell, Sloan and Pearce, 1944.
2. National Opinion Research Center, Report No. 37a, Cincinnati Looks Again.
3. Root, A. R., and A. C. Welch, The continuing consumer study: a basic method for the engineering of advertising, *Jour. Marketing* 7, July 1942.
4. Hughes, E. C., *French Canada in transition*, 86, Univ. of Chicago Press, 1943.
5. Newcomb, T., *Personality and social change*, N.Y., Dryden Press, 1942.
6. Bruner, Jerome S., *Mandate from the people*, N.Y., Duell, Sloan and Pearce, 1944; Cantril, Hadley, *Gauging public opinion*, Princeton Univ. Press, 1944.
7. Lazarsfeld, P. F., The change of opinion during a political discussion, *Jour. Ap. Psychol.* 23: 131–147, 1939.
8. Interested readers will find such a discussion and concrete examples in chapter 10, The panel, in *Say it with figures*, H. Zeisel, N.Y., Harpers, 1946.
9. An especially rich source for such explanatory variables will be found in a housing study organized by the Lavanburg Foundation under the direction of Robert K. Merton.
10. The interested reader will find a thoroughgoing discussion of important intervening variables in Sherif, M., *An outline of social psychology*, N.Y., Harpers, 1948.

7

Classifying and Building Typologies

Some Remarks on Typological Procedures in Social Research

Empirical social research produces daily crops of problems which students attempt to solve with out-of-pocket measures. After some time, a body of procedures accumulates; these techniques are handed down until they form a well established methodological tradition. However, it often takes years before these techniques are systematically reviewed with an eye to their logical underpinnings.

A book by Carl G. Hempel and P. Oppenheim "Der Typusbegriff im Licthe der Neuen Logik" (The Concept of Types in the Light of the New Logic)[1] offers such an opportunity. This book attempts to analyze the logic of typological procedures where these procedures are used in the social and natural sciences. Since the establishment of types is one of the recent developments of social research, a systematic discussion of the problems involved is very appropriate. The following discussion attempts to present and to enlarge upon the ideas of Hempel and Oppenheim, applying them to the practical problems of social research. As a result, these remarks are less than a summary, inasmuch as they do not report the whole book, and more than a review, inasmuch as they introduce additional experiences and considerations.

One is safe in saying that the concept of type is always used in referring to special compounds of attributes. In speaking of the midwestern type of American, one may have in mind certain physical features, certain attitudes and habits, certain affiliations and talents attributed to the inhabitants of this region. In speaking of types of books or of types of governments, a special combination of attributes

Reprinted from "Some Remarks on Typological Procedures in Social Research," in *Continuities in the Language of Social Research,* edited by Paul F. Lazarsfeld, Ann Pasanella, and Morris Rosenberg (New York: Free Press, 1972), pp. 99–106. Abridged by Ann Pasanella from *Zeitschrift für Sozialforschung* 6 (1937): 119–39.

is thrown into relief. Sometimes not all the attributes entering a typological combination can be enumerated. When the psychologist describes the extrovert type, he hopes that subsequent research will find more and more attributes which enter into this particular combination. There can and will be much discussion on how such a special combination of attributes is found, delineated and justified.

First it is necessary to introduce the concept of attribute space. Suppose that for a number of objects, several attributes are taken into consideration. Let it be these three: size, beauty, and the possession of a college degree. It is possible to visualize something very similar to the frame of reference in analytic geometry. The X-axis, for instance, may correspond to size; in this direction, the object can really be measured in inches. The Y-axis may correspond to beauty; in this direction the objects can be arranged in a serial order, so that each object gets a rank designation, rank No. 1 being the most beautiful. The Z-axis may correspond to the academic degree; here each object has or has not a degree. Those two possibilities shall be designated by plus and minus, and shall be represented arbitrarily by two points on the Z-axis on the two opposite sides of the center of the system. Each object is then represented by a certain point in this attribute space, for instance, by the following symbolism: (66″; 87%; plus;). If the objects to be grouped are the women in a certain sample, then this particular woman would be 5½ feet tall, would rank rather low in a beauty contest, and would have a college degree. To each individual would correspond a certain point in the space (though not every point would correspond to an individual). The reader is invited to familiarize himself by examples of his own with this very useful concept of attribute space; each space will, of course, have as many dimensions as there are attributes in the classifying scheme.

In the frame of an attribute space, the operation of *reduction* can be defined and explained. In order to have a simple example, the case of three characteristics will be discussed first. They might be this: To have (+) or not to have (−) a college degree, to be of white (+) or colored (−) race, and to be native (+) or foreign-born (−) resident of the United States. Evidently only the following eight combinations are possible (thus combination 6 is, for example, the white, foreign-born without a college degree):

Combination Number	College Degree	White	Native Born
1	+	+	+
2	+	+	−
3	+	−	+
4	+	−	−
5	−	+	+
6	−	+	−
7	−	−	+
8	−	−	−

By reduction is understood any classification as a result of which different combinations fall into one class.

Suppose that one tries to estimate the social advantages which correspond to these eight combinations of college degree, race, and nativity. It is possible (no question of the actual facts shall be implied here) to argue in the following way: To be a Negro is such a disadvantage in this country that college degree and nativity make little difference. Therefore, the combinations 3, 4 and 7, 8 fall into one class of greatest discrimination. For the whites, nativity is much more important than education, because one can substitute self-education for formal training, but one cannot amend foreign birth. Therefore, the combinations 2 and 6 form the next class—the foreign-born white—which is presumably less discriminated against than the Negroes. Among the native-born whites, education may be an important factor. Therefore, a special distinction is introduced between the combinations 1 and 5. Thus an order of social advantage is established: the native white with college degree, the native white without college degree, the foreign-born white irrespective of education, and the Negro irrespective of nativity and education.

By merging some of our original eight combinations, we now have four classes. We have reduced the attribute space.

There are at least three kinds of reduction which should be distinguished:

1. The functional;
2. The arbitrary numerical;
3. The pragmatic.

1. In a functional reduction there exists an actual relationship between two of the attributes which reduces the number of combinations. If, for instance, Negroes cannot acquire college degrees, or if

tall girls are always judged more beautiful, certain combinations of variables will not occur in actuality. In this way, the system of combinations is reduced. The elimination of certain combinations can either be complete or these combinations may occur so infrequently that no special class need be established for them.

2. Arbitrary numerical reduction is best exemplified by index numbers. In the analysis of housing conditions, for instance, the following procedure is frequently used: Several items, such as plumbing, central heating, refrigeration, etc., are selected as especially indicative, and each is given a certain weight. Central heating and ownership of a refrigerator, without plumbing, might be equivalent to plumbing without the other two items, and, therefore, both cases get the same index number.

The weights for such a procedure can originate in different ways, of course.

3. In the case of functional reduction, certain combinations are eliminated in view of relationships existing between the variables themselves. In the case of pragmatic reduction, certain groups of combinations are assigned to one class in view of the research purpose. The example of degree-race-nativity, given above, offers such a pragmatic reduction. In considering the concrete problem of discrimination, no distinction was made between the other qualifications of the Negroes, and all were regarded as one class. . . .

Reduction[2] is a grouping of attribute combinations involving more than one attribute. To make the matter quite clear, we can examine the simplest case, two attributes, x and y, both of which might be visualized as ranks. Take, for example, the situation in which a large sample of married couples are studied with respect to two variables: (1) the attitude of the wives toward their husbands and (2) the economic success of the husband. y, the attitude of the wife, is ranked from very favorable to distinctly unfavorable and x, the success of the husband, is ranked from very great to very little. It would be possible to set up three grades for each variable, designated as high, medium, and low. As a result, there would be nine possible combinations of attitude and success. As yet, no reductions have taken place. Suppose, however, that as a result of a further analysis, we find that if the wife's attitude toward the husband is favorable, then the economic success will not influence marital relations, whereas, if the wife has only a medium attitude toward him, he needs at least medium success to make the marriage a success, and only great success can save the marriage if the wife's attitude is altogether unfavorable. If the problem is to classify all the marriages in two groups—one for which the attitude-success combinations are favorable for good marital relations, and one for which the combinations are unfavorable—the [following] diagram of a reduction would ensue:

X: Economic Success of Husband

	High	Medium	Low
High			
Medium			
Low			

Y: Attitude of Wife toward Husband

If one keeps to the more geometrical representation of these combinations he would say that the combinations resulting from a reduction always "turn the corner," because they involve more than one axis. . . .

It is by no means alleged that typological systems ought to originate in such a combination procedure as has been exemplified so far. Quite the contrary, it would be very worthwhile to analyze the different ways and means by which types have been established in different fields of research. The only claim made here is that once a system of types has been established by a research expert, it can always be proved that, in its logical structure, it could be the result of a reduction of an attribute space.

This procedure of finding, for a given system of types, the attribute space in which it belongs and the reduction that has been implicitly used is of such practical importance that it should have a special name; the term *substruction* is suggested.

When substructing to a given system of types the attribute space from which and the reduction through which it could be deduced, it is never assumed that the creator of the types really had such a procedure in mind. It is only claimed that, no matter how he actually found the types, he could have found them logically by such a substruction. . . .

The most common use of types is made when a writer gives an impressionistic classification of the material he has at hand. Here is a student who groups different types of criminals, another who classifies reasons for marital discord, a third one who deals with types of radio programs, and so on. These types are conceived as expedient tools and serve the study if they yield a valuable numerical distribution or correlation with other factors. . . .

Whenever a writer uses such a typological classification, he should substruct to it a corresponding attribute space and the reduction connected therewith, in order to be aware of what is logically implied in his enumeration of types. There would be many advantages in this discipline. The writer would see whether he has overlooked certain cases, he could make sure that some of his types are not overlapping, and he would probably make the classification more valuable for actual empirical research. This practical value of a substruction deserves special attention. If a student invents types of family discord, his contribution is valuable only if in any concrete case it is possible to say whether the given discord belongs to a certain type or not. For this purpose, criteria have to be worked out. These criteria, in general, point directly to the attribute space from which the type was reduced. Therefore, the substruction of the adequate attribute combinations to a given system of types adapts them better to actual research purposes.

As an example, there is reported here an adventure in substruction which summarizes once more all the points made so far. For a study of the structure of authority in the family, conducted by the International Institute of Social Research, a questionnaire was devised pertaining to authoritarian relations between parents and children. E. Fromm, the director of the study, suggested as a theoretical basis in outlining the study, four types of authoritarian situations:

Complete authority;
Simple authority;
Lack of authority;
Rebellion.

By using the procedures of reduction and substruction, it was possible to attain a thorough research procedure, and at the same time to exhaust all possible significance of Fromm's types.

An authoritarian situation in a family is determined by the way the parents exercise their authority, by the way in which the children accept it, and by the interrelations between exercise and acceptance. Two main categories in the questionnaire covered the matter of exercise: Questions were asked to discover whether parents used corporal punishment and whether they interfered with such activities as recreation, church attendance, etc. Two groups of indices were used in regard to acceptance: The children were asked if they had confidence in their parents, and whether conflicts with them in various fields of activity were frequent. Each index had two possible scores: high ($+$)

and low $(-)$. By this means, the following four combinations were reached:

	Corporal Punishment	
Interference	+	−
+	1	2
−	3	4

It was then possible to reduce this scheme to a rough one-dimensional order of intensity of exercise. The combination No. 1 (corporal punishment is used and interference is frequent) is apparently the strongest form and No. 4, the weakest. The type in which corporal punishment is used but no interference in the child's activities was attempted (No. 3) can be eliminated as practically contradictory. The combination No. 2 was left to describe a moderate degree of exercise. These three combinations, plus-plus, minus-minus, and minus-plus, can then be reduced to a one-dimensional order, X, Y and Z, with X as the strongest degree.

The same procedure may be applied to the indices pertaining to acceptance of authority:

	Conflicts	
Confidence	+	−
+	1	2
−	3	4

Combination No. 2 (absence of conflicts and existence of confidence) is readily seen to be the highest degree of acceptance. The inverse combination, No. 3, is the weakest. The combination No. 1 can practically be disregarded as confidence will hardly co-exist with persistent conflicts.[3] The combination minus-minus (no conflicts and no confidence) is roughly a median grade. The three grades of acceptance are then labeled A, B, and C, with A as the highest degree.

Here two separate reductions have been carried through: The two-dimensional space consisting of corporal punishment and interference has been reduced to one dimension "exercise of authority." In the same way, conflict and confidence were reduced to "acceptance of authority."

A further step leads to the drawing of a chart which constitutes the attribute space into which the four initial types of authority will have to be placed. It turns out that nine combinations are logically possible, while Fromm suggested only four types. By the procedure of substruction, the last scheme will have to be matched with Fromm's types (which were, of course, conceived in a wholly different way).

| | | Acceptance | |
Exercise	A	B	C
X	1	2	3
Y	4	5	6
Z	7	8	9

It may be assumed that Fromm's type "complete authority" is covered by the combinations 1 and 2. Simple authority is covered by combinations 4 and 5. The lack of authority is represented by combination 8 and rebellion by 3 and 6. For greater clarity the substruction is repeated in another form:

Combination	Type	Exercise	Acceptance
1 and 2	Complete authority	Strong (X)	Voluntarily accepted (A) or just accepted (B)
4 and 5	Simple authority	Medium (Y)	Voluntarily accepted (A) or just accepted (B)
8	Lack of authority	Weak (Z)	Just accepted (B)
3 and 6	Rebellion	Strong (X) or medium (Y)	Refused (C)

Combinations 7 and 9 are not covered. Apparently it was assumed that neither voluntary acceptance nor rebellion against an authority which is scarcely exercised is possible. The substruction, however, may be used as a tool for discovery. It discloses the possibility that children might long for an authority which no one offers them. These discovered combinations suggest further research.

The reader may disagree with the above substruction and may think that other combinations should be matched with Fromm's types. Then he may try to improve the types on the basis of the general scheme suggested above. He will see for himself that the procedure of substruction can lead to improvements in typologies which have been construed on the basis of theoretical considerations or intuitions. The proof of the success of the procedure lies, of course, in concrete applications which lie beyond the scope of the present exemplification.

It may again be stressed strongly that this whole analysis does not limit the research man in the actual sequence of his work. It is by no means postulated that he should start by deciding what attributes he wants to use, then proceed with the reduction, and so finally get his system of types. Often, especially if many attributes are at stake, it might be much better for the student to become deeply acquainted with his material and then bring order into it by first blocking out a few main types on a completely impressionistic basis. Only thereafter would he reconsider the matter and substruct to his own typological intuitions an adequate attribute space and bring into relief the reduction which he has used implicitly. The best results probably will be gained in just this combination of a first general survey and a subsequent systematic analysis. The elaborate example just given provides a good illustration.

The problem comes up whether to every given system of types there corresponds only one attribute space and oné mode of reduction. The answer is probably "no." The typological classifications used in current social research are somewhat vague and, therefore, more than one logical substruction can usually be provided for them. The different attribute spaces originating from these substructions can be transformed one into another, however. The procedure of transformation is very important because it is the logical background of what is generally termed "an interpretation of a statistical result." It could be shown that such an interpretation is often nothing more than transforming a system of types from one attribute space into another with different coordinates, and therewith changing simultaneously one reduction into another. There is no opportunity here to discuss this question beyond giving one example.

Several hundred pupils were grouped in a rough way, according to their physical development and according to their scholastic achievements. Combinations of these two attributes yielded five rather distinct empirical types. The physically underdeveloped children were either especially bright or especially unsuccessful. The same was true for well developed children; most of them also appeared among the two scholastic extremes. The children of medium physical development were, on the whole, medium in their scholastic achievement as well. Relatively few children were of medium physical development and especially good or bad in their school work; and relatively few children of unusually good or bad physical condition were medium in their ability in school.

The result was interpreted in the following terms. Among the physically underdeveloped children there are two types: those who were too handicapped to be successful in school; those who overcompensated for their physical weakness and did especially well in school. Every teacher knows those two types from his own experience. Among the especially well developed children, one group was the all-around type, combining mental with physical maturity. The other group was the "hoodlum" type which, on the basis of strength, has such a good position in class that it does not consider it necessary to make an effort in school work. If this interpretation is analyzed in the light of the previous considerations, it turns out that these types can be described in two completely different sets of dimensions. Instead of the original attributes of physical and mental developments, new terms are used. These are overcompensations, parallelism between physical and mental activity, and peer recognition versus peer neglect. Such an interpretation consists logically of substructing to a system of types an attribute space different from the one in which it was derived by reduction, and of looking for the reductions which would lead to the system of types in this new space. That is what transformation means.

The operations of reduction, substruction, and transformation could be called "typological operations," because their application links any system of types with an attribute space. (We use the word "type" for those systems where more than one attribute is at stake and where the reductions cut across the axis of the attribute space.) The logic of these typological operations has not been given enough attention so far; its careful study could improve considerably the use of types in practical research.

These remarks have been mainly concerned with illustrating those typological operations. The focus was the reduction of an attribute space to a system of types. Three kinds of reduction were distinguished: the functional, the arbitrary numerical, and the pragmatic. The latter is the most important in empirical research; its inversion is called substruction. Substruction consists of matching a given system of types with that attribute space and that reduction from which it could have originated logically. This substruction of an attribute combination to a given system of types permits one to check the omissions or overlappings in this system and points the way to its practical applications.

Notes

1. A. W. Siythoff, W. V. Leiden, 1936.
2. The first two procedures of reduction and the concept of reduction itself are clearly discussed by Hempel and Oppenheim. They lay much less stress upon them,

however, than is given in these remarks. In a logical analysis of typological operations, the process of reduction ought to have a commanding place.

When it comes to empirical social research, pragmatic reduction overshadows the other two kinds. Hempel and Oppenheim have not included it in their analysis. The desire to discuss the method of pragmatic reduction has given rise to the present paper.

3. If a few such cases come up, they might first be eliminated or else lumped together with the moderate degree of acceptance. Later, they might be studied separately.

A Digression on Disposition Concepts

Before going further, the role of dispositions in empirical action analysis has to be clarified. I have already referred to the distinction between motive as a causally assessed disposition and the merely descriptive use of terms like "needs" or "goals," which are often summarized under the catchall heading of "motivation." No general classification of disposition concepts exists. An author is usually interested in one of them; he tries to define it carefully and then gives a list of comparisons with "related concepts." Thus Allport concentrates on attitudes and discusses how they differ from values, interests, opinions, etc.[1] Kluckhohn focuses on values and tries to differentiate them from attitudes, needs, goals, beliefs, etc.[2] The literature along this line is practically endless.

But, by starting from shifting linguistic usages, one misses just those distinctions which lead to essential variations in research procedures and in interpretations. It is more fruitful to bring out the dimensions along which distinctions have been proposed so that the intent of various authors becomes more comparable and the terminology loses its importance. A scrutiny of various texts shows that three dimensions dominate the discussion. One is generality and specificity (e.g., a personality trait that can be exhibited in many substantive spheres versus an interest usually directed toward a limited object). Another may be described as degree of directiveness (e.g., an attitude toward versus a desire for something, the former being more of the passive, the second more of the driving kind). A third dimension relates to the time perspective (e.g., a plan or an expectation spans the future; an urge or a perceptual bias focuses on the present). If we dichotomize these three dimensions of substantive scope, dynamics, and time

Reprinted with editorial adaptations from "Reflections on Business," *American Journal of Sociology* 65, no. 1 (1959): 1–31 [8–10]. This paper was originally initiated by the Direction on Economic Development of the Ford Foundation.

TIME RANGE

Dynamics	Present Mainly Scope			Dynamics	Future Referents Included Scope	
	Specific	*General*			*Specific*	*General*
Passive	1	2		*Passive*	5	6
Driving	3	4		*Driving*	7	8

FIG. 1

range, we get eight combinations which can serve classificatory purposes and at the same time show what other aspects are involved in the linguistic tradition of these disposition concepts (Fig. 1). (In a more detailed discussion the three dimensions would be treated as continuous, so that finer distinctions could be made.)

Most terms have been used differently by various authors, and most readers will attach their own private associations to them. This should be remembered in reading a few examples that illustrate the relatively simple three-dimensional scheme, which for our purpose seems useful.

1. *Preferences* as for specific foods and *opinions* on specific issues are specific, passive, and current.

2. *Traits* like broad-mindedness, more general *attitudes* like economic liberalism, as well as such "frames of reference" as looking at issues from a "businessman's point of view" are general, passive, and current.

3. What are usually called *wants* or needs, like being hungry or looking for a new car to replace a worn-out one, are specific, driving, and current.

4. More *directional traits* like vitality and energy or aggressiveness may be described as general, driving, and current.

5. *Expectations* as to future prices and customer demands that are important in modern economic analysis are typical examples of the specific, passive, future-oriented dispositions.

6. *Tendencies* to consider longer chains of possible consequences and *inclinations* like optimism come to mind as examples of the more general, passive, and future-oriented dispositions.

7. Investment *intentions*, occupational *plans*, and schemes for getting promoted to an impending executive vacancy may be described as specific, driving, and future-oriented.

8. The ubiquitous term "motivation" should become less ambiguous here. In the present paper I shall restrict the term "motivation" to a disposition of rather *general scope* and with the implication that it *directs* its bearer toward activities that bridge the present and the *future*.

Type 8 is the one most relevant for present purposes, but, as a by-product, a number of worthwhile distinctions can be distinguished. Types 2, 4, and 6 are usually lumped together as traits. We can assume that businessmen are more conservative (Type 2) than, say, university professors and more energetic (Type 4). Whether the businessmen are more optimistic as to future events (Type 6) than professors is hard to guess and might change according to circumstances. The specific (odd numbered) dispositions are more pertinent in the present context. Types 5 and 7, expectations and plans, have acquired importance in recent econometric studies of business intentions.[3] They can both be introduced as variables in time-series studies. There the double role of time becomes especially clear. For any expectation we have to know at what time it is held and to what future period it refers. The relation between the "passive" expectation and the "driving" plan is complex. While plans lead to action, expectations affect plans; we know from voting studies that intentions often color expectations.[4] Type 3, wants or needs, are traditional in consumer studies. Types 5 and 7 often seem more accessible to simple interviews than Type 3; the latter were the entering wedge for projective techniques. Type 1 includes the typical objects of polls.

Thus we see that even this simple classification of dispositions leads to differences in problems and research techniques which can be derived from the position of the types in the dimensional scheme. Additional variations can be handled more casually because they do not seem to be of much consequence for our subject matter; this holds for the means-end relation, for instance, and the separation of a state (angry) from a trait (irascible). The distinction between physiological and culturally induced wants will become relevant at one point only. But one other complication has to be introduced. It came about when anthropologists and sociologists began to scan these concepts of disposition. A goal may be pursued or a selection made with or without the feeling that doing so is morally desirable or will be socially rewarded. This leads to the notion of norm or value. All the categories listed above can take on a normative element, although some may do so more easily than others. Intentions (Type 7) and wants (Type 3) seem to be more often "affected by public interest" than expectations (Type 5) and frames of reference (Type 2). For most purposes it is enough to refer to the normative element when needed, without doubling the terminology.

Every one of the eight types of dispositions can become a motive in the study of specific acts. One finds in the literature statements to the effect that people are motivated by optimism, by a specific goal, by a cultural orientation, by an expectation, etc. Inasmuch as these refer to concrete acts where the causal role of any of the dispositions is assessed, the phrasing is consistent with our terminology. The term "motivation," on the other hand, will be reserved for a rather broad, driving, and future-oriented disposition of Type 8 in our scheme. Often it is used in a much broader and looser sense, sometimes being applied to all dispositions, sometimes to all those of great scope or all those with strong directive implications. In references to such usage in this paper the word "motivation" will be put in quotation marks, but, with or without quotation marks, the term will refer to a described disposition which at best has a good probability of becoming a motive in a specific act.

Notes

1. Allport, Gordon. "Attitudes," in Carl Murchison (ed.), *Handbook of Social Psychology,* pp. 798–844. Worcester, Mass.: Clark University Press, 1935.

2. Kluckhohn, Clyde. "Values and Value Orientations in the Theory of Action," in Talcott Parsons and E. A. Shils (eds.), *Toward a General Theory of Action,* pp. 388–433. Cambridge, Mass.: Harvard University Press, 1951.

3. Modigliani, Franco, and Balderston, F. E. "Economic Analysis and Forecasting: Recent Developments in the Use of Panel and Other Survey Techniques," in Eugene Burdick and A. J. Brodbeck (eds.), *American Voting Behavior,* pp. 372–98. Glencoe, Ill.: Free Press, 1959.

4. Berelson, Bernard, Lazarsfeld, Paul F., and McPhee, William. *Voting.* Chicago: University of Chicago Press, 1954.

8

Analyzing the Relations between Variables

On the Relation between Individual and Collective Properties

Introductory Considerations

1. *Purpose*

Social scientists often make use of variables to describe not only individual persons but also groups, communities, organizations, or other "collectives."[1] Thus one reads, for example, of "racially mixed census tracts," of "highly bureaucratized voluntary organizations," or of a "centrally located rooming-house district." At other times the variables, although describing individuals, are based on data about certain collectives, as in a comparison of "graduates of top-ranking medical schools" with "graduates of other medical schools." This paper attempts to clarify some of the operations involved in the construction and use of such variables in empirical research, and provides a nomenclature for the different ways in which information about individuals and about collectives may be interwoven in these properties. The properties will be classified according to the measurement operations involved in their construction.

2. *Some Features of Generalizing Propositions*

The intended meaning of the variables often remains ambiguous if they are not examined in the context of the propositions in which they are used. It is therefore necessary at the outset to highlight certain features which are common to all generalizing propositions, whether or not they involve collectives. (As an illustration, reference is made

Reprinted from Paul F. Lazarsfeld and Herbert Menzel, "On the Relation between Individual and Collective Properties," in *Complex Organizations: A Sociological Reader,* edited by Amitai Etzioni (New York: Holt, Rinehart and Winston, 1961), pp. 422–40. Written in 1956. The Etzioni edition omits the final section of the original article.

to the proposition "Children of rich parents go to college in greater proportion than do children of poor parents.")

a. Generalizing propositions assert something about a set of *elements* (children).
b. For the research purposes at hand, these elements are considered *comparable*. In other words, the same set of *properties* (wealth of parents; going to college) is used to describe each element.
c. Each element has a certain *value* on each property. The values (rich parents, poor parents; going to college, not going to college) may be quantitative or qualitative.
d. The propositions assert interrelationships between the properties of the elements.

3. *Present Concern*

The propositions with which the present discussion is concerned have the additional characteristic that their elements are dealt with either as collectives or as members of collectives. An example of the first kind is "There is a negative correlation between the rate of juvenile delinquency of American cities and the proportion of their budget given over to education." An example of the second kind is "Those recognized as leaders do not deviate very far from the norms of their group."

4. *Special Meaning of "Collective" and "Member"*

The terms "collective" and "member" are used here in a specific sense which needs clarification. A collective may be an element of a proposition; that is, it is one of a set of units which are regarded as *comparable* in the sense specified above: the same set of properties is used to describe all the elements. These elements are *collectives* if each is considered to be composed of constituent parts, called *members*, which are regarded as comparable in their turn. "Comparable" is used in the same sense as before: all members are described by a single set of properties. (This is usually not the same as that used to describe the collectives.)

In other instances members are the elements of the propositions. Elements will be called "members" if they are considered to be constituent parts of larger units, called "collectives," which are regarded as comparable in the same sense as before.

Thus one set of properties is always used to describe or classify all the members, and another single set of properties is used to characterize all the collectives. It is clear that under these definitions one can

speak of "collectives" only when their "members" are also being referred to, and of "members" only when their "collectives" are also
involved. Furthermore, there must be a multiplicity of members if the
term "collective" is to be meaningful. It is perhaps less obvious but
will be seen later that there must also be a multiplicity of collectives—i.e., the members of more than one collective must be referred
to—if the distinctions between properties to be described below are
to be relevant.

By contrast, the notion of "element" is needed to characterize any
generalizing proposition whatsoever. It is applicable even in situations
where the notions of "member" and "collective" are not involved at
all.

5. Distinction between "Individuals" and "Members"

In the examples that come to mind most easily, the members of collectives are individual persons. Thus, for example, cities are the collectives and people are the members in the following two propositions:
(1) "The oldest settlers of cities are most likely to hold political
office," or (2) "The more industry there is in a city, the higher the
proportion of Democratic voters." The first proposition has members
and the second has collectives as elements. In the same sense, a precinct can be treated as a collective, with the inhabitants as members.
However, the members of a collective are not necessarily individual
persons. A city, for example, can be described as a collective with the
voting precincts as members. It follows that what appears as a collective in one context (e.g., precincts), can appear as a member in another. In any analysis of a piece of writing in which some of the
elements are collectives, it is always necessary to specify clearly of
what members the collectives are composed (for the purposes at
hand).[2]

The following graph will help to keep this terminology in mind:

The circles symbolize the collectives, the crosses within them their
members. The dots indicate that we are dealing with collectives as
elements of a proposition. This is the situation with which we deal in
the first part of this paper. In Sections 10 and 11 we discuss research
where members are the focus of attention. They are then the elements

of propositions, but their membership in one of a series of collectives is one of their characteristics.

6. *Possibility of "Three-Level" Propositions*

In some studies, more than two levels appear: for example, inhabitants, precincts, and cities may all be elements of the same study. This whole matter could, therefore, be elaborated by pointing out the various relationships which can exist between inhabitants, precincts, and cities. The next few pages are restricted to collectives which have only one kind of member; the members in most illustrations will be individual persons, but we will also present some examples in which the members themselves are larger units. Only much later (in Section 16) will examples of "three-level" propositions be taken up, in which units, e.g., "union shops," are simultaneously considered to be both members of their locals *and* collectives of individual workers.

7. *Propositions about Collectives as Substitutes and in Their Own Right*

Propositions about collectives are sometimes made as substitutes for propositions about individual persons, simply because the necessary data about individual persons are not available. For example, a high Republican vote in "silk-stocking" districts is sometimes accepted to show that wealthy people are likely to vote Republican, when no records about individual votes and individual incomes are available.[3] For this reason it is often not realized that a large number of sociologically meaningful empirical propositions can be made of which only collectives are intended to be the elements. Thus, for example, an anthropologist may show that the political independence of communities is correlated with their pattern of settlement. A student of social disorganization may ask whether city zones with a high incidence of juvenile delinquency also show a high incidence of commitments for senile dementia. A small-group experimenter may hypothesize that "the probability of effective utilization of the insights that occur is greater in certain communication patterns than in others."[4] Much discursive writing also consists, in a hidden way, of such propositions.

A Typology of Properties Describing "Collectives" and "Members"

8. *Properties of Collectives*

It is often useful to distinguish three types of properties which describe collectives: analytical properties based on data about each member; structural properties based on data about the relations among members; and global properties, not based on information about the properties of individual members.[5] The following examples may clarify these distinctions:

a. *Analytical*. These are properties of collectives which are obtained by performing some mathematical operation upon some property of each single member.[6]

> The average rental paid in a precinct and the proportion of its inhabitants who have "Old Immigrant" (English, German, Scottish, Scandinavian) names are analytical properties of a collective (precinct) composed of individuals.[7] The proportion of the communities of a given state that have their own high school is an analytical property of a collective (state) the members of which are communities. The diffusion of a message in a city, defined as the per cent of the target population knowing the message, is an analytical property of the city.[8]

> The standard deviation of incomes in a nation appears as an analytical property in the following example. The effect of postwar legislation in Great Britain was to make the income distribution much narrower. Economists have predicted that under these conditions people will save more, because they will spend less money on display consumption which might help them be socially acceptable in the higher strata.

> Correlations are sometimes used to characterize collectives and then also constitute analytical properties. The correlation of age and prestige in a given community, for example, has been used as a measure of its norms regarding old age. Sometimes more indirect inferences are involved. MacRae shows that in urban areas voting is highly correlated with occupation, while this is not the case in rural districts. He concludes from this vote that in rural districts there is a stronger spirit of community and cohesion.[9]

b. *Structural*. These are properties of collectives which are obtained by performing some operation on data about the relations of each member to some or all of the others.

> Assume, for example, that a sociometrist has recorded the "best-liked classmate" of each student in a number of classes. He can then describe the classes by the degree to which all choices are concentrated upon a few "stars." Or he might, alternately, classify them according to their cliquishness, the latter being defined as the number of subgroups into which a class can be divided so that no choices cut across subgroup lines. In these examples the collective is the school class, and the members are the individual students; "concentration of choices" and "cliquishness" are structural properties of the classes.

For an example in which the members are larger units, consider a map of the precincts of a city, which indicates the number of Negroes residing in each. Let a "Negro enclave" be defined as a precinct in which some Negroes live, but which is completely surrounded by precincts without Negroes. The proportion of the precincts of a city which are Negro enclaves would then be a structural property of the city.

c. *Global*. Often collectives are characterized by properties which are not based on information about the properties of individual members.

American Indian tribes have been characterized by the frequency with which themes of "achievement motive" make their appearance in their folk tales.[10] Societies have been classified as to the presence of money as a medium of exchange, of a written language, etc.[11] Nations may be characterized by the ratio of the national budget allotted to education and to armaments. Army companies may be characterized by the cleanliness of their mess equipment.

Voting precincts have been classified according to the activities and attitudes of their Republican and Democratic captains, including hours spent on party duties, number of persons known to the captain personally, and his expressed commitment to the party.[12] In experiments in message diffusion by leaflets dropped from airplanes, cities have been treated to different degrees of "stimulus intensity," defined as the per capita ratio of leaflets dropped.[13] All these are global properties.

The density of settlement is a global property of a district. Having a city manager form of government is a global property of a city. The insistence on specified initiation rites as a prerequisite to membership is a global property of a religious cult or of a college fraternity. Accessibility from the nearest big city is a global property of a village. A scale score assigned to each state according to the combination of duties assigned to the state board of education (rather than left to local authorities) is a global property of each state.[14]

"Emergent," "integral," "syntalic" and other terms have been used in meanings very similar to that of our term "global." It is not at all certain which term is most useful.[15]

Notice that all three of the above types of properties—analytical, structural, and global—describe collectives.

9. A Subsidiary Distinction among Analytical Properties of Collectives

An interesting distinction may be made among the analytical properties. The first two examples given above were the average income of a city, and the proportion of the communities of a given state that have their own high school. These properties of collectives have what one might call a similarity of meaning to the properties of members on which they are based. The wealth of a city seems to be the same sort of thing as the wealth of an inhabitant. The endowment of a community with a high school and the rate of high-school endowed communities in a state have a parallel meaning. This is not true for the remaining examples of analytical properties given above—the standard deviation of incomes in a nation, or correlations like that between age and prestige in a given community. Correlations and standard deviations can apply only to collectives and have no parallel on the level of members. The standard deviation of incomes in a city, for example, denotes something quite different—lack of homogeneity, perhaps—from individual income, the datum from which it is computed.

Another variable of this sort is "degree of consensus." When a Democrat and a Republican are competing for the mayoralty, the degree of political consensus in a particular club might be measured by the extent of the club's deviation from a fifty-fifty split. In this instance the analytic property is measured by a proportion, but it is not the simple proportion of adherents of either party; clubs which are 80 per cent Democratic and those which are 20 per cent Democratic are regarded as equal in consensus.

Whereas correlations, standard deviations, and similar measures always have a meaning peculiar to the group level, averages and proportions may or may not have a parallel meaning on the individual and collective levels.[16] Lack of parallel meaning is perhaps most clearly illustrated in the concept of a "hung jury," that is, a jury rendered indecisive by its inability to reach the required unanimity. Such a state of affairs is most likely when the individual jurors are most decisive and unyielding in their convictions.

10. *Properties of Members*

Another set of distinctions can be made between properties describing members in contexts where collectives have also been defined.

    a. *Absolute* properties are characteristics of members which are obtained without making any use either of information about the characteristics of the collective, or of information about the relationships of the member being described to other members. They thus include most of the characteristics commonly used to describe individuals.

        In the proposition, "Graduates of large law schools are more likely to earn high incomes at age 40 than graduates of small law schools," income is an absolute property of the members (the individual students).

b. *Relational* properties of members are computed[17] from information about the substantive relationships between the member described and other members.

> Sociometric popularity-isolation (number of choices received) is a relational property. Many other sociometric indices fall into this category. For example, if each member of a small group has rated each other member on a 5-point scale of acceptance-rejection, each member can be characterized by the total score he received (popularity), by the total score he expressed (active sociability), by the average deviation of the scores he accorded the others (discrimination in his acceptance of other members), etc.[18] In a study of the diffusion of the use of a new drug through a community of doctors, the physicians were classified according to whether or not they had a friend who had already used the new drug on a certain date.[19]

Some investigators have clarified the structure of relational properties by the use of matrices.[20] This new device can be fruitfully applied to some older papers.[21]

The distinction between relational properties of individuals and structural properties of collectives deserves emphasis. The former characterize members of collectives in their relations to one another. The latter characterize collectives and are aggregates over the relational properties of their members.

c. *Comparative* properties characterize a member by a comparison between his value on some (absolute or relational) property and the distribution of this property over the entire collective of which he is a member.

> Sibling order is a comparative property of individuals in the proposition, "First-born children are more often maladjusted than intermediate and last-born children." Note that each individual is characterized by comparison with the age of the other individuals in his family; in the resulting classification, many of the "last-born" will be older in years than many of the "first-born." Being a "deviate" from the majority opinion in one's housing project unit is a comparative property.[22]

> Another example is contained in the following proposition: "Students who had the highest I.Q. in their respective high school classes have greater difficulty in adjusting in college than students who are not quite at the top in high school, even when their actual I.Q. score is equally high." Here the comparative property (being at the top in high school or not) is established in terms of the I.Q. distribution

in each student's respective high school; the proposition pertains to a set of college students which includes boys from several high schools (collectives).

d. *Contextual* properties describe a member by a property of his collective.

Consider an example cited previously: "Graduates of large law schools are more likely to earn high incomes at age 40 than graduates of small law schools." In this proposition, "being a member of a large law school" is a contextual property of individuals.

Contextual properties are also used in the following propositions: "Union members in closed shops are less militant than union members in open shops." "Residents of racially mixed districts show more racial prejudice than those of racially homogeneous districts." "The less the promotion opportunity afforded by a branch (of the army), the more favorable the opinion (of soldiers) tends to be toward promotion opportunity."[23] In these propositions, being a member of a closed shop, residing in a mixed district, or being a soldier in a branch with frequent promotions are all examples of contextual properties.

Contextual properties are really characteristics of collectives applied to their members. Thus the classification of "collective properties" developed above could be repeated here as a subdivision of contextual "individual properties."[24] Note also that a contextual property, unlike a comparative property, has the same value for all members of a given collective.

11. *Contextual and Comparative Properties Meaningful Only Where More Than One Collective Is Involved*

It is not meaningful to speak of contextual or comparative properties when the elements under study are all members of the same collective—for instance, when only graduates of one law school are being studied—for the following reasons. Any *contextual* property would, in that case, have the same value for all the elements; hence nothing could be said about the interrelationship of this property and any other property. Any *comparative* property would, under these circumstances, classify the elements in exactly the same way as the absolute property from which it was derived, except that the calibration may be grosser. (If only children of one family are considered, the classification into "first-born," "intermediate," and "last-born" differs from that by age only in the grosser calibration. Similarly, if I.Q. scores of graduates of one law school are replaced by classification into lowest, second, third, and highest I.Q. quartile within their school, nothing will change except that the number of categories is reduced.)

12. *Special Case Where the Typology Can Be Applied in Two Alternate Ways*

A difficulty comes about when all the members of a set of collectives (or a representative sample of the members of each) constitute the elements of a proposition which includes a contextual property. Suppose, for instance, that the income ten years after graduation is recorded for all who graduate from fifty law schools in a certain year. A possible finding might be, "The income of law school graduates is correlated with the size of the school they graduated from." This is a proposition about students, relating their income (an absolute property) to the size of their law school (a contextual property). The same proposition could be interpreted also as one where the elements are the law schools; the average income of the students would then be an analytical property of each law school; its size would be a global property of these collectives.

13. *The Present Classification Is Formal Rather Than Substantive*

As stated at the outset, the scheme suggested above is intended for the classification of properties according to the operations involved in their measurement. Although a classification by the underlying concepts or forces that the properties may be intended to represent might have numerous parallels to the present classification, it would not be the same.[25] In the present methodological context, for example, "number of libraries in a community" and "occurrence of aggressiveness themes in folk tales current in a tribe" are classified as global properties because they are not based on information about the properties of individual members. Yet it would be convincing to argue that these properties are relevant to the behavioral sciences only because properties of individuals, of the relations among individuals, or of the resulting social structures are inferred from them. Similarly, the title of office held by a person in a hierarchy would here be classified as an "absolute" property, even when the researcher is actually interested in the incumbent's power over subordinates which the title implies.

At some points arbitrary decisions have to be made. On an intuitive basis we decided to consider the number of members in a collective (e.g., population size) as a global property, although one might argue that it is analytical, obtained by counting the "existence" of each member. Even more ambiguous is the classification of rates, based on the behavior of ex-members—e.g., suicide rates. No definitive practice is proposed for such borderline cases.

Combinations of Types of Properties

The types of properties which have been defined can appear in various forms of combinations.

14. *Several Types in the Same Proposition*

Very commonly, as many of the above examples have shown, one proposition will make use of properties of several types. An additional illustration of this can be drawn from a study of political processes within the International Typographical Union, which has been operating under an internal two-party system for many decades. The shops of this union were classified according to their degree of "political consensus"; shops in which 67 per cent or more of the members favored the same party were regarded as high in consensus, the remainder as low. Individual members were graded according to the amount of union political activity they engaged in. It was expected that men in shops where political consensus was high would be more active in politics than those in shops where consensus was low. The hypothesis, however, was borne out only in small shops (i.e., those with thirty men or less). The finding could therefore be expressed in the following proposition: "For workers in small shops, there is a correlation between consensus of the shop and degree of political activity of the men; for workers in large shops, there is no such correlation." In this proposition there appear two contextual properties (size and consensus of each man's shop) and an absolute property (political activity).[26]

The following hypothetical example again shows the use of several types of variables in one proposition—in fact, in each of several propositions. Ten preliterate tribes living in a certain country are classified according to the number of wars they have fought during the last hundred years. This characteristic, in the present terminology, is a global property of each tribe. A representative sample of one hundred men from each tribe is given a test of "aggressiveness"—an absolute property, from which a summary score for each tribe is computed, as an analytical property. At this point, the correlation between average aggressiveness and the number of wars can be computed. One may regard this computation as either a correlation between an analytical and a global property of ten collectives, or a correlation between an absolute and a contextual property of one thousand individual persons.

Now a factory is opened in the district, and some men from each of the ten tribes find employment there as laborers. Each is given the test of "aggressiveness"; each is also observed for a period of one month, and the number of fights he starts with other employees is recorded. Then the following two correlations can be computed:

a. The correlation between the score on the aggressiveness test and the number of fights. This is a proposition the elements of which are people and the properties of which are conventional psychological characteristics—absolute properties, in the present terminology.

b. The correlation between the number of fights and the number of wars reported for the tribe from which each individual came. This is again a proposition the elements of which are people. But one of the variables (number of wars) now is a contextual property.

The comparison between these two propositions is interesting. In proposition (a) actual fighting is related to the psychological trait of aggressiveness. In proposition (b) actual fighting is related to something that one might call the normative background of each person.

15. Properties of One Type Constructed from Properties of Another Type

The types of properties outlined can also be compounded in that a property of one type may be constructed from properties of another type. Contextual properties, for example, have been defined as properties describing a member by a property of his collective. But what property of his collective is to be used? In most of the examples given, contextual properties of members were based on global properties of their collectives, as in the phrase "men from tribes that have engaged in many wars." But contextual properties can equally well be based on any other kind of property of a collective—for example, on a structural property, as when doctors are classified according to whether or not they ever practiced in cities ridden by medical cliques. One might test whether those who formerly practiced in cliqueless cities have less tendency to form cliques in their new location.

This compounding is also illustrated by examples, cited earlier in another connection: "being a worker in a big shop" and "being a worker in a shop with high consensus." The first of these is a contextual property constructed from a global property; the second is a contextual property constructed from an analytical property.

16. Several Types from the Same Data

In some instances one body of research will construct properties of several different types from the same data, as in the following excerpts from a report on the adoption of modern farming practices by Kentucky farmers.

> 393 farm operators . . . in thirteen neighborhoods were interviewed. . . . Information was obtained on the extent to which each of the operators had tried and was following 21 farm practices recommended by the agricultural agencies. For each respondent, an adoption score was calculated. This score is the percentage of applicable practices which the operator had adopted. For example, if 18 of the practices applied to the farm operations being carried on and the operator had adopted 9, his score was 50. Neighborhoods varied widely in the mean adoption scores of residents, which range from a low of 25 in one neighborhood to a high of 57 in another. . . . The neighborhoods were combined . . . into three types of neighborhoods: "low adoption areas," "medium adoption areas," and "high adoption areas." . . .
>
> The following operational hypothesis . . . is suggested: In areas of high adoption, those from whom other farmers obtain farming information have higher adoption rates than farmers in general; but, in areas of low adoption, the adoption rates of leaders are similar to adoption rates of farmers in general . . . the hypothesis is supported by data. In the "low adoption areas" the mean score of all farmers was 32 and that of the leaders 37, while in the "high adoption areas" the mean score of all farmers was 48 and that of the leaders 66.[27]

Here the farm operator's "adoption score" is used as an absolute property of information leaders and of farmers in general. It is also used as the datum from which the classification of neighborhoods into "high adoption areas" and "low adoption areas" is computed. This classification is an analytical property of the neighborhoods; when used, as in the proposition quoted, to characterize the farmers resident in the neighborhoods, it becomes a contextual property of the farmers.

17. Simultaneous Characterization of the Same Elements as Collectives and as Members

Complexity of another sort arises when one set of elements appears both as members and as collectives in the same proposition. Up to this point examples of such "three-level propositions" have deliberately been excluded. It is now appropriate to introduce such examples. Consider, for instance, the following assertion: "Women's clubs which are internally divided into cliques have less easy-going relationships with other women's clubs than have clubs which are not so divided." Here the elements (women's clubs) are first categorized according to a structural variable (internal division into cliques), and then an assertion is made about a relational property (relationship with other clubs) of the elements in each structural category.

In the study of political processes within the International Typographical Union, which was cited earlier, each printer's vote in a union election was recorded. A liberal and a conservative candidate competed for union office. Each printer's vote was compared with his own conservative-liberal predisposition, determined by an attitude scale. The individuals could thus be classified as voting according to or contrary to their own predisposition. Up to this point, no collective is involved; there is merely a combination of two absolute properties into one. This combined absolute property of each printer was then compared with two contextual properties: the majority vote in his shop, and the majority vote in the local to which his shop belonged. The question was whether the climate of opinion in a man's shop or that in his entire local is more important in affecting his decisions. The answer could be determined only by examining cases where the shop and the local were in conflict. It was found that more people voted contrary to their own predisposition when it was in conflict with the majority of their shop (but not of their local) than when it was in conflict with the majority of their local (but not of their shop). In this instance each person is first characterized as voting according to or contrary to his predisposition. This absolute variable is then correlated with two contextual variables, both describing the same members (persons), but each having reference to a different level of collectives (shops or locals).[28]

18. *Outlook*

The preceding analysis can be extended in many directions; three of them shall be briefly sketched. For one we can introduce status differences among the members of the collectives. Colleges have professors and administrators, factory teams have workers and foremen, platoons have soldiers and noncoms. This may call for extending the notion of structural properties if, e.g., we distinguish various types of supervision; or analytical properties may be generalized if we classify colleges according to the degree to which the administration and the faculty share the same values. Stouffer has made ingenious use of such status differences by developing what one could call partitioned analytical properties. He wanted to know whether the food provided for army units had an effect on soldiers' morale. If he had asked the soldiers to rate the food he would not have known whether their morale did not affect their rating of the food. So he asked the noncommissioned officers to judge the food and correlated their average rating with the average morale score of the soldiers; the elements of the correlation were of course the army units studied.[29]

A second line of analysis opens up if the elements of a proposition are pairs of individuals: people who are friends tend to vote the same way; egalitarian relationships are more enduring than those which are hierarchic. It would be artificial to call such notions "propositions about collectives." Obviously dyads can be characterized in an even more complex way: pairs of doctors who commonly discuss cases with each other as equals are more likely to use the same type of drug than are pairs of doctors who stand in an advisor-advisee relationship to each other.[30] A scrutiny of recent sociometric literature is likely to provide distinctions going beyond those offered in this paper.

Finally, the utility of the present approach deserves argument. Obviously no one wants to make methodological classifications for their own sake. They are, however, useful in reminding us of the variety of research operations that are possible, and in clearing up misunderstandings. It can, for example, be shown that many arguments about atomism versus "holistic" approaches in current sociological literature can be clarified by an explication of the formal types of properties which enter into speculative or empirical propositions. In another publication, the senior author has summarized passages from several recent works of social research which relate, often in quite complex ways, the characteristics and attitudes of individuals, their propensity to choose friends inside and outside of variously overlapping collectives, the composition of these collectives in terms of members' background and perceptions, and the recent occurrence of certain events in the history of the collectives. He attempted to show that such "contextual propositions" go a long way toward satisfying the frequently heard demand that social research should "consider structures" or "take the total situation into account."[31]

Notes

1. Individuals and collectives made up of individuals do not, of course, exhaust the matters which social scientists describe. Social-science propositions may, instead, have various other units for their subjects. Not infrequently the subjects are acts, behavior patterns, customs, norms, "items of culture," and the like, as in the assertion that "items of culture that are . . . not much woven into a pattern . . . are least likely to encounter resistance to their diffusion."—Ralph Linton, *The Study of Man* (New York: Appleton, 1936), pp. 341–342. "Beliefs and practices" have been sorted into four classes according to the pattern of their differential distribution among mobile and nonmobile holders of high and low positions in a stratification system."—Peter M. Blau, "Social Mobility and Interpersonal Relations," *American Sociological Review*, 21 (1956), 290–295.

2. It is, of course, also possible to make propositions about cities without reference

to any members at all, just as it is possible to make propositions about individuals without reference to any collectives. Thus one may, e.g., correlate city size with number of churches, or location with building materials used, just as one can correlate individual income and education. In neither case are the distinctions made in the present paper relevant, because the individuals are not treated as "members" and the cities are not treated as "collectives" as here defined (i.e., as composed of "members"—constituent units described by their values on some one set of properties). It is thus clear that the typology of properties here presented is not always pertinent.

3. This procedure can lead to very misleading statistics, as pointed out by W. S. Robinson in "Ecological Correlations and the Behavior of Individuals," *American Sociological Review,* 15 (1950), 351–357. Sounder methods for inferring individual correlations from ecological data are proposed by Leo A. Goodman, "Ecological Regressions and Behavior of Individuals," *American Sociological Review,* 18 (1953), 663–664, and by Otis Dudley Duncan and Beverly Davis, "An Alternate to Ecological Correlation," *ibid.,* pp. 665–666.

4. For details on these and additional examples, see Paul F. Lazarsfeld and Morris Rosenberg (eds.), *The Language of Social Research* (Glencoe, Ill.: Free Press, 1955), pp. 302–322. Compare also Herbert Menzel, "Comment," *American Sociological Review,* 15 (1950), 674.

5. This classification of properties of collectives corresponds closely to the classifications presented earlier by Cattell and by Kendall and Lazarsfeld and reprinted in Lazarsfeld and Rosenberg (eds.), *op. cit.,* pp. 291–301. Analytical properties are Cattell's population variables and Kendall and Lazarsfeld's Types I, II, and III. Structural properties are Cattell's structural variables and Kendall and Lazarsfeld's Type IV. Our global properties are Cattell's syntality variables and Kendall and Lazarsfeld's Type V. See also n. 25.

6. It should be understood that the distinctions here proposed do not depend on who performs the operations involved. For example, "average income of a city" would be classified as an analytical property regardless of whether the investigator (a) obtains individual income data from all inhabitants directly and then computes the average, (b) obtains individual income data from the files of the tax collector and then computes the average, or (c) looks up the average income in the published census reports. Compare also n. 17.

7. Phillips Cutright and Peter H. Rossi, "Grass Roots Politicians and the Vote," *American Sociological Review,* 23 (1958), 171–179.

8. Melvin L. DeFleur and Otto N. Larsen, *The Flow of Information* (New York: Harper, 1958).

9. Duncan MacRae, Jr., "Occupations and the Congressional Vote, 1940–1950," *American Sociological Review,* 20 (1955), 332–340. For another example, see the evidence used to demonstrate differences in the norms of two housing projects in Leon Festinger, Stanley Schachter, and Kurt Back, "The Operation of Group Standards," in Lazarsfeld and Rosenberg, *op. cit.,* pp. 373–377.

10. See David C. McClelland and G. A. Friedman, "A Cross-cultural Study of the Relationship between Child Training Practices and Achievement Motivation Appearing in Folk Tales," in Guy E. Swanson, Theodore M. Newcomb, and Eugene L. Hartley (eds.), *Readings in Social Psychology* (New York: Holt, Rinehart and Winston, 1952), pp. 243–249.

11. See, e.g., Linton C. Freeman and Robert F. Winch, "Societal Complexity: An Empirical Test of a Typology of Societies," *American Journal of Sociology,* 62 (1957), 461–466.

12. Cutright and Rossi, *loc. cit.*

13. DeFleur and Larsen, *op. cit.*

14. Robert Redfield, *The Folk Culture of Yucatan* (Chicago: U. of Chicago Press, 1941); and Margaret J. Hagood, and Daniel O. Price, *Statistics for Sociologists* (rev. ed., New York: Henry Holt and Company, 1952), pp. 144–152.

15. Although global properties of collectives are not based on information about members, the above examples are, of course, listed here on the assumption that assertions about the members are made somewhere in the same proposition or at least in the same body of work; otherwise the distinction between "global" and "absolute" properties would become pointless (cf. n. 2). It may also bear repeating here that any discussion of a "collective" requires clear specification of what its members are considered to be. The proportion of the buildings of a city which are devoted to cultural activities was given as an example of a "global property" of a city on the assumption that the city is treated as a collective of inhabitants; i.e., that statements involving the inhabitants are made in some connection with this measure of "cultural level." It is, of course, also possible to treat a city as a collective of buildings; then the proportion of buildings devoted to cultural activities would become an analytical property. Which of these two types of property it is can be judged only from the context. (See also Section 13.)

16. Compare the notion of "counterpart" in Edgar F. Borgatta, Leonard Cottrell, Jr., and Henry J. Meyer, "On the Dimensions of Group Behavior," *Sociometry,* 19 (1956), 233.

17. It may be worth repeating here that the distinctions proposed are independent of who performs the operations involved. Thus, e.g., "sociometric popularity" would be classified as a relational property when measured in any of the following three ways: (a) the investigator counts the number of choices accorded to a member by his colleagues in answer to a sociometric questionnaire; (b) the investigator observes the frequency of interactions between the member and his colleagues; (c) the member is asked, "How many visits did you receive from colleagues during the last week?" These distinctions are, of course, important in themselves but not relevant to the present typology (cf. n. 6).

18. Some sociometric indices are listed in Hans Zeisel, *Say It with Figures* (4th ed.; New York: Harper, 1957), pp. 110–114, 148–153. The list includes indices not only of relational properties but of comparative and structural properties as well.

19. Herbert Menzel and Elihu Katz, "Social Relations and Innovation in the Medical Profession: The Epidemiology of a New Drug," *Public Opinion Quarterly,* 19 (1956), 337–352.

20. See Zeisel, *loc. cit.,* and Leon Festinger, Stanley Schachter, and Kurt Back, "Matrix Analysis of Group Structures," in Lazarsfeld and Rosenberg, *op. cit.,* pp. 358–367. In both instances matrices are also used to develop indices for structural properties of groups.

21. See, e.g., Robert R. Sears, "Experimental Studies of Projection," *Journal of Social Psychology,* 7 (1936), 151–163.

22. Festinger, Schachter, and Back, *loc. cit.,* pp. 367–382.

23. S. A. Stouffer, *et al., The American Soldier* (Princeton, N.J.: Princeton, 1949), I, 256.

24. It is sometimes helpful to talk of "collective properties" instead of the cumbersome "properties of collectives"; the same holds for "individual properties." It is important, however, not to be misled by this linguistic condensation.

25. Cattell's classification of population, structural, and syntality variables (cf. n. 5

above), which is closely paralleled in form by our analytical-structural-global distinction, seems to be based on a mixture of measurement criteria and considerations of causality. The latter gain the upper hand in the critique of Cattell's scheme by Borgatta, Cottrell, and Meyer: e.g., "Aggregate measures, to the extent that they cannot be accounted for as population variables (in direct parallel measures), may be considered syntality variables. . . . Further, changes in population variables attributable to social interaction should be regarded as syntality variables."—Borgatta, Cottrell, and Meyer, *loc. cit.*, p. 234. Peter M. Blau's "Formal Organization: Dimensions of Analysis," *American Journal of Sociology*, 63 (1957), 58–69, contains an analysis in terms of intended underlying concepts which parallels the present discussion of measurement operations in certain respects.

In addition, the literature contains, of course, classifications of group properties which are based on quite different criteria. See, e.g., John K. Hemphill and Charles M. Westie, "The Measurement of Group Dimensions," in Lazarsfeld and Rosenberg, *op. cit.*, pp. 323–324; and Robert K. Merton, "Provisional List of Group Properties," in his *Social Theory and Social Structure* (rev. ed.; Glencoe, Ill.: Free Press, 1957), pp. 310–326. The Hemphill-Westie categories are subjected to a factor analysis and compared with certain other schemes in Borgatta, Cottrell, and Meyer, *loc. cit.*, pp. 223–240.

26. See S. M. Lipset, Martin Trow, and James Coleman, *Union Democracy: The Inside Politics of the International Typographical Union* (Glencoe, Ill.: Free Press, 1956).

27. C. Paul Marsh and A. Lee Coleman, "Group Influences and Agricultural Innovations: Some Tentative Findings and Hypotheses," *American Journal of Sociology*, 61 (1956), 588–594. Other varying examples of the use of properties describing or referring to collectives will be found in Lazarsfeld and Rosenberg, *op. cit.*, pp. 287–386.

28. Adapted from Lipset, Trow, and Coleman, *op. cit.*

29. Stouffer, *et al.*, *op. cit.*, I, 353–358.

30. James Coleman, Herbert Menzel, and Elihu Katz, "Social Processes in Physicians' Adoption of a New Drug," *Journal of Chronic Diseases*, 9 (1959), 18.

31. Paul F. Lazarsfeld, "Problems in Methodology," Robert K. Merton, Leonard Broom, and Leonard S. Cottrell, Jr. (eds.), *Society Today* (New York: Basic Books, 1959), pp. 69–73.

Mutual Relations over Time of Two Attributes: A Review and Integration of Various Approaches

The Problem of Mutual Effect

Over the last 40 years an increasing number of publications have dealt with the problem of how to make causal inferences from nonexperimental data. This literature has helped to clarify the vague notion of cause and has at the same time provided a variety of useful techniques. The present chapter deals with only one specific approach, the so-

Reprinted with editorial adaptations from *Psychopathology*, edited by M. Hammer, K. Salinger, and S. Sutton (New York: Wiley and Sons, 1972), chap. 25, pp. 461–80.

called panel technique; its main feature is repeated observations on the same people. The discussion will cover its history and its rationale and will contribute some new ideas to its execution. Other types of causal analysis will only be mentioned inasmuch as they are related to the problem on hand. No comparison of merits will be attempted, and certainly no claim of superiority for the panel technique is implied.

The basic issue will be demonstrated by a set of data that is easily accessible. Rosenberg (1957) interviewed Cornell sophomores to ascertain their occupational choices and what he called their occupational values. He divided the occupational choices into those that were people oriented (PO)—for instance, teaching and medicine—and those that were not people oriented (NPO)—for instance, engineering and business. The occupational values were divided in the same ways: for example, rendering a service versus getting rich. The details of this classification are irrelevant here; we shall accept the two dichotomies as they appear in Rosenberg's book.

The topic of the present chapter begins with a cross tabulation of the replies given by Cornell sophomores. The interrelation between their occupational choices and values is given in Table 1. It is clear that choices and values are positively associated. But the table does not permit a causal interpretation. It might be that peoples' choices are caused by their values; it might also be, however, that, once a choice has been made for whatever reason, the student acquires the appropriate values—and of course there can be a continuous feedback between the two items; finally, third factors might play a decisive role—for instance, people from certain types of families might develop PO choices as well as PO values.

In the late 1930s the present author suggested that the unraveling of the causal process involved might be facilitated by obtaining the same information from the same people a second time. This procedure, the panel study, was applied in a study of the 1940 election.

TABLE 1. CROSS-SECTIONAL RELATION BETWEEN OCCUPATIONAL CHOICE AND OCCUPATIONAL VALUE, 1950

| | | Value | | |
		PO	NPO	Total
Choice	PO	226	89	315
	NPO	166	231	397
	Total	392	320	712

TABLE 2. "People-Oriented" Occupational Values and Occupational Choices in 1950 and 1952—Full Cross Tabulation

Occupational Values and Choices, 1950	Occupational Values and Choices, 1952				
	PO Choice-PO Value	PO Choice-NPO Value	NPO Choice-PO Value	NPO Choice-NPO Value	Total
PO choice-PO value	163	15	30	18	226
PO choice-NPO value	21	29	8	31	89
NPO choice-PO value	36	8	73	49	166
NPO choice-NPO value	6	14	43	168	231
Total	226	66	154	266	712

The data then obtained and the way in which they are treated were reported in *The People's Choice,* especially in the introduction to the third edition, where a more detailed account is given (Lazarsfeld, 1968).

An "index of mutual interaction" was developed to describe the influence of two factors upon each other. We shall come back to this index presently. At the moment what matters is to see what kind of information is obtained by repeated interviews. We stay with Rosenberg's material: Table 2 is a so-called 16-fold table, which resulted when he reinterviewed the same students two years later as seniors. Since the appearance of *The People's Choice* this type of 16-fold table has been subjected to a variety of treatments. In addition to the original development of the index of mutual interaction two main trends can be distinguished. Coleman (1964) and Boudon (1968) accepted the use of dichotomies and developed more refined types of analysis. Campbell (1963) and Pelz and Andrews (1964) proposed to apply the panel technique to quantitative variables, which led them to use traditional correlation analysis. Their approach was then converted into the use of path analysis, especially by Duncan (1966) and Heise (1969).

It is the contention of the present chapter that all these authors made valuable contributions. But the relation between their procedures and approaches to the original analysis has never been brought out. These connections will be explored now with one proviso: the whole discussion will be in terms of dichotomies. This makes the structure of the problem much clearer. Once the main results are obtained, it is quite easy to translate some of them into the language of regression or path analysis. The inverse is not possible. The statistics of dichotomies lead to results that cannot be covered by the algebra of linear equations.

The algebraic treatment of a system of interconnected dichotomies has received only scant attention in the literature. It can be greatly simplified by using a specific symbolism. Although this author has already presented the symbolism on various occasions, it will be helpful to introduce here a brief summary.

A Symbolism for the Analysis of Dichotomous Systems

1. Dichotomies are numbered arbitrarily, and "responses" are arbitrarily designated as positive ($+$) or negative ($-$). A "response pattern" to four items might be, for example, ($+ + - +$); this could refer to four objects and to a person who owns all but the third, or it could refer to a test in which all but the third question are answered correctly.

2. The proportion of people showing a specific response pattern is given by p_s, where s, the *signature*, is a sequence of indices corresponding to the list number of the dichotomies. Thus p_{1234} would be the proportion of people giving the response pattern mentioned in (1). A bar over an index means a negative response for the item thus numbered.

3. If an item is listed but not considered in a specific count, it does not appear in the signature. Thus $p_{2\bar{3}4}$ is the proportion of people having the response pattern ($+ - +$) for the last three items, irrespective of their response to item 1. Obviously $p_{2\bar{3}4} = p_{12\bar{3}4} + p_{\bar{1}2\bar{3}4}$ and also $p_{2\bar{3}4} = p_{24} - p_{234}$.

4. In the present context attributes can be ordered in a sequence according to the time at which they were observed. It is often important to know what difference an earlier attribute makes on the frequency of a later one. This "effect" of item 1 on item 2 may then be measured by

$$f_{12} = \frac{p_{12}}{p_1} - \frac{p_{\bar{1}2}}{p_{\bar{1}}} = \frac{(1 - p_1)p_{12} - p_{\bar{1}2}p_1}{p_1 p_{\bar{1}}}$$

$$= \frac{p_{12} - p_1(p_{12} + p_{\bar{1}2})}{p_1 p_{\bar{1}}} = \frac{p_{12} - p_1 p_2}{p_1 p_{\bar{1}}}.$$

Thus f_{12} is the difference between the conditional probability that item 2 is $+$, given that item 1 is $+$, and the conditional probability that item 2 is $+$, given that item 1 is $-$.

5. In the preceding formula $p_1 p_{\bar{1}} = c_1$ can be considered a measure of the symmetry in the cut of the item; $c_1 = 0.25$ when $p_1 = p_{\bar{1}}$ and

decreases as $|p_1 - p_{\bar{1}}|$ increases. In a formal way one can construct

$$f_{21} = \frac{p_{12} - p_1 p_2}{p_2 p_{\bar{2}}} = \frac{f_{12} c_1}{c_2}.$$

It is easily shown that $f_{12} \cdot f_{21}$ equals the square of the traditional phi coefficient between the two items.

6. The numerator in f_{12} can be put into the form of a determinant:

$$p_{12} - p_1 p_2 = \begin{vmatrix} p_{12} & p_1 \\ p_2 & 1 \end{vmatrix} = \begin{vmatrix} p_{12} & p_{1\bar{2}} \\ p_{\bar{1}2} & p_{\bar{1}\bar{2}} \end{vmatrix}.$$

This determinant will be symbolized by [12] and called the *cross product*. Any two dichotomous items form a fourfold table; their cross product [*ik*] will turn out to be a very fundamental computing device. It vanishes if the relative frequency of *k* is the same in the two subsets created by item *i*.

7. Conditional probabilities within subsets are symbolized by Greek letters. Thus, for example,

$$\frac{p_{12}}{p_1} = \pi_{2,1} \quad \text{and} \quad \frac{p_{1\bar{2}3}}{p_{1\bar{2}}} = \pi_{3,12},$$

or, more generally,

$$\frac{p_{si}}{p_s} = \pi_{i,s},$$

where *s* stands for any signature, and *i* for the item on which we focus.

8. If a sample is stratified by the response to an item, say item 3, *contingent* cross products may be computed for the two ensuing subsets. They would be symbolized thus:

$$[12; 3] = \begin{vmatrix} p_{123} & p_{13} \\ p_{23} & p_3 \end{vmatrix} \quad \text{and} \quad [12; \bar{3}] = \begin{vmatrix} p_{12\bar{3}} & p_{1\bar{3}} \\ p_{2\bar{3}} & p_{\bar{3}} \end{vmatrix}.$$

Actually we shall mainly use the conditional effect coefficients, to wit:

$$f_{12;3} = \frac{[12; 3]}{p_{13} p_{\bar{1}3}} \quad \text{and} \quad f_{12;\bar{3}} = \frac{[12; \bar{3}]}{p_{1\bar{3}} p_{\bar{1}\bar{3}}}.$$

9. Joint relative frequencies will be classified according to their *level* of stratification, that is, by the number of indices that appear in the signature. When cross products are formed, we speak of their *order*, to stay with the traditional terminology of correlation analysis.

Thus [12; 34] is a cross product of second order; its highest entry is p_{1234}, a relative frequency of fourth level.

10. To obtain an easier flow we shall talk interchangeably of dichotomies. attributes, or items. Also interchangeable will be the terms proportions, probabilities, and (relative) frequencies. When we want to stress numbers in their unadjusted form, we shall always talk of raw frequencies.

The Formulation of the Problem

We now return to the question of how a 16-fold table can be fully analyzed. It is assumed that two attributes under study interact and that their interaction is clarified by repeated interviews. In the emerging tables, as in Table 2, the cases where the position on both dichotomies remains unchanged can be found in the main diagonal of the 16-fold table. Cases in the minor diagonal have changed on both attributes, and their number is usually small. In the other eight cells we find the cases that changed on one attribute only; for reasons to be explained later we shall call these the "critical" cells.

Assuming that we are dealing with a process of interaction between two attributes, we can raise the question as to which of the two is stronger. This is a vague term that covers a variety of possibilities: one attribute might affect the other, it might make the other change, it might drag the other along when it itself changes, etc. Each of these ideas can be translated into a combination of cells, and the possible variations are very numerous indeed. The problem is to bring some order into the way in which a 16-fold table can be analyzed. The following four principles will be applied to facilitate this task:

1. We shall concentrate on the relative strengths of the two attributes. All indices are developed with the purpose of *comparing* the two factors with each other; no statement about each one separately is intended.

2. Therefore all the processes to be considered will be symmetrical; this means that in any formula describing some kind of mutual influences the signatures pertaining to the two attributes will appear in the same algebraic form. If they are interchanged, the index will only change its sign.

3. Terms like "relative strength," "influence," and "effect" are used interchangeably; they are supposed to evoke an intuitive imagery. Their precise meaning derives from the algebraic procedures by which corresponding indices are derived. The algebra can lead in turn to finer distinctions within the originating imagery.

4. The level of stratification will be the guiding principle of organization. Each index to be developed will be classified according to whether the highest joint frequency in it is of the second, third, or fourth level.[1]

The Coleman-Boudon Model (Second-Level Analysis)

If we restrict ourselves to second-level joint frequencies, we can just determine which attribute observed the first time predicts better the other one at the second observation. In this situation the f coefficient is the best indicator, and so our final criterion will be the difference between f_{14} and f_{23}. In our concrete example the two figures are 0.31 and 0.35, respectively, and therefore in these terms "value" is somewhat stronger than "choice" in their mutual interaction. This, incidentally, is the approach that Campbell (1963) took in his original comments. (Because he discussed quantitative variables, he, of course, compared correlation coefficients and not f coefficients.)

After some reflection one will notice that this approach neglects an important point. An item might appear to be stronger because the other item that it predicts is more unstable. The literature, therefore, soon abandoned this elementary form of using the cross-lagged correlation approach. The idea that has been pursued explicitly or implicitly by all authors concerned is best represented by the following scheme:

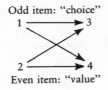

For quantitative variables this imagery is easily translated into a set of linear equations. For dichotomies, however, a different way, first introduced by Coleman and later simplified by Boudon, proved necessary.

Let us focus on the proportion of students who, the second time, make a people-oriented choice of occupation. Their relative frequency p_3 can be divided into four subsets according to choices and values expressed the first time. For each of these four subsets, we can compute separate conditional probabilities that the second choice will be people-oriented. The same can be done for the second expression of values. Our main example then produces the conditional probabilities shown in Table 3.

Now assume that these proportions observed at the second interview come from three sources: the persistence of an earlier position; the influence of the two factors on each other, as it is exercised over

TABLE 3. CONDITIONAL PROBABILITIES OF EXPRESSING PO CHOICES AND PO
VALUES FOR SUBGROUPS FORMED BY FIRST CHOICE AND FIRST VALUE

Pattern of First Choice and Value	Signature s	Row Totals	Relative Row Frequencies	
			$\pi_{3,s}$	$\pi_{4,s}$
+ +	1 2	226	0.79	0.85
+ −	1 $\bar{2}$	89	.56	.33
− +	$\bar{1}$ 2	166	.27	.66
− −	$\bar{1}$ $\bar{2}$	231	.09	.21
		712		

time; and finally changes that cannot be accounted for by just considering the two factors and their mutual effect. This idea can be succinctly summarized in the model of Schema I.

Schema I

Pattern Frequencies
at First Observation   At Second Observation

(1)	(2)	% $p_3 : \pi_{3,s}$	% $p_4 : \pi_{4,s}$
+ +	p_{12}	$a_{13} + a_{23} + e_3$	$a_{14} + a_{24} + e_4$
+ −	$p_{1\bar{2}}$	$a_{13} \qquad + e_3$	$a_{14} \qquad + e_4$
− +	$p_{\bar{1}2}$	$a_{23} + e_3$	$a_{24} + e_4$
− −	$p_{\bar{1}\bar{2}}$	e_3	e_4

The first two columns classify respondents according to the choices
(1) and the values (2) which they express at the first interview. The
other two columns refer to the proportions of respondents who at the
second interview express, respectively, people-oriented choices and
people-oriented values. These conditional probabilities are decom-
posed into three parts. The letters a_{13} and a_{24} pertain, respectively,
to the contribution that the first observation makes to the second
observation on the same item. The letters a_{14} and a_{23} symbolize the
contribution that the first item makes to the other item the second
time. The letters e_3 and e_4 give the proportion of people with PO
choices and PO values who had neither of these people-oriented responses the first time. The top line of these conditional frequencies in
Schema I implies clearly an assumption; the contributions of the two

observations the first time are the same for one attribute irrespective of whether the other attribute was people oriented before. We shall come back to this assumption in the next section. For the moment the task is to analyze this model in more detail.

Any model imposes restrictions on the empirical data it is supposed to represent. If in the schema of the model we subtract the second line from the first, we get a_{23} and a_{24} in the first and second columns, respectively. But the same results are obtained if we subtract the fourth line from the third. This means that in the case where the data fit the model exactly we would have to find that

$$\pi_{3,12} - \pi_{3,1\bar{2}} = \pi_{3,\bar{1}2} - \pi_{3,\bar{1}\bar{2}}.$$

This condition can be put into the form

$$f_{23;1} = f_{23;\bar{1}}. \tag{1a}$$

This means that the stability of choice is the same for students with and without people-oriented values.

By repeating the same operation, beginning with lines 1 and 3, we obtain the equivalent restriction

$$f_{13;2} = f_{13;\bar{2}}. \tag{1b}$$

By applying the same operations to the even item (last column of the model) we obtain

$$f_{14;2} = f_{14;\bar{2}} \quad \text{and} \quad f_{24;1} = f_{24;\bar{1}}. \tag{1c}$$

Empirical data have to satisfy these conditions at least approximately in order that they can be represented by the model of Schema I. This result deserves the name of *Theorem A*.

What equations exist between the parameters of the model and empirical data that would fit it perfectly? We shall derive the answer for the "odd" attributes only; the result for the "even" attribute is established by replacing index 3 by index 4. Schema I can be rewritten so that it pertains to simple proportions and not to ratios, as shown in Schema II.

Schema II

$$p_{123} = p_{12}(a_{13} + a_{23} + e_3)$$
$$p_{1\bar{2}3} = p_{1\bar{2}}(a_{13} \qquad + e_3)$$
$$p_{\bar{1}23} = p_{\bar{1}2}(\qquad a_{23} + e_3)$$
$$p_{\bar{1}\bar{2}3} = p_{\bar{1}\bar{2}}(\qquad\qquad e_3)$$

TABLE 4. THE PARAMETERS FOR THE MODEL OF SCHEMA II APPLIED TO TABLE 2

	Stability	Susceptibility	$e_3(e_4)$
Value	0.51 (a_{13})	0.20 (a_{23})	0.08
Choice	.48 (a_{24})	.16 (a_{14})	.21

An inspection of Schema II permits us to derive the following set of equations:

$$p_3 = a_{13}p_1 + a_{23}p_2 + e_3, \tag{2a}$$

$$p_{13} = p_1(a_{13} + e_3) + p_{12}a_{23}, \tag{2b}$$

$$p_{23} = p_{12}a_{13} + p_2(a_{23} + e_3). \tag{2c}$$

These three equations in turn can be combined to form cross products. As a result we now have a new set of equations wherein the parameters of the Coleman-Boudon model are the coefficients in a series of linear equations:

$$[13] = p_{13} - p_1 p_3 = a_{13}p_1 p_{\bar{1}} + a_{23}[12], \tag{3a}$$

$$[23] = p_{23} - p_2 p_3 = a_{23}p_2 p_{\bar{2}} + a_{13}[12]. \tag{3b}$$

If we now divide Equations 3a and 3b by $p_1 p_{\bar{1}}$ and $p_2 p_{\bar{2}}$ respectively, we obtain *Theorem B:*

$$f_{13} = a_{13} + f_{12}a_{23}, \tag{4a}$$

$$f_{23} = a_{23} + f_{21}a_{13}. \tag{4b}$$

The f coefficients are empirical data. The a values can now be computed from Equations 4a and 4b. This links the latent parameters of the Coleman-Boudon model to manifest observations. As mentioned before, the equations for the even item emerge if in Equations 4 we replace index 3 by index 4.

It will be helpful to fix the terminology for the four main coefficients of the model. We call a_{13} and a_{24} the *stability* of each attribute; a_{23} and a_{14} will be called the *susceptibility* of each to the influence of the other. The main substantive result for the present example is that "values" are relatively more susceptible to the influence of "choice" and at the same time more stable. This can be seen from Table 4.

No estimation is needed in this case because Equations 4a and 4b and the corresponding equations for the even item have just the right number of unknowns to permit solution by Cramer's rule. However, as we shall see presently, various conventional significance tests can

TABLE 5. COMPUTED AND ACTUAL JOINT PROPORTIONS

	p_{34}	$p_{3\bar{4}}$	$p_{\bar{3}4}$	$p_{\bar{3}\bar{4}}$
Computed	0.27	0.07	0.32	0.34
Actual	.32	.09	.22	.37

be applied if manifest higher-level frequencies are compared to those that would be derived from the Coleman-Boudon model.

If the linear model were to satisfy the whole process, we could compute the cross product between the two second observations. It can be shown in a variety of ways that the following equations would have to hold:[2]

$$[34] = [13]a_{14} + [23]a_{24} \tag{5}$$
$$= [14]a_{13} + [24]a_{23} = 0.07.$$

The values of p_3 and p_4 are not determined by the model and can therefore be taken from the empirical data. As can be seen, the values are $p_3 = 0.41$ and $p_4 = 0.53$. This permits computation of the model value of $p_{34} = p_3 p_4 + [34]$, $p_{3\bar{4}} = p_3 p_{\bar{4}} - [34]$, and so on.

Table 5 gives in the first line the data fitted to the model, and in the second line the actual data. It can be seen that the actual association is greater than would be accounted for by the parameters of Equation 5. Thus further analysis is needed.

Causal Interpretation of Differential Associations
(Third-Level Analysis)

We saw that the Coleman-Boudon model implies a restrictive assumption. If attributes 1 and 2 affect attribute 3, their contributions are independent of each other. The consequence is that in a strict sense $f_{13;2} = f_{13;\bar{2}}$ and $f_{23;1} = f_{23;\bar{1}}$. If their joint contribution is larger than $a_{13} + a_{23}$, then an additional term has to be introduced into the first equation of Schema I:

$$\pi_{3,12} = a_{13} + a_{23} + d + e_3. \tag{6}$$

The value of d is easily computed by substituting Equation 6 for the first line of Schema I. It can then be seen directly that

$$d = f_{13;2} - f_{13;\bar{2}} = f_{23;1} - f_{23;\bar{1}}. \tag{7}$$

The parameter d is usually called the "interaction" between items 1 and 2. It is very important not to confuse this notion with the mutual effects of a pair of attributes. The statistical notion of interaction refers to two independent items observed at the same time. The mutual effect problem refers to the relation between the two items across time, where each is both dependent and independent. The fact that the terminology is confusing is regrettable, but it is too well established to permit change. At the moment the imagery for the two cases is distinct, and the algebra can make the matter perfectly clear.

To be concrete we exhibit in Table 6 the conditional relations of 2 and 4 if the sample is stratified by item 1 (the figures are taken, of course, from Table 2). For Table 6, the f coefficient on the left side, $f_{24;1}$, equals 0.52; on the right side, $f_{24;\bar{1}} = 0.44$. Therefore $d_4 = f_{24;1} - f_{24;\bar{1}} = 0.52 - 0.44 = 0.08$, which by Equation 7 equals $f_{14;2} - f_{14;\bar{2}}$. We have given d the index 4 to indicate that the "dependent" item here is the value system of the respondent.

It is not difficult to give a substantive interpretation to $f_{24;k}$. It measures the stability of the even attribute under the two conditions of the odd attribute being positive or negative the first time. Or, in terms of the concrete example, if students made a people-oriented occupational choice in 1950, they are less likely to change their value systems than if they made a non-PO choice.

It is obviously possible to compute the same index for the odd attribute. The figures can be taken directly from Table 2 and would have to be arranged as in Table 6, using item 1 instead of item 2, and item 3 instead of item 4. The computation shows that $d_3 = f_{13;2} - f_{13;\bar{2}} = f_{23;1} - f_{23;\bar{1}} = 0.05$, somewhat smaller than d_4. Forgetting significance problems, we can see that the odd attribute observed the first time predicts changes in the even attribute somewhat better than "the other way around."

TABLE 6. STRATIFICATION BY CHOICE IN 1950

| | | PO (+) Value in 1952 (Item 4) | | | NPO (−) Value in 1952 (Item 4) | | |
		PO (+)	NPO (−)	Total	PO (+)	NPO (−)	Total
Value in 1950 (Item 2)	PO (+)	193	33	226	109	57	166
	NPO (−)	29	60	89	49	182	231
	Total	222	93	315	158	239	397

Some authors have considered $d_4 - d_3$ as another index of mutual effect. The literature is reviewed by Rees (1971), who correctly raises an objection: In this approach we fail to take into account what happened to the "independent" item between the two observations. If we consider the change in one attribute and the first value of the other, we deal with prediction and not with interaction over time. The idea should be abandoned, therefore, just as the simple cross-lagged correlation idea was (Yee & Gage, 1968). Rees is right in saying that three observations would be needed: then one could compare changes in one item between the first two observations with changes in the other item between times 2 and 3. At the end of this chapter a solution for the case with only two observations available will be discussed.

Thus we conclude that the analysis of third-level data provides useful insights but no new index of mutual effect.

Two additional remarks should be helpful. First, $d_4 - d_3$ is a second-order difference for which various significance tests are available. In dichotomous algebra it corresponds to the third-level symmetric parameter—a generalization of the cross product. In the Coleman-Boudon model it vanishes because $d_3 - d_4 = 0$. In conventional correlation analysis it cannot be expressed at all, because it uses data which would correspond to a triple covariance Σxyz. Most certainly it should not be confused with partial correlations.

Second, a 16-fold table in terms of proportions has 15 degrees of freedom. We have so far consumed 11 of them. This leaves 4 more for discussion; they are obviously implied in the fourth-level data. The simplest way to put it is this: the four cross products in the four rows of 16-fold Table 2 are still free. How would we use them for mutual effect analysis on that level?

The Index of Mutual Effect (Fourth-Level Analysis)

To build up an appropriate analysis we start with the students who at the first interview gave "inconsistent" responses—either "choice" or "value" was people oriented, but not both. Some of them had become consistent at the second round. In which direction did this harmonization come about? In terms of choice and value they were originally either $(+ -)$ or $(- +)$; at the second interview some of those students had become consonant, that is, either $(+ +)$ or $(- -)$. The four cells containing these dissonant to consonant cases have been marked by an asterisk (*) in Schema III (for the moment the letters and triangles in the schema should be neglected).

Schema III. The eight "critical cells" containing the case where there is change on one but not on both attributes between two interviews.

Time 2

	O / E	+ / +	+ / −	− / +	− / −	Row total
Time 1	+ +		Δ E_1	Δ O_1		p_{12}
	+ −	* O_2			* E_2	$p_{1\bar{2}}$
	− +	* E_3			* O_3	$p_{\bar{1}2}$
	− −		Δ O_4	Δ E_4		$p_{\bar{1}\bar{2}}$
	Column total	p_{34}	$p_{3\bar{4}}$	$p_{\bar{3}4}$	$p_{\bar{3}\bar{4}}$	1

Obviously, two extreme cases can happen: (*a*) all students who move from dissonant to consonant positions adjust their second choices to conform to their first values; or (*b*) they all end up with the values one would expect from their earlier choices. In the imagery of a harmonization process it will make intuitive sense to say: In the first case values dominate choices; in the second case choices are dominant.

To facilitate the following discussion we use the letters O_i and E_i as shown in Schema III instead of the dichotomous symbolism. Obviously $E_1 = p_{123\bar{4}}$, $O_3 = p_{\bar{1}2\bar{3}\bar{4}}$, and so on.

Most concrete cases will represent a mixture of the two extremes. In Schema III we have marked with O and E the proportions in those cells which indicate, respectively, the dominance of the odd item (the choice) or the even item (the value); the numerical subscript serves to indicate the row in which the cell can be found. (How the dominance can be explained in rows 1 and 4 will be detailed below.) Using the dichotomous symbolism, we can express the probability, for example, of $(-\,+)$ moving to $(+\,+)$ as follows:

$$\frac{E_3}{p_{\bar{1}2}} = \frac{p_{\bar{1}234}}{p_{\bar{1}2}} = \pi_{34,\bar{1}2}.$$

The probability of a movement from $(+\,-)$ to $(+\,+)$ is of course $\pi_{34,1\bar{2}}$. If $\pi_{34,1\bar{2}} > \pi_{34,\bar{1}2}$, then in this respect the odd item dominates the even one. As usual, the difference can be put into a more symmetric form if, from Schema III, we introduce the determinant

$$\Delta_1 = \begin{vmatrix} O_2 & E_2 \\ E_3 & O_3 \end{vmatrix}.$$

Then

$$\pi_{34,1\bar{2}} - \pi_{34,\bar{1}2} = \frac{\Delta_1}{g_{1\bar{2}} \cdot g_{\bar{1}2}} = h_1,$$

where $g_{1\bar{2}} = O_2 + E_2$ and $g_{\bar{1}2} = E_3 + O_3$. We shall call h_1 the *index of relative concurrence* and justify the term presently. If h_1 is positive, the odd item is dominant on this level; if h_1 is negative, the even item is stronger.

But such an index would not yet properly describe the relative importance of the two factors in maintaining consistency, because the following consideration enters. Suppose we find that the value of h_1 indicates that choice (O) is stronger than value (E). The numerical result might still be due to the fact that values are less attached to a consonant pattern than choices, that they oscillate more, irrespective of the choice pattern. Index h_1 would then overrate the relative importance of choice.

How do we take this problem into account? Again attachment is a vague notion and needs to be specified in the present context. The appropriate way is to look at the first and the last rows of Schema III, which contain the students who at the first interview were consonant, either $(++)$ or $(--)$. The cases in the two middle cells of the two rows are those that break away from the original consonance and end up dissonant at the second interview. These cells are marked by a triangle in Schema III.

The disruption of an initial consonance might be due to a variety of reasons: other factors impinge on the people outside the choice-value pattern; accidental factors that influence the answers enter at the time of the two interviews; technical errors affect the data processing. For the present purpose, however, the sources of the shift are irrelevant. The essence is that the four triangle cells permit us to define what we mean when we decide that one factor is less attached than the other. The less attached factor is the one where more cases break away from consonance. For each factor two such cells come into play to describe the "breakaway"; in regard to choice, for instance, it is the people who move from $(++)$ to $(-+)$ and those from $(--)$ to $(+-)$. In both cases the choice changes but not the value.

Now in the light of our preceding discussion we want to be sure that an item does not appear dominant just because it is more attached to the congruent pattern. In Schema III we have, therefore, marked as O_1 and O_4 the cells which *do not* support the relative influence of the even item; figuratively speaking, O_1 and O_4 are "good" for the odd item. A reasonable *index of relative attachment* is now based on these breakaway cases. By analogy it will use their determinant:

$$\Delta_2 = \begin{vmatrix} E_1 & O_1 \\ O_4 & E_4 \end{vmatrix}.$$

The index will be

$$h_2 = \frac{\Delta_2}{g_{12} \cdot g_{\bar{1}\bar{2}}},$$

where $g_{12} = E_1 + O_1$ and $g_{\bar{1}\bar{2}} = O_4 + E_4$. But h_2 should be weighed negatively when a total *index of mutual effect* is formed. Combining all these considerations, we find that such an index was originally proposed by the formula

$$I = h_1 - h_2,$$

and it still seems appropriate. Here I is positive if the odd item is stronger, and negative if the even item is stronger.[3]

Our basic example (Table 2) provides the following data:

$$\Delta_1 = \begin{vmatrix} 21 & 31 \\ 36 & 49 \end{vmatrix}, \quad \Delta_2 = \begin{vmatrix} 15 & 20 \\ 14 & 43 \end{vmatrix};$$
$$h_1 = -0.03, \qquad\qquad h_2 = 0.08;$$

and therefore

$$I = h_1 - h_2 = -0.11.$$

Thus to a small extent values affect choices relatively more than choices affect values, as far as an analysis of the fourth stratification level is concerned. It is important to compare this result with the findings in Table 4. There we found choices to be stronger than values in the sense that earlier choices contributed more to later values than the other way around. Now we are analyzing which of the two factors contributes more to a cohesive pattern; here the values are relatively dominant.

It obviously would not make any sense to raise the question of which finding is more important. Clearly the two results deal with different parts of the total process. The answer depends on the problem in hand. Suppose that our two items are children's exposure to television and their propensity to violence and that in an initial survey the two attributes were found to be positively associated. We would make a second set of interviews in order to see "what makes for what." The correct approach would be to analyze the resulting 16-fold table in terms of the Coleman-Boudon model to compare the two relative susceptibilities. But suppose we find marked positive associations within each row of the 16-fold table. This would show that an enduring pattern has acquired functional autonomy, so that we mainly want to know what, relatively, the two attributes contribute to pattern maintenance; then the index of mutual effect would be appropriate.

In both cases we try to approximate a controlled experiment to obtain leads for action. In the second case we might want to know how to break the pattern; in the first we might want to argue that television watching does not lead to violence—it is the other way around. In both cases, incidentally, we might go on to look for spurious third factors, but this is outside of the program we set for this chapter.[4]

It is algebraically clear that the results on the second and the fourth level of analysis can vary independently from each other. Helpful insights can be gained by constructing "custom-tailored" 16-fold tables with paradoxical combinations. A general procedure has been developed for such construction, but space does not permit its inclusion here.

Our analysis is not yet complete. As a result of introducing the two terms of the index of mutual effect, 13 degrees of freedom are now consumed. In what way should the 2 remaining ones be used?

It is obviously useful to know how many people altogether break away from or join the consistent pattern. This would mean adding the number of cases in all eight critical cells and computing this figure as a proportion of the total sum. In our original example this figure is 0.34. This is then proposed as an additional index because the index of mutual effect is of greater information value if the proportion that shifts on one item but not on both is large.

We are free and need to choose one more index. Intuition suggests filling one gap, alluded to in the discussion of third-level data: the simultaneous consideration of change in both attributes.

The Anderson Index

If we don't have a third wave of interviews, we can make the simplifying assumption that the relation between the second and third observations would be the same as that between the first and the second. The only difference would be that the outcome of the first 16-fold table would be the initial stage of the second one. The original figures would be the transition probabilities if recomputed as proportions of each row (Anderson, 1951). We can use Schema III as background for our further discussion because we shall only use the probabilities of one step move at a time—but so that two steps lead to a complete reversal of the original pattern. Then E_i and O_i can be used as transition probabilities, provided they are considered divided by their respective row totals.

Then the relative roles of the two attributes could be described in terms of the time sequence of their changes: if a two-step full change comes about, we could have here a new index of relative importance: Which attribute "leads," that is, which changes first?

The change from $(++)$ to $(--)$, for instance, could come about in two different ways. The odd item could change first: $(++) \rightarrow (-+) \rightarrow (--)$. In terms of Schema III the probability of this sequence is O_1O_3. The alternative sequence, $(++) \rightarrow (+-) \rightarrow (--)$, could also occur; it would have the probability E_1E_2. The probability for a lead of the odd item is, therefore, $O_1O_3 - E_1E_2$. We have to consider three other changes: from $(+-)$ to $(-+)$, from $(-+)$ to $(+-)$, and from $(--)$ to $(++)$. If the odd item is in the lead, then the probabilities for these three sequences are, respectively, E_2E_4, E_3E_1, and O_4O_2. A similar computation can be carried out for the three remaining cases, where the even item has the lead. The corresponding path probabilities are, respectively, O_2O_1, O_3O_4, and E_4E_3.

We then may use as the new index the difference between the probabilities that the odd item leads and the probabilities of the sequences that give the lead to the even item. After reordering terms this index turns out to be

$$A = (O_1 - O_4)(O_3 - O_2) + (E_1 - E_4)(E_3 - E_2).$$

If A is positive, then in terms of this imagery the odd item is "stronger" than the even; if A is negative, the even item is stronger. A possible intuitive interpretation of A would be as follows. Any probability of increasing the frequency of the odd attribute has a positive sign. A probability that a step decreases the total positive frequency of the odd item is counted as negative in index A. This can be seen by comparing the index formula with Schema III.

The Anderson index is not the only way of relating change to change. If observations at three time periods are available, one could apply the whole analysis of this chapter to a 16-fold table in which the basic units are two subsequent shifts in two attributes. However, this would exceed the program of the present discussion.

We can compute for our example of Table 2 the Anderson index A by dividing the numbers in the critical cell through their respective row totals. The value is $A = 0.01$. In a weak way the odd-item choice is leading in a process in which the original 16-fold table is seen as a Markov chain of interaction between the two attributes. It would be interesting to study the equilibrium state of this process and the manner in which it depends on the values of O_i and E_j. The problem is complex and could only be approached by computer simulation.

The index A uses the entries in the critical cells differently from I, the index of mutual effect. The two indices cannot be transformed into each other. Thus A consumes the last degree of freedom in the description of a 16-fold table.

Conclusions

The model delineated in this chapter applies to two complementary situations. On the one hand, it can be used merely to describe a 16-fold table in a concise and intuitively helpful way. The 15 parameters and indices introduced contain exactly the same amount of information as the 15 free cells of a 16-fold table. However, they facilitate decision making if one wants to condense the available information. One might, for instance, make simplifying assumptions, as in the case of the Coleman-Boudon model; or one might concentrate on the index of mutual effect and forget about additional information available on the fourth stratification level. Many other such simplifications can also be useful.

Instead, one can proceed in a reverse way. One might for systematic reasons be interested in certain structural problems. Then one would start with assumptions on the parameters and indices and would raise the question of what kind of 16-fold table would emerge from such assumptions. The answer would give leads to further interpretation.

From a more substantive point of view this chapter has had two purposes. One was related to the general problem of how to interpret empirical data. Authors are likely to use terms like "process" and "interaction" rather loosely. The analysis here has tried to show that, given a specific procedure (in this case panel analysis), such terms acquire more precise meaning or are shown to cover several meanings indiscriminately. The reader will certainly have sensed also a hidden claim to have contributed to the "chicken and egg" problem.

A second purpose was to eliminate some old misunderstandings and avoid some future ones. Thus, for instance, it has occasionally been intimated that there is a contradiction between what Campbell calls the "cross-lagged panel correlation" and this author's work on the index of mutual effect. The present treatment shows that they are compatible because the analyses refer to different stratification levels. Similar considerations come into play with a number of recent publications applying path analysis to panel data. By definition path analysis is concerned only with second-level data and neglects higher stratification levels. The content of a 16-fold table includes data on the third and fourth stratification levels, which path analysis in its present form cannot analyze; whether such data are empirically worth while or should be neglected is a different question.

The discussion here was restricted to the algebra of dichotomous systems. Some of the resulting formulas bear obvious parallels to equations emerging from regression and path analysis; others do not. An investigation of the parallels between the two algebraic approaches has not been attempted here. Excluded also has been the question of whether dichotomous data or quantitative variables are more subject to error. This can really be answered only after one has discussed the problem of how to deal with variates that are not directly accessible to empirical observation.

Finally a word about the organization of the chapter is in order. At first reading it may seem rather pedantic to make the distinction of stratification levels the guiding idea. But there are at least two grounds on which to defend this procedure. On the one hand, such organization seems the best way to interrelate the indices for panel analyses that have been proposed by various authors. And, second, the stratification levels seem to lead to conceptual distinctions that otherwise might be overlooked or clouded; this has been repeatedly emphasized in the preceding pages.

Much traditional statistical analysis uses data where normal distributions are assumed; this assumption makes the use of higher-level data unnecessary. In social research, however, these higher-level data are certainly indispensable, and how to deal with them succinctly and economically constitutes an urgent problem. The author does not want to prejudge whether the ideas discussed in this chapter could be helpful to the study of relations between continuous variates; on the other hand, he also does not want to conceal his optimism in this regard.

Notes

1. The main example in the following pages will be Table 2. For the convenience of the reader the symbols linking the algebra with the table can be summarized as follows:

1 = PO choice time 1	3 = PO choice time 2
$\bar{1}$ = NPO choice time 1	$\bar{3}$ = NPO choice time 2
2 = PO value time 1	4 = PO value time 2
$\bar{2}$ = NPO value time 1	$\bar{4}$ = NPO value time 2

2. This is a special case of a general theorem that is proved elsewhere (Lazarsfeld, 1961). In the present case it is assumed that the association between items 3 and 4 is due solely to their connection with items 1 and 2 as established by equations of the type of Equation 4.

3. Actually Δ_1 and Δ_2 were standardized somewhat differently in the original study. But this has no bearing on the general discussion. The present way of dividing by g_k is more in keeping with the spirit of time direction, which suggests preference for the directional type of f indices. Also, h_k varies between -1 and $+1$, while the older standardization made for less fixed bounds.

4. Since the resurrection of path analysis several authors have applied it to the findings of *The People's Choice*. But most writers knew the material only from an early publication by D. Campbell, which did not discuss the full 16-fold tables. Thus they did not become aware that we wanted to study relative depth of attitudes—the second case. Path analysis is a parallel to the Coleman-Boudon model and cannot contribute anything to the analysis of fourth-level data.

References

Anderson, T. W. *Probability models for analyzing time changes in attitudes.* The Rand Corporation, 1951.

Boudon, R. A new look at correlation analysis. In H. M. Blalock & A. B. Blalock (Eds.), *Methodology in social research.* New York: McGraw-Hill, 1968. Pp. 199–235.

Campbell, D. T. From description to experimentation: Interpreting trends as quasi-experiments. In C. W. Harris (Ed.), *Problems in measuring change.* Madison: University of Wisconsin Press, 1963. Pp. 212–242.

Coleman, J. S. *Introduction to mathematical sociology.* Glencoe, Ill.: The Free Press, 1964.

Duncan, O. D. Path analysis: Sociological examples. *American Journal of Sociology,* 1966, 72 (1), 1–16.

Heise, D. R. A model for causal inference from panel data. Unpublished manuscript, University of Wisconsin, 1969.

Lazarsfeld, P. F. The algebra of dichotomous systems. In H. Solomon (Ed.), *Studies in item analysis and prediction.* Stanford: Stanford University Press, 1961. Pp. 111–157.

Lazarsfeld, P. F. *The people's choice.* (3rd ed.) New York: Columbia University Press, 1968.

Pelz, D. C., & Andrews, F. M. Detecting causal priorities in panel study data. *American Sociological Review,* 1964, 29, 836–848.

Rees, M. B. A comparison of cross-lagged path, and multivariate causal inference techniques applied to interest, information, and aspiration among high-school students. Unpublished doctoral dissertation, Northwestern University, 1971.

Rosenberg, M. *Occupations and values.* Glencoe, Ill.: The Free Press, 1957.

Yee, A. H., & Gage, N. L. Techniques for estimating the source and direction of causal influence in panel data. *Psychological Bulletin,* 1968, 70, 115–126.

9

Qualitative Analysis

Some Functions of Qualitative Analysis in Social Research

Qualitative Data Suggesting Relationships: Quasi-Statistics

[I have dealt elsewhere] with operations of qualitative analysis which are essentially prior to quantitative research: observations which raise problems, the formulation of descriptive categories, the uncovering of possible causal factors or chains of causation for a particular piece of behavior.[1] These operations stimulate and focus later quantitative research, and they set up the dimensions and categories along the "stub" of the tables, into which quantitative research may fill the actual frequencies and measurements.

However, one encounters very frequently in social science literature, studies which do not use the mechanism of quantitative data-collection and statistical analysis, and still make the kind of statements which quantitative research makes. These statements may be simply frequency distributions (i.e., "most Trobrianders" or even "the Trobriander" knows or believes or does so-and-so); they may be correlations (corner boys have a spending economy, while college boys have a saving economy); they may be statements of causal relationships ("If [the politician] concentrates upon serving his own group, he will never win widespread support . . . In order to win support, he must deal with important people who influence other groups"). Such statements, based on a body of observations which are not formally tabulated and analyzed statistically, may be termed "quasi-statistics."

Reprinted with editorial adaptations from Allen H. Barton and Paul F. Lazarsfeld, "Some Functions of Qualitative Analysis in Social Research," in *Sociology: The Progress of a Decade*, edited by Seymour Martin Lipset and Neil J. Smelser (Englewood Cliffs: Prentice-Hall, 1961), pp. 95–122 [12–13 and 116–19]. First published in 1955 in *Frankfurter Beiträge zur Soziologie* 1:321–61.

They include "quasi-distributions," "quasi-correlations," and even "quasi-experimental data."

Non-quantitative research of this sort is no longer logically prior to statistical research. It rather directly substitutes for statistical research, making the same kind of statements but on the basis of a recording and analysis of cases which takes place largely within the mind of the observer. This kind of research has obvious shortcomings, but it also has a place in the research process, viewed as a continuing and increasingly refined pursuit by the whole community of social scientists.

An example of the dangers of impressionistic "quasi-statistics" is given by Bernard Barber in an article on participation in voluntary associations:

> American observers themselves were overwhelmed by what they did not fully understand: instance the following from Charles and Mary Beard's *The Rise of American Civilization:* "The tendency of Americans to unite with their fellows for varied purposes . . . now became a general mania . . . It was a rare American who was not a member of four or five societies . . . Any citizen who refused to affiliate with one or more associations became an object of curiosity, if not suspicion." Although in comparative perspective the United States may well be a "nation of joiners," a survey of the available data on the number of people with memberships in voluntary associations reveals the little-known fact that many have not even a single such affiliation. This uniformity too holds for all types of areas in the United States, whether urban, suburban, small city, small town or rural.[2]

Barber then quotes statistics showing that in these various areas and strata of the population from one third to over two thirds of the people do not belong to any voluntary associations. As one proceeds from simple frequency distributions to correlations and then to systems of dynamic relationships between several variables, impressionistic "quasi-statistics" becomes steadily less adequate.

On the other hand it is argued that a careful observer who is aware of the need to sample all groups in the population with which he is concerned, who is aware of the "visibility bias" of the spectacular as opposed to the unspectacular case, who becomes intimately familiar with his material over a long period of time through direct observation, will be able to approximate the results of statistical investigation, while avoiding the considerable expense and practical difficulty of quantitative investigation. It has been claimed, for instance, that to provide a fully statistical basis for the conclusions which Whyte was able to draw from his observation of corner gangs and college boys groups, would require hundreds of observers studying hundreds of gangs and neighborhoods over many years.

There are some situations in which formal quantitative methods are apparently less necessary than others. When one is dealing with primitive groups with a nearly homogeneous culture, in which one set of prescribed roles is just about universally carried out by the population, it may require only the observation and interviewing of relatively few cases to establish the whole pattern. The same argument can be applied to studies of a quite homogeneous subculture within a civilized society. These methods seem to have succeeded in presenting a good first approximation at least in the description of the culture and behavior of such groups. When anthropologists now call for formal sampling, data-recording, and statistical analysis it is either to catch up finer details—the small number of deviant individuals, for instance—or to deal with situations of culture groups with less homogeneity—with groups in process of acculturation, breakdown of old norms, or the development of strong internal differentiation.

In situations of less homogeneity and simplicity, it is doubtful that quasi-statistics are anything like a full substitute for actual statistics. However, they can still play an important "exploratory" function. Statistical research is too expensive and time-consuming to be applied on all fronts at once; like the 200-inch telescope it must focus on a few areas of particular interest for intensive study. Quasi-statistical studies can run ahead of the more cumbersome quantitative procedures to cover wide areas of social phenomena, and to probe into tangled complexes of relationship in search of possible "processes." They serve as a broad scanner and "finder" like the wide-angled but less powerful Schmidt telescope of Mount Wilson and Palomar. Moreover, the gathering and analysis of "quasi-statistical data" can probably be made more systematic than it has been in the past, if the logical structure of quantitative research at least is kept in mind to give general warnings and directions to the qualitative observer.

[· · ·]

Matrix Formulations

Sometimes the analysis of qualitative observations confronts a mass of particular facts of such great number and variety that it seems quite unworkable to treat them individually as descriptive attributes or in terms of their specific interrelationships. In such a situation the analyst will often come up with a descriptive concept on a higher level which manages to embrace and sum up a great wealth of particular observations in a single formula. Take, for instance, Ruth Benedict's description of the Zuni Indians, which mentions their avoidance of drugs and alcohol, their lack of personal visions, their placid response to divorce, their "mild and ceremonious" relation to their gods, and so on. After presenting a great many such particular facts, Benedict is able to sum them up in a single formula: The Zuni culture has an Apollonian pattern—that is, a central theme of avoidance of emotional excess. This pattern or theme permeates every aspect of Zuni life.[3] Such a formula capable of summing up in a single descriptive concept a great wealth of particular observations may be called a matrix formulation. This definition covers the notion of a "basic pattern" of a culture, a "theme," an "ethos," a "zeitgeist" or "mentality of the time," a "national character," and on the level of the individual person a "personality type."

Matrix formulations may be applied to complex units at any level. In a study of a village of unemployed in Austria, the researchers made a collection of separate "surprising observations." Although they now had more time, the people read fewer library books. Although subject to economic suffering, their political activity decreased. Those totally unemployed showed less effort to look for work in other towns than those who still had some kind of work. The children of unemployed workers had more limited aspirations for jobs and for Christmas presents than children of employed people. The researchers faced all kinds of practical difficulties because people often came late or failed to appear altogether for interviews. People walked slowly, arrangements for definite appointments were hard to make, "nothing seemed to work any more in the village."

Out of all these observations there finally arose the over-all characterization of the village as "The Tired Community." This formula seemed clearly to express the characteristics which permeated every sphere of behavior: although the people had nothing to do, they acted tired—they seemed to suffer from a kind of general paralysis of mental energies.[4]

In a study of a particular group—people who had been designated as "influentials" in an American community—Merton confronted the problem of explaining their diverse behaviors. Various classifications proved of no avail in accounting for the wide range of observations available. The particular behavior on which the research was focussed—the reading of news magazines—remained unexplained. In trying to order the "welter of discrete impressions not closely related one to the others," the researchers finally came up with one general theme" which distinguished the influentials: some were "cosmopolitan," primarily interested in the world outside the local community, while others were "local," primarily interested in the local community itself. Merton clearly indicates the typical function of such a matrix formulation when he declares:

> All other differences between the local and cosmopolitan influences seem to stem from their difference in basic orientation . . . The difference in basic orientation is bound up with a variety of other differences: (1) in the structures of social relations in which each type is implicated: (2) in the roads they have travelled to their present positions in the influence-structure; (3) in the utilization of their present status for the exercise of interpersonal influence; and (4) in their communications behavior.[5]

The bulk of the article is then taken up with an elaboration of this dual matrix formulation in terms of all the specific behaviors which fit into one or the other type of orientation, the local or the cosmopolitan.

Matrix formulations can thus vary in the level of the unit which they describe, from a whole culture to a community and to a status group within a community. They are used right down to the level of individual personalities, where, for instance, a great variety of particular behaviors will be summed up in the matrix formula of an "anal personality" or a "cerebrosonic temperament." At the personality level they are often referred to as "syndromes," a term arising out of the physiological level where it refers to just the same kind of complex of individual facts all of which can be summed up in one single formula.

Another way in which the matrix formulations can vary is in terms of the relations between the elements. The elements which went into Benedict's formulation of an Apollonian culture were all alike in terms of the variable "emotional tone"—their emotional tone was low in intensity. They all went together in the same sense that one can classify in a single group all regions with a very even temperature, or all people with a high blood pressure. In a matrix formulation such as Tönnies' "Gemeinschaft," the elements seem to be involved in causal relations and processes with one another.[6] The elements of "reciprocal trust" for example can be considered as growing out of the element of "prolonged face-to-face association with the same people," as can a great many of the other characteristics of a "Gemeinschaft"-situation. In the matrix formulation of an "anal personality," the behavior characteristics are thought of as all arising out of a single basic factor, the fixation of the erotic development at a certain childish stage. In many of the culture-pattern formulations since Benedict's purely descriptive ones, we find the idea that all of the elements in the pattern are products of the pattern of child training—or even of a single element in the child training pattern. Some matrix formulations involve a mixture of descriptively related and causally related elements.

Yet another way in which matrix formulae can be differentiated could be called their "projective distance." The following examples should indicate what is meant by this dimension. In Merton's study of *Mass Persuasion,* it was found that a wide variety of remarks made by the Kate Smith devotees could be summed up in the notion of "submissiveness to the status quo."[7] They believed that it was right for some to be poor and others rich, they accepted their position in the system of stratification, they rationalized that the rich had so many troubles that it was just as well to be poor. The more general descriptive concept follows very directly from the manifest content of the respondent's statements; they could almost have made the generalization themselves.

In Cantril's study of the *Psychology of Social Movements,* he confronted a collection of interviews and observations of people who join all sorts of marginal political cults like the Townsend groups, Moral Rearmament, the Coughlinites, and so on.[8] Out of the welter of characteristics there emerged the general notion that all of these people were suffering from a lack of orientation to the complexities of the modern world, a need for a frame of reference within the events of their lives and for world affairs could be understandable. The matrix formulation of "need for orientation" seemed to tie together a great many diverse forms of behavior, attitudes and beliefs on the part of the members of these groups. Now this matrix formulation is further removed from the manifest content of the material than was the formulation in the previous example. There is a greater gap between the formula and what the people actually said, in talking about troubles they had and how good it made them feel that their movement told them what was wrong with the world and how it could be corrected. Here the statements and observations collected by the field work are interpreted as projections of a somewhat complex psychological state, which very few of the respondents themselves could directly articulate.

A still greater distance between the manifest content of the material and the matrix formulation which is constructed to express its basic pattern is often found in the characterization of personality types or of the ethos of a culture. In these cases, guided by general theoretical orientations, one may use subtle indicators as a basis for a formulation which appears in some ways contradictory to the manifest content of the material. Verbal expressions and actual behavior patterns apparently indicative of feelings of superiority are interpreted, when seen in the context of more subtle indicators, as evidence of quite the opposite basic outlook. In Benedict's characterization of the Zuni as basically Apollonian, she has to explain away—on the basis of looking beneath the surface—various apparently "Dionysian" elements.[9]

There is a good deal of similarity between the rationale of the matrix formulation and Parson's discussion of the place of "secondary descriptive systems" in his scheme of social systems based on the unit act:

> When a certain degree of complexity is reached, however, to describe the system in full in terms of the action scheme would involve a degree of elaboration of details which would be very laborious and pedantic to work out. This is true even if description is limited to "typical" unit acts and all the complex detailed variations of the completely concrete acts are passed over. Fortunately, as certain degrees of complexity are reached, there emerge other ways of describing the facts, the employment of which constitutes a convenient "shorthand" that is adequate for a large number of scientific purposes.
>
> . . . It has been seen that the acts and action systems of different individuals, in so far as they are mutually oriented in one another, constitute social relationships. In so far as this interaction of the action systems of individuals is continuous and regular these relationships acquire certain identifiable, relatively constant properties or descriptive aspects . . . It is not necessary to observe all the acts of the parties to a relationship, or all their attitudes, etc., but only enough to establish what is for the purpose in hand the relevant "character" of the relationship . . .
>
> Thus the primary function of such a secondary descriptive scheme as that of social relationship is one of scientific economy, of reducing the amount of labor of observation and verification required before adequate judgements may be arrived at. A second function . . . [is] to state the facts in a way that will prevent carrying unit analysis to a point where it would destroy relevant emergent properties.[10]

Parsons gives as examples of secondary descriptive schemes typologies of social relationships, personality types, and descriptive categories applied to groups. While Parsons' concept is not entirely identical with that of the matrix formulation, it illustrates much of the reasoning behind such complex descriptive concepts, which sum up and render manageable a large and varied body of individual points of data.

Notes

1. Editor's note: see the original version of this essay in the Lipset and Smelser volume, pp. 95–122.

2. Bernard Barber, "Participation and Mass Apathy in Associations," in [Alvin W. Gouldner, ed., *Studies in Leadership,* New York, 1950], pp. 481 *seq.*

3. Ruth Benedict, *Patterns of Culture,* New York, 1946, Ch. IV.

4. [Marie] Jahoda and [Hans] Zeisel, [*"Die Arbeitslosen von Marienthal,"* Leipzig, 1932, quoted in M. Jahoda, M. Deutsch, and S. W. Cook, *Research Methods in Social Relations,* New York, 1951].

5. [Robert] Merton, "Patterns of Influence," [in Paul Lazarsfeld and Frank Stanton, eds. *Communications Research 1968–69,* New York, 1969], p. 191.

6. Ferdinand Toennies, *Gemeinschaft und Gesellschaft,* Leipzig, 1887. A brief summary is found in Parsons [*The Structure of Social Action,* Glencoe, Ill., 1969], pp. 686 *seq.*

7. Merton, *Mass Persuasion,* pp. 152 seq.

8. Hadley Cantril, *The Psychology of Social Movements,* New York, 1941.

9. Benedict, *op. cit.,* see pp. 80, 83, 85, 94, 107, 112 for instances.

10. [Talcott Parsons and Edward A. Shils, *Toward a General Theory of Action,* Cambridge, Mass., 1951, 2d part], pp. 743 *seq.*

10

Macrosociology

Macrosociology

In the present section I am dealing with another tend where clear phases can be distinguished, but where the interplay between various factors is somewhat more complicated. The origin of formal sociology is closely connected with the industrialization of Western Europe. The development of an economically powerful middle class, the destitution of the new masses of wage workers, and the growth of democratic political institutions were the main topics of the early 19th century European classics. The two World Wars slowed down the development of the social sciences in Western Europe. No major work in the classical tradition was published in Europe between 1920 and 1950.

In the United States, no corresponding transition had ever taken root. When the country emerged from the colonial stage, industrialization had already set in. The problem of how to adjust to it was complicated by the appearance of recurring waves of immigrants. Daily concerns were too urgent to allow time for historical perspective. The study of ethnic minorities, the improvement of social services, the understanding of the huge new urban centers were the background against which sociology developed. Empirical research techniques became an indispensable tool in America and were taught in hundreds of colleges.

Slowly, however, uneasiness became noticeable. Even before the Second World War, some American authors called for more "social theory." Later, these voices became much louder. Some sociologists regretted that broad social issues were not dealt with in most studies. They feared that the investigation of specialized topics might contribute to maintenance of the status quo. Translation of the works by Weber, Durkheim and Simmel made the American pioneers look rather provincial. The new international role of the United States di-

Reprinted with editorial adaptations from "Sociology." In *Main Trends of Research in the Social and Human Sciences*. Part 1, *Social Sciences* (Paris, The Hague: Mouton, UNESCO, 1970), pp. 61–165 [76–90].

rected attention to underdeveloped countries. All these elements coalesced into a trend which for lack of a better name we might call the *macrosociological movement*.

A new breed of studies now begins to appear, dealing with broad social units. Topics are complex: what does it mean to live under socialism in the USSR? Why has democracy no deep roots in Germany? Why was the Common Market successful while it seems so difficult to unify the Arab world? Such questions suggest a revival of the classical tradition, but there are two marked differences: the issues while large are more circumscribed in time and space; concrete evidence is much more plentiful and handled with more circumspection. We can talk of a movement not only because so many studies became available, but because we can see similarities with the survey movement. The first macrosociological phase is the rather general interest in social analysis represented by 19th century European sociology. The second phase will be described here as a movement in which sociologists of all countries try to develop their goals, sharpen their research techniques, and delineate the ways of reaching conclusions.

The third phase, the stage of codification, has not yet been reached. Actually, the present section is intended to help begin it. The procedure will be an inductive one. I shall not try to define macrosociology; instead I shall briefly describe a number of studies in order to draw out the basic procedures they seem to have in common. The examples will be taken from a list which is appended to this section. The list of titles may serve as a temporary implicit definition of the field.[1]

The specific sociological aspect of the new macrosociology movement seems to derive from two elements. Workers in this field are quite aware that they usually concentrate on a rather small number of variables. Their selection is clearly influenced by the traditions of general sociology. The very fact that a kind of generalized variate language is used shows the strong influence of survey analysis. The second feature characterizing the work of macrosociologists is not as obvious, but a careful scrutiny of the writing shows that selected notions of process influence the choice of topic and the interpretation of same.

These two observations dictated the outline of this section. I shall first use four specific studies to carve out in some detail four types of macrosociological variates. Additional studies treated more briefly, will then strengthen the original examples.

. . . In macrosociological work there does not yet seem to be a clear-cut relation between individual variates and the explanation sketches into which they enter. The best I could do was therefore to make an inventory of the main paths along which the macrosociological trend seems to move.

Macrosociological Variates

We begin with the relatively simple case of a single macrosociological variate. Eckstein analyses why Norway is such a prime example of a stable democracy. Among other factors, he stresses the country's long *profound sense of community*. What are the cues he uses for this characterization? The basic concept is divided into three elements: Norwegians a) avoid treating other people as utilities, and wish their social relations to be exempt from economic considerations; b) avoid competitive situations; c) are prone to cooperative activities and favour organizations which serve this purpose. Here are some of the cues Eckstein used to establish the preference for non-economic social relations: medical doctors do not fight public medical care and like salaried jobs; having spent some time in public service is almost a prerequisite for political success. Eckstein draws on a cross-national public opinion survey where people were asked whether their countrymen could be trusted; Norway leads the list with 77% positive answers. Eckstein uses personal interviews to exemplify how Norwegians avoid humiliating other people; he interprets their proverbial desire for solitude as a way of suppressing their own hostilities.

The non-competitiveness is inferred from similar cues. Norwegians prefer such sports as skiing where they are not pitted against each other. Many Norwegian organizations follow the procedure of trial votes in order to end up with a unanimous decision. In parliament, arrangements are made to play down antagonism between parties.

The importance of organizations is attested to by their numbers and the broad range of activities they cover. Even much commercial research and marketing is done on a cooperative basis. Trade unions and employer organizations are highly centralized; Eckstein believes that this facilitates negotiations. (Here is an interesting parallel with Lipset who, as we shall note, uses the decentralization of American unions as a cue for their essentially asocial militancy.)

To fill out this notion of "sense of community" Eckstein draws on a number of other cues among which material on suicide is the most interesting. Compared to other Scandinavian countries, the Norwegian suicide rate is especially low; psychiatric case studies seem to show that it is guilt feelings rather than frustrated success which account for suicidal tendencies. We now turn to a second example.

Runciman not only introduces macrosociological variates, but attempts to show that their values change over time. In one chapter, he seeks to demonstrate the thesis that *the inequality of status* between manual and non-manual workers in England has objectively decreased since World War II, while the sense of relative deprivation among manual workers has increased. I do not discuss the second part of the proposition—the increase in relative deprivation. Moreover, Runciman does not make a serious effort to prove this. The change in objective status, however, is well documented. From a large number of surveys he shows that the number of students from labour class parents has increased. An increasing number of labour children desire and acquire white collar jobs. Inversely, from budget figures and employment data, Runciman shows that the use of servants in middle class families has decreased. Intermarriage between wage earners and white collar workers is on the increase. A cue to lack of change comes from community studies which continue to show strong residential segregation between manual and non-manual workers.

It is characteristic for the British tradition that many data are available on behaviour related to stratification; direct opinion and attitude questions which would play a major role in American surveys seem to be rare. Runciman also uses cues from a loose kind of content analysis. Cartoons in *Punch* increasingly lampoon the affluent worker and the middle class family who must do their own household work while the autobiographies of labour leaders show satisfaction in the ascent to a middle class style of life.[2]

A comparison between the Eckstein and Runciman studies leads to one distinction. If changes in a macrosociological variate are to be observed, the cues to these shifts must be intrinsically flexible: the content of mass media, the social composition of a student body, etc. If, on the other hand, some more enduring characteristic of a society is at stake, cues from organizational arrangements and preferences which have found institutional expression will be more appropriate.

In a third type of study, the macrosociological variates grow out of observing differences not over time but between countries. Lipset, in his book *The First New Nation*, defends a rather complex thesis. All through the history of the United States, two values have been dominant: the right to equality and the reward for achievement. These two macrosociological variates are first introduced through references to the writings of historical observers. No cues are proposed to establish the two variates directly, although stimulating speculations are given on their interplay. For example, the point is made that such a society leads to more conformism than one which accepts more stratification and stresses style rather than success. Empirical data come into play only when Lipset characterizes institutions and tries to explain them on the basis of these two basic concepts. Consider the impressive variety of cues he offers for comparing American unions with the unions in other modern western countries: strike statistics demonstrate that U.S. unions are more militant; the number of salaried officials in American unions surpasses that of other countries; lay committees do not have much control over American union officials; the wage differential between skilled and unskilled workers is much greater in the U.S. special provisions in U.S. unions give skilled members more power in the organization.

Most of the cues are of a quantitative nature derived from operational statistics; occasionally institutional arrangements are drawn upon. Comparisons with other countries stress the business character of American unions in contrast to the ideological elements in the European scene; Australian and Canadian unions stand somewhere in the middle. Often the link between a concrete cue and the macrosociological variate it represents, requires several steps. An equalitarian, achievement-minded society will not be overly-concerned with the means by which success is achieved. On the one hand, this can lead to tolerance of corruption in unions—one of Lipset's cues—and on the other, to a feeling that the absolute amount of personal income is more important than the source from which it is derived. On the latter point, the crucial cue is an interesting set of opinion surveys comparing European and American respondents. The question at issue was whether people preferred a higher income as workers or white-collar status with a lesser income. European workers prefer the latter, Americans the former.

The most direct use of a system of macrosociological variates is by Dahrendorf when he raises the question of why democracy in Germany has always been endangered. He starts with four major factors, one of which is the German value system. While Eckstein restricted himself to Norway, Dahrendorf bases his argument on a comparison between Germany and the Anglo-Saxon countries. In this sense, his procedure is similar to Lipset's. But while Lipset does not convert the value system into a macrosociological variate, Dahrendorf does. He distinguishes between public and private values. Public values include exhortations to keep smiling, to be fair in dealings with others, to respect the rights of others, and so on. Among the chief private values are truthfulness to oneself, devotion to one's family, steadfastness under adversity. An especially good cue was found in a comparison of the ways Germans and Anglo-Saxons think about loneliness. For the German, to be lonely is a kind of heroic posture; for an Anglo-Saxon, it is a sign of deficient socialization. Dahrendorf recognizes that this is aphoristic and establishes as his mission the demonstration that private values are predominant in German culture. He employs the general argument that private values are likely to be transmitted by the family, and public values through the schools. Thereafter, he must find evidence that in Germany, the family has priority over the school by being able to compare the weights of these two social structures.

Here is a brief summary of his cues. The Constitution of the Federal Republic is the only one which mentions the right and the responsibility of the family to educate its children; if conflicts between school and family come before the courts, the decision is usually in favour of the family. Dahrendorf adds to this certain features of school organization: instruction covers only half the day, so that children can go home for lunch and remain there the afternoon; sports and other social activities are not included in the school curriculum.

As in every country, controversies on education create a vast quantity of documents. In scrutinizing their content, one finds a prevailing position: the school, especially on the more advanced level, takes care of a general molding of the mind, not related to any specific use or to any special responsibility. The remaining socialization process is left to the family. Statements by teachers about students who have been dismissed from the *Gymnasium* mention lack of substantive interest and insufficient motivation; the implication is always that it is not the task of the school to develop such attitudes, which must be rather imparted by the family. The author also mentions some public opinion polls on the subject of what respondents consider their own most desirable qualities. Almost half the respondents give priority to *Familiensinn* (deep attachment to the family).[3]

The use of linguistic cues in Dahrendorf's study deserves special comment. Social linguistics has become a new field of interest. In its more elementary form sociolinguists ask how social structures are reflected in language habits. At a more sophisticated level, they examine the reverse flow. That is, whereas the language which children learn affects the way in which they perceive their social environment, what they perceive affects their mode of handling social relations. Therefore, over the generations, language affects social structures. Study of the interaction between language and social structure is a new topic of sociological analysis. For the macrosociologist, linguistic cues deserve special attention, even if they must be bolstered by other types of cues. The American candidate "runs" for election; the Britisher "stands" for Parliament; the Frenchman "presents himself" to the electorate. Distinction among these terms is certainly more subtle than merely noting that Eskimos have as many words for snow as the Arabs have for camels. However, it will require a considerable collection of examples before a systematic analysis will be possible.[4]

Finally a word on the role of sampling surveys in macrosociological work. . . . The marginal distribution of answers to a single question is only a starting point for survey analysis. To make a single survey significant, elaborate cross-tabulation between answers to different questions and their relation to background data is indispensable. In the context of the present discussion, a few marginal distributions can provide an important cue. Eckstein showed that Norwegians are more ready to trust their compatriots; Lipset's evidence that white collar jobs are not prestigious in the United States, and Dahrendorf's reference to the importance of family sentiments in Germany are good examples.

The preceding discussion of how macrosociological variates are formed included examples of the kind of propositions into which they enter. It will round out the whole picture if I parallel each of the four cases just described with supplementary examples.

Macrosociological Propositions

Eckstein's study was concerned with the stability of a social system. This time-honoured sociological topic has in recent years been an object of controversy. Authors like Coser request more attention to the study of conflict,[5] and this has penetrated macrosociological work through another set of variates, usually called *contradiction*. A good example is Eisenstadt's study of what he calls historical centralized bureaucratic empires, like medieval China and the Ottoman Empire. He sees them as systems better organized than the feudal states but less differentiated than modern industrial countries. Unless they can develop a modern form of economic organization, they will revert to their feudal past. Their transitional character is due to a number of contradictions. One set of contradictions arises from the ruler's policies, directed against some strata of the population while favouring others. Another set centers on the fact that the bureaucratic organs developed special orientations and interests of their own which often contradicted the interests of the rulers. Two areas in which contradictions were most pronounced were those of legitimation and stratification in which the new middle groups, unable to free themselves from traditional symbols, simply aristocratized themselves. Further, within the economic and administrative field, there was the opposition between long-range and short-range policies. Together with the growing trends towards an autonomous bureaucracy which played a central regulative function in these systems, these contradictions laid the foundations for an "anti-system" denoting the built-in tendency to change.

Runciman's study echoes the sociologists' interest in the *segmentation of systems*. The term really has two meanings. In one, it refers to the study of special groups within a population; indeed, the comparison of manual and non-manual workers is a cornerstone in Runciman's book. Recent work in studies of the elite deal with segments in this sense.[6]

But sociologists are also concerned with a second meaning of the term segmentation; they speak of the political, the economic, the spiritual subsystems. A person can have much power and little money or wealth without power. It was Max Weber who proposed distinguishing between income, prestige, and political power. While often united, they may vary independently. The idea itself appears in many forms. The most influential modern version is Thomas Marshall's study on the development of citizenship in England. According to this author, civil rights emerge first in the frame of incipient capitalism. To preserve these rights, courts are established with seats far away from the local communities. The way in which the courts operate is a political problem, and so, the fight for political rights comes next. Social rights develop partly as a result of education, partly through the instrumentation of political and civil rights. Marshall's essay is probably one of the most often quoted items in macrosociological literature.

The example taken from Lipset is a special case of a third sociological concern: *the role of values in the working of a social system*. People feel that certain goals and certain ways to act are right; these values then become determinants of their choices and their relations to each other. It is certainly not quite clear how the coercive role of values develops. There is agreement that it has its origin in the socialization of the child. But it can be maintained in a variety of ways: by fear of sanctions, by imitation of others, by a super-ego, etc.[7] Despite this ideological uncertainty, values play a considerable role in many macrosociological studies. As one further example I choose Lucian Pye's discussion of politics in Burma. I cannot do justice to the breadth of his analysis, and quote only one item because it refers to a linguistic use.

Pye discusses two values in detail. One connotes the notion of leadership powerfully exercised. In Burma, all strata consider this highly desirable; leadership is romantic and dangerous—somewhat like love in Western society. At the same time, one is supposed to be compassionate, considerate of one's neighbour, inoffensive, and not disruptive to others' peace of mind. The other connotes "an emotion that wells up inside the Burmese preventing him from pushing himself for his own interest and compelling him to accede to the demands of others." The parallel to Lipset's values of equality and success is obvious. Pye's study relates the ensuing value conflict to a special family structure and in turn derives from it many of the difficulties Burma has in organizing its political life.

A fourth macrosociological variate is the *organization*. Dahrendorf tries to "measure" the importance of two institutions—the family and the school. This is organizational research writ large. Increasingly, sociological literature characterizes organizations in the same way as a psychologist characterizes personalities. Many efforts are under way to describe how many levels of authority an organization has, how its efficiency is related to the morale of its staff, and so on.[8]

In its application to whole countries this art is only beginning. One of the most interesting examples is provided by Shils in his study of Indian intellectuals. It is his notion of center and periphery. The center consists of those institutions and roles which exercise authority of any kind or are role models for the rest of the system. The periphery consists of those parts of society which are the recipients of commands and of beliefs which they do not themselves create or cause to be diffused. The two notions can have a spatial meaning as when we talk of the "provinces," they can have a social meaning implied in the notion of "establishment." Or they can have a more psychological connotation when we impute inferiority feelings to Western-trained intellectuals who come from undeveloped countries. Shils discusses in detail the possible relations between periphery and center. The distance between them can vary, the autonomy of the periphery can be different, the flow of information between the two can be more or less unilateral, and so on. This is a truly macrosociological variate which will certainly arouse increasing attention.[9]

Macrosociological Processes

The topic of the next few pages falls between two extremes. We may have a precise definition of social process when dealing with specific variates observed repeatedly. . . . At the other end, we have an extensive literature on the logic of explanation in history.[10] Among modern logicians Hempel has taken a position which, in its attenuated form, seems most helpful for the present purpose. He starts with a rigourous definition adapted from the natural sciences. The explanation of a simple event proceeds in the following steps: there is a general law connecting a number of variables and containing several free parameters; a specific event is characterized by specific values of these parameters; the combination of the "covering law" and the specific parameters provides the explanation.

Hempel is aware that, for a variety of reasons, this formula cannot be exactly applied to complex historical phenomena. He therefore introduces the notion of *"explanation sketches."* These are schemata in which the covering law is not really known, the parameters of the concrete situation are vague, and in which therefore any concrete explanation is more or less distant from a rigourous analysis. As the name indicates, explanation sketches are above all incomplete forms of explanation, they require further "filling-out" by empirical research, for which the sketch suggests the direction. As our examples will show, the incompleteness and vagueness can be found *in various dimensions*. There are hidden assumptions which are not brought out; there is segmentation of a process with emphasis on one part, neglect of another; and there is great variation in the empirical "filling-out." The common element in our examples is a movement or a process leading from one structural element at an earlier point in time to a changed structural element at a later point in time. Connecting the two, some causal agent is imputed, which either sets the process into motion, determines its direction, relates several causal factors or maintains its flow in some other way.

It is useful to apply this notion of explanation sketches to the work of the macrosociologist. In the light of the present review, one can go one step further. Hempel concluded his discussion in the rather unspecific, permissive manner just described. Scutiny of concrete studies permits us to single out a few major types of explanatory sketches. Such a classification reflects well the spirit of much current sociological analysis. Just as the macrosociologist likes to work with a rather small number of basic concepts, so he tends to apply relatively few explanation sketches. I shall single out three types: the linear sketch, the strategy mode and the dialectic type.

a. The most primitive and basic form of all explanation sketches are *patterns of simple linearity*. This supposes a process in which the first element is seen to be the cause for the second, which in turn is the cause for the third, which in turn is the cause for the fourth. Very often such a multi-stage causal change is developed with little attention to the links between cause and effect, which tend to remain highly specific or historically bound. The incompleteness of this sketch lies partly in its highly specific nature, which tends to resort to monocausal explanations even if the independent variate is some vaguely described, supposedly powerful "factor," partly in its segmented nature, which assumes that all other conditions are unchanged, insignificant or in other ways held constant. It is precisely these hidden assumptions which have to be brought out if one looks for generalizations.

Inkeles deals with a sequential change that was introduced in the Soviet Union in the 1930s. At that time, the authority pattern in the industrial production process was altered from collective to individual responsibility. This in turn led to a reorganization of authority relations in the school system as the major recruiting reservoir for the factory. The former quasi-egalitarian relations between teachers and students gave way to a more clear-cut hierarchical structure, discipline returned to the classroom, and various forms of experimentation with progressive ideas met an abrupt end. The final wave of change occurred in the family, which responded mainly to the changed authority pattern of the school system. Parents were urged to exercise stricter control over their children, and the former freedoms, expressed legally by the ease with which abortion and divorce could be obtained, had to make way for strict state controls. The inference is that these changes take place in a system with strict political control, where a change in law or status is crucial. It also presupposes a relatively low level of organizational complexity so that other institutions whose authority patterns might contradict the general trend are either absent or ineffectual.

b. The second mode of explanation might be called the *strategy type*. The imagery is taken from the behaviour of a single individual who finds himself in a specific situation and must decide how next to proceed.

Etzioni studies unification as a process which leads from units with separate boundaries to some larger community. During this process, many strategic decisions must be taken. Some emerge, with empirical hindsight, as steps in the right direction, while others lead to failure. One such *strategic* decision in times of a crisis, is whether to accelerate or decelerate unification efforts. Consequences are defined as direct outcomes of the decision: acceleration is likely to retard the prospect of final unification, and may even destroy previously taken measures, while deceleration is much more favourable to unification in the long run. While this decision is only one of many, Etzioni's problem is not so much to account for why a particular decision was taken, but to interrelate the various consequences that resulted from previous bifurcations and to assess their relative weight in the overall final outcome.

While the decision-making organ could easily be identified in the previous example, this is not true when the crucial determinant lies with a ruling elite or some other stratum of society. Here, it is said that certain crucial attitudes have developed which found expression in concrete actions. Moore compares the reaction of the English and French landed aristocracy to the newly opened possibilities of commercial farming. While the process of transition from an agricultural society to a modern, industrialized one could proceed in various ways, in cases where the landed aristocracy took up commercial farming, the consequences were more favourable to the emergence of democracy than in cases where they did not. Here, the strategy sketch is linked with a linear scheme. Moore attributes the English nobleman's willingness to engage in these new activities to his greater independence from the crown; the French counterpart did not possess this autonomy.

c. The strategy sketch is more varied than the linear pattern because it considers different strategies even if only one is actually carried out. A greater scope can be introduced if the consequences of a choice can feed back on the first decision and lead to a different choice. In the same way, the linear pattern may be enriched. A variate growing out of a preceding one may in turn affect its trend. In these cases we shall talk of *dialectic explanation sketches*. They focus simultaneously on several lines of development. Processes unfold and interact. Resistances emerge and are either overcome, or deflect the original trend or force retraction. Because of its feedback element, the dialectic mode is likely to introduce additional sociological ideas: the boundaries of systems which separate them from surroundings and the important notion of unanticipated consequences.

Diamond's study of the transformation of Virginia from an organization into a society provides a first example. Here, the dissatisfaction or disturbances created after the organization had been set up after the model of the East India Company resulted from a frustration of various expectations: difficulties in recruitment due to the scarcity of indigenous labour and lack of mineral resources which forced the company to engage in agricultural activities rather than in an exploitation of mineral resources as originally planned. Additional incentives had to be provided for the labour force imported from England, notably the granting of land after a specified period of time. This solution in turn led to a fundamental change in the character of the organization by rendering its monopoly character obsolete and by engendering a "multiplicity of statuses" which laid the foundations for a societal network. From the point of view of those who had initiated what was thought to be the only feasible remedy to a pressing problem, the result was quite unanticipated. The impact of the environment had shaped new problems and by excluding the feasibility of various alternative solutions, the solutions led to the structural change.

Greater preciseness in identifying structural referents brings with it greater preciseness in timing the process which is described. This is also a characteristic of Smelser's analysis of the process which led to the differentiation of the family during the Industrial Revolution in Great Britain. At the beginning of the Industrial Revolution, the family was still in an undifferentiated stage with a variety of functions and with traditionally defined relationships between adults and children. Through various changes in the larger social context, particularly the introduction of technological changes in the cotton industry, the traditional structure of the family economy was threatened. Various disturbances erupted. Solutions were sought in a new legislative regulation of working hours and conditions in the factories. After two unsuccessful attempts, the legislation of 1847 completed the process of differentiation of the family by eliminating child work altogether and by reducing working hours for women in order to free them for socialization tasks of the children. Previous legislative attempts had been unsuccessful and only led to further disturbance and agitation: the first reduction of children's working hours resulted in a relay system to maintain them under the supervision of parents in the factory; the second accomplished the abolition of child labour, but did not bring a reduction in adult working hours. Both solutions were incomplete and unsuccessful, as they destroyed the traditional relationship between parents and children without providing a new level of consolidation. The final legislative act provided a new equilibrium point for the family. The family was able to adjust to the industrial age, but only after a new balance between family ideology and the demands of industrialization had been achieved.

d. Closely related to the notion of explanation sketches is the tendency to propose *sequences* which are treated partly as "laws" and partly as explanations of specific cases. Early sociologists tried to discern specific phases through which societies moved. This effort has not been abandoned but modern macrosociologists give it a more specific term. Thus Smelser proposes seven steps for the change of a "subsystem" like the family. A malfunction starting from within or without, sets in motion search, remedial efforts and further disturbances, until a new "equilibrium" is reached where a number of new or changed subsystems take on the function which was originally performed by one. But Smelser stresses that often some of his steps may be omitted. Bendix stresses that changes may be quite different according to the time at which they occur. Industrialization in England was bound to be a different process than in Germany where later some of the social and technological elements were imported from England. While the beginning of industrialization in Germany and Japan was nearly simultaneous, the preceding history of the two countries greatly affected the pattern of change.

An ingenious example of the need for flexible thinking on patterns of change has been provided by an Indian scholar.[11] It is well known that after some time, what once were innovations can come to have retarding effects. Thus, the first city to introduce electric streetcars will have an outmoded system by the time that another city, acting later, installs a more efficient one. Deva applies this schema to newly developing countries in the following way. Countries which became industrialized at an early date were required to stress the free market system in order to overcome vestiges of the medieval economy. Now that their economic systems have become highly complex, considerable central planning is necessary. But this meets with ideological difficulties because of the earlier emphasis on free competition. In contrast, the new countries which imported complex industries had no traditional aversion to state intervention or central planning. They may bypass a liberal market economy, not for political reasons, but because they want to move directly to a more advanced mechanism.

e. One more type of reasoning deserves to be reported here: the transfer of findings made in a more restricted context to a macrosociological level. We have already mentioned how Runciman uses the notion of "relative deprivation," which was first developed to interpret specific survey results. Peter Hofstätter argues that small groups, because they are more easily analysed, can be "used as models for the study of more complex collectives, such as the state: they can be considered groups of groups." Borrowing a finding from Bales that small groups have two kinds of "heroes," a popular one and an efficient one, Hofstätter notes that the Germans as a nation are perceived as efficient leaders. Since they cannot conceal their efficiency, they should ally themselves with the French, representing the well-liked type in the group of nations.[12]

Etzioni has discussed this whole matter in a systematic way. He uses the term "theorem" for "a statement about the relation between two or more variables which is supported by some data." His main contention is that a theorem can be transferred from one subfield to another, using quite different data. This requires considerable reinterpretation of indicators, but involves the same basic variables.[13] His illustrations come from the field of peace research. At one point he starts from a theorem that friends are often similar in their social characteristics as well as in their attitudes and preferences. Inversely, groups formed of people who share many characteristics are likely to be more cohesive, as their friendship is more resistant to disintegration. Etzioni then moves this idea from the intrasocietal to the intersocietal level. He reviews the various unification efforts among European countries; why has the Common Market been more successful than other similar schemes? One of the reasons should be the greater homogeneity of the six participants. They have a similar political structure—no socialist, no authoritarian government; none is overwhelmingly Protestant, none neutralist. Similar observations can be made about common market efforts in Africa and Latin America. Finally, Etzioni applies the theorem to world government. In the beginning one might have to be content with the formation of regional communities. After a time, the members of this regional combine will become more similar to each other—industrialization and world-wide communication work in the direction of increasing world-wide homogeneity. This will in the end make world government possible. Thus the extrapolation of a simple sociological theorem becomes more than an explanation sketch for past events—it leads to ideas for future action on a macrosociological scale.

A variation on the "transfer of theorems" is introduced in cases where the jump from the original statement to a higher level of aggregation is not as great as in the preceding examples. Authors then often talk about the "application" of a theorem. Sociologists and social psychologists stress that in face to face groups behaviour is strongly guided by a desire to gain or maintain the approval of peers. Janowitz and Shils apply this idea to explain why German soldiers kept on fighting when they knew the war was lost; they lived in small units where no one wanted to be the first to call it quits. A Columbia study gave the same interpretation of how faculties in American universities successfully resisted the red hunt of the late Senator Joe McCarthy: the danger of his attack was great but remote, the attitude of one's colleagues who would have frowned on "collaboration with the enemy" had the strength of immediacy and thus added up to the stronger pressure. Seemingly the broader phenomenon is "derived" from a basic law, but the derivation is loose and omits so many steps that here, too, it is better to think of a transfer.

The discussion of variates and explanation sketches as the building blocks of macrosociology is now completed. A word on the strategy of this section should be added. The mandate given to the authors of the various chapters comprising the present Study provided that each could stress those trends which seemed to him most characteristic of the contemporary scene. Therefore, the emphasis on macrosociology does not require special justification; it reflects the author's judgment. But why stress the methodological aspects of this movement?

In the introduction of this section we mentioned as one root of the macrosociological movement a concern with "big" issues and their political implications. One cannot overlook the danger of a resulting obscurantism: better to guess about important matters than to study "little" issues, merely because we understand the methods by which they can be approached. There is a way to meet this danger. Let us accept the new trend as it is represented by authors who not only argue for it, but who also have performed the hard labour of providing concrete studies. Understandably, they were not inclined to discuss their procedures at the time they created the new style. But the observer from the outside should see it as a task to "explicate" what is going on. In this way he can reconcile the creative urge of a movement with the tradition of a social science that wishes to overreach all actual trends by general systematics.

Notes

1. Here I do not include comparative studies based on large international data banks which are covered in Chapter 10 ("Cross-cultural, Cross-societal and Cross-national Research") of [*Main Trends of Research*]. Macrosociological authors deal with a small number of cases and their emphasis is on many qualitative details. Still it is difficult to draw boundaries. Eisenstadt had sufficient historical bureaucratic studies to present actual numerical tabulations; Etzioni deals only with four cases but he presents propositions in quasi-quantitative language. Nevertheless, their emphasis is so strongly on interpretation that they have been included in this review.
2. Runciman's chapter could be considered part of the British discussion on the *embourgeoisement* of the manual worker. The cues for such a concept are still rare, especially as they would have to come from different time periods and be rather sensitive to change. It is therefore not surprising that the matter is still controversial.
3. All these cues are not subject to quick change. In the United States, at this moment, Negro activists request greater participation of family organizations in the administration of local schools. The reason now is the protection of civil rights, but as an unanticipated consequence the balance between family and school might shift. If

one were to watch for such changes in the coming years, Dahrendorf's type of data would not be too helpful, though very convincing in depicting an existing basic structure.

4. I wish to draw special attention to a reflective and informative auxiliary paper by J. A. Fishman on "Sociolinguistics and the Language Problems of Developing Countries", subsequently published in: *International Social Science Journal* 20 (2), 1968, p. 211.

5. L. Coser, *The Study of Conflict*, Glencoe (Ill.), Free Press, 1962.

6. S. Keller, *Beyond the Ruling Class*, Toronto, Random House, 1968.

7. A very good discussion of the problems here involved can be found in S. Nowak, "The Cultural Norms as Elements of Prognostic and Explanatory Models in Sociological Theory," *The Polish Sociological Bulletin* 14 (2), 1966.

8. A review of this literature may be found in A. Barton, *Organizational Measurement*, New York, College Entrance Examination Board, 1961.

9. E. Shils, "The Macrosociological View," in T. Parsons, *et al.* (eds.), *American Sociology*, New York, Basic Books, 1968.

10. Fortunately it is now possible to obtain a quick overview of the present state of this discussion. A number of readers on the philosophy of science include writings on history. In addition, two readers on historical analysis have recently appeared, each edited by a protagonist of very different points of view: W. Dray (ed.), *Philosophical Analysis and History*, New York, Harper & Row, 1966; P. Gardiner (ed.), *Theories of History*, New York, The Free Press of Glencoe, 1959.

11. I. Deva, "The Course of Social Change: A Hypothesis," *Diogenes*, 1966, p. 74.

12. P. Hofstätter, *Gruppendynamik*, Hamburg, 1957.

13. A. Etzioni, "Non-conventional Uses of Sociology as Illustrated by Peace Research," in: P. F. Lazarsfeld, *et al.* (eds.), *Uses of Sociology*, New York, Basic Books, 1967.

References

Almond, G. and Coleman, J. (eds.), *The Politics of Developing Areas*, Princeton (N.J.), Princeton University Press, 1969.

Almond, G. and Verba, S., *The Civic Culture*, Boston (Mass.); Toronto, Little, Brown and Co., 1963.

Apter, D., *The Politics of Modernization*, Chicago (Ill.), University of Chicago Press, 1965.

Aron, R., *18 Leçons de la Société Industrielle*, Paris, Gallimard, 1966.

Bailyn, B., "The Origins of American Politics" in: *Perspectives in American History*, Vol. I, 1967.

Bellah, R., *Tokugawa Religion*, New York, The Free Press, 1957.

Benedict, R., *The Chrysanthemum and the Sword*, Cleveland; New York, The World Publishing Company, 1967 (1st ed. 1946).

Bendix, R., *Nation-Building and Citizenship*, New York, John Wiley & Sons (Inc.), 1964.

Coulborn, R. (ed.), *Feudalism in History*, Princeton (N.J.), Princeton University Press, 1965.

Dahrendorf, R., *Gesellschaft und Demokratie in Deutschland*, Munich, Piper & Co., 1966.

Diamond, S., "From Organization to Society: Virginia in the 17th Century," *American Journal of Sociology,* 63, March 1958, p. 457.

Eckstein, H., *Division and Cohesion in Democracy,* Princeton (N.J.), Princeton University Press, 1966.

Eisenstadt, S. N., *Political Systems of Empires,* New York, The Free Press, 1963.

Etzioni, A., *Political Unification,* New York, Holt, Rinehart & Winston, 1965.

Geertz, C., *Agricultural Involution,* Berkeley (Calif.), University of California Press, 1966.

Goldthorpe, J., "Social Stratification in Industrial Society" in: R. Bendix and S. Lipset, *Class, Status and Power,* New York, The Free Press, 1966, pp. 648–660.

Inkeles, A. and Bauer, R., *The Soviet Citizen,* Cambridge (Mass.), Harvard University Press, 1959.

Leach, E. R., *Political Systems of Highland Burma,* Boston (Mass.), Beacon Press, 1954.

Levy, M., *Modernization and the Structure of Societies,* Princeton (N.J.), Princeton University Press, 1966, 2 Vols.

Lipset, S. M., *The First New Nation,* New York, Basic Books, 1963.

Marsh, R., *Comparative Sociology,* New York, Harcourt, Brace & World, 1967.

Marshall, T. H., *Class, Citizenship and Social Development,* New York, Doubleday & Co., 1964.

Mendras, P. (ed.), *Société et Volonté Générale,* Paris, Gallimard, 1966.

Moore, Jr., B., *Social Origins of Dictatorship and Democracy,* Boston (Mass.), Beacon Press, 1966.

Porter, J., *The Vertical Mosaic,* Toronto, University of Toronto Press, 1965.

Pye, L., *Politics, Personality and Nation Building,* New Haven (Conn.); London, Yale University Press, 1963.

Runciman, W. G., *Relative Deprivation and Social Justice,* University of California Press, 1966.

Shils, E., "Political Development in the New States," *Comparative Studies in Sociology and History* 2 (3, 4), 1960.

Smelser, N., *Social Change in the Industrial Revolution,* Chicago (Ill.), University of Chicago Press, 1959.

Van den Berghe, P., *Race and Racism,* New York, John Wiley & Sons, 1967.

Wittfogel, K. A., *Oriental Despotism,* New Haven (Conn.), Yale University Press, 1957.

11

The Relevance of Methodology

Methodological Problems in Empirical Social Research

The Nature of Modern Methodology

The sociologist is supposed to convert the vast and ever-shifting web of social relations into an understandable system of knowledge. To discover and appraise the way in which this is being done is the object of methodological analysis. Sociologists study man in society; methodologists study the sociologist at work. In the world of the natural sciences this is a major activity which at certain turning points, for instance, the years preceding Einstein's theory of relativity, has had a major influence on the course of science itself. For comparison's sake it is worthwhile to recall for a moment what is usually done by the philosophers of science. Their activities centre around the notion of *explication*. Hempel, a leading German representative of this group who now works in the United States, has described this idea as follows:

> Explication aims at reducing the limitations, ambiguities, and inconsistencies of ordinary usage of language by propounding a reinterpretation intended *to enhance the clarity and precision of their meanings* as well as their ability to function in the processes and theories with explanatory and predictive force.[8]

When we transfer terms like "personality" or "law" or "cause" from everyday language into scientific usage, we must always make decisions for which we ourselves take the responsibility. We give up certain connotations of these terms in order to make the remainder more precise and more easily amenable to verification and proof. In

Reprinted with editorial adaptations from "Methodological Problems in Empirical Social Research," in *Transactions of the Fourth World Congress of Sociology*, vol. 2: *Sociology: Applications and Research* (London: International Sociological Association, 1959), pp. 225–49 [232–49]. The general theme of the Congress, held in Milan and Stresa, September 8–15, 1959, was "society and sociological knowledge."

this sense, as Hempel points out, an explication cannot be qualified simply as true or false; but it may be judged as more or less adequate according to the extent to which it attains its objectives.

Social scientists who are interested in methodology can easily find occasion for such explication, applied both to the older speculative writings on social phenomena and to bodies of contemporary empirical studies. It is instructive to examine the work of a classical writer, say, in the field of public opinion research, and to see how his statements might be translated into the language of modern research procedures.[10] It will be found, on the one hand, that such writings contain a great richness of ideas which could profitably be infused into current empirical work; on the other hand, it will be found that such a writer tolerates great ambiguity of expression. By proper explication, we can bring out the more precise meanings which might be imputed to him. As social scientists we would be especially interested to see which of his statements permit verification. The task of such explication is not to criticize the work, but rather to bridge a gap, in this case between an older humanistic tradition and a newer one which is more empirically oriented. Our French colleagues will recognize that this is an application of "*explication des textes*" to sociological writings and to empirical social research.

As a matter of fact, the need for such explication is particularly urgent in the social sciences. When the natural scientist makes a discovery, it usually turns out to be so different from everyday experiences that the very nature of the phenomenon forces him to develop precise and sharp terminology; the extreme example of this, of course, is mathematics. But in speaking about human affairs we are accustomed to common sense, to everyday language, and we cannot avoid transferring these colloquialisms to the classroom and to the debating halls where we discuss social matters. Everyday language is notoriously vague, however, and therefore clarification and purification of discourse are very important for the social scientist. We must make deliberate efforts toward semantic analysis.

Another and related line of intellectual activity has been called the "*critique of theory*." The word critique has been taken over from German philosophy, and can be easily misunderstood. When Kant wrote his *Critique of Pure Reason,* he obviously did not mean to be critical of rational thinking; by "critique" he meant an analysis of the conditions under which such thinking is possible. The same meaning is found also in the field of literary and artistic criticism; here, too, the idea is not that the critic necessarily disapproves of a piece of art, but that he analyzes its structure. In the same way, criticism of theoretical systems implies only that their foundations and tacit assumptions are clearly brought to light.

The main American representative of critical analysis is Bridgman, and a short essay of his provides what is perhaps the best introduction to critiques of this kind. In his introductory statement, Bridgman puts the task quite clearly:

> The attempt to understand why it is that certain types of theory work and others do not is *the concern of the physicist as critic, as contrasted with the physicist as theorist.* The material for the physicist as critic is the body of physical theory, just as the material of the physicist as theorist is the body of empirical knowledge.[3]

The distinction between "theory" and "critique" is important. The critic deals with empirical material—but once removed. By bringing out clearly what the theorist (or analyst) does with his primary data he contributes in his way to the progress of research. In the introduction and conclusion of his essay, Bridgman brings to the American reader an understanding of the general intellectual influences which emanated, at the turn of the century, from writers like Poincaré in France and Mach in Germany. If one were to write the intellectual history of the generation of European students who grew up during the first decades of the twentieth century, one would probably rank this kind of critique, along with psycho-analysis and Marxism, as the main intellectual influences which shaped the climate of thinking in the period.

It is interesting that Bridgman places great emphasis on the educational value of such critiques. He points out that the difficulty of assimilating the creative ideas of others has been greatly underrated in modern education. And he feels that if more stress were put on the development of critical faculties, the creativeness and inventiveness of the young natural scientist would be considerably enhanced.

There is some good reason to talk of methodology rather than philosophy of science in our field. From the quotation I have just given, it can be seen that in the natural sciences the emphasis is on the explication of theories. We do not yet have really developed theories in our field. What is called social theory are either systems of concepts, as exemplified by the work of von Wiese or of Parsons, or they are directives pointing out the aspects of social phenomena to which we should pay special attention, an intellectual activity best exemplified by Merton's explication of functional analysis.[16] Rather than talking about a "philosophy of the social sciences," I prefer to talk about its methodology, a term which is more modest and which corresponds better to the present state of affairs. It implies that concrete studies are being scrutinized as to the procedures they use, the underlying assumptions they make, the modes of explanation they consider as satisfactory. Methodological analysis in this sense provides the elements from which a future philosophy of the social sciences may be built. If my linguistic feeling is adequate, the term should convey a sense of tentativeness; the methodologist codifies ongoing research practices to bring out what is consistent about them and deserves to be taken into account the next time.

Methodology and the related activities of explication and critical analysis have developed as a bent of mind rather than as a system of organized principles and procedures. The methodologist is a scholar who is above all *analytical* in his approach to his subject matter, whether his own or other people's research work. He tells other scholars what they have done, or might do, rather than what they should do. He tells them what order of finding has emerged from their research, not what kind of result is or is not preferable. This kind of analytical interest requires self-awareness, on the one hand, and tolerance, on the other. The methodologist knows that the same goal can be reached by alternative roads, and he realizes that instruments should be adapted to their function, and not be uselessly sharp.

A reminder is perhaps needed on the ways in which methodology is *not* defined here. For example, it is probably less rigorous than formal logic; on the other hand, it has less substantive content and is more formal than what has been called the psychology or sociology of knowledge. Likewise, the methodologist is not a technical advisor; he does not tell research workers the specific procedures of sampling or measuring which they should follow in the conduct of an investigation. Neither is it his task to indicate what problems should be selected for study. But once the topic for investigation has been chosen, he might suggest the general types of procedures which, in the light of the stated objectives, seem more appropriate. I want to give you two examples of the kind of methodological efforts which I think has proved clarifying, and as I proceed I shall simultaneously bring out the points which still need further elucidation.

The Flow from Concepts to Measurement Procedures

My first example deals with the relation between concepts and their representation by empirical research operations. I shall restrict myself to classificatory concepts like the cohesion of a group or the ambition of a person which are essentially developed in order to classify groups and people by their degree of cohesion or ambition, respectively. The attribution of such properties is interchangeably called description, classification, or measurement. The ultimate purpose is to develop propositions to the effect, for instance, that cohesive groups of workers are more productive or that ambitious persons are more likely to lack warm human relations with other people. We will call the indices or tests by which such classifications are achieved "variates"; it is a term which reminds one properly of the better-known mathematical term of a variable, but includes ranking and other qualitative attributions. The process by which concepts are translated into variates, as they are used in empirical study, consists in general of four steps: an initial imagery of the concept, the specification of dimensions, the selection of observable indicators, and the combination of indicators into indices.

(a) *Imagery.* The flow of thought and analysis which ends up with a measuring instrument usually begins with something which might be called imagery. Out of the analyst's immersion in all the detail of a theoretical problem, he creates a rather vague image or construct. The creative act may begin with the perception of many disparate phenomena as having some underlying characteristic in common. Or the investigator may have observed certain regularities and is trying to account for them. In any case, the concept, when first created, is some vaguely conceived entity that makes the observed relations meaningful.

Suppose we want to study industrial firms. We naturally want to measure the management of the firm. What do we mean by management? The notion probably arose when someone noticed that, under the same conditions, a factory is sometimes well run and sometimes not well run. Something was being done to make men and materials more productive. This "something" was called management, and ever since students of industrial organization have tried to make this notion more concrete and precise. The same process takes place in other fields. By now the development of intelligence tests has become a large industry. But the beginning of the idea of intelligence was that, if you watch little boys, some strike you as being alert and interesting and others as dull and uninteresting. This kind of originating observation starts the wheels rolling for a measurement problem.

(b) *Concept specification.* The next step is to take this original imagery and divide it into components. The concept is specified by an elaborate discussion of the phenomena out of which it emerged. We develop "aspects," "components," "dimensions," or similar specifications. They are sometimes derived logically from the over-all concept, or one aspect is deduced from another, or from empirically observed correlations. The concept is shown to consist of a complex combination of phenomena, rather than a simple and directly observable item.

Suppose you want to know if a production team is efficient. You have a beginning notion of efficiency. Somebody comes and says, "What do you really mean? Who are more efficient—those who work quickly and make a lot of mistakes, so that you have many rejections, or those who work slowly but make very few rejects?" You might answer, depending on the product, "Come to think of it, I really mean those who work slowly and make few mistakes." But do you want them to work so slowly that there are no rejects in ten years? That would not be good either. In the end you divide the notion of efficiency into components such as speed, precision, continuity, etc., and suddenly you have what measurement theory calls a set of dimensions.

(c) *Selection of indicators.* After we have decided on these dimensions, there comes the third step: finding indicators for the dimensions. Here we run into a number of problems. First of all, how does one "think up" indicators? The problem is an old one.

William James has written in *The Meaning of Truth:*

> . . . Suppose, e.g., that we say a man is prudent. Concretely, that means that he takes out insurance, hedges in betting, looks before he leaps . . . As a constant habit in him, a permanent tone of character, it is convenient to call him prudent in abstraction from any one of his acts . . . There are peculiarities in his psychophysical system that make him act prudently . . .

Here James proceeds from an image to a series of indicators suggested directly by common experience. Today we would be rather more specific about the relation of these indicators to the underlying quality. We would not expect a prudent man always to hedge in betting, or to take out insurance on all possible risks; instead we would talk about the probability that he will perform any specific act as compared with a less prudent individual. And we would know that the indicators might vary considerably, depending on the social setting of the individual. Among students in a Protestant denominational college, for instance, we might find little betting and rare occasions for taking out insurance. Still a measure of prudence could be devised which was relevant to the setting. We might use as indicators whether a student always makes a note before he lends a book, whether he never leaves his dormitory room unlocked, etc.

The fact that each indicator does not have an absolute but only a probabilistic relation to our underlying concept requires us to consider a great many possible indicators. The case of intelligence tests furnishes an example. First intelligence is divided into dimensions of manual intelligence, verbal intelligence, imaginativeness and so on. But even then there is not just one indicator by which imaginativeness can be measured. We must use many indicators to get at it.

There is hardly any observation which has not at one time or another been used as an indicator of something we want to measure. We use a man's salary as one indicator of his ability; but we do not rely on it exclusively, or we would have to consider most businessmen more able than even top-ranking university professors. We take the number of patients a doctor has cured as another indicator of ability in that setting; but we know that a good surgeon is more likely to lose a patient than a good dermatologist. We take the number of books in a public library as an indicator of the cultural level of the community; but we know that quality of books matters as much as quantity.

(d) *Formation of indices.* The fourth step is to put Humpty Dumpty together again. After the efficiency of a team or intelligence of a boy has been divided into six dimensions, and ten indicators have been selected for each dimension, we have to put them all together, because we cannot operate with all those dimensions and indicators separately.

For some situations we have to make one over-all index out of them. If I have six students and only one fellowship to give, then I must make an over-all rating of the six. To do this I must in some way combine all the information I have about each student into an index. At another time we must be more interested in how each of several dimensions is related to outside variables. But, even so, we must find a way of combining the indicators, since by their nature the indicators are many, and their relations to outside variables are usually both weaker and more unstable than the underlying characteristic which we would like to measure.

To put it in more formal language, each individual indicator has only a probabilistic relation to what we really want to know. A man might maintain his basic position, but by chance shift on an individual indicator; or he might change his basic position, but by chance remain stable on a specific indicator. But if we have many such indicators in an index, it is highly unlikely that a large number of them will all change in one direction by chance, when the man we are studying has in fact not changed his basic position.

To put the matter in another way, we need a lot of probings if we want to know what a man can really do or where he really stands.

This, however, creates great difficulties in the fourth step of the measurement sequence which we described above. If we have many indicators and not all of them move in the same direction, how do we put them together in one index? Only recently have we raised the question: can we develop a theory to put a variety of indicators together? The subject is a large one, and it is impossible to go into details here. The aim always is to study how these indicators are interrelated with each other, and to derive from these interrelations some general mathematical ideas of what one might call the power of one indicator, as compared with another, to contribute to the specific measurement one wants to make. In the formation of indices of broad social and psychological concepts, we typically select a relatively small number of items from a large number of possible ones suggested by the concept and its attendant imagery. Louis Guttman speaks aptly of a universe of possible indicators and a sample of them which is actually used.[7]

Some Unsolved Problems in the Relation of Concepts and Indices

What are some of the problems involved in this flow from concepts to index formation? To begin with it is not easy to be precise in the distinction between classificatory and other types of concepts. A definition of the concept of "role" or "frame of reference" probably cannot be subsumed under the explication just proposed. They are of a more abstract nature, preceding any incorporation into an empirical proposition. Nevertheless, some explication is needed and possible.

Until quite recently, for instance, role behaviour was defined as the expectation society has in regard to the occupants of certain positions. But when it came to studying empirically what kind of expectation "society" has about the role of, say, a school superintendent, it turned out that one had to distinguish between very different members of what came to be called the role set.[15] The member of the school board had expectations about the school superintendent which were different from those of the teachers.[6] Not only is the role player, here the school superintendent, forced to find a compromise between these different expectations, but the various members of the role set have to work out their relations to each other.

A frame of reference was usually defined as those social and biographical experiences which affect the way a person perceives or judges a specific situation. When empirical studies on frames of reference were made, it turned out that the concept really covered two quite different meanings. Sometimes it referred to the fact that a single object was perceived differently according to what comparisons were implicitly made: the same sum of money is a lot for a poor man and little for a rich man. This is the notion of an anchorage point on a single dimension. But in other contexts a frame of reference meant the choice of one dimension among several. A forest is a multi-dimensional object characterized by its colours as well as by the animals who live in it. But the painter uses only the one and the hunter the other dimension.

These, however, are rather random examples. The relation of non-classificatory concepts to empirical data is by no means clear. As a matter of fact the problem itself is not easily formulated, as we shall see when we later come to talk about the notion of structure.

The next difficulty comes at the second phase, when we specify the dimensions of a concept. When do we want to deal with a rather complex notion as a whole, and when do we want to divide it into separate variates? Durkheim's concept of cohesion, for instance, contains at least two dimensions; one has to do with frequency and closeness of contact between people, the other with agreement among their values. We could either look at contacts and value integration as two sets of indicators for the same concept; or we could propose that two different notions, say, social cohesion and value cohesion, should be distinguished. Again, no general ideas have been developed to guide one on this point, or to explicate the consequences of different choices.

The same problem appears in reverse when it comes to the listing of indicators. There is a famous American study which shows that people who have an authoritarian personality are more likely to discriminate against ethnic minorities like Jews and Negroes. The indicators for the authoritarian personality are of great diversity: mistrust, inability to tolerate ambiguity, superstition, etc. The question, however, could be raised whether discrimination against ethnic minorities is not a part of the universe of indicators by which the concept of authoritarianism is operationally represented. To put it in the more general terms: it is not easy to say what should be the indicators and what should be the correlates of a concept. Probably only in the course of time will one be able to know how broad or how specific concepts should be.

The nature of the indicators themselves requires further clarification. Compare the two following cases: in the one we want to know whether a businessman who is widely travelled has more liberal economic views than one who never left his home. How would we characterize a widely travelled businessman? By the number of trips he took, the length of time he travelled, the number of countries he visited? By present practice we would probably combine all those indicators into one index. For the other case take one of the projective tests by which anxiety is being measured. We show a person a vague picture of a moving man which can be interpreted either as a man in flight or a man taking his exercise. In practice there will, of course, be several such unstructured pictures. People can be classified according to how often they interpret the situation as one of danger or stress.

This pair of examples suggests some possible distinctions among sets of indicators. Interpreting the responses to projective tests implies, for example, many more psychological assumptions than we make when we develop an index of "wide-travelledness." The indicators of wide-travelledness are directly related to their concept, while projective measures are indirect and depend for their interpretation on much prior substantive knowledge. In the physical sciences with their highly developed theory, indirect measurements are of course most common—for example, the use of light spectrograms to measure temperature or velocity. Another distinction might be that the concept of wide-travelledness has a conventional quality—its indicators are put together because the researcher thinks they are experiences which may have similar effects on a criterion variable, political attitudes. The different indicators are not assumed to hang together in the real world, or to reflect an underlying trait. The concept of anxiety on the other hand has a realistic quality; it is not so much created as discovered by the researcher and may be thought of as representing some underlying attribute of a person. In a more or less explicit way the investigator has a theory relating the indicators to this attribute. All these are merely suggestions; so far we have no good classification of the major types of indicators. Probably a whole theory of signs will be needed before order is brought into this field.

For the time being we can take refuge in a rule of thumb which has been called the interchangeability of indices. If we have a universe of reasonable indicators for a concept it seems to make little difference which subset we choose for the formation of a final index. In the study of social scientists mentioned before we found that the more eminent professors were likely to be politically more progressive.[12] We measured eminence in a variety of ways, e.g., once by using a man's publications as indicators, and once using the honours which had been bestowed upon him. While the two indices were not highly correlated with each other they were interchangeable in the sense that they showed the same correlation with an index of progressiveness. At the same time we could show that progressiveness itself could be measured in a variety of ways without the main empirical proposition being affected. But even here a problem lurks. What is a universe of reasonable indicators? Obviously we could pick unreasonable ones which would violate the rule of interchangeability. It is not clear whether we shall be able to answer the question beyond referring to the good judgement of the investigator.

We are probably best off with the fourth step, the combination of indicators into one overall instrument, an index or scale. Quite explicit mathematical models are available for such procedures, but space forbids discussing this point further.

One might ask, how are we helped by the initial analysis of the flow from concept to index when each step represents as yet unsolved problems? The answer, I think, is a two-fold one. The problems themselves could not be precisely formulated without the initial analysis. And second, the explication, even if it is not complete, will save us from vague, general and acrimonious discussion as to whether it is possible to use measurements in the social sciences. Comparisons between the natural and social sciences are not likely to be useful, but one who feels compelled to engage in them will also find that a precise analysis of what we do in the social sciences will locate the points of similarity and difference between the various fields.

The Measurement of Collective Properties

The preceding analysis of measurement applies to characteristics of collectives as well as to those of individuals. It is true that until lately the largest amount of research concerned individual properties. But in recent years increasing efforts have been made to describe collectives—small groups, larger organizations, communities, etc.—along quantitative dimensions. We shall call such variates "collective properties" just to avoid the clumsy term "properties of collectives." Examples are easily given: Educational sociologists have measured the quality of schools by using as indicators a list of practices which are considered as desirables; others have developed quality indices by combining the training of the teachers, the size of the school library, the budget available per student, and so on. Some industrial sociologists have classified factories according to the power the unions have in their management. The procedure was to select a list of decision areas in which the unions might or might not participate: wage setting, grievances, safety devices, promotions, etc. Others have worked on a classification of patterns of supervision. An inventory was made of the kind of decisions which foremen took in the course of a day's work. The decisions were rated as either more oriented towards the needs of the workers or more oriented towards the technical productivity of the plant. The separate items were combined into an index which corresponds to a broad characteristic of supervision, going from "worker orientation" on the one end to "efficiency orientation" on the other end.

It is not surprising that the most frequent efforts at measuring collective properties are made around organizations where many comparable units exist and where data are relatively easily available. But there is a rapidly increasing trend to measure collective properties of a variety of other organizations like church parishes, local party organizations, and housing projects. As more funds for this relatively expensive type of work become available, we can count on an ever-increasing experience with this kind of measurement. The importance of this development for sociological analysis is very great and leads to the second example of methodology I want to present.

Contextual Propositions

All through our theoretical literature one can find the desire to bring out the specific nature of sociological thinking. It comes up in a variety of ways. Durkheim insisted on the special nature of sociological facts. Modern critics of microsociological work complain that it leaves out the specifically sociological attributes of social institutions. More philosophically-oriented colleagues always yearn for a discussion and definition of the term "structure" which seems to symbolize the essence of truly sociological units of analysis. All these efforts are undoubtedly justified, but it is doubtful whether their merits will come to light if the discussion is pursued on a general and merely verbal level. I shall propose one possible formulation which is very concrete and derived from empirical research experience. I do not claim that it satisfies the full concern of those who struggle in the service of truly sociological and structural thinking. But I submit that carving out one specific type of structural thinking will help everyone concerned to express better his own concern, even if it is only by explicit opposition to the paradigm I am proposing.

Let me give you the following definition of a contextual proposition:

(a) It contains at least three variates.
(b) At least one of them is a collective property—that is, a characterization of individuals by the types of collective to which they belong.
(c) The interrelation between two of the variates is itself affected by the variation of the collective property.

In order not to be too abstract, I shall first give a concrete example. I have earlier referred to a recent study of American social scientists. The professors studied were teaching in 165 colleges.[12] The colleges were classified according to how progressive their social scientists were on the average. (There is no need here to go into the details of this measurement.) We thus dealt with a collective property: the colleges were divided according to whether they were conservative, progressive, or somewhere in between. We also knew, of course, the progressiveness of each individual teacher, which was measured on a scale ranging from 0 to 6.

Now, it has been known for a long time that, in the American population at large, older people were more conservative than younger people. But the interpretation of this general finding was not clear. It might mean that growing older made for a loss of vitality and hence led to a decline in seeking social change; or it might be that the phenomenon was a purely social one—that growing up in an essentially conservative society necessarily leads to increasing conformity. Maybe in a communist society people become more pro-communist, that is, more orthodox in terms of the communist regime, as they grow older.

Our data permitted a preliminary test of these interpretations, in that we know what the immediate social context is in which the professors are passing their lives; we know whether their colleagues at their college are progressive or conservative. If the increased conservatism of the older people was an adjustment to the prevailing national climate of opinion, then the decline of progressivism with age should be smallest in progressive colleges where the local climate counteracts the national, and largest in conservative ones where both climates work together. The following table shows what we found:

THE AVERAGE LEVEL OF PROGRESSIVENESS ACCORDING TO AGE
IN THREE GROUPS OF COLLEGES

College "Climate"	Age of Professors		
	Up to 40	41–50	51 or older
Progressive	3.13	2.98	2.76
Medium	2.81	2.49	2.13
Conservative	1.90	1.54	1.46

Comparing the first two columns, we find that the decline in the progressive colleges is 15 points on our measuring scale; in the medium colleges, 32 points; and the conservative ones, 36 points. Thus, indeed, the decline in progressiveness is markedly smaller in liberal colleges and greatest in conservative ones. Comparing the second and third columns, we find that the tendency continues also after the age of 50, with the seeming exception of the most conservative colleges. This, however, is probably due to the fact that our scale did not permit a low enough range to measure fully the conservatism in the very conservative institutions. What we then find here is that the correlation between age and progressivism depends upon the context in which these teachers work.

Recent literature provides an increasing number of examples for such contextual propositions. Especially outstanding is a study of my colleague Lipset, who compared the attitude of printers in 80 different shops.[13] The collective property which appears in his propositions is the size of the shop. The larger the shop, for example, the more active in and the better informed about union politics are the printers. But the effect of size is more marked upon the chairmen of the local union unit than upon the rank and file. The increase of union activity with shop size is also more pronounced for printers whose primary friendship groups are mainly composed of fellow printers than for those whose social relations are away from their place of work. In an unpublished study, H. Zeisel found that the greater the average wealth of a county, the larger are the awards juries make in accident cases; but within counties the richer jurors vote for smaller awards than the poorer jurors, perhaps because they identify more closely with the insurance companies while the poorer jurors identify with the injured parties. The interpretation points to an interplay between collective norms and individual frames of reference. In the same class of results belongs Stouffer's famous finding that within military units, morale is higher among soldiers who have been promoted; but, between units, morale decreases with the overall number of promotions, presumably because the nonpromoted soldiers feel especially deprived when a general expectation is frustrated for them individually.[18]

It seems to me that such empirical findings go very far toward catching what social theorists have in mind when they urge that one take total situations into account or emphasize the importance of structures as opposed to the atomistic approach of empirical studies. The essence of a contextual proposition is that it proceeds simultaneously on two levels. It interrelates individual properties, and at the same time takes into account variation in the characteristics of a higher level collective in which the individuals are located. It is, of course, not always possible to design studies so that enough collectives are available to create variates on both the individual and the collective level. Sometimes we can only compare two situations, which we have to select skillfully to represent extreme cases of the contextual situation. Sometimes, when we cannot carry our study beyond one context, we have to be satisfied with an imaginative interpretation of its probable role. Many of you, I am sure, know of the experiments of Professor Solomon Asch showing that students are willing to misstate the length of physical objects if enough people in their surroundings insist that the facts are contrary to the perceptions of the experimental subjects.[1] It has been claimed that this is not a general psychological phenomenon, but is characteristic for American students, who grow up in a conformist culture. It is justified to raise this contextual objection, but whether it is true or not will have to be decided by repeating the Asch experiments in another culture.

By carving out the notion of a contextual proposition the work of the methodologist has only begun. It would now be necessary to turn to writings of a more theoretical or philosophical nature and to study line by line the statements made by these authors. Which of them can be reproduced by the formulation here proposed? In cases where this is not possible, it would be necessary to look for further clarification. It might be, for instance, that not every characteristic of a collective is to be considered a structural property. They might . . . experience the degree of hierarchy in social relations in a college or a printing shop as structural properties, but not the size of these collectives or the attitude distribution (opinion climate) within them. The purpose of my example is not to claim that it brings full clarity into a confused discussion, but that it shows the way by which such clarity could be increased.

Outlook

Let me end up with a few brief references to other methodological developments. Some of them will probably come up in the special sessions of this division of our congress. If not I will at least have given bibliographical suggestions to those participants who are interested in pursuing my topic in more detail. I bypass the role of mathematical models because few sociologists today have the training to use and appraise them. But there are very simple formalisms hardly deserving the name of mathematics which have proved very useful. One is the use of simple combinations of attributes to test and develop descriptive typologies.[20] Another is the presentation of data in matrix form. Without the use of any matrix algebra, just being aware of rows and columns and averages within them, quite a number of sociological concepts can be clarified, for example those involving social mobility, or relationships among individuals within a group.[23] The notion of transition probabilities is also a very simple one. If applied to repeated observations, e.g., of attitudes or social behaviour, they render to the discussion of social processes the same service as the notion of contextual propositions renders to the notion of structures.[11]

Another area which has been greatly clarified by recent discussions is the whole complex of causal analysis. How can we distinguish between a spurious correlation and one which corresponds to a causal sequence? Quite simple techniques of classifying people simultaneously on several variates can help to illuminate the relationships between them.[24] What is the relation between the explanation of a single case and the application of a statistical regularity?[19] If one wants to get a feeling for the progress introduced by the careful explication of social research procedure, one might look at the recent discussion between two philosophers of history, Dray and Gardiner.[4,5] The two philosophers disagree on many things but they agree that intentions are not subject to empirical analysis. Neither of them has heard of the careful empirical studies done to discover the factors which are related to people's carrying out or failing to carry out various intentions, for instance, to vote, to work in certain occupations, to make capital investments.[22] One is a little bit reminded of Hegel's proof that only seven planets can exist, just before the eighth one was discovered.

I just mentioned studies which predict people's behaviour from their intentions. This would not make sense if we want to predict success in marriage or in an occupation.[21] There everyone wants to succeed and therefore the chances of success have to be inferred from correlates like length of engagement in the first case or kind of training in the second case. The logic of these various prediction studies has been greatly clarified by recent methodological analysis.[9] It is more difficult to compare statistical predictions with those made in individual cases by clinical psychologists or occupational counsellors. Paul Meehl has collected the available evidence, which does not seem to give either of the two procedures a clear advantage.[14] His monograph also raises the question whether the individual prediction really uses hidden statistical knowledge or whether it applies qualitative procedures in their own right. The matter is still controversial, as is the role of qualitative methods in empirical research altogether. Dr. Barton and I reviewed a large number of qualitative studies and came to the conclusion that here is an area where explication is especially lacking and needed.[2]

I mentioned before that in my opinion no social theory in the strict sense of the term yet exists. Still, efforts at theorizing are being made and they deserve and need explication. My colleague Robert Merton has set down a careful analysis of the work done by functional analysts.[16] His essay has been translated into French and so I assume that it is known by many Europeans. It may not be known that an American philosopher Ernest Nagel carried Merton's achievement a step further.[17] He translated Merton's formulation into mathematical language and thereby was able to show its similarity to systems analysis as it is carried out by biologists. Another aspect of theory formation was studied by Hans Zetterberg.[25] He took fourteen empirical findings from small group studies and showed that they could be derived from only four of them. His emphasis is on the fact that various combinations of four of the findings could form the axiomatic basis for all the others.

It might well be that some of these hurried references sound more interesting than the two examples I developed in more detail. The discussion of this paper should provide an opportunity for further elaboration. Whatever the emphasis I should not conceal from our European colleagues that my whole approach is not without opponents in the United States. Quite a number of my American colleagues feel that concern with methodology thwarts the ability for substantive investigations. No one, of course, knows the answer, but I try to defend myself by referring to an old saying that poetry is emotion recollected in tranquility. I consider methodology creative work recollected in the same mood. I do not see any reason why one cannot shuttle back and forth between creative substantive work and reflections on the procedures by which it is best guided.

Another objection is the futility of methodological efforts: it is said that social scientists are either gifted or not, and that you cannot teach creativity. Here I usually counter with a parallel from the world of sports. It is sometimes hard to understand how it happens that sports records, like those of the Olympic Games, are continually bettered—runners run faster miles, pole vaulters clear greater heights, and so on. It is unlikely that, over the last fifty years, the capacities of *homo athleticus* have improved in any Darwinian sense. But training techniques, styles of running, and athletic equipment have steadily been refined. Great athletic stars are born; but good coaches can so raise the average level of technique that when a star appears he starts from a higher level than the star of a generation ago. He therefore is able to reach greater peaks of achievement, even though his individual capacities need not be superior to those of his predecessors. In the same sense, methodology, self-awareness of the field, provides a better starting background for the individual creative scholar.

I have at one occasion used a parable with which I might end this paper. There is a well-known story about the centipede who lost his ability to walk when he was asked in which order he moved his feet. But other details of the story are buried in conspiratorial silence. First of all, there is no mention of the fact that the inquiry came from a methodologist who wanted to improve the walking efficiency of the centipede community. Then, little attention is paid to the other centipedes who participated in the investigation. Not all of them reacted with such disastrous effects. Some were able to give rather reasonable answers; from these the investigator worked diligently to arrive at general principles of walking behaviour.

When the methodologist finally published his findings, there was a general outcry that he had only reported facts which everyone already knew. Nevertheless, by formulating this knowledge clearly, and by adding hitherto unobserved facts at various points, he eventually enabled the average centipede in the community to walk better. After a generation or so, this knowledge was incorporated into textbooks, and so filtered down to students on a lower level of scholarship. In retrospect this was the outstanding result. Of course, the great centipede ballet dancer and other creative walking artists continued to require hereditary endowments, and could not be produced by the school system. But the general level of walking, characteristic of the centipede in the street, was improved. And because of this those few individuals endowed with great personal gifts started out at a higher level, and achieved creative performances unparalleled in the past.

References

Of the studies mentioned in this paper, I quote only those which in my opinion will give the reader the easiest access to the points I tried to stress.

1. Solomon Asch, *Social Psychology* (New York: Prentice-Hall, 1952).

2. Allen Barton and Paul F. Lazarsfeld, "Some Functions of Qualitative Analysis in Social Research," in Sociologica, V. I, *Frankfurter Beitrage zur Soziologie,* 1955, pp. 321–351.

3. P. W. Bridgman, *The Nature of Physical Theory* (Princeton: Princeton University Press, 1936).

4. William Dray, *Laws and Explanations in History* (London: Oxford University Press, 1957).

5. Patrick Gardiner, *The Nature of Historical Explanation* (London: Oxford University Press, 1952).

6. Neal Gross et al., *Explorations in Role Analysis* (New York: Wiley, 1958).

7. Louis Guttman, "The Problem of Attitude and Opinion Measurement," Ch. II of *Measurement and Prediction,* Samuel Stouffer et al. (Princeton: Princeton University Press, 1950).

8. C. G. Hempel, *Fundamentals of Concept Formation in Empirical Science* (Chicago: University of Chicago Press, 1952), International Encyclopedia of Unified Science, Vol. II, no. 7.

9. Paul Horst et al., *The Prediction of Personal Adjustment* (New York: Social Science Research Council, 1941).

10. Paul F. Lazarsfeld, "Public Opinion and the Classical Tradition," *Public Opinion Quarterly,* Vol. 21 (1957), pp. 39–53.

11. Paul F. Lazarsfeld and Robert K. Merton, "Friendship as Social Process: A Substantive and Methodological Analysis," in *Freedom and Control in Modern Society,* edited by M. Berger, T. Abel, and C. H. Page (New York: Van Nostrand, 1954).

12. Paul F. Lazarsfeld and Wagner Thielens, *The Academic Mind* (Glencoe, Illinois: The Free Press, 1958).

13. Seymour Lipset, Martin Trow and James Coleman, *Union Democracy* (Glencoe, Illinois: The Free Press, 1956).

14. Paul E. Meehl, *Clinical vs. Statistical Prediction* (Minneapolis: University of Minnesota Press, 1954).

15. Robert K. Merton, "The Role-Set: Problems in Sociological Theory," *British Journal of Sociology,* v. 8, pp. 106–120 (June 1951).

16. Robert K. Merton, *Elements de Methode Sociologique* (Paris: Librairie Plon, 1953), Ch. 3.

17. Ernest Nagel, "A Formalization of Functionalism," in *Logic without Metaphysics* (Glencoe, Illinois: The Free Press, 1956).

18. Samuel Stouffer et al., *The American Soldier* (Princeton: Princeton University Press, 1949), Vol. I, pp. 250–258.

19. Hans Zeisel, *Say It with Figures* (New York: Harper, revised, 4th edition, 1957), Chs. VI and VII.

Together with a colleague, Dr. Morris Rosenberg, I edited a volume of 60 annotated papers on methodology under the title, *The Language of Social Research* (Glencoe, Illinois: The Free Press, 1955). The most pertinent ones for present discussion are:

20. Allen H. Barton, "The Concept of Property Space in Social Research," pp. 40–53.

21. Ernest W. Burgess and Leonard S. Cottrell, Jr., "The Prediction of Adjustment in Marriage," pp. 268–276.

22. John A. Clausen, "The Prediction of Soldiers' Return to Pre-War Employment," pp. 260–267.

23. Leon Festinger, Stanley Schachter, and Kurt Back, "Matrix Analysis of Group Structures," pp. 358–367.

24. Paul F. Lazarsfeld, "The Interpretation of Statistical Relations as a Research Operation," pp. 115–124.

25. Hanz Zetterberg, "On Axiomatic Theories in Sociology," pp. 533–539.

III

HISTORY AND SOCIOLOGY OF SOCIAL RESEARCH

12

Sociology of Social Research

The Sociology of Empirical Social Research

To choose a topic for a presidential address is a rather frightening experience. More irrevocable than marriage, more self-revealing than a dream, it forces one to assign priorities to a variety of interests which have long remained lazily undecided. Between the time when the American Sociological Society was organized in 1906 and the first world war, its presidents were more fortunate. Elected for two years, they could give two addresses. One was usually devoted to a specific sociological problem that concerned them, and the other to a kind of state of the union message, in which they discussed matters currently of concern to our profession at large. At first, I thought I would have to make a choice between the two types. Recently I completed a preliminary survey of organized research in this country wherein I investigated where we stand with respect to our research centers, social relations laboratories, our bureaus of applied social research. This seemed to me an urgent professional problem and a good topic for tonight's discussion. But I also had a theoretical candidate. You all know the old saying: those who can, do; those who cannot, teach; and those who have nothing to teach, become methodologists. I always felt that this is an unfair misunderstanding of methodology, and tonight's occasion seemed an opportunity for clarification. I finally decided to combine the two topics and to center my remarks on the interrelation between the organization of social research and methodology. This involves the following five points:

    1. Empirical research requires a specific kind of organization which I shall call "institutes." These institutes in turn generate a bent of mind, a way of reflecting on research procedures which I shall call "methodology."

    2. Such induced sensitivity to methodology can be fruitful for general

Reprinted from "The Sociology of Empirical Social Research," *American Sociological Review* 27, no. 6 (1962): 757–67. First presented as the presidential address at the fifty-seventh annual meeting of the American Sociological Association, Washington, D.C., September 1, 1962.

sociological analysis in areas far afield from what we think of as empirical studies.

3. To understand the contemporary scene it is necessary to provide some facts and raise additional questions on the history of empirical social research in Europe, as well as in the United States.

4. Today's social research institutes in this country are a very recent development, raise interesting organizational problems of their own, and have broad implications for the teaching of sociology and, perhaps, even for the future of our university administration in general.

5. The substantive work these institutes carry out needs to, and soon will, undergo a considerable broadening which I shall specify at the end of my remarks.

There is not time enough to elaborate any of these points in detail. Consequently, I shall occasionally use, as a device for speedier communication, illustrations taken from my own academic career. I have repeatedly advocated that sociologists should give accounts of the way their interests and writings actually develop and I am ready, therefore, to take my own prescription and trace back some of the things you know I stand for. In a way, this is an effort to draw generalizations from a single case. And my first point is indeed best introduced by a personal reminiscence.

The Methodology—Institute Syndrome

When I joined the staff of the University of Vienna, some thirty-five years ago, one of my first assignments was to review a large body of data on the occupational choices of young people. It was easy to see the regularities of their choices. They were linked with social stratification, and permitted one to interpret age differences in terms of a general theory of adolescence. The available studies also contained many tabulations of the *reasons* for the choices. But this material was contradictory; no sense could be made of it. My attention shifted to the problem of what was wrong with the mode of investigation. And here I noticed an ambiguity in the question "why." Some youngsters answered in terms of the influences to which they had been subjected, while others talked about the attractive features of the jobs under consideration. Still others referred to broader personal goals which they hoped would be served by a particular occupation. An investigator's lack of skill in the art of asking "why" led to meaningless statistical results.

The study was originally inspired by a program of research on adolescents laid out by my Viennese teacher, Charlotte Bühler. But, in my own biography, it led to a sequence of studies on choices: how could one find out why people bought one product rather than another, why they voted the way they did, why they listened to certain radio programs, and so forth. Ever since, I have continued to search for sound ways for making empirical studies of action. When can one use retrospective interviews? When is it better to use panel studies (repeated observations of people in the process of choice)? When are decisions best understood by considering the social context—the school, the factory or other organizations—within which the choice was made? And in all this, of course, I find myself puzzled by a theory of action where no one ever acts, and by modern mathematical decision theory where people act on probabilities of future events and utilities of outcomes, but where no one ever asks from which social and experimental background these estimates arise.

A program for the empirical study of action required a staff of collaborators trained to collect and analyze data whenever a research opportunity offered itself. I obtained permission from my academic superiors to create, in Vienna, a research center very similar to the kind of American institutes I shall discuss presently. It antedates, as far as I know, all such university institutions in this country except the one at the University of North Carolina created by Howard Odum. Now, supervising even a small research staff makes one acutely aware of the differences between various elements of a research operation and of the need to integrate them into a final product. Some assistants are best at detailed interviews, others are gifted in the handling of statistical tables, still others are especially good at searching for possible contributions from existing literature. The different roles must be made explicit; each has to know what is expected of him and how his task is related to the work of the others. Thus, staff instruction quickly turns into methodological explication. Maintaining the intellectual standards of an institute is tantamount to codifying empirical social research as an autonomous intellectual world.

But this is not the end of the story. When one is responsible for directing research, abstract sociological issues turn into down-to-earth challenges. It is not enough to develop constructive typologies; one must decide under which type a particular person or group actually should be classified. One cannot just ponder over the nature of causality; one must give concrete evidence as to why a certain election was won or lost. At this point the tables are often turned. The research operation can provide the model which helps to clarify and unify problems that arise in spheres of inquiry far removed from empirical social research in its narrower sense. And this is my second point: Methodology can often give aid to social theory.

Relations between Methodology and Social Theory

Permit me to consider with you one example of the relation between methodology and social theory. Many of you, I am sure, are acquainted with the notion of an attribute space. It starts with the observation that objects can be described along a number of dimensions. Think, for example, of an IBM card on which people are described by sex, race, education, etc. In such a space, regions can be combined to form typologies. Thus sex and employment status permit many combinations; but for certain purposes it makes sense to distinguish just three; men, irrespective of their work, and women according to whether they are housewives or work outside.

This reduction of a combinatorial system of attributes to a smaller number of types has a counterpart which I have called a *substruction*. Beginning with a typology, or simply a list of objects, we ask ourselves in what way they have originated from an attribute space. The linguists do that today. They take the basic sounds of languages—the phonemes—and look for the minimum number of attributes of which these phonemes are combinations. Such a "binary description" of language leads to characteristics such as nasal/oral, strident/mellow, tense/lax. Any real language occupies only certain regions of the attribute space and leaves others empty.

In empirical social research we come across this substruction whenever we wish systematically to classify people or groups according to a proposed typology. My first encounter with this problem occurred when I worked with Erich Fromm on a study of authority in European families. He had distinguished four types: complete authority, simple authority, lack of authority, and rebellion. In order to use his ideas for an empirical study, we had to introduce criteria or, more specifically, questionnaire items along two dimensions: the degree of authority the parents wanted to exercise and how much of it their children accepted. Each of the two dimensions was divided into three levels, giving nine combinations. Seven of them were easily reduced to Fromm's types, but two of them forced us to acknowledge a fifth type: families in which the children wanted more authority than the parents were inclined to impose. Substruction helped us discover a new type.

The relation between typologies and attribute spaces will be obvious to anyone who has converted people into questionnaires and finally into cross-tabulations. But what matters most now is the way such a formal observation clarifies more general sociological issues. You will remember that Max Weber gave ten criteria for a pure bureaucracy. We cannot deal tonight with a ten dimensional space, so suppose we arbitrarily select two of the ten criteria. Each officer has a clearly defined sphere of competence and he is appointed on the basis of technical qualification. This gives a two dimensional space you can visualize easily as a traditional system of x-y coordinates drawn on a piece of paper. Actual organizations will be points in this system according to the degree to which they exhibit the two characteristics, which we shall assume have been scaled from 0 to 5. And as a free gift we now know what an ideal type is: it is the region in the upper right corner, around the point with the coordinates 5/5.

How about the diagonally opposite point, the one with the coordinates 0/0? No one, as far as I know, has worked out in detail what a non-bureaucracy looks like. But in another area the relation of these two points is very familiar. I refer to Toennies' "Gemeinschaft and Gesellschaft," Durkheim's "Société Mécanique and Organique," Becker's "Sacred and Secular Society," and Redfield's "Folk and Urban Continuum." The most seminal effort to provide a substruction for this typology is Parsons' "Pattern Variables." For the sake of simplicity, let us take two of the many dimensions which have been proposed for this typology—say, isolation and social homogeneity. Assume that they are somehow measured and entered respectively on the two axes. Then the pure folk society is at 0/0 and the pure urban mass society is diagonally opposite at 5/5. Now a good model is supposed to generate more ideas than were put into it to begin with, and this one does. Our two corner points can be connected by any number of lines that can vary in shape and length. They turn out to be the paths along which the transition from the traditional to the modern social system can be found. I suggest to you an instructive parlor game. Take your favorite theory of social change—telling how one aspect of society affects other social dimensions—and translate it into lines connecting points in an attribute space. While you will not obtain an empirical answer, you will be helped by the clearer formulation of problems and by seeing unexpected connections between possible solutions.

I hope the example I have given has helped to back up the second item in the five point plan which guides me tonight. The technical and organizational nature of empirical social research leads to formal ideas, to distinctions and interconnections relevant for many sociological pursuits well beyond the realm of strictly empirical research. My position is akin to the kind of sociology of knowledge which Marxists employ when they stress that new tools of production are often reflected in new ways of intellectual analysis. I look at empirical research as an activity which is especially conducive to x-raying the anatomy, the basic logical framework of general social inquiry. This is, of course, not the only way to look at the situation. One could focus on the content of the empirical studies produced in recent years, and my concluding remarks are devoted to this substantive aspect. But let me elaborate for a moment on the context in which I see my formal emphasis—formal both in intellectual and in institutional terms. I have always been most curious about the *process* of production, the *structure* of a piece of work, the *way* people reach a specific intellectual goal. As an amateur musician, I find my enjoyment of music considerably enhanced if an expert explains the theoretical structure of a quartet. Knowing little about *belles lettres,* I am indebted to the "new criticism" because its internal analysis of a piece of writing opens an experience to which I would not otherwise have access. This interest in "explications" was reinforced during my student days. It was in that period that the theory of relativity had come to the fore. We were greatly impressed by the fact that it came about not just through substantive findings, but also through the conceptual clarification of basic notions. I remember vividly the delight in discovering that it is not obviously clear what is meant when one says that two events, one on the sun and one on earth, occur "simultaneously." I should add that reading a mathematical paper reinforces this tendency. Hours are spent on one page, trying first to guess what the author is driving at, then why he is concerned with this objective, and, finally, the understanding of his proof. (Proofs are usually presented in a direction opposite from the way in which a theorem was originally discovered.)

In my teaching, I try to convey this mood to students in various ways. We read empirical research closely and try to reconstruct how the author was led from one step to the next: what data he might have inspected but not reported; how the order of his final presentation might have developed from an originally vague and quite different imagery. Often an hour is spent just on analyzing a table of contents. It comes very close to what the French call *"explication de texte,"* a training which gives them such great expressive strength. Dilthey's notion of hermeneutics, his general principles for interpreting philosophical systems, is echoed in this effort to make students understand that writing a term paper and publishing a book have more in common than they suppose. I have no evidence for the educational value of this methodological approach, but this does not keep me from being very convinced of its merits.

I now want to turn to some institutional problems and consequences which are indigenous to the way empirical studies are typically set up in contemporary American universities. This is more easily explained if I first insert some remarks on the history of social research.

A Note on History of Social Research

There are two leading facts in this history. First, its origins lay in early modern Europe (it may be dated as far back as the Seventeenth Century), but in Europe it failed to develop as a regular branch of professional sociology. Second, in the United States, where it was destined to flourish, it existed long before it found organizational setting in our universities. Permit me to digress sufficiently to explain some of the remarkable circumstances these bare generalizations cover.

A series of studies now under way at Columbia University shows that practically all modern empirical techniques—our Latin American friends sometimes summarize them as Yankee Sociology—were developed in Europe. Sampling methods were derived as a sequence to Booth's survey of life and labor in London. Factor analysis was invented by the Englishman, Spearman. Family research, with special emphasis on quantification, came of age with the French mineralogist, Le Play. Gabriel Tarde advocated attitude measurement and communications research. (Looking at the contemporary French scene, one might well speak of his posthumous victory in his epic battle with Durkheim.) The idea of applying mathematical models to voting was elaborately worked out by Condorcet during the French Revolution. His contemporaries, Laplace and Lavoisier, conducted social surveys for the Revolutionary Government, and their student, the Belgian, Quetelet, finally and firmly established empirical social research under the title of "*physique sociale.*" He did this, incidentally, to the great regret of Comte, who claimed that he had invented the term and now had to substitute for it a much less desirable linguistic concoction, to wit, sociology. In Italy, during the first part of our century, Niceforo developed clear ideas on the use of measurement in social and psychological problems, brilliantly summarized in his book on the measurement of progress. The Germans could claim a number of founding fathers: Max Weber was periodically enthusiastic about quantification, making many computations himself; Toennies invented a correlation coefficient of his own; and, during Easter vacations, von Wiese regularly took his students to villages so that they could see his concepts about social relations acted out in peasant families.

And yet, before 1933, nowhere in Western Europe, did empirical research acquire prestige, a home in universities, financial support, textbooks, or enough devotees to form what I should like to call a critical mass: the number of people sufficient to maintain each other's interest by providing a reciprocal reference group. What accounts for this discontinuity in European sociology? All of these countries have today a large, albeit somewhat ambivalent, interest in empirical research, but why is it now experienced as an American invasion rather than what it is in reality: a revival of an autonomous European development? I do not know. Perhaps the ravages of two wars and the intervening fascist period kept western European sociology from taking the "operational jump" for which it was ready; or perhaps structural features of university life or of the general intellectual climate in Europe made it necessary for the breakthrough to come in a new country. Only a very careful analysis of the material published around 1930, here and in Western Europe, could give an answer.

In the United States another historical problem is puzzling. We know that concern with underprivileged groups led to various fact-finding efforts here, such as the work of the American Social Science Association around 1870, and the survey movement which began at the turn of the century and was later supported by the Russell Sage Foundation. But why did it take so long for the universities to find their proper place in this broad trend? The question will not be fully answered but the issue is well illustrated by the efforts of the University of Chicago to develop means by which ameliorative activities in the community and the research interests of academia could join forces. The facts I shall summarize have been assembled by Mr. Vernon Dibble as part of the Columbia University history program mentioned before.

You all know of Albion Small, the founder of the *American Journal of Sociology,* and one of our early presidents. He began his chairmanship of the Department of Sociology at the University of Chicago in 1893. One of the professors in this Department, a former minister, was appointed because of his knowledge, based on previous activities, of the needs of the Chicago community. I refer to Charles R. Henderson, who, indeed, lived up to everyone's expectations. He wrote manuals for social workers on how to collect information that would help advance social legislation; he organized networks of social informants; he trained students who later became prominent in their own right. But, at that time in Chicago, it was assumed that the role of the University was to help the community solve its problems; the sociologist was not to carry out research himself. This was not a meaningful division of labor, however, and Henderson was soon forced to collect and analyze his own data. And yet the University structure had made no provision for this turn of affairs. Consequently, one day, Henderson, in a mood of desperation, wrote Albion Small that he just had to have an assistant at $100 a month. He listed ten arguments in favor of this revolutionary idea. As a typical illustration let me quote his argument No. 8:

> My department of study suffers unjustly in comparison with those of the physical sciences, with their costly equipment and corps of permanent assistants. I do not hope to be put on an equality with them, nor do I wish for them any diminution of equipment, but I want a little chance to demonstrate what can be done for the science of human welfare and furtherance of the higher life, with even a meagre supply of help.

The typewritten letter, dated February 1902, has a handwritten post-script: "Since writing the above I have learned that a similar arrangement to this proposal has been successfully tried at Columbia by Professor Giddings."

In March, Small wrote a three page letter to President Harper supporting Henderson's request as "part of a large program which we are all feeling that it is time to work out." This large program was empirical sociological research which would entitle "the University of Chicago to the leading place in that subject in the world, at least until some of the European universities shall realize the readjustment of interests that is going on."

Henderson obtained his assistant, but Small did not realize his great design. In 1914, a committee wrote a sixty page report on the need for a "bureau of social research" in Chicago. The bureau was not visualized as a University activity. The plan was sponsored by the City Club of Chicago and signed by a committee of four, consisting of three businessmen and George Herbert Mead. As far as I can tell, it was never implemented.

In 1922, Small was willing to join forces with a man with whom he shared nothing but an institutional conviction. The then dean of the Business School at Chicago proposed a central research institute, ignoring all departmental divisions. In a letter to the president, Small not only approved the idea but stated that "It makes my heart bleed to fear that our own social science group will miss its birthright by failure to qualify for the opportunity." And he added his own version of how the system would work:

> There should be "genuine commissions of inquiry" with a hierarchical order of work: graduate students would do the "assorting of materials and of organizing them in accordance with the findings of their more experienced seniors." But, so that this not become mere routine, "regular sessions of the seniors would be held with the graduate students present for thrashing out all the questions of principle involved." He wanted a cumulative continuity of such work. "The minutes of each inquiry, properly filed and indexed in the archives of the institution, would form an object lesson in the methodology of that type of inquiry and would be permanently instructive, both as to mistakes to be avoided in subsequent inquiries, and as to methods which proved to be useful. All this in addition to the substantive results of the investigation."

But even in 1922, the University was not ready for such a radical step. As a matter of fact, at about the same time, they refused a similar institute which Merriam had proposed for political science.

But, short of this, Small made great strides. He succeeded, often in the face of great resistance, in appointing men like Robert Park who introduced the guided dissertation into the Department of Sociology. Until then, the doctoral candidate followed the German pattern; he chose his topic, wrote his thesis in solitary confinement, and presented the final product to a professor who judged its intellectual merits. In Chicago in the 1920's the dissertation became part of a general program and was carried out in close contact with the sponsor. This was facilitated by Beardsley Ruml who deliberately used the Spellman Fund to make empirical research a regular part of the graduate curriculum.

That was the time when the sociological work being done at Chicago was prominent in American Sociology. But, after the initiative of the great pioneers like Park, Burgess, Thomas, and Ogburn, this dominance waned. It is my guess that a more formal organization for social research would have extended the influence of these great Chicago leaders even after other graduate schools began to make their bid.

Small always stressed that empirical research did not concern him personally, but that the future of sociology as a discipline depended upon the discovery of an appropriate institutional form for its exercise. It is interesting, incidentally, that this part of his work is nowhere mentioned in the many papers written about him. And yet, it is to his great credit, as a sociologist, that he sensed something which has since been documented by historical investigation. Turning points in higher education have often hinged on some institutional innovation. The medieval universities became permanent institutions once Paris established the disputation as a way of training students. The humanist revolution revolved around the scrutiny of classical texts. The idea of the modern university began with the Berlin seminar, a group of students who did more than just listen, who, in fact, also conducted their own research under the guidance of a master. And the contemporary sciences—of nature as well as of society—required the laboratory.

It took fifty years before we began to face this problem realistically in sociology, and much research will be needed to clarify what delayed and what finally led to the social research institute becoming imbedded in the university structure. Among the early handicaps one can easily think of are reasons like these: too few graduate students to form teams with division of labor; lack of seniors who had themselves risen from the ranks of empirical research; and, of course, lack of funds. But only monographic studies of places like North Carolina, Wisconsin, and Columbia will bring light onto the issue. Let me now turn to a review of the contemporary scene.

The Social Research Institute in the American University

There are about one hundred universities in the United States which today give at least ten PhDs in all fields combined, including the natural sciences. Slightly less than two-thirds of these institutions have made arrangements to carry out social research. We draw our definition rather liberally: it can be either a unit specifically attached to a Department of Sociology; or an interdepartmental setup including the Department of Sociology; or, finally, a fairly permanent project to which at least one sociologist is attached, even though the Department does not participate officially. The programs of these agencies are either *specialized,* or they cover a broad range of topics and are, so to say, *general purpose* units. The former outnumber the latter by more than two to one. The "general purpose" units, in turn, divide rather evenly into those which are *autonomous,* in the sense that they develop their own programs, and those which see themselves mainly as *facilitating* the research activities of individual faculty members. The distinction is somewhat difficult to make because academic tradition favors the rhetoric of facilitation, while the inner dynamics of such institutes press towards increasing autonomy and self-direction.

You are all aware of the controversies which have grown up around these institutes. On the positive side, we may note the following. They provide technical training to graduate students who are empirically inclined; the projects give students opportunities for closer contact with senior sociologists; the data collected for practical purposes furnish material for dissertations through more detailed study, or what is sometimes called secondary analysis; the members of a Department with an effective institute can give substance to their lectures with an enviable array of actual data; skills of intellectual cooperation and division of labor are developed; chances for early publications by younger sociologists are enhanced.

On the other side of the debate, the argument goes about as follows. Students who receive most of their training on organized projects become one-sided; instead of developing interests on their own, they become mercenaries of their employers; where institutes become influential, important sociological problems are neglected because they do not lend themselves to study by the "research machinery"; people who work best on their own find themselves without support and are regarded as outsiders.

The situation, as I see it, is promising but confused. We allow these institutes to develop without giving them permanent support, without integrating them into the general university structure, without even really knowing what is going on outside our immediate academic environment. As a bare minimum it is imperative that a more detailed study of the current situation be carried out. This would hopefully lead to recommendations for university administrators, for members of our own Association, and for all others concerned with the basic problem of how the avalanche of empirical social research can be fitted into current educational activities without having careless institutional improvisations destroy important traditional values or hinder creative new developments. True, we have no perfect formula for incorporating institutes into our graduate education. But pluralism is not the same as anarchy, and it is anarchy with which we are faced at the moment. Some form of permanent core support, assimilation of teaching and of institute positions, a better planned division of the students' time between lectures and project research, a closer supervision of institute activities by educational officers, more explicit infusion of social theory into the work of the institutes—all this waits for a systematic discussion and for a document which may perform the service which the Flexner report rendered to medical education fifty years ago.

In such a report the role of the institute director will have to figure prominently. Let me place him in a broader framework. We are confronted, nowadays, in our universities, with a serious problem which can be classified as an "academic power vacuum." When graduate education in this country began, no one doubted that the university president was an important figure. Gilman at Johns Hopkins and White at Cornell were intellectual as well as administrative leaders. Stanley Hall at Clark was impressive both as a president and as a psychologist. Inversely, individual professors were deeply involved in organizational innovation. John W. Burgess forced the creation of a graduate faculty upon the Columbia trustees. In his autobiography he describes movingly what this meant to him as a teacher and scholar. Silliman sacrificed his private fortune to establish a physical laboratory in his home and finally convinced the trustees at Yale that natural sciences were not a spiritual threat to young Americans.

Today, however, we witness a dangerous divergence: academic freedom is more and more interpreted in such a way as to keep the administration out of any truly academic affairs; and the faculty, in turn, has come to consider administration beneath its dignity. But educational innovations are, by definition, intellectual as well as administrative tasks. And, so, they have fallen into a no-man's land: the President and his staff wait for the faculty to take the initiative; the professors on their side consider that such matters would take time away from their true scholarly pursuits. As a result, many of our universities have a dangerously low level of institutional development.

One institutional consequence of research institutes is that they inevitably train men who are able and willing to combine intellectual and administrative leadership. An institute director, even if his unit only facilitates faculty research, must train a staff able to advise on important research functions. It is not impossible that, on specific topics, the collective experience of the institute staff exceeds the skills of the individual faculty member. One who has lived with scores of questionnaires can help write a better questionnaire on a subject matter in which he is not expert. Having helped to dig up documents and sources of data on many subjects makes for greater efficiency even on a topic not previously treated. In an autonomous unit this is even more pronounced. Here the staff carries out a self-contained work schedule. A hierarchy is needed, proceeding often from assistants to project supervisors, to program director, and, finally, to the director himself. The latter is at least responsible for reports and publications. But the director is also concerned with maintaining what is sometimes called the "image" of his operation. Its prestige, its attraction for staff and students, and its appeal for support are self-generated, not derived only from the reputation of the teaching departments. The professional staff sees its future career closely bound up with the destiny of the unit, a fact which sometimes makes for challenging problems in human organization.

At the same time, the director must develop the coordinating skills so necessary in a modern university. Often the place of his unit in the organization chart is not well defined. The novelty of the whole idea makes for instability and requires considerable institutional creativity. And, finally, we should frankly face the fact that in our system of higher education the matching of budgetary funds with substantive intellectual interests is a characteristic and enduring problem. The institute director knows the skills and interests of the faculty members, and he brings men and money together. This is not badly described as the role of "idea broker." Often he will have to work hard to obtain funds for a more unusual research idea suggested to him; at other times a possible grant looks so attractive that he will try to discover, among some of his faculty colleagues, what he would diplomatically call a "latent interest."

I am afraid this is not the appropriate forum for reforming university presidents. But I can at least try to convince some of you that directing a research institute is no more in conflict with scholarly work than is teaching. The director is faced with a variety of research problems which permit him to try out his intellectual taste and skills, while the individual scholar might find himself committed to a study prematurely chosen. The multitude of data passing through the director's hands considerably broadens his experience. Staff conferences provide a unique sounding board for new ideas. Even negotiations for grants open vistas into other worlds which a sociologist can turn to great advantage in his own work. Undoubtedly not every personality type is suited for this role, and even the right type of man needs proper training. But the opportunities for self-expression and for intellectual growth are considerable, and sociologists, in particular, should not be misled by the prevalent stereotype of administration.

I have now sketched out my main theme: empirical social research tends toward an organizational form of work which has two consequences: on an intellectual level, it forces one to be explicit about the work in hand. This, in turn, leads to a methodological awareness which radiates ideas into general fields of social inquiry. On an institutional level, institutes are, in themselves, a highly interesting innovation. They affect the organization and curriculum of departments of sociology, and they focus attention on the broader problem of what I have called the power vacuum in American universities.

This brings me to my last point. To what does all this empirical research add up? In a way, this is related to the main theme of this convention: "the uses of sociology." First, a reminder: until 1937 our annual meetings always had a central theme; then a resolution was adopted that because the field had become too diversified, this practice was no longer possible. By now, it would seem that diversification has reached such a point that the annual meetings should perhaps try to review common denominators, one by one. In any case, I used the feeble authority of the President and persuaded the Council that the problem of utilization is an urgent one. Actually, it would be better to talk of a utility spectrum. At the one end, you have the idea, most clearly represented by contemporary Soviet opinion, that the only justified use of social research is the advancement of social revolution. Having grown up in an exciting and constructive period of socialist optimism, I have never quite lost my hope for radical social change. But I do not believe that empirical social research of the type we are discussing tonight can contribute much to it.

At the other end of the spectrum, one finds utility in the narrowest sense. This includes studies for government agencies, for business firms, labor unions or other voluntary organizations which pay for them in the expectation that they will advance their purposes. But do they really help? As you know, we hope to publish the main contributions of this convention in a volume under some title such as "Applied Sociology." From watching the period of preparation for this program, I gather that a kind of curvilinear relation exists. The greatest difficulty in providing concrete examples comes at the two extremes of the utilization spectrum: the exponents of basic social change and the people who want guidance for immediate policy and action are most often disappointed.

Within this continuum many points could be singled out for discussion. Having little time left, I want to select two of them, one because the record of the past is impressive, and the other because the needs of the future are urgent.

Achievements and Hopes of Empirical Social Research

It has been said that the most sociologists can hope for at the moment are theories of the middle range. My colleague who coined this phrase gave his presidential address on multiple discoveries. So he will not mind if I report that fifty years ago, during the early phases of the Chicago school, the hope was expressed that their field studies would contribute to "intermediate scientific truth." And, indeed, empirical social research has proved most useful in serving this function.

Let me bring in at this point a final reminiscence. When I began to conduct studies of consumers as part of my Austrian program of research on choice, I often had to defend their scientific dignity. On one occasion, I pointed out that a series of such studies permitted important generalizations, and chose, as an example, the notion of the "proletarian consumer." Comparing him with his middle class counterpart, I described him as:

> ... less psychologically mobile, less active, more inhibited in his behavior. The radius of stores he considers for possible purchases is smaller. He buys more often at the same store. His food habits are more rigid and less subject to seasonal variations. As part of this reduction in effective scope the interest in other than the most essential details is lost; requirements in regard to quality, appearance and other features of merchandise are the less specific and frequent the more we deal with consumers from low social strata.

Notice that this is a summary of a large number of studies, no one of which, in its own right, is very interesting. But, together, they led to the notion of effective scope. This concept became subsequently useful in many ways—be it to distinguish between local and cosmopolitan roles, between lower and better educated social strata, or just between people whose radius of interests could be small or large. Stouffer's notion of relative deprivation was similarly developed from a variety of seemingly unconnected attitude surveys. Many other examples could be given to show the possible contributions of empirical studies, however narrow, to theories of the middle range. As a matter of fact, this is almost implied in the very idea of mediating between descriptive data and higher order generalizations. Inversely, there probably would not be much theory of the middle range without the steady supply of specific studies, a growing proportion of which comes from various social research institutes.

At another segment along the utility spectrum we meet the question whether major social improvements have been facilitated by the available techniques and the existing organizational forms of empirical social research. I do not refer to the continuous efforts to improve recognized trouble spots such as delinquency or racial discrimination. The issue is rather whether it is possible to do what Robert S. Lynd once called research for the future—studies which are generated by a sociological analysis of unrecognized social needs. We have tried for years to clarify this challenging idea at Columbia University. When Allen Barton became Director of the Bureau of Applied Social Research at Columbia, he put some order into our collective thinking by developing types of studies which would satisfy Lynd's criterion. Let me give you two examples from his list. One type can be called the investigation of *"positive deviant cases."* We take it for granted that certain types of situations usually take unfavorable turns. And yet sometimes exceptions occur: local or regional elections in which a good candidate wins in spite of the fact that his adversary has the power of the machine on his side; a really independent small town newspaper which survives in spite of opposition by the "interests"; a faculty successfully resisting infringements on academic freedom; escape of youngsters from temporary associations with criminal gangs. While the content of these examples varies from case to case, they all converge on the central task of finding generalizations centered on the problem of how to stem an undesirable social drift. It is muckraking in reverse.

Another type of study can be called the *pretesting of new social ideas*. A new notion of creative reform—especially if it has just been formulated—often needs studies to check on its assumptions and to perfect its design, partly to improve its feasibility and partly to facilitate its public acceptance. At the present moment, for example, it appears that structural unemployment can be solved only by a large-scale relocation of workers. The idea often meets great resistance from local commercial, church, and union interests. Some legislative aid for specialized re-training even precludes the use of federal funds for relocation. In addition, many workers themselves seem to resist relocation, although the extent and the relative weight and interconnection of all this is by no means known. Parallel to the need for pertinent sociological and psychological data, one must ask whether, from an economic and a technical point of view, it is easier to move people or to move factories.

The mere size of such studies might be enough to outgrow the capacity of a single research group. They require an interweaving of quantitative and qualitative technique, of simultaneous research on individual and organizational levels, together with some historical analysis. Furthermore, such inquiries are time consuming. But there is nothing prohibitive in itself about such an extension of current research practices. And yet the fact that it has not been done is by no means accidental. Having been director of an institute for some years, I cannot avoid a feeling of regret. It is a great temptation to undertake a study for which funds are available, on topics which require the kind of skills one has developed in one's staff, under sponsorship which promises continuity. My generation has had to worry a great deal about the mere survival of our organizations and their acceptance by university administrations. The new generation of directors, whom we have trained, work under better conditions. They should have the courage to strike out in the direction of some of the more complex areas that I have just tried to exemplify. I seriously hope that they will take the flames, and not the ashes, from the fires we have kindled.

As I come to the end of my remarks I become aware that the difficulty of writing a presidential address is equalled only by the prospect of leaving the rostrum and hearing one's friends say that it was all very interesting, but the main themes were not quite clear, that the examples might have been more pointed, the organization of the points was somewhat confusing.

It is a little like the case of the man who asks for a divorce and gives, as his reason, the fact that his wife talks and talks and talks. The judge asks what she talks about and the man replies: "Your honor, that's just the problem, she doesn't say." My sympathies to-night are naturally with the woman. There are situations where one wants to express ideas that can hardly be communicated to others who have not undergone comparable experience. I have done my best to say what I am talking about. It is my conviction that, as time goes on, a growing number of sociologists will meet the problems and situations to which I have been exposed. If some of them find that, in retrospect, my observations make sense and that, as they face a concrete decision, some of my suggestions prove of help, then the purpose of this address will have been achieved.

13

History of Social Research

Notes on the History of Quantification in Sociology: Trends, Sources, and Problems

Hermann Conring and German Universitätsstatistik

It is difficult to visualize intellectual life in Germany in the decades following the Thirty Years' War. The educated layman knows the connection between Locke and the Glorious Revolution; he is aware of the brilliance of the French theater when Louis XIV established his hegemony in Europe through a series of wars. But who remembers that at about the same time (1683) the imperial city of Vienna was beseiged by the Turks and saved in the nick of time by a Polish army—except, perhaps, if he has heard that this brought coffee to Europe and thus greatly affected the intellectual life of London?

The physical devastation of large parts of Germany at the time of the Westphalian Peace (1648) and the drastic decline in the population would lead one to expect a complete blackout of the mind. And yet, recovery had to come; and indeed, it did come, but it gave German intellectual activities a peculiar complexion. First of all, there was abject poverty. It is true that both Petty and Conring were involved in shady financial transactions, but the differing social contexts affected the scale of their misdeeds. Petty dealt in huge fortunes, while Conring's correspondence resounds with begging and waiting for a few gold pieces promised to him for some political service. In the two-score German universities, professors remained largely unpaid and the life of the students was at an all-time low. No middle class existed, no intellectual center, no national aristocracy which might have supported the work of artists and scientists. Whatever help there was had to come from the three hundred princes who ruled their ruined little countries with absolute power.

These princes were, by and large, all concerned with the same

Reprinted with editorial adaptations from "Notes on the History of Quantification in Sociology: Trends, Sources and Problems," *Isis* 52, no. 168 (1961): 277–333 [286–92].

problems. One was to maintain their independence against the Emperor whose power had been greatly weakened by the great war. At the same time, there was enough national feeling to make a possible invasion by France a common concern, especially in the western part of the realm. The relation between Catholics and Protestants, although formally settled by the peace treaty, was still very much in flux. And finally, the jealousies and battles for prestige between the various courts kept everyone on the move. This competition is especially relevant for my narrative. As one could expect in as many as three hundred principalities, there was a typical distribution of ability and culture among the rulers; for the better kinds, the advancement of knowledge and the improvement of government was a serious concern or at least an important competitive tool. It may sound somewhat strange to compare this situation with what happened in the Italian city states during the Renaissance. There was, of course, little money and probably less taste to build palaces, to paint murals, or to collect sculptures. But people were cheap. Therefore, if a man acquired some intellectual renown, several courts might bid for his services. The natural habitat for an intellectual was still the university corporation; so a relatively large number of small universities were created (and disappeared) according to the whims of some of the more enlightened rulers.

But again, what was expected from the learned doctors was colored by the peculiar situation. All in all, the critical German problem of the time was civic reconstruction. Problems of law and of administration had high priority. The competition between the principalities pressed in the same direction: the struggle over a little piece of territory; the question of which prince should have which function in imperial administration; questions of marriage and succession among ruling houses were discussed and settled in the light of precedent, and by the exegesis of historical records. International law started a few miles from everyone's house or place of business. No wonder then that it was a spirit of systematically cataloguing what existed, rather than the making of new discoveries that made for academic prestige. This, in turn, prolonged the life of the Scholastic and Aristotelian traditions which had dominated the medieval universities and by then had withered away in most other parts of Western Europe. In the second half of the 17th century, when English and French intellectuals wrote and taught in their own language, the form of communication among German academicians was still exclusively Latin, even in the numerous "position papers" they were asked to publish by the princes whom they served.

The life and work of Hermann Conring must be examined against this background. He was born in 1606 in Friesland, son of a Protestant pastor. His gifts were soon recognized and he was taken into the house of a professor at the University of Helmstaedt. This town belonged at the time to the Duchy of Brunswick which in turn was part of the general sphere of influence of the Hanoverian Duchy.[1] In 1625, Conring went to the University of Leyden, probably because his family still had many connections with the Netherlands from which they had originally come. (Four years before, Grotius, who was also a student at Leyden, had fled his native country because he had been involved on the liberal side of religious and political controversy.) The best source on Conring's study period in Holland is Moeller.[2] Conring stayed in Leyden for six years and was greatly attracted by the breadth of its intellectual life. He tried very hard to get a Dutch professorship, but did not succeed. So in 1631, he returned to Helmstaedt as professor of natural philosophy and remained there for the rest of his life.

From what we know about him today, we can conclude that he would undoubtedly have become a European figure like Grotius who was twenty years his elder and Leibnitz who was forty years his junior, if like them, he had spent part of his mature life outside Germany. I have no space here to document in detail what is known about Conring as a person. Instead, I shall briefly compare him with these two men with whom we are so much more familiar. Conring never met Grotius, but he came back to Helmstaedt imbued with his ideas. Whenever it was not too dangerous for him, he stood up for religious tolerance and if possible, for reunification of all Christian churches. In many respects the two men seem to have been similar, as may be seen, for example, from a character sketch of Grotius by Huizinga.[3] Huizinga described how Grotius was "permeated in every fiber with the essence of antiquity": that in his writings on public affairs he mixed contemporary cases and "examples from antiquity in order to give advice to his own day"; that his knowledge in all spheres of learning was so great that "the capacity and the alertness of the humanist memory has become almost inconceivable." Practically the same terms are used of Conring by his contemporaries and by the historians who tried to reconstruct his image from his very extensive correspondence. The only difference is one of morality. All authorities on Conring agree on his venality and servility, although some point out that this was characteristic of German academicians of the time.

Leibnitz and Conring had repeated personal contact. A brief summary of how this came about will bring the description of Conring's life one step further. From early in his Helmstaedt career, Conring lectured on politics although officially he was made professor of this subject only in 1650. One of his students was the young Baron J. C. Boineburg (1622–1672) who defended the dissertation he had written under Conring in 1643. A few years later, after having changed his religion, Boineburg entered the service of the Archbishop Elector of Mainz, who was one of the leading rulers of Germany in the period after the Westphalian Peace; and Boineburg became possibly the most prominent German statesman of the time. The crucial problem of the principalities in the Rhine area was how to contain the power of Louis XIV. The Mainz Elector changed his position, being first in favor of appeasement, and then in favor of organizing defensive alliances with Protestant countries. Boineburg remained an appeaser throughout his political career which brought him repeatedly into conflict with his own prince, but at the same time made him an important bridge between Germany and the West. Whenever he had to make a political decision, he turned to his old teacher for advice. Many times he asked Conring to write pamphlets on current issues to support a specific position. Boineburg was also very much concerned with the possibility of reunifying the Christian churches which, incidentally, was also Grotius' main interest towards the end of his life (1645). At one time, Boineburg suggested an exchange of statements by relatively conciliatory representatives of the Catholic and Protestant positions. Again, he called upon Conring who wrote a number of monographs from the Protestant point of view; the whole affair came to nothing. These "expert opinions," always based on extensive historical and legal research, are one of the sources of knowledge about Conring. An instructive and well organized inventory can be found in Felberg.[4]

At the same time that Boineburg turned to his teacher either for advice or for backing of his various political schemes, he was on the outlook for other intellectuals he could use for similar purposes. His attention was drawn to a young Saxonian who, at the age of 24, had written a treatise on "A New Method of Teaching Jurisprudence" (Methodus Nova), a work in which he wanted to apply to legal studies and research the same ideas which Bacon had sketched in his Novum Organum for the natural sciences. Boineburg prevailed upon Leibnitz to enter the service of the Elector of Mainz; he accepted, and remained in this position for ten years—from 1666 to 1676. Boineburg wanted to be sure of his judgment and sent Leibnitz' drafts to Conring.[5] The latter was not overly impressed, but Boineburg retained Leibnitz nonetheless. As a result, Leibnitz and Conring came into continuous contact with each other. Both were Protestants, and the one was directly, the other indirectly, attached to a Catholic court. Boineburg called on Conring for informal or formal expression of expert opinion. He used Leibnitz more as a personal representative. For four years, beginning in 1672, Leibnitz was Boineburg's representative in Paris, a stay which was interrupted only by a brief visit to London. This was the period in which Leibnitz made contacts with French and British academicians and laid the foundations for his international fame. The only return Conring got out of it was a small French pension for which he was expected to contribute to the fame of Louis XIV in his public writings.

Leibnitz never completely escaped Conring's shadow. When he moved to Hannover in 1676 to become court librarian, a position he held until the end of his life (1716), his administrative superior was a man who again had been a student of Conring.[6] Between Conring and Leibnitz an atmosphere of mutual respect and ambivalence prevailed. The former was probably jealous of the rising fame of this new, and last, German polyhistor. He may also have had the feeling that he had been born a few decades too early. When he was thirty, Germany was still in the middle of the great war, and the main problem of a German professor was to keep out of the hands of various occupying armies and to clothe and feed his family. When Leibnitz was thirty, the agent of a German statesman could make trips all over Europe and take active part in public affairs. By then, Conring was old; and while he was famous, his participation in the recovery period was restricted to the written word.

Conring's isolation during a crucial intellectual period may also explain a final disagreement between Conring and Leibnitz. By the middle of the 1670's, Leibnitz was already deeply involved in mathematical studies and his reputation in this field, however controversial, was at least as great as his reputation as a social scientist. Conring thoroughly disapproved of all such mathematical ideas and advised Leibnitz not to waste his time on them.[7] This blind spot in Conring cannot, however, completely be attributed to Conring's age. All in all, he seems to have had only a limited understanding of mathematical thinking. A careful and systematic compilation of everything which Conring wrote on population problems[8] shows that he had a static view of the problems involved. While interested in studying size and social structure of populations in relation to public policy, he had no conception of or interest in birth and death rates or any of the other dynamic ideas so characteristic of contemporary British political arithmeticians.[9] Whether further research could explain these blind spots, I cannot tell. One rather obvious root is Conring's continuous concern with Aristotle's writings. They were the topic of his dissertation; later, he published many commentaries on and new editions of Aristotle's political texts; his own work, which created the tradition of German university statistics, was deeply influenced by Aristotelian ideas. I feel it was necessary to sketch this general background before I could turn to this part of Conring's efforts.

Conring wants to bring order into the available knowledge about various countries. His purpose is explicitly threefold: he looks for a system which should make facts easier to remember, easier to teach, and easier to be used by men in the government. To this end it is necessary to have categories of description which are not accidental, but are deduced, step by step, from basic principles. His "model," as we would say today, is *the state as an acting unit*. The dominant categories are the four Aristotelian causae. His system is consequently organized under four aspects.

The state as an acting body has a goal or *causa finalis*. The second aspect is a *causa materialis* under which Conring subsumes the knowledge of people and of economic goods. The *causa formalis* is the constitution and the laws of a country. The *causa efficiens* is its concrete administration and the activities of its elite. Under each of these main categories, Conring systematically makes further subdivisions. The causa efficiens, for example, describes the concrete ways by which the state is governed. They are either principales or instrumentales. The former are the statesmen themselves; the latter are again subdivided into animatae (staff) and inanimatae. At the point where he has arrived at a "causa efficiens instrumentalis inanimata," his main example is money. And under this rubric he then develops elaborate monetary ideas which, I gather, were quite advanced for his time.

One should notice, behind this forbidding terminology, a number of very modern topics. Thus, contemporary social theory is much concerned with the goals (causa finalis) and subgoals of organizations, their possible conflict and the duty of the "peak coordinator" to attempt their integration. The distinction between causa formalis and efficiens corresponds almost textually to the distinction between formal and informal relations, which is fundamental for all modern organizational analysis. The many examples which Conring attaches to his definition can be gleaned from Zehrfeld.[10] And Conring does not stop at a merely descriptive presentation of his categories. He often adds what we would call today speculative "cross-tabulations." For example, consider his conjoining the causa formalis and the causa materialis: in a democracy, all people should be studied; in an aristocracy, knowledge of the elite is more relevant.

These ideas are first developed as a general system and then applied consistently to one country after another. Stress is laid on interstate comparisons. Conring's richest material pertains to Spain, which he still considered the leading European power. It would not be too difficult to reconstruct from his very extensive comments an "Anatomy of Spain." By comparing it with Petty's work on Ireland, one should get a better picture of the difference in style of thinking which distinguishes these two authors. Conring himself, incidentally, was very explicit about his method. He classifies the type of sources available to him and gives detailed criteria as to how to judge their reliability; he tries to separate his own work from that of the historian, the geographer, the lawyer, etc.; and again in the frame of Aristotelian logic, he discusses elaborately the kind of inferences which can be drawn from descriptive facts of rules of conduct for the responsible statesman.[11]

The first publication of Conring's on the "notitia rerum publicarum" were unauthorized notes by one of his students; the original manuscripts were published only after Conring's death. Soon, his students began to give the same course at other universities. Various compendia appeared, usually under a title such as "Collegium Political-statisticum." (It is controversial when and how the term "statistics" was introduced for this tradition.) By the beginning of the 18th century, the Conring system was taught all over Germany.[12] It had the advantage of being eminently teachable even by minor men, and gave an academic frame of reference to the training of civil servants, which remained a common problem to all the little German states up to the end of their existence in the Napoleonic era. Conring's political activities helped in the diffusion of his main idea. He spent some time in about ten other German principalities in his capacity as temporary advisor; it can be taken for granted and could probably be proven from a perusal of his correspondence that on such occasions he established academic contacts.[13]

In any case, when Achenwall was a student at various German universities in the years around 1740, he met a well-established tradition. He began to collect statistical information in the Conring sense and when in 1748 he received a call to Göttingen, he was prepared to make it the base of his main course. As a matter of fact, his inaugural lecture was a defense of the whole system against representatives of related disciplines who feared the competition with their own prerogatives. I have already mentioned that Achenwall's writing in German helped to focus attention upon his work. But the image of a "Göttingen school of statistics," which got abroad rather quickly, was much strengthened by an institutional factor.

Notes

1. It should be remembered that not long after the death of Conring in 1681, Hannover and Brandenburg were competing for top prestige in Germany. When the Brandenburg Elector acquired the title of Prussian King by a legal trick, the Hannoverian tried to balance this success by accepting somewhat reluctantly, the crown of England.

2. Ernst V. Moeller, *Hermann Conring* (Hannover: Ernst Geibel, 1915).

3. Johann Huizinga, *Men and Ideas* (New York: Meridian Books, 1959).

4. Paul Felberg, *Hermann Conring's Anteilam Politischen Leben Seiner Zeit* (Trier: Paulinus-Druckerei, 1931).

5. It is possible to trace all this in some detail in Guhrauer's biography of Leibnitz. (G. C. Guhrauer, *Gottfried Wilhelm Freiherr V. Leibnitz* [Breslau: Ferdinand Hirt's Verlag, 1846].) This two-volume book puts great emphasis on Leibnitz' personal contacts and either quotes directly from correspondence or gives at least references as to where further information can be found. It is, of course, written with Leibnitz as the central figure and therefore the many allusions to Conring are often brief. It should be worthwhile to follow up Guhrauer's references and to piece the picture together with Conring in mind. Among the monographs on Conring, I have not found one with this emphasis.

6. Guhrauer, *op. cit.,* p. 212.

7. Guhrauer, *op. cit.,* pp. 213f.

8. Reinold Zehrfeld, "Hermann Conring's Staatenkunde" in *Sozialwissenschaftliche Forschungen,* 1925, 5: 79ff.

9. As far as I know, political arithmetic is about the only topic of contemporary knowledge on which Leibnitz himself did not write. It is therefore well possible that Conring did not even know of the work of his English contemporaries. He was, however, informed on English developments in at least one other field; among his medical writings, I found mention of a treatise on Harvey's discovery of the circulation of blood (in addition to texts on skorbut, fractured skulls and iatrochemistry).

10. Zehrfeld, *op. cit.,* pp. 15ff.

11. Zehrfeld, *op. cit.,* pp. 46ff.

12. One day the history of universities should be rewritten from a social scientist's point of view. Stephen D'Irsay (*Histoire des Universités* [Paris: Auguste Picard, 1933]) is altogether too superficial, although his footnotes on sources are very valuable. Paulsen's "History of Academic Instruction in Germany" is a fine piece of analytical writing and contains much information on the period after the Thirty Years' War (Friedrich Paulsen, *Geschichte des Gelehrten Unterrichts* [Leipzig: Veit & Comp., 1919]). His main interest, however, is with the ups and downs of the classical studies and he pays less attention to the men and institutions relevant to my narrative.

13. Several princes gave him the title of "Personal Physician and States Counselor" which shows how the many facets of his reputation were fused. I do not discuss here the similar positions he held for a while in Denmark and in Sweden. There is evidence that in 1651 he hoped to move to Sweden permanently; but again nothing came of this effort to escape the small town atmosphere of Germany.

Max Weber and Empirical Social Research

Six times during his life Max Weber was closely involved in empirical social research. [One of the purposes of the present paper is] to provide a narrative description of what actually happened . . . .[1]

We use the term "empirical social research" in a way that has recently become conventional, to mean studies of a contemporary situation using various techniques, such as questionnaires, field observations, existing records, and generally giving priority to quantitative data, though without excluding case studies and other qualitative material. Obviously a historical study is also empirical research; it is merely for terminological convenience that we distinguish between these two types of inquiry.

Agricultural Labor

The first episode took place when Weber was about 27 years old. He was then a member of the *Verein für Sozialpolitik,* an association that had existed in Germany since 1872. Its core was a group of university professors who were worried about the growing antagonism of German workers, organized in socialist unions, toward the German state. On the one hand they wanted to impress upon industrialists the need for social reforms, and on the other hand they wanted to minimize the influence of Marxist thinking on the workers. To achieve these aims, they organized studies of social problems, such as the cost of living, taxes, tariffs, and so on, and they discussed their findings at annual meetings in which representatives of unions, industry, and government were invited to participate. The association's hope was that studies and discussions would lead to social legislation and what today we would call improved labor-management relations.[2]

Around 1890 the *Verein* launched an inquiry into conditions of rural labor in Germany. Somewhat more than 3,000 landowners received detailed questionnaires requiring a description of the situation within their particular areas; an astonishing 70 per cent replied. In addition, 600 questionnaries were sent to individuals who were believed to have a more general view of the topic. This specialist's questionnaire inquired into general trends rather than asking for specific description; approximately 50 per cent were completed and returned.

The custom of the association was to sort these replies by geo-

Reprinted from Paul F. Lazarsfeld and Anthony R. Oberschall, "Max Weber and Empirical Social Research," *American Sociological Review,* 30, no. 2 (1965): 185–99 [185–193].

graphic region and to ask members to volunteer in the analysis of each set. Weber undertook the report on Eastern Prussia. Publications on the report started in 1892. They were rather uniform in character: for one district after another there were voluminous tables on income, budgets, and so on; the reporters probably did most of the computations themselves. Weber's report (890 pages) contains about 120 pages of such descriptive tabulations. (7)[3] It is distinguished from the other summaries by one interesting feature: Weber was the only analyst from the *Verein* who compared his material with the results of earlier studies, to provide an historical perspective.

At the annual meeting of 1893, in Berlin, summaries of these detailed reports were submitted for discussion by the whole membership. (2) Instead of presenting the traditional resumé of his findings, Weber placed the political implications of his material in the foreground. He created a sensation by pointing out that, for economic reasons, East Prussian landowners imported Polish agricultural laborers, thereby endangering the German character and the national security of this frontier of the German Reich. Even when his emphasis was on the political implications of his data, however, Weber could not refrain from introducing some methodological considerations. The design of the study had been fixed before he took on the analysis, and he disagreed with several aspects of it. For example, he sharply criticized the fact that only landowners had been used as informants, a criticism in which he was joined by many others. He also objected to the content of the questionnaires, stating that the *Verein* had put too much emphasis on the material condition of the laborers, whereas "the problem which the condition of the rural laborers presents lies predominantly in the subjective area." By that he meant concretely that

[the question is not how high the income of the workers really is, but whether as a result of (the level of wages) an orderly economy is possible for the workers, whether he and his employer are satisfied according to their own subjective evaluation, or why they are not, what direction their wishes and aspirations are taking, for future development will depend upon these factors. (7, p. 5)]

A year later, in 1893, Weber conducted another survey of rural laborers on behalf of the Evangelical-Social Congress. A group of Protestant ministers had become aware that, to be successful in their missionary work among low-income groups, they needed to know more about the living conditions of these strata. A number of surveys resulted, one of them again concerned with the conditions of rural labor. By then Weber had become a kind of patron saint for people interested in empirical work. The research director of the ministers' organization solicited his advice, and Weber remained closely connected with the study.[4] He hesitated as to whether to send questionnaires to rural ministers or to doctors, but he decided on the ministers because the Congress had a central register of all parish ministers and because they might be better suited to report on psychological problems. About 1,000 questionnaires were returned, out of more than 10,000 sent out.

The ministers' questionnaire itself was not a radical departure from the 1891 *Verein* questionnaire. It was, however, much shorter, divided into meaningful units, and the questions were more precise. In the following pair of questions the shift toward precision, and the increased concern with psychological factors, are evident.

Verein, 1891. Questionnaire II, question 4:[5]
The relations of employer to the workers. Do patriarchical relationships still prevail in the good meaning of the word, that is paternal caretaking on the one side, and loyal attachment on the other? Is discipline becoming looser? Breaks in contract. Do the landowners take into account the greater self-consciousness of the workers, or do they miss the right tone in their dealings (with the workers)? What manner of punishment prevails?

Ministers' study, 1893. Part IVb, question 3:[6]
Are the relations between employer and employee patriarchical? That is, caretaking on the one side and attachment on the other? What do the employees say about their employers, about officials of the estates and the foreman? What punishment is given in cases of poor performance, does corporal punishment occur? fines? deductions from wages?

Weber omitted many questions on the forms of land-tenure and kept the section on the material and living conditions short. Instead he concentrated on social and occupational mobility, migratory labor, and the origin of the various peasant groups. Previous surveys had included questions on whether or not a laborer might get ahead; Weber was also interested in the social changes that mobility and migratory labor might bring about:

To what extent does emigration into foreign countries and movement into industrial regions take place? Single individuals or entire families? Are these the hard workers or the lazy ones? Are they changed in any way when they return and does the change have any effect upon the community?

In another innovation for this type of survey Weber tried to tap attitudes. After a series of questions on the living quarters of the laborers, he asks: "Do the workers put any value at all upon the condition of the tenements, and in what respect?" He also wanted to know the workers' attitudes toward non-traditional forms of work: "What is the people's outlook toward work in side-occupations such as sugar factories. . . . What is their outlook toward the introduction of machines?" Weber did not, on the other hand, include questions on the laborers' hopes and aspirations, or their satisfaction with their wages and general lot in life.

The ministers' replies were superior to the answers the *Verein* had received from the landowners. "A large part of the reports give a detailed account of how the data were obtained . . . ," Weber wrote. (1, p. 540) "These are systematic monographs that have an enduring value for cultural history." Weber was no better able than his contemporaries to find a suitable mode of analysis for the reports, and in 1893 he made a remark that might apply to all the surveys of this period (1, p. 540):

> . . . nonetheless we face all this material as a puzzle, for we have not so far been able to find a way in which it is to be worked over. He who has not collaborated in such a venture cannot draw a picture of the magnitude of such an undertaking. The authentic freshness of the accounts which the reader can enjoy in the original reports will mostly be lost.[7]

At this point Max Weber had concentrated in his methodological thinking on two problems: the correct choice of informants and the improvement of questionnaires. He was explicitly worried about analyzing what today we would call replies to open-ended questions, and he was still convinced that low-income people could not be interviewed directly because he assumed that they were unable to describe properly their own situation, and that the more advanced ones would be reluctant to supply information for an inquiry sponsored by a middle-class organization.

At about this point Weber's activities were interrupted by the onset of his mental illness, which lasted from 1897 to 1902. It was not until 1904, at the age of 40, that he resumed fully his scientific activities. In that year his study of the Protestant ethic appeared, and in that year also he participated in the World Congress of Arts and Sciences at St. Louis where the study of agricultural labor was a main topic for his report. In the next few years he engaged in two concurrent empirical research enterprises.

Industrial Labor

In 1907, at the suggestion of Weber's younger brother, Alfred, the association decided to undertake a series of studies on "Selection and Adjustment (Occupational Choice and Experience)" of workers in large industries. Weber's formulation of the two problems implicit in the title of the program is as follows:

> What is the effect of big industry on the personal characteristics, the occupational destiny and the private style of life of its workers; what physical and psychological qualities do they develop?
>
> To what extent is the potential and actual development of large industries determined by characteristics of the labor force rooted in its ethnic, social and cultural origins, its traditions and living conditions?

The investigations were to be based on data available in the offices of selected factories, on observations made by collaborators, and on direct interviews with workers. The association appointed a committee to direct the study. Max Weber was not a member; nonetheless (the reasons for this are unknown), he wrote the basic documents, which are now published in his *Gesammelte Aufsätze zur Soziologie und Sozialpolitik*. Included among these documents is a 60-page "methodological introduction" for the survey (3). In another context this would deserve detailed analysis, because it clarifies Weber's conception of the relation between economics and sociology, on the one hand, and between factual information and theory, on the other. For present purposes, special attention should be drawn to his emphasis on the need to investigate the workers' "subjective attitude" toward their work situation (pp. 53–56). He felt that if possible such information should be presented in tabular form.

In addition to this general rationale for the study, two research instruments were worked out, presumably also by Max Weber.[8] One is a 2,000-word "working plan" listing 27 topics to which the regional directors of the study should give special attention. It set forth the following instructions for the collaborators: They should start by describing the technological features of the factories under study. Then they should analyze the composition, geographic origin and work history of the labor force, the qualifications for work and difficulties in satisfying them, with special emphasis on recent changes. The third and largest set of problems is devoted to the activities of the worker in the factory: chances for advancement and for satisfying special work interests; experience with various wage systems; mobility; training facilities; effect of aging, etc. A final set of items refers to sociological problems: social distinctions among types of workers, degree of cohesion, features of daily life different from other population groups with similar income, aspirations for their children, etc.

Much of this information was to be obtained from experts or by participant observation. But attached to the general plan was a formal questionnaire containing 27 questions to be asked of workers in personal interviews. The questions pertained either to topics on which statistics were desired (such as occupation of parents and leisure time activities), or to topics on which it was assumed that only direct interrogation could provide information (such as reasons for occupational choice, goals in life, and so on).

Preoccupation with this enterprise gave rise to a very important fourth episode in the "quantitative life" of Max Weber. He himself carried out a detailed study of workers' productivity in a textile factory belonging to his wife's family. He obviously attached much importance to it. His report was published at once, and he later described how hard he had worked on it; he made endless computations himself "because only during the continuous and personal analysis of figures will the investigator hit upon those ideas which he needs to interpret his findings and to develop new problems."[9] The title of the paper is "Regarding the Psycho-Physical Aspects of Industrial Work" (4). Its starting point is that differential qualifications of various types of workers are obviously of interest to social scientists. Can they be measured? Does contemporary work in experimental psychology suggest ways of doing so? What other procedures could be used to answer such questions as: Are there innate abilities to work? Do they differ among various races? How are they affected by sex and age of the workers, their social origin, and so on?

The first hundred pages of the paper (Sections 1–5) are devoted to a detailed review of the existing literature, with special emphasis on the work of Weber's colleague, Kraepelin. He had published five volumes of papers, reporting laboratory experiments dealing with concepts which today are still part of the foundation of industrial psychology: learning curves, fatigue, monotony, effect of interruptions, etc.

In a sixth section on "methodological problems," Weber asks whether the results of laboratory studies, based mainly on paper-and-pencil tests, can be applied to the much more complex factory situation. He is doubtful and wishes that experiments on real working machines could be carried out. This he considers financially impossible, because such experiments would cost at least 20 dollars a day (sic! p. 119). So the next best thing is to look at records of piece-rate earnings and of production as they are kept in the natural course of industrial production. The next 120 pages are devoted to a secondary analysis of such data.

We have no space here to convey the brilliance of his procedure. He begins by looking for variations during the day, in the course of the week, and over longer periods. The findings are partly interpreted in terms of Kraepelin's psychological categories. In discussing individual variations, however, he introduces the workers' desire to influence the piece rate, the role of the rate booster, and the attitudes of organized workers and of pietistic women (Section 9). His analysis of marriage as a stabilizing influence is strikingly similar to Durkheim's interpretation of suicide rates, though the latter is not mentioned (Section 10). At one point he analyzes the behavior of a few workers who simultaneously attend two weaving machines which differ in regard to difficulty and to piece rate. He shows that after a period of trial and error the worker finds an optimum balance between effort and earning; his data and discussion could be directly translated today into a mathematical learning model (pp. 209–217). The monograph anticipates in every respect the modern approach to analyzing voting, radio listening, buying, or any other action performed by large numbers of people under comparable circumstances. Careful statistical analysis is used to deduce as many generalizations from the data as possible and to interpret them in the light of appropriate concepts already available or newly advanced for the purpose at hand.

At the association's Dresden meeting in 1911, the leading labor economist, Herkner, gave a summary of the factory survey, and another speaker reported additional productivity figures, using Weber's approach and corroborating his findings,[10] but Weber himself had by then completely withdrawn from both enterprises.[11] He seems not even to have remained in contact with the men who collected and analyzed the regional material for the factory studies: none of the authors referred to him in the published reports. At the general summary meeting of 1911 he was not included in the list of discussants that the chairman announced in advance, though in the end he did intervene at length. The leading German statistician, Bortkiewich, criticized politely but incisively various shortcomings in the studies.[12] Thereupon Weber got up, acknowledged some mistakes in the statistical procedures, and defended other procedures in considerable detail. But his general tone was one of skepticism. All other participants reiterated their admiration for the great importance of the studies, while Weber stressed his opinion that nothing much came of the whole affair. At best it resulted in a few hypotheses and the "high probability that, with the help of future material, after a long, long while valuable and crucial results might ensue."[13]

Counting the statistical analysis of productivity data and the planning of the labor survey as two concurrent but distinct ventures, we have now reported on four of Weber's encounters with empirical research. The last two added new elements to his self-education: the systematic use of statistical cross-tabulation and the conviction that direct interviews of low-income people are as desirable as reliance on informants.

The Study of Attitudes

A fifth episode is based on material collected by another person, Adolf Levenstein, who had an intense desire to present to the world the living thoughts and hopes of his fellow workers. For years before he hit upon the idea of a questionnaire survey he held weekly discussions with co-workers. Then, between 1907 and 1911 he sent out 8,000 questionnaires to three categories of workers—miners, steelworkers and textile workers—in eight industrial locations, 1,000 questionnaires intended for each location. He first sent a number of questionnaires to his many friends and contacts, then corresponded with those who returned questionnaires and sent them others to be distributed. He thus achieved a very high rate of return (63 per cent) which might have been higher still had not the socialist press condemned his undertaking midway through, for reasons that are not clear.

Levenstein at first published only essays and poems by some of his more literate friends and respondents. But he showed the questionnaires to some professors, including Max Weber, and they tried to persuade Levenstein to let some of their students collaborate in further analysis of the survey. After oral persuasion had failed Weber published a brief article in 1909—"On the Methodology of Social-Psychological Surveys and on Their Analysis" (5)—in which he publicly called on Levenstein to undertake a numerical analysis of his data, at the same time giving him advice on how to do it. Apparently this form of pressure was effective, though Levenstein did not follow all the advice and categorically refused to have his coding and tabulating checked by university students and professors.

The Levenstein questionnaire explored the workers' attitudes on all the burning questions of the day. Even though the questions were phrased in clumsy fashion, and sometimes quite different items were lumped together, they covered a wide range of the workers' motivations, satisfactions, aspirations, and general attitude toward their situation in life. The questionnaire was later divided by Levenstein into five sections for purposes of analysis. The first section contained background data such as name, age, occupation, marital status, number of children, income, manner of payment, and length of the work day. Weber in his critique (5) suggested that more background information was needed, such as place of birth, father's occupation, and a detailed job history. The second section dealt with such matters as fatigue, monotony, preference for piece rates or hourly wages, thoughts during work and other topics that were also important in the *Verein für Sozialpolitiks* study of factory workers. The second section ended with the loaded question number 20: "What depresses you most, the low level of pay, or that you are so dependent upon the employer, that you have such limited prospects to advance in life, that you have nothing to offer to your children?"[14] The third section dealt with hopes and wishes, preferred hours of work, what the worker would do if he had the spare time, what he would buy if he had the money, and what occupation he would choose given the opportunity. The remaining two sections were on cultural and political matters such as reading, political interests, and belief in God. Question number 25: "Do you go often into the forest? What do you think of when you lie on the ground, and everything is still and quiet all around?" which Weber thought "grotesque" actually turned out to be an interesting projective question for those who answered it.

Weber advised Levenstein on a number of technical points indicating that he had acquired an acute sensitivity to what one would today call the techniques of survey analysis. The most interesting aspects of this discussion concern the use of typologies. Levenstein classified his respondents into a number of types which he had conceived intuitively and for which gave no clear basis of classification. Weber was highly critical of this unsystematic approach and wanted him to adopt a more logical procedure. His thinking on the construction of empirical typologies was very modern, totally different from that associated with the controversial ideal types.

> Only after the material has been quantitatively exploited and various parts of it brought into relationship with each other, only then may one try to use this foundation as the basis for constructing types of proletarian mentality and awareness, formal as well as substantive types. . . . At any rate, one must approach this problem on the basis of numbers, that is to say, investigate differences in the frequency of certain styles of expression and of thought-orientation by age, income, and place of origin of the respon-

dents. Dubious cases should be excluded, while the indisputable ones, if that seems possible, should be brought together carefully into types (and also combinations of types and transitional types), all this, however, very carefully, and with constant re-examination of the original data. (5, p. 956)

This passage indicates that Weber favored a quantitative approach to the building of typologies from qualitative data. Moreover, his notion of arriving at the correct dimensions after constructing provisional "transitional" types and "combinations" of them, is in the spirit of contemporary typological procedures.

Levenstein's work may legitimately be considered one of the earliest efforts to study attitudes. But neither he nor Weber made explicit the idea that attitudes can be measured, that questionnaire materials can be combined so as to form variables along which people are classified. This brings us back once more to Weber's psycho-physical paper. In a few pages (4, pp. 132–136) Weber tried to make a threefold distinction that seemed to him as important as it was difficult for him to express clearly.

In the attempt to analyze causally the fluctuations in production, whether they be expressed in terms of piece-rate earnings, or "exactly" in terms of the figures established through the output-measuring registers, one has to take into account that several categories of components come into play, quite distinct in their manner of "being given" even though trespassing upon each other's boundaries.

At one extreme there are factors involving the rational actions of men, "workers who regulate their output according to plan for material reasons [i.e., gain]. . . . The 'maxims' which such purposeful regulation follows we can 'interpret pragmatically.' " At the other extreme are factors involving physiological and psychophysical changes which become visible only through their effect, a change in output, and which the workers experience as facilitating or impeding production, without even being aware of the mechanisms behind it. Weber cited as an example the Zeiss experiment of Abbe where the working day was reduced and production was slightly increased just in such an automatic, unconscious way, independent of the good will or ill will of the workers. Such factors can be "explained" by knowing the psychophysical laws derived from experiments. Between these two extremes are attitudes and frames of mind of which the workers are aware, but which they do not consciously experience as being related to a change in output. The researcher can make such factors psychologically "understandable" by reconstructing them introspectively.

Weber used the term *"Attitüde"* repeatedly in his essay, but he missed the idea that attitudes as variables could be cross-tabulated against behavioral items just as one did with external factors such as the amount of light and heat in a workroom. Obviously the matter was of considerable concern to him because he made a very clear terminological distinction in all his writings. If a worker was angry at his employer or disliked the wage system, this was an attitude. But as far as we can see, the term never appears in his historical writings. In Parsons's translation of *The Protestant Ethic,*[15] for example, the term "attitude" appears about 40 times in the translation, and the context makes its appearance seem quite natural in each case. Still, in none of these instances did Weber himself use the word; instead, he used a variety of other nouns: *Anschauung, Gesammtstimmung, Gesinnung, Art des Empfindens,* etc. He obviously felt that the action of historical persons or groups, as reconstructed from letters, recorded customs, and so on, should be described in a terminology different from what a "psychologist" uses when he studies living human beings. There is, indeed, an important methodological problem here. But Weber did not solve it, nor, as a matter of fact, did he even formulate it clearly.

Other Efforts

Weber's sixth and final empirical effort began in 1910 when he became secretary-treasurer of the newly formed German Sociological Society. From the first it was contemplated that this professional group undertake research itself. Weber outlined a project on the sociology of the press which he intended to direct (6). In his usual manner, he located the problem in its historical and comparative perspectives; he discussed the inner organization and the distribution of power in newspapers; and he also got down to asking some specific questions and suggesting concrete methods of investigation that resembled modern content analysis: "What type of reading do the newspapers accustom men to? . . . What kinds of mass beliefs and mass hopes are created and destroyed, what kinds of point of view?" (6, pp. 440–441). He suggested that the research begin by exploiting the content of the newspapers themselves:

> We shall have to start with measuring, in a pedestrian way, with the scissors and the compass, how the contents of the newspapers has quantita-

tively shifted in the course of the generation, between light literature and editorial, between editorial and news, between what is or is no longer [into the paper] as news. . . . And from these quantitative investigations we will have to move on to qualitative ones. We will have to pursue the style of presentation in the papers, how the same problems are treated inside and outside the papers, the apparent repression of emotional presentation. (6, p. 441)

Weber secured funds for a survey of the press. But in 1912 at the second meeting of the Sociological Society he announced that he was withdrawing as project director for personal reasons, and he could find no one to replace him.

Our narrative would not be complete if we did not stress a trend in Weber's writings which cannot be located neatly along a timeline but which certainly adds to the picture of his interest in quantification. We refer to his repeated use of the notion of probability, especially during the later part of his life.

In all the social sciences clarity about the nature of "disposition concepts" has developed only slowly. The pragmatists made the initial start by pointing out the importance of indicators. Thus, William James would say that a prudent man is one who looks before he jumps, buys insurance, etc. Slowly the notion of probability was introduced; the prudent man is *likely* to look before he jumps, etc. Finally it became clear that prudence is not an all-or-none matter—people have to be ranked according to this and other concepts in which we are interested. And various combinations of indicators provided the basis for this ranking.[16]

In 1895 Durkheim tried to write a Magna Charta for the new science of sociology. In his *Rules of Sociological Method* the central and reiterated proposition was that "social facts are to be treated as things." And when, in the introduction to the second edition, he wanted to defend his ideas against the words of his critics he sought to do so by sharpening his definitions:[17]

> Things include all objects of knowledge that cannot be conceived by mental activity, those that require for their conception data from outside the mind, from observations and experiments, those which are built up from the more external and immediately accessible characteristics to the less visible and more profound.

But Durkheim, like James, still thought of indicators as "all or nothing." One of the "corollaries" to his first rule is:

The subject matter of every sociological study should compromise a group of phenomena defined in advance by certain common external characteristics, and all phenomena so defined should be included within this group.[18]

From the context in which this is stated one can infer Durkheim's imagery. A "social milieu" would be characterized by certain indicators, *all* of which were necessary to establish its existence. Durkheim never faced the problem of what one should do if only *some* of the required indicators were present.

Weber, however, recognized the probabilistic nature of indicators, and he expressed this in his sociological concepts. Passages like the following occur frequently:[19]

. . . it is only the existence of the probability that a certain type of action will take place which constitutes the "existence" of friendship. Thus that a *friendship exists* or has existed *means this and only this:* that we, the observers, judge that there is or has been a probability that on the basis of known subjective attitudes of certain individuals there will result in the average sense a certain specific type of action.

Weber specifically stresses that only in such probabilistic terms can the meaning of social relationships be caught. They cease to exist, he says, "whenever there is no longer a probability that certain kinds of meaningfully oriented social action will take place." Elsewhere he defines power as the *probability* that a person is "in a position to carry out his own will despite resistance" or that a command will be obeyed "by a given group of people."[20]

And yet, one final problem Weber did not face. What if a variety of indicators do not behave in the same way? For instance, mutual support in emergencies might be more "essential" for friendship than similar tastes in food. "Certain commands" can apply to a variety of topics: some of them, if not obeyed, might show that "imperative control" is not present; others might be flaunted with various degrees of frequency without undermining the control structure. And what is more serious: if we have data on such a set of indicators, how do we combine them—if combining be desirable—into one index that would permit us to order classes of friendships and to distinguish degrees of authority?[21]

In a way Weber's failure on this point also kept him from full clarity on the nature of attitude measurement. It should be recalled, however, that his systematic work was interrupted by the beginning of the world war in 1914, and that between the end of the war and 1920, when he died, events in Germany made scientific work especially difficult. Without the war's interruption, Weber's increasing clarity on the nature of empirical social research might very well have led him to a level of comprehension the field as a whole did not begin to develop until the late 1920's.[22]

Notes

1. We assume that the reader is acquainted with the main facts of Weber's life. A good summary can be found in the foreword in Hans H. Gerth and C. Wright Mills, *From Max Weber: Essays in Sociology,* New York: Oxford University Press, 1946. Reinhard Bendix provides a brief sketch in his *Max Weber: An Intellectual Portrait,* New York: Doubleday Anchor Books, 1962. The book was written by his wife, Marianne Weber (*Max Weber, Ein Lebensibild,* Tübingen: J. C. B. Mohr, 1926) contains the largest number of details, though of course her story is colored by her personal attitude toward Weber.

2. We shall refer to this organization as the "association" or "the *Verein.*" It published a long series of monographs, and its history was written in 1938 as the last publication after its dissolution by Hitler: (Franz Boese, *Geschichte des Vereins für Sozialpolitik,* Berlin: Duncker und Humbolt, 1939.) Nominally, the association was revived and its publications continued after the second World War.

3. The publications by Max Weber on which this essay is based are listed below. Numbers in parentheses will be used in the text to refer to this list. So far as we know, none of these sources has been translated from German.

4. Unfortunately, most of the literature on this survey is in periodicals, newspapers, or reports of the Evangelical-Social Congress which are not available in the U.S. The discussion will be based mainly on a six-page newspaper article written by Weber in 1893 (1).

5. The *Verein* questionnaire is printed in *Schriften des Vereins für Sozialpolitik,* Vol. 53 (1891), pp. 14–24.

6. The 1893 questionnaire is partially reproduced in Eugen Katz, "Landarbeiter und Landwirtschaft in Oberhessen," *Münchner Volkswirtschaftliche,* Studien 64 (1904). Katz used an abbreviated form of this questionnaire in a small study of his own conducted in 1901–02.

7. A few years later Weber conducted a seminar in Heidelberg in which students used the questionnaires for their dissertation; but these too lacked a novel mode of analysis. The typical procedure was that each student chose one province or region and wrote a brief 50-page essay, faithfully following the topics outlined in the questionnaire. No attempt was made to quantify the questions on social relations and intellectual needs through coding of answers or any other method. Starting in 1899 Weber published these essays in a series entitled *Die Landarbeiter in den evangelischen Gebieten Norddeutschlands,* Tübingen: H. Laupp, 1899–1902. Unfortunately, Weber's own 11-page introduction to the series was not accessible to us.

8. *Schriften des Vereins für Sozialpolitik,* Vol. 133, preface.

9. *Ibid.,* Vol. 138 (1911).

10. *Ibid.,* Vol. 138 (1911), pp. 139ff.

11. There is one reference to the psycho-physical paper in a later edition of the *Protestant Ethic,* and, conversely, in section 9 of the paper there is a reference to "the larger context in which I have tried to analyze these things elsewhere" (4, p. 162).

12. In discussing the occupational choices made by women, Bortkiewich pointed out that really two questions are in order: Why do they work at all? Why in a specific occupation?

13. *Schriften des Vereins für Sozialpolitik,* Vol. 138 (1911), p. 190.

14. A similarly loaded pair of questions appeared in a questionnaire distributed by Karl Marx in 1888: "In case of accident, is the employer obliged by law to pay compensation to the worker or his family? If not, has he ever paid compensation to those who have met with an accident while working to enrich him?"

15. Max Weber, *The Protestant Ethic and the Spirit of Capitalism* (trans. by Talcott Parsons), New York: Charles Scribner's Sons, 1958.

16. For a general discussion of disposition concepts see Carl Hempel, *Concept Formation,* Chicago: University of Chicago Press, 1948. For a brief review of their history in psychology see Paul F. Lazarsfeld, "Latent Structure Analysis," in Sigmund Koch (ed.), *Psychology: A Study of a Science,* New York: McGraw-Hill, 1959, Vol. 3.

17. Emile Durkheim, *Rules of Sociological Method* (trans. and ed. by George E. G. Catlin), Chicago: University of Chicago Press, 1938, p. xliii.

18. *Ibid.,* p. 35.

19. *The Theory of Social Economic Organization* (trans. and ed. by Talcott Parsons and A. M. Henderson), New York: Oxford University Press, 1947, p. 119 (italics ours).

20. *Ibid.,* p. 152.

21. Actually Weber was not quite consistent in his use of probability notions. He defined a bureaucratic organization by a set of criteria, including hierarchy, separation of professional and personal obligations, separation of membership from ownership of the tools of work, etc. He defined as "ideal-typical" those organizations which satisfied all the criteria. But what about those which satisfied only a proportion of them? Carl J. Friedrich, in a critique, correctly pointed out that omission of an answer to this question precluded empirical study of concrete organizations. He wanted to compare bureaucracies in various countries. He had to use Weber's criteria—or similar ones—as "measuring rods for determining the degree of bureaucratization"; he needed "the judgment of more or less." See his "Some Observations on Weber's Analysis of Bureaucracy," in Robert K. Merton, *et al.* (eds.), *Reader in Bureaucracy,* Glencoe, Ill.: Free Press, 1957, p. 27, and Weber's "The Essentials of Bureaucratic Organization," *ibid.,* pp. 18ff.

22. Weber was well acquainted with contemporary writing on probability theory, as is evident in the footnotes to his paper "Objective Possibility and Adequate Causation in Historical Explanation," in *The Methodology of the Social Sciences* (trans. and ed. by Edward A. Shils and Henry A. Finch), Glencoe, Ill.: Free Press, 1949, pp. 167ff.

Untranslated Papers by Max Weber on Which This Essay Is Based

(1) "Die Erhebungen des Evangelisch-Sozialen Kongresses über die Verhältnisse der Landarbeiter Deutschlands," in *Christliche Welt* (1893), pp. 535–540.

(2) "Referat: die ländliche Arbeitsverfassung," in *Verhandlungen von 1893* (Vol. 58 of *Schriften des Vereins für Sozialpolitik*), pp. 62–86.

(3) "Erhebungen über Anpassung und Auslese (Berufswahl und Berufsschicksal) der Arbeiterschaft der geschlossenen Gross Industrie," in *Gesammelte Aufsätze zur Soziologie und Sozialpolitik,* Tübingen: Mohr, 1924, pp. 1–60.

(4) "Zur Psychophysik der industriellen Arbeit," in *Gesammelte Aufsätze zur Soziologie und Sozialpolitik,* Tübingen: Mohr, 1924, pp. 61–225.

(5) "Zur Methodik Sozialpsychologischer Enqueten und ihrer Bearbeitung," in *Archiv* 29 (1909), pp. 949–958.

(6) "Geschäftsbericht der Deutschen Gesellschaft für Soziologie," in *Schriften der Deutschen Gesellschaft für Soziologie I* (1911), pp. 39–62.

(7) *Die Verhältnisse der Landarbeiter im Osterlbischen Deutschland* (Vol. 55 of *Schriften des Vereins für Sozialpolitik*), Berlin: Duncker und Humbolt, 1892.

The Writings of Paul F. Lazarsfeld

This bibliography, which aims at exhaustivity with the exception of the unpublished materials and of the forewords, consists of a chronological listing of Paul F. Lazarsfeld's writings, books, articles, and his research reports for the Bureau of Applied Social Research (the BASR's reports, originally in mimeographed form, were published in microfiche by Clearwater Publishing in 1979). It is based mainly on two earlier compilations: a bibliography compiled by Lazarsfeld himself for my edition of his selected writings, published in France under the title *Philosophie des Sciences Sociales* (Paris: Gallimard, 1970); and for his later work and for unpublished materials, the *Guide to the Bureau of Applied Social Research*, edited by Judith S. Barton (New York: Clearwater Publishing, 1984). The topical bibliography compiled by Paul M. Neurath and published in *Qualitative and Quantitative Social Research: Papers in Honor of P. F. Lazarsfeld*, edited by R. K. Merton, J. S. Coleman, and P. H. Rossi (New York: Free Press, MacMillan, 1979), will also be consulted with profit.

1920

"Heilpädagogische Gruppierung in einer Anstalt für verwarloste Kinder." *Zeitschrift für Kinderheilkunde* 27.

1923

"Die sozialistische Erziehung und das Gemeinschaftsleben der Jugend." *Die Sozialistische Erziehung* 3, no. 8 (August): 191–94.

1924

with L. Wagner. *Gemeinschaftserziehung durch Erziehungsgemeinschaften: Bericht über einen Beitrag der Jungendbewegung zur Sozialpädagogik.* Leipzig: Anzengruber.

1925

"Über die Berechnung der Perihelbewegung des Merkur aus der Einsteinschen Gravitationstheorie." *Zeitschrift für Physik* 35, no. 2: 119–28.

1927

a. "Die Berufspläne der Wiener Maturanten." *Mitteilungen aus Statistik und Verwaltung der Stadt Wien,* pp. 21–25.
b. "Marxismus und Individual-Psychologie." *Die Sozialistische Erziehung* 7 (May): 89–101.
c. "DINTA (Deutsches Institüt für Technische Arbeitschulung)." *Arbeit und Wirtschaft* 5, no. 11 (June): 437–40.
d. "Ergebnis der de Man Debatte." *Arbeit und Wirtschaft* 5, no. 16 (August): 684–90.
e. "Die Psychologie in Hendrik de Man's Marxkritik." *Der Kampf* 20: 270–75.

1928

a. "Die Berufspläne der Wiener Maturanten des Jahres 1928." *Mitteilungen aus Statistik und Verwaltung der Stadt Wien,* pp. 311–15.
b. "Anhang: Zur Normierung Entwicklungspsychologischer Daten." *Zeitschrift für Psychologie* 107: 237–53.
c. *On Choosing an Occupation.* Berlin: S. Fischer.

1929

a. "Der Anwendungsbereich der Ruppschen Koeffizienten." *Psychotechnische Zeitschrift* 4: 9–15.
b. *Statistiches Praktikum für Psychologen und Lehrer.* Jena: G. Fischer.
c. "Hinter den Kulissen der Schule." In *Technik der Erziehung,* edited by Sofie Lazarsfeld, pp. 212–36. Leipzig: Hirzel.
d. "Körperliche und geistige Entwicklung." *Die Quelle* 9: 803–9.
e. "Die Bedeutung der normalen Verteidigung für die Leistungsmessung." *Psychotechnische Zeitschrift* 4: 104–7.
f. with Karl Reininger and Marie Jahoda. "Das Weltbild des Jugendlichen." In *Technik der Erziehung,* edited by Sofie Lazarsfeld, pp. 94–104. Leipzig: Hirzel.

1930

a. "Die Bedeutung der normalen Verteidigung für die Leistungsmessung." *Ber. den XI. Kongress für experimentelle Psychologie,* pp. 108–11.
b. *Six Papers on Statistical and Educational Psychology.* Berlin: S. Fischer.

1931

a. *Umgang mit Zahlen.* Vienna: Psychologisches Institut.
b. with contributions from C. Bühler, B. Biegeleisen, H. Hetzer, and K. Reininger. *Jugend und Beruf: Kritik und Materials.* Jena: G. Fischer.
c. with R. J. Cone. "Der Einfluss der Interessen auf die Wahrnehmung." Typescript. 93 pp.

1932

a. "Die Kontingentzmethode in der Psychologie—Zur Erinnerung an Wilhelm Betz." *Zeitschrift für angewandte Psychologie* 41, nos. 1–3: 160–66.
b. "Neue Wege der Marktforschung." *Mitteilungen der Industrie und Handels Kammer zu Berlin,* October 25. 4 pp.
c. "Marktuntersuchungen auf Psychologischer Grundlage." *Mitteilungen der Gesellschaft für Organisation,* pp. 127–28.
d. "Jugend und Beruf." *Ber. Kongr. disch. Ges. Psychol.* 12: 379–82.

1932–33

"An Unemployed Village." *Character and Personality,* no. 1: 147–51.

1933

a. *Der Milchverbrauch in Berlin.* Gutachten der Wirtschaftspsychologischen Forschungsstelle. Berlin: Milchversorgungsverband.
b. with Marie Jahoda and Hans Zeisel. *Die Arbeitslosen von Marienthal: Ein Soziographisher Versuch über die Wirkungen langdauern der Arbeitslosigkeit.* Leipzig: Hirzel. 2d ed., with a new preface by Lazarsfeld. Allensbach and Bonn: Verlag für Demoskopie, 1960. American edition. *Marienthal: The Sociography of an Unemployed Community.* Chicago: Aldine-Atherton, 1971.

1934

a. "The Psychological Aspect of Market Research." *Harvard Business Review* 12 (October): 54–71.
b. "Die NRA und der Konsument." *Der Oesterreichiche Volkswirt* 26, no. 22 (February): 479–82.

c. with D. R. Graig. "Some Measurement of the Acceptance and Rejection of Rayon by Pittsburgh Women: An Experimental Study of 800 Women." American Society for Testing Materials. 30 pp.

1935

a. "The Art of Asking Why." *National Marketing Review* 1, no. 1 (Summer): 32–43.
b. "The Factor of Age in Consumption." *Market Research* 3: 13–16.
c. with Arthur W. Kornhauser. "The Techniques of Market Research from the Standpoint of a Psychologist." *Institute of Management,* series 16. New York: American Management Association.
d. with B. Zawadski. "Psychological Consequences of Unemployment." *Journal of Social Psychology* 6: 224–51.
e. with various coauthors. "A Study of the Psychological Factors Influencing the Drinking of Plain Milk by Adults." Report to the Milk Research Council, Inc., by the Psychological Corporation of New York. 71 pp.

1936

a. "Public Attitude toward Economic Problems." *Market Research* 5, no. 2 (August): 13–15.
b. "How Cities Differ in Their Magazine Reading Habits." *Sales Management* 38 (February 15): 218–20, 262.
c. "Factors Influencing Length of Unemployment as Found in the Occupation: Characteristics Survey." Typescript. 40 pp.
d. with E. Fisher Brown. "Dislike of Milk among Young People and Development of a Method to Measure and Analyse This Dislike: A Psychological Study." Milk Research Council, Inc., and the University of Newark Research Center. 63 pp.
e. with Kaethe Leichter. "Erhebung bei Jugendlichen Autorität und Familie." In *Studien über Autorität und Familie,* edited by Max Horkheimer, pp. 353–415. Paris: Alcan.

1937

a. [1935] "The Outlook for Testing Effectiveness in Advertising." *Management Review* 25, no. 1 (January): 3–12.
b. Four essays on psychological techniques in marketing research in *The Technique of Marketing Research,* edited by Ferdinand C. Wheeler, Louis Bader, and J. George Frederick, chaps. 3, 4, 11, 15. New York: McGraw-Hill.

c. "The Study of Job Hunting." Report to the Eastern Psychological Association. National Youth Administration (NYA).
d. "Logical Analysis of Unemployment Indices." Paper presented to the American Sociological Society, Atlantic City. 19 pp.
e. "Coming of Age in Essex County: An Analysis of 10,000 Interviews with Persons 16–24 Years Old." Office of Essex County Superintendent and the University of Newark Research Center. 126 pp.
f. "Some Remarks on Typological Procedures in Social Research." *Zeitschrift für Sozialforschung* 6, no. 1: 119–39.
g. "The Use of Detailed Interviews in Market Research." *Journal of Marketing* 2 (July): 3–8.
h. with David Craig. "Purchase of Gasoline and Oil." *Market Research* 6.
i. with R. Ripin. "Tactile Kinaesthetic Perception of Fabrics with Emphasis on Their Relative Pleasantness." *Journal of Applied Psychology* 21, no. 2: 198–224.
j. with Samuel A. Stouffer. "Research Memorandum on the Family in the Depression." *Social Science Research Council Bulletin* 29. Reprint, New York: Arno Press, 1972.
k. with Rowena Wyant. "Magazines in 90 Cities—Who Reads What?" *Public Opinion Quarterly* 1, no. 4 (October): 29–41.

1938

a. with E. F. Brown. "Milk Drinking Habits of Young People: A Psychological Study." Milk Research Council, Inc., and the University of Newark Research Center. 100 pp.
b. with P. Eisenberg. "The Psychological Effects of Unemployment." *Psychological Bulletin* 35: 358–88.
c. with Marjorie Fiske. "The 'Panel' as a New Tool for Measuring Opinion." *Public Opinion Quarterly* 2, no. 4 (October): 596–613.

1939

a. "The Change of Opinion during a Political Discussion." *Journal of Applied Psychology* 23, no. 1 (February): 131–47.
b. "Interchangeability of Indices in the Measurement of Economic Influences." *Journal of Applied Psychology* 23, no. 1 (February): 33–45.
c. "Radio Research and Applied Psychology." *Journal of Applied Psychology* 23, no. 1 (February): 1–7.
d. [Elias Smith, pseud.] "A Difficulty in the Feature-Analysis of a Radio Program." *Journal of Applied Psychology,* 23 no. 1 (February): 57–60.
e. [Elias Smith, pseud.] with Ollry Francis. "An Index of 'Radio-Mindedness' and Some Applications." *Journal of Applied Psychology,* 23, no. 1 (February): 8–18.

1940

a. "American Station Sampler and How to Use It." BASR. 6 pp.
b. "Description of Discerning." In *The Unemployed Man and His Family,* edited by Mirra Komarovsky, pp. 135–46. New York: Dryden Press.
c. "Progress in Radio Research: Introduction by the Guest Editor." *Journal of Applied Psychology* 24, no. 6 (December): 661–64.
d. "'Panel' Studies." *Public Opinion Quarterly* 4, no. 1 (March): 122–28.
e. "The Use of Mail Questionnaires to Ascertain the Relative Popularity of Network Stations in Family Listening Surveys." *Journal of Applied Psychology* 24, no. 6 (December): 802–16.
f. "Studies in the Change of Political Opinions." *Psychological Bulletin* 37: 460.
g. [ed.] *Radio and the Printed Page: An Introduction to the Study of Radio and Its Role in the Communication of Ideas.* Contributions by Samuel A. Stouffer and staff members of the Office of Radio Research. New York: Duell, Sloan and Pearce. Reprint, New York: Arno Press, 1971.
h. with Marjorie Fleiss. "Progress Report on the Development of a Spending Test." BASR. 53 pp.
i. with Marjorie Fleiss. "The Age Stratification of Department Store Customers as a Basis for a Policy Decision." BASR.
j. with William S. Robinson. "The Quantification of Case Studies." *Journal of Applied Psychology* 24, no. 6 (December): 817–25.
k. with William S. Robinson. "Some Properties of the Trichotomy 'Like, No Opinion, Dislike' and Their Psychological Interpretation." *Sociometry* 3, no. 2: 151–78.
l. with Hans Zeisel. "A Study of Giving to Federation." BASR. 68 pp.
m. [Elias Smith, pseud.] with Edward A. Schuman. "Do People Know Why They Buy?" *Journal of Applied Psychology* 24, no. 6 (December): 673–84.

1941

a. "Reports to Curtis Publishing Company." BASR. 77 pp.
b. "General Statistical Analysis of Joint Newspaper-Radio Ownership." BASR. 35 pp.
c. "Joint Ownership of Radio Stations and Newspapers in 1-1 Communities: A Statistical Analysis." BASR. 34 pp.
d. "Audience Building in Educational Broadcasting." *Journal of Educational Sociology* 14, no. 9 (May): 533–41.
e. "Evaluating the Effectiveness of Advertising by Direct Interviews." *Journal of Consulting Psychology* 5 (July/August): 170–78.
f. "Remarks on Administrative and Critical Communications Research." *Studies in Philosophy and Social Science* 9, no. 1: 2–16. New York: Institute of Social Research.

g. "Repeated Interviews as a Tool for Studying Changes in Opinion and Their Causes." *American Statistical Association Bulletin* 2 (January): 3–7.

h. "Some Notes on the Relationship between Radio and the Press." *Journalism Quarterly* 18, no. 1 (March): 10–13.

i. "Studying the Effect of Radio." *Transactions of the New York Academy of Sciences,* series 2, 3, no. 5 (March): 126–29.

j. with M. Bayne and Edward A. Schuman. "Use of Government Officials Concerned with Broadcasting." BASR. 60 pp.

k. with Hazel Gaudet. "Who Gets a Job." *Sociometry* 4: 64–77.

l. with Edward A. Schuman. "Initial Report on an Exploratory Study of Coverage by American Radio Stations." BASR. 6 pp. plus charts.

m. edited with Frank M. Stanton. *Radio Research, 1941.* New York: Duell, Sloan and Pearce. Reprint, New York: Arno Press, 1979.

1942

a. "The Daytime Serial as a Social, Commercial, and Research Problem." BASR. 51 pp.

b. "What We Really Know about Daytime Serials." Notes of a talk delivered on "The Pulse of New York," October 21, pp. 3–14. New York: Columbia Broadcasting System.

c. "Should She Have Music?" BASR. 40 pp.

d. "Magazine Reading before and after Pearl Harbor: Report to the Office of War Information." BASR. 22 pp.

e. "The Daily Newspaper and Its Competitors." *Annals of the American Academy of Political and Social Science* 219 (January): 32–43.

f. "The Effects of Radio on Public Opinion." In *Radio and Film in a Democracy,* edited by Douglas Waples, pp. 66–78. Chicago: University of Chicago Press.

g. "Statistical Analysis of Reasons as Research Operation." *Sociometry* 5, no. 1 (February): 29–47.

h. with Ruth Durant. "National Morale, Social Cleavage, and Political Allegiance." *Journalism Quarterly* 19, no. 2 (June): 150–58.

i. with Herman S. Hettinger. "Are Newspaper Stations Different from Others?" *Testimony and Analysis of Certain Exhibits before the Federal Communications Commission* (April), pp. 3–11. New York: Newspaper Radio Committee.

1943

a. with Raymond Franzen. *Solution of the Selection of the Best Combination of Dichotomous Arrangements to Distinguish a Categorical Criterion.* Washington: Civil Aeronautics Administration. Report 12, pp. 19–24.

b. with Robert K. Merton. "Studies in Radio and Film Propaganda." *Transactions of the New York Academy of Sciences* 6, no. 2 (November 22): 58–79.

1944

a. "On the Postwar Future of Radio." Typescript. 16 pp.
b. "The Controversy over Detailed Interviews: An Offer for Negotiation." *Public Opinion Quarterly* 8, no. 1 (Spring): 38–60.
c. "The Election Is Over." *Public Opinion Quarterly* 8, no. 3 (Fall): 317–30.
d. with others. "Polls, Propaganda, and Politics." *The Nation*. A series of articles appearing from August 12 through November 4. 28 pp.
e. with Bernard Berelson and Hazel Gaudet. *The People's Choice: How the Voter Makes Up His Mind in a Presidential Campaign.* New York: Duell, Sloan and Pearce. 2d ed., New York: Columbia University Press, 1948. 3d ed., New York: Columbia University Press, 1968.
f. with R. Franzen and T. Ehrlich. "Sampling Procedures for Measurement of Station Coverage." BASR. 87 pp.
g. with Robert K. Merton. "The Psychological Analysis of Propaganda." *Proceedings of Writers' Congress Conference,* pp. 362–80. Berkeley and Los Angeles: University of California Press.
h. edited with Frank M. Stanton. *Radio Research, 1942–43.* New York: Duell, Sloan and Pearce. Reprint, New York: Arno Press, 1979.

1945

a. "CBS Study." BASR. 48 pp.
b. "Who Influences Whom—It's the Same for Politics and Advertising." *Printer's Ink* 211, no. 10 (June 8): 32–36.
c. "Research Problems in the Field of Public Relations." *Public Relations Directory and Yearbook* 1: 93–95.
d. with Bernard Berelson. "Women: A Major Problem for the PAC." *Public Opinion Quarterly* 9, no. 1 (Spring): 79–82.
e. with Marjorie Fiske. "The Columbia Office of Radio Research." In *How to Conduct Consumer and Opinion Research,* edited by Albert Blankenship, pp. 137–50. New York: Harper and Brothers. Also *Hollywood Quarterly* 1, no. 1 (October): 51–59.
f. with Marjorie Fiske. "The Office of Radio Research: A Division of the Bureau of Applied Social Research, Columbia University." *Educational and Psychological Measurement* 5, no. 4 (Winter): 351–69.
g. with Raymond Franzen. "Mail Questionnaire as a Research Problem." *Journal of Psychology* 20: 293–310.

h. with Raymond Franzen. "Prediction of Political Behavior in America." *American Sociological Review* 10, no. 2: 261–73.

i. with Raymond Franzen. *The Validity of Mail Questionnaires in Upper Income Groups.* Time, Inc., Research Report no. 940, October 1. 6 pp.

j. with Patricia Kendall. "The Listener Talks Back." In *Radio in Health and Education,* pp. 48–65. New York Academy of Medicine. New York: Columbia University Press.

k. with Geneviève Knupfer. "Communications Research and International Cooperation." In *The Science of Man in the World Crisis,* edited by Ralph Linton, pp. 465–95. New York: Columbia University Press.

l. with Helen Schneider. "The Social Psychology of the Morning Radio Audience." BASR. 107 pp.

1945–46

with Patricia J. Salter. "Problems and Techniques of Magazine Research." *Magazine World,* August 1945–June 1946 (12 articles). 39 pp.

1946

a. "Radio and International Cooperation as a Problem for Psychological Research." *Journal of Consulting Psychology* 10, no. 1 (January/February): 51–56.

b. with Harry Field. *The People Look at Radio.* Chapel Hill: University of North Carolina Press. Reprint, New York: Arno Press, 1980.

1947

a. "Latent Attribute Analysis." Paper presented to the American Sociological Society. Atlantic City.

b. "Audience Research in the Movie Field." *Annals of the American Academy of Political and Social Science* 254 (November): 160–68.

c. "Some Remarks on the Role of Mass Media in So-Called Tolerance Propaganda." *Journal of Social Issues* 3, no. 3 (Summer): 17–25.

d. "Factor Analyses of Qualitative Attributes." *American Psychologist* 2: 306.

e. with Thelma Ehrlich. "Experiment with Two Methods of Measuring Magazine Readership." BASR. 65 pp.

f. with Geneviève Knupfer. "Portrait of the Underdog." *Public Opinion Quarterly* 11, no. 1 (Spring): 103–14.

1948

a. "The Role of Criticism in the Management of Mass Media." *Journalism Quarterly* 25, no. 2 (June): 115–26.
b. "The Use of Panels in Social Research." *Proceedings of the American Philosophical Society* 92, no. 5: 405–10.
c. Review of *Public Opinion and Propaganda,* by Leonard Doob. *Public Opinion Quarterly* 12, no. 3 (Fall): 496–98.
d. "What Is Sociology?" Oslo: Skrivemaskinstua Universitets Studentkontor. Mimeograph. 20 pp.
e. "The Concept of Latent Attribute." Typescript. 18 pp.
f. "The Qualitative Study of Larger Cross Product Matrices with Positive Entries." Typescript. 42 pp.
g. "The Use of Indices in Social Research." Typescript. 32 pp.
h. with Bernard Berelson. "The Analysis of Communication Content." BASR. 149 pp.
i. with Patricia Kendall. *Radio Listening in America: The People Look at Radio—Again.* New York: Prentice-Hall. Reprint, New York: Arno Press, 1979.
j. with Robert K. Merton. "Mass Communication, Popular Taste, and Organized Social Action." In *Problems in the Communication of Ideas,* edited by Lyman Bryson, pp. 95–118. Institute for Religious and Social Studies. New York: Harper and Brothers.

1949

a. "Religious Voting in New York." Paper delivered at the Institute for Religious and Social Studies. 23 pp.
b. "The American Soldier: An Expository Review." *Public Opinion Quarterly* 13, no. 3 (Fall): 377–404.
c. "Should Political Forecasts Be Made?" In *The Polls and Public Opinion: The Iowa Conference on Attitude and Public Opinion Research,* edited by Norman C. Meier and Harold W. Saunders, pp. 278–86. New York: Henry Holt.
d. "Unsettled Problems of Survey Methodology." In *The Polls and Public Opinion: The Iowa Conference on Attitude and Public Opinion Research,* edited by Norman C. Meier and Harold W. Saunders, pp. 322–28. New York: Henry Holt.
e. "Motion Pictures, Radio Programs, and Youth." In *Youth Communications and Libraries,* edited by Frances Henne, Alice Brooks, and Ruth Ersted, pp. 31–45. Chicago: American Library Association.
f. with Allen Barton et al. *The Psychology and Sociological Implications of Economic Planning in Norway.* Oslo: Skirbemaskinstua.

g. with Helen Dinerman. "Research for Action." In *Communications Research, 1948–1949,* edited by Paul F. Lazarsfeld and Frank M. Stanton, pp. 73–108. New York: Harper and Brothers. Reprint, New York: Arno Press, 1979.

h. with Patricia Kendall. *Radio Listening in America.* Englewood Cliffs, N.J.: Prentice-Hall.

i. edited with Frank M. Stanton. *Communications Research, 1948–1949.* New York: Harper and Brothers. Reprint, New York: Arno Press, 1979.

1949–50

with Morris Rosenberg. "The Contribution of the Regional Poll to Political Understanding." *Public Opinion Quarterly* 13, no. 4 (Winter): 570–86.

1950

a. "The Interpretation and Computation of Some Latent Structures." In *Studies in Social Psychology in World War II.* Vol. 4, *Measurement and Prediction,* edited by Samuel A. Stouffer et al., pp. 413–72. Princeton: Princeton University Press.

b. "The Logical and Mathematical Foundation of Latent Structure Analysis." In *Studies in Social Psychology in World War II.* Vol. 4; *Measurement and Prediction,* edited by Samuel A. Stouffer et al., pp. 362–412. Princeton: Princeton University Press.

c. "Votes in the Making." *Scientific American* 183: 11–13.

d. with Patricia Kendall. "Problems of Survey Analysis." In *Continuities in Social Research: Studies in the Scope and Method of "The American Soldier,"* edited by Robert K. Merton and Paul F. Lazarsfeld, pp. 133–96. Glencoe: Free Press.

e. with Robert K. Merton. "Proposal to Establish an Institute for Training in Social Research." BASR and the Columbia University Planning Project for Advanced Training. 97 pp.

f. edited with Robert K. Merton. *Continuities in Social Research: Studies in the Scope and Method of "The American Soldier."* Glencoe: Free Press.

1950–51

"The Obligations of the 1950 Pollster to the 1984 Historian." *Public Opinion Quarterly* 14, no. 4 (Winter): 618–38.

1951

a. [1948] "Communication Research and the Social Psychologist." In *Current Trends in Social Psychology,* edited by Wayne Dennis, R. Lippitt, et al., pp. 218–73. Pittsburgh: University of Pittsburgh Press.
b. "Methodological Considerations in International Broadcasting Research." BASR. 181 pp.
c. with Allen H. Barton. "Qualitative Measurement in the Social Sciences: Classification, Typologies, and Indices." In *The Policy Sciences,* edited by D. Lerner and H. D. Lasswell, pp. 155–92. Stanford: Stanford University Press.
d. with J. Dudman. "The General Solution of Latent Class Case." In *The Uses of Mathematical Models in the Measurement of Attitudes.* Santa Monica: The Rand Corporation.
e. with Morris Rosenberg and Wagner Thielens. "The Panel Study." In *Research Methods in Social Relations,* edited by M. Jahoda, M. Deutsch, and S. Cook, pp. 587–609. New York: Dryden Press. 4th ed., 1956.
f. with Peter Rossi. "A Simple Model for Attitude Tests." In *The Uses of Mathematical Models in the Measurement of Attitudes.* Santa Monica: The Rand Corporation.

1952

with David G. Hays. "A System of Scales Derived from a Standard Trace Line Model." Typescript. 75 pp.

1952–53

"The Prognosis for International Communications Research." *Public Opinion Quarterly* 16, no. 4 (Winter): 481–90.

1953

a. "A Formalization of Robert K. Merton's Explanation of 'Value Homophyly.'" BASR. 41 pp.
b. Papers from the Dartmouth Seminar on Concepts and Indices, July 11–25. Typescript. 222 pp.
c. "Report from the Implementation Committee to the Citizen's Group on Television Regarding Plans for a Television Development Center." BASR. 62 pp.
d. "Dynamics of Response to Mass Communications: Comparative Study of Meaning and Formation of Public Opinion" and "Remarks on Projec-

tion and Identification as Mechanisms of Response." In *Mass Communications Seminar, May 11–13, 1951,* edited by Hortense Powdermaker, pp. 55–57, 108–13. New York: Wenner-Gren Foundation.

e. "Some Historical Notes on the Empirical Study of Action." BASR and the Columbia University Planning Project for Advanced Training.

f. [ed.] "Concepts and Indices." BASR. 222 pp.

1954

a. "The Analysis of Repeated Interviews." BASR and the Columbia University Planning Project for Advanced Training.

b. "The Analysis of Repeated Interviews: Panel Analysis Exemplified through Studies of Voting Decisions." Paper from the Dartmouth Conference on Social Progress. 41 pp.

c. "A Conceptual Introduction to Latent Structure Analysis." In *Mathematical Thinking in the Social Sciences,* edited by Paul F. Lazarsfeld, pp. 349–87. Glencoe: Free Press.

d. [ed.] "Analysis of Social Progress." Papers from the Dartmouth Seminar on Social Progress. BASR. 459 pp.

e. [ed.] *Mathematical Thinking in the Social Sciences.* Glencoe: Free Press. Reprint, New York: Russell and Russell, 1969.

f. with Allen H. Barton, S. M. Lipset, and Juan J. Linz. "The Psychology of Voting: An Analysis of Political Behavior." In *Handbook of Social Psychology,* edited by G. Lindzey, 2: 1124–75. Boston: Addison-Wesley. 3d ed., 1959.

g. with Bernard Berelson and William N. McPhee. *Voting: A Study of Opinion Formation in a Presidential Campaign.* Chicago: University of Chicago Press. Phoenix Edition, 1966.

h. with Charles E. Lindblom. "A Case Study of Methods in Social Science." Typescript. 57 pp.

i. with Robert K. Merton. "Friendship as Social Process: A Substantive and Methodological Analysis." In *Freedom and Control in Modern Society,* edited by M. Berger, T. Abel, and C. Page, pp. 18–66. New York: Van Nostrand.

1955

a. [1946] "Interpretation of Statistical Relations as a Research Operation." In *The Language of Social Research: A Reader in the Methodology of Social Research,* edited by Paul F. Lazarsfeld and Morris Rosenberg, pp. 115–25. Glencoe: Free Press.

b. "Communication Problems in Sociology." *Report of the Fifth Conference of the Association of Princeton Graduate Alumni* (December): pp. 17–26.

c. "Progress and Fad in Motivation Research." *Proceedings of the Third Annual Seminar on Social Science for Industry—Motivation.* Stanford Research Institute, March 23, San Francisco, pp. 11–23.

d. "Why Is So Little Known about the Effects of Television on Children and What Can Be Done?" Testimony before the Kefauver Committee on Juvenile Delinquency. *Public Opinion Quarterly* 19, no. 3 (Fall): 243–51.

e. "A Logical Analysis of the Measurement Problem in the Social Sciences." *Conference Proceedings on Measurement of Management,* Society for Advancement of Management, New York, November 3–4, pp. 21–30.

f. "Mutual Effects of Statistical Variables." BASR and the Columbia University Planning Project for Advanced Training.

g. "Recent Developments in Latent Structure Analysis." *Sociometry* 18, no. 4 (December): 391–403.

h. "An Algebraic Introduction to Latent Structure Analysis." Typescript. 142 pp.

i. with Allen H. Barton. "Some Functions of Qualitative Analysis in Social Research." *Frankfurter Beiträge zur Soziologie* 1: 321–61.

j. with Elihu Katz. *Personal Influence: The Part Played by People in the Flow of Mass Communication.* Glencoe: Free Press. Reprinted 1964.

k. edited with Morris Rosenberg. *The Language of Social Research: A Reader in the Methodology of Social Research.* Glencoe: Free Press. Reprinted 1965.

l. [Elias Smith, pseud.] with Lotte Radermacher. [1932] "The Affinity of Occupation and Subject Matter among Adult Education Students." In *The Language of Social Research: A Reader in the Methodology of Social Research,* edited by Paul F. Lazarsfeld and Morris Rosenberg, pp. 100–105. Glencoe: Free Press.

m. [Elias Smith, pseud.] with Hortense Horwitz. [1945] "The Interchangeability of Socio-Economic Indices." In *The Language of Social Research: A Reader in the Methodology of Social Research,* edited by Paul F. Lazarsfeld and Morris Rosenberg, pp. 73–76. Glencoe: Free Press.

1956

a. "Comments" on Walter J. Blum and Harry Kalven, Jr., *The Art of Opinion Research. University of Chicago Law Review* 24: 65–69.

b. "Some New Results and Problems in Latent Structure Analysis." Typescript. 49 pp.

c. "Recent Developments in Latent Structure Analysis." *Sociometry* 18: 647, 659.

1957

a. "The Historian and the Pollster." In *Common Frontiers of the Social Sciences,* edited by Mirra Komarovsky, pp. 242–62. Glencoe: Free Press.

(A slightly revised version of Lazarsfeld's 1950 article "The Obligations of the 1950 Pollster to the 1984 Historian.")

b. "'Public Opinion' and the Classical Tradition." *Public Opinion Quarterly* 21, no. 1 (Spring): 39–53.

c. Review of *Union Democracy*, by S. M. Lipset, M. Trow, and J. S. Coleman. *Public Opinion Quarterly* 21, no. 1 (Spring): 212–14.

d. "Concluding Remarks." In *Mathematical Models of Human Behavior: Proceedings of a Symposium*, pp. 97–103. Stamford, Conn.: Dunlap and Associates.

1957–58

with Wagner Thielens, Jr. "Social Scientists and Recent Threats to Academic Freedom." *Social Problems* 5, no. 3: 244–66.

1958

a. "Who Are the Marketing Leaders?" *Tide*, May 9, pp. 53–57.

b. "Evidence and Inference in Social Research." *Daedalus* 87, no. 4: 99–130.

c. with Wagner Thielens, Jr. *The Academic Mind: Social Scientists in a Time of Crisis*. With a field report by David Riesman. Glencoe: Free Press. Reprint, New York: Arno Press, 1974.

1959

a. "Amerikanische Beobachtungen eines Bühler-Schülers." *Zeitschrift für experimentelle und angewandte Psychologie* 6: 69–76.

b. "Problems in Methodology." In *Sociology Today: Problems and Prospects,* edited by Robert K. Merton, Leonard Broom, and Leonard S. Cottrell, Jr., pp. 39–78. New York: Basic Books.

c. *Report on a Project to Map Out the General Area of Non-Intellectual Factors in the Prediction of College Success*. College Entrance Examination Board. 51 pp.

d. "Sociological Reflections on Business: Consumers and Managers." In *Social Science Research on Business: Product and Potential,* with Robert A. Dahl and Mason Haire, pp. 99–155. New York: Columbia University Press.

e. "Latent Structure Analysis." In *Psychology: A Study of a Science,* vol. 3, edited by Sigmund Koch, pp. 476–543. New York: McGraw-Hill.

f. "Latent Structure Analysis." *Contributions to Scientific Research in Management*. Proceedings of the Scientific Program following the dedication

314

The Writings of Paul F. Lazarsfeld

of the Western Data Processing Center, Graduate School of Business Administration, University of California, Los Angeles, January 20–30, pp. 1–8.

g. "Methodological Problems in Empirical Social Research." *Transactions of the Fourth World Congress of Sociology.* Vol. 2, *Sociology: Applications and Research,* pp. 225–49. London: International Sociological Association.

h. "Reflections on Business." *American Journal of Sociology* 65, no. 1 (July): 1–31. Expanded as "Sociological Reflections on Business: Consumers and Managers." In *Social Science Research on Business: Product and Potential,* with Robert A. Dahl and Mason Haire. New York: Columbia University Press.

i. *Some Aspects of Human Motivation in Relation to Distribution.* Report of the Thirty-First Annual Boston Conference on Distribution, pp. 61–63.

j. [1958] Tendances actuelles de la sociologie des communications et comportement du public de la radiotélévision américaine." *Cahiers d'Etudes de Radio Télévision,* no. 23: 243–56. Originally prepared as a paper for a conference at the Sorbonne, Paris, January 17, 1958.

k. with Robert A. Dahl and Mason Haire. *Social Science Research on Business: Product and Potential.* New York: Columbia University Press.

l. with Robert E. Mitchell. "Point of Purchase Advertising: A Report on the Model Twenty-700 Cigarette Vending Machine." BASR. 47 pp.

1960

a. "Latent Structure Analysis and Test Theory." In *Psychological Scaling,* edited by H. Gulliksen and S. Messick, pp. 83–95. New York: John Wiley and Sons.

b. "A Researcher Looks at Television." *Public Opinion Quarterly* 24, no. 1 (Spring): 24–31.

c. Review of *Delay in the Court,* by Hans Zeisel, Harry Kalven, Jr., and Bernard Buchholz. *Public Opinion Quarterly* 24, no. 4 (Winter): 694–700.

1961

a. "The Algebra of Dichotomous Systems." In *Studies in Item Analysis and Prediction,* edited by H. Solomon, pp. 111–57. Stanford: Stanford University Press. Abridged in *L'Analyse empirique de la causalité,* edited by Paul F. Lazarsfeld and R. Boudon, pp. 255–75. Paris: Mouton, 1966.

b. "Notes on the History of Quantification in Sociology: Trends, Sources, and Problems." *Isis* 52, no. 168 (June): 277–333.

c. "An Extended Solution of Discrete Class Case." Typescript. 10 pp.

d. with Herbert Menzel. [1956] "On the Relation between Individual and Collective Properties." In *Complex Organizations: A Sociological Reader,* edited by Amitai Etzioni, pp. 422–40. New York: Holt, Rinehart and Winston.
e. with Sydney S. Spivak. "Observations on the Organization of Empirical Social Research in the United States." *International Social Science Council Information* 29 (December): 1–35.

1962

a. [1960] "Philosophy of Science and Empirical Social Research." In *Logic, Methodology and Philosophy of Science: Proceedings of the 1960 International Congress,* edited by E. Nagel, P. Suppes, and A. Tarski, pp. 463–73. Stanford: Stanford University Press.
b. "The Sociology of Empirical Social Research." *American Sociological Review* 27, no. 6 (December): 757–67.
c. with Allen H. Barton. "The Methodology of Quantitative Social Research." In *A New Survey of the Social Sciences,* edited by B. N. Varma, pp. 151–69. Asia House.
d. with Ruth Leeds. "International Sociology as a Sociological Problem." *American Sociological Review* 27, no. 5 (October): 732–41.

1963

a. "Trends in Broadcasting Research." In *Studies in Broadcasting,* no. 1 (March), edited by Katagiri and Motono, pp. 49–64. Tokyo: Theoretical Research Center of the Radio and TV Culture Research Institute, Nippon Hoso Kyokai.
b. "Political Behavior and Public Opinion." In *The Behavioral Sciences Today,* edited by Bernard Berelson, pp. 176–87. New York: Basic Books.
c. with Jane Hauser. "Sociological Aspects of Planning." *Social Science Information* 2, no. 1 (March): 82–88.
d. with H. Menzel. "Mass Media and Personal Influence." Voice of America Forum Lectures, *Mass Communication Series 8.* Also in *The Science of Human Communication,* edited by Wilbur Schramm, pp. 1–10. New York: Basic Books.

1964

a. "Some Problems of Organized Social Research." In *The Behavioral Sciences: Problems and Prospects,* edited by Ozzie G. Simmons, pp. 9–19. Boulder: Institute of Behavioral Science, University of Colorado.

b. "A Note on Empirical Social Research and Interdisciplinary Relationships." *International Social Science Journal* 16: 529–33.

c. "Note sur la recherche sociale empirique et les liens interdisciplinaires." *Revue Internationale des Sciences Sociales* 16: 573–78.

d. "Sociology vs. Common Sense." In *Contemporary Sociology,* edited by Milton L. Barron. New York: Dodd, Mead.

e. with Jack Ferguson. "Social Science Information Services: Progress Report on a Survey." *American Behavioral Scientist* 7, no. 10 (June): 20–22.

f. with Jane Z. Hauser. "The Admissions Officer in the American College: The Study of an Emerging Occupation." New York: College Entrance Examination Board. Mimeograph.

g. with Jane Z. Hauser. "The Admissions Officer: Fulcrum for Academic Leadership." *Journal of the Association of College Admissions Counselors* 10, no. 2 (Fall): 3–6.

h. with Sam D. Sieber. *Organizing Educational Research: An Exploration.* Englewood Cliffs, N.J.: Prentice-Hall.

1965

a. [1961] "Repeated Observations on Attitude and Behavior Items." In *Mathematics and Social Sciences,* collected by V. Capecchi, Paul Sternberg, T. Kloeck, and C. T. Leenders, pp. 121–42. Paris and The Hague: Mouton, with the collaboration of UNESCO, the Rockefeller Foundation, and the Ecole Pratique des Hautes Etudes.

b. "Latent Structure Analysis" and "Repeated Observations on Attitude and Behavior Items." In *Mathematics and Social Sciences I,* collected by V. Capecchi, Paul Sternberg, T. Kloeck, and C. T. Leenders. Paris and The Hague: Mouton, with the collaboration of UNESCO, the Rockefeller Foundation, and the Ecole Pratique des Hautes Etudes.

c. "The Seminars and Graduate Education." In *A Community of Scholars: The University Seminars at Columbia,* edited by Frank Tannenbaum, pp. 74–85. New York: Praeger.

d. with Raymond Boudon. "Remarques sur la signification formelle de deux indices." In *Le Vocabulaire des sciences sociales: concepts et indices,* edited by Raymond Boudon and Paul F. Lazarsfeld, pp. 224–28. Paris and The Hague: Mouton.

e. with Terry Clark and B. Lécuyer. "Memorandum on Progress and Plans for Study of the History of Empirical Social Research in France, 1660–1914." BASR. 49 pp.

f. with Amitai Etzioni. "Innovation in Higher Education." Typescript. 36 pp.

g. with Neil W. Henry. "The Application of Latent Structure Analysis to Quantitative Ecological Data." In *Mathematical Explorations in Behavioral Science,* edited by F. Massarik and P. Ratoosh, pp. 333–48. Homewood, Ill.: Irwin Press.

h. with Antony R. Oberschall. "Max Weber and Empirical Social Research." *American Sociological Review* 30, no. 2 (April): 185–99.

i. with Jean Stoetzel. "Définition d'intention et espace d'attributs." In *Le Vocabulaire des sciences sociales: concepts et indices,* edited by Raymond Boudon and Paul F. Lazarsfeld, pp. 189–93. Paris and The Hague: Mouton.

j. edited with Raymond Boudon. *Le Vocabulaire des sciences sociales: concepts et indices.* Paris and The Hague: Mouton.

1966

a. "Communications Research." *Grassroots Editor* 8: 3–6.

b. "Concept Formation and Measurement in the Behavioral Sciences: Some Historical Observations." In *Concepts, Theory, and Explanation in the Behavioral Sciences,* edited by Gordon J. Di Renzo. New York: Random House.

c. "Innovation in Higher Education." In *Expanding Horizons of Knowledge about Man,* pp. 12–21. New York: Yeshiva University.

d. with Neil W. Henry. "Models for Opinion Change." Typescript.

e. with Sam D. Sieber. *The Organization of Educational Research.* New York: BASR Monograph.

f. edited with Raymond Boudon. *L'Analyse empirique de la causalité.* Paris and The Hague: Mouton.

g. edited with Neil W. Henry. *Readings in Mathematical Social Science.* Chicago: Science Research Associates.

1967

a. "Some Recent Trends in United States Methodology and General Sociology." *First International Conference of the Social Sciences* (September), pp. 653–88. Bologna.

b. with Neil W. Henry. "Modelli matematici per lo studio dei panels." In *Metodologia e ricerca sociologica: saggi sociologici,* edited and with an introduction by Vittorio Capecchi. Bologna: Societa Editrice il Mulino.

c. in collaboration with George Nash. "New Administrator on Campus: A Study of the Director of Student Financial Aid." BASR. 367 pp.

d. edited with William H. Sewell and Harold L. Wilensky. *The Uses of Sociology.* New York: Basic Books.

1968

a. *Am Puls der Gesellschaft.* Edited and with a foreword by Gertrude Wagner. Vienna: Europa Verlag.

b. "Measurement." In *American Society: Perspectives, Problems, Methods,* edited by Talcott Parsons, pp. 101–14. New York: Basic Books.

c. "An Episode in the History of Social Research: A Memoir." In *Perspectives in American History,* 2: 270–337. Cambridge: The Charles Warren Center for Studies in American History, Harvard University. Republished in *The Intellectual Migration: Europe and America, 1930–1960,* edited by Donald Fleming and Bernard Bailyn. Cambridge: Harvard University Press, 1969.

d. "Survey Analysis: The Analysis of Attribute Data." *International Encyclopedia of the Social Sciences,* 15: 419–29. New York: Macmillan and Free Press.

e. "The Place of Empirical Social Research on the Map of Contemporary Sociology." In *The Social Sciences: Problems and Orientations,* pp. 223–41. Paris and The Hague: Mouton/UNESCO.

f. with Neil W. Henry. *Latent Structure Analysis.* Boston: Houghton-Mifflin.

g. with David Landau. "Adolphe Quetelet." *International Encyclopedia of the Social Sciences,* 13: 247–57. New York: Macmillan and Free Press.

1969

a. "From Vienna to Columbia." *Columbia Forum* 12, no. 2 (Summer): 31–36. Part of this essay was published in *Perspectives in American History.* Cambridge: The Charles Warren Center for Studies in American History, Harvard University, 1968.

b. "Uber die Brauchbarkeit der Soziologie." In *Soziologie: Forschung in Oesterreich,* edited by Leopold Rosenmayr and Sigurd Hoellinger, pp. 13–31. Graz: Hermann Böhlau's Nachf.

1970

a. *Qu'est-ce que la sociologie?* Paris: Gallimard.

b. *Philosophie des sciences sociales.* Edited and with an introduction by Raymond Boudon. Paris: Gallimard.

c. "A Memoir in Honor of Professor Wold." In *Scientists at Work— Festschrift in Honor of Herman Wold,* edited by T. Dalenius, G. Karlson, and S. Malmquist, pp. 78–103. Uppsala: Almqvist and Wiksells Boktryckeri AB.

d. "Sociology." In *Main Trends of Research in the Social and Human Sciences.* Part 1, *Social Sciences,* pp. 61–165. Paris and The Hague: Mouton/UNESCO. Published separately as *Main Trends in Sociology.* New York: Harper and Row, 1973.

e. "A Sociologist Looks at Historians." In *Public Opinion and Historians: Interdisciplinary Perspectives,* edited by Mevin Small, pp. 39–59. Symposium at Wayne State University, May 8–9. Detroit: Wayne State University Press.

f. with Jeffrey G. Reitz. "Toward a Theory of Applied Sociology." Report for the United States Office of Naval Research. BASR. 78 pp.

g. edited with Raymond Boudon and François Chazel. *L'Analyse des processus sociaux.* Paris and The Hague: Mouton.

1971

a. "The Mathematical Revolution and the Management of Marketing Communications." In *Sixteenth Annual Conference Proceedings,* edited by W. S. Hale. Advertising Research Foundation.

b. "Accounting and Social Bookkeeping." In *Accounting in Perspective: Contributions to Accounting Thought by Other Disciplines,* pp. 88–101. Cincinnati: South-Western Publishing.

c. "Measurement in Today's Sciences." Typescript. 27 pp.

d. in collaboration with Sam D. Sieber. "Reforming the University: The Role of the Research Center." BASR. 180 pp. Published by Praeger, 1972.

1972

a. [1946] "Mutual Effects of Statistical Variables." In *Continuities in the Language of Social Research,* edited by Paul F. Lazarsfeld, Ann K. Pasanella, and Morris Rosenberg, pp. 388–98. New York: Free Press.

b. [1950] "Development of a Test for Class Consciousness." In *Continuities in the Language of Social Research,* edited by Paul F. Lazarsfeld, Ann K. Pasanella, and Morris Rosenberg, pp. 41–43. New York: Free Press.

c. [1954] "Mass Media of Communication in Modern Society." In *Qualitative Analysis: Historical and Critical Essays,* pp. 106–20. Boston: Allyn and Bacon.

d. [1958] "Historical Notes on the Empirical Study of Action: An Intellectual Odyssey." In *Qualitative Analysis: Historical and Critical Essays,* pp. 53–105. Boston: Allyn and Bacon.

e. [1968] "The Problem of Measuring Turnover." In *Continuities in the Language of Social Research,* edited by Paul F. Lazarsfeld, Ann K. Pasanella, and Morris Rosenberg, pp. 358–62. New York: Free Press.

f. *Qualitative Analysis: Historical and Critical Essays.* Boston: Allyn and Bacon.

g. "Regression Analysis with Dichotomous Attributes." *Social Science Research* 1, no. 1 (April): 25–34.

h. "Reply to Comments on Lazarsfeld's 'Regression Analysis with Dichotomous Attributes.'" *Social Science Research* 1: 425–27.
i. "Mutual Relations over Time of Two Attributes: A Review and Integration of Various Approaches." In *Psychopathology,* edited by M. Hammer, K. Salzinger, and S. Sutton, pp. 461–80. New York: John Wiley and Sons.
j. "Algebra of Dichotomies." In *Notes of Lectures on Mathematics in the Behavioral Sciences,* edited by Henry A. Selby, pp. 162–96. Boston: Mathematical Association of America.
k. with Robert K. Merton. [1950] "A Professional School for Training in Social Research." In *Qualitative Analysis: Historical and Critical Essays,* pp. 361–91. Boston: Allyn and Bacon.
l. edited with Ann K. Pasanella and Morris Rosenberg. *Continuities in the Language of Social Research.* New York: Free Press.

1973

a. "The Policy Science Movement (An Outsider's View)." *Policy Sciences* 6: 211–22.
b. "Working with Merton." In *The Idea of Social Structure: Papers in Honor of Robert K. Merton,* edited by Lewis A. Coser, pp. 35–66. New York: Harcourt Brace Jovanovich.
c. "Zwei Wege der MassenKommuniKationsforschung." In *Die Elektronische Revolution,* edited by Oskar Schatz, pp. 197–222. Graz: Styria Verlag.
d. with Martin Jaeckel. "The Uses of Sociology by Presidential Commissions." In *Sociology and Public Policy,* edited by Mirra Komarovsky, pp. 117–42. New York: Elsevier.
e. with J. G. Reitz. *An Introduction to Applied Sociology.* New York: Elsevier.

1975

a. *Main Trends in Sociology.* New York: Harper and Row.
b. "Toward a History of Empirical Sociology." In *Méthodologie de l'histoire et des sciences humaines: Mélanges en l'honneur de Fernand Braudel,* pp. 289–301. Paris: Gallimard.
c. "The Social Sciences and the Smoking Problem." In *Smoking Behavior: Motives and Incentives,* edited by William L. Dunn, Jr., pp. 283–86. Washington, D.C.: V. M. Winston and Sons.
d. with A. S. Meyer and Lucy M. Friedman. "Motivational Conflicts Engendered by the Ongoing Discussion of Cigarette Smoking." In *Smoking Behavior: Motives and Incentives,* edited by William L. Dunn, Jr., pp. 243–54. Washington, D.C.: V. M. Winston and Sons.

e. with Douglas McDonald. "Some Problems of Research Organization." BASR. 67 pp.

1976

"Evaluation of Social Experiments: Commentary." In *The Evaluation of Social Programs,* edited by C. Clark, pp. 60–61. Beverly Hills: Sage.

1977

"Some Episodes in the History of Panel Analysis." In *Longitudinal Research in Drug Use: Empirical Findings and Methodological Issues,* edited by Denise Kandel, pp. 249–65. New York: John Wiley and Sons.

Introductions and Forewords

1940. Mirra Komarovsky, ed. *The Unemployed Man and His Family.* New York: Dryden Press. Reprint, New York: Arno Press, 1971.
1945. Ernest Greenwood. *Experimental Sociology: A Study in Method.* New York: King's Crown Press.
1947. Hans Zeisel. *Say It with Figures.* New York: Harper and Row.
1953. Bernard Stern, ed. "Historical Materials on Innovation in Higher Education." Typescript.
1955. Herbert Hyman. *Survey Design and Analysis.* New York: Free Press.
1959. Allen H. Barton. *Studying the Effects of College Education.* New Haven: The Edward W. Hazen Foundation.
1959. N. Jacobs, ed. *Culture for the Millions: Mass Media in Modern Society.* Princeton, N.J.: Van Nostrand and Co.
1960. Rose K. Goldsen and collaborators. *What College Students Think.* Princeton, N.J.: Van Nostrand and Co.
1961. *Organizational Measurement and Its Bearing on the Study of College Environments.* New York: The College Entrance Examination Board.
1962. Samuel Stouffer. *Social Research to Test Ideas.* New York: Free Press.
1965. S. Sternberg, ed. *Mathematics and Social Sciences.* Debates of Menthon–Saint Bernard (July 1–27, 1960) and seminar in Gösing, Austria (July 3–27, 1962). Paris: Mouton. Published with the collaboration of UNESCO, the Rockefeller Foundation, and the Ecole Pratique des Hautes Etudes.
1965. Ecole Pratique des Hautes Etudes. "Les Intellectuels et la culture de masse." Special Issue of *Communications* 5: 3–12. Paris: EHESS.
1965. Anthony Oberschall. *Empirical Social Research in Germany, 1848–1914.* Paris: Mouton.

1966. "Mathematics and the Social Sciences." In *Readings in Mathematical Social Science*, edited by Paul F. Lazarsfeld and Neil W. Henry, pp. 3–18. Chicago: Science Research Associates.

1966. Gordon J. Di Renzo, ed. *Concepts, Theory, and Explanation in the Behavioral Sciences*. New York: Random House.

1967. Paul F. Lazarsfeld, William H. Sewell, and Harold L. Wilensky, eds. *The Uses of Sociology*. New York: Basic Books.

1968. Morris Rosenberg. *The Logic of Survey Analysis*. New York: Basic Books.

1968. Hans Zeisel. *Say It with Figures*, 5th ed. New York: Harper and Row.

1968. Hans Zeisel. *Ditelo con i numeri*. Padova: Marsilio.

1970. Charles Y. Glock, Gertrude J. Selznick, and Joe L. Spaeth. *The Apathetic Majority*. New York: Harper and Row.

1971. Bernard Rosenberg and David Manning White, eds. *Mass Culture Revisited*. New York: Van Nostrand Reinhold.

1972. Anthony Oberschall, ed. *The Establishment of Empirical Sociology: Studies in Continuity, Discontinuity, and Institutionalization*. New York: Harper and Row.

1972. "An Introduction." In *Some Problems in the Organization and Use of Social Research in the U.S. Navy*, by Douglas C. McDonald. BASR. 147 pp.

1973. Sam Sieber. *Reforming the University: The Role of the Research Center*. New York: Praeger.

1973. J. G. Reitz. *The Gap between Knowledge and Decision in the Utilization of Social Research*. Report for the U.S. Office of Naval Research. New York: BASR.

1973. "The Use of Social Science in Business Management." In *Views from the Socially Sensitive Seventies*. Seminars presented to the Supplemental Training Program. New York: American Telephone and Telegraph.

1973. Wolf Heydebrand. *Hospital Bureaucracy: A Comparative Study of Organizations*. New York: Dunellen Publishers.

1973. Ann K. Pasanella and Janice Weinman. *The Road to Recommendations*. Report for the U.S. Office of Naval Research. New York: BASR.

1976. Caroline U. Persell. *Quality, Careers, and Training in Educational Research*. New York: General Hall.

Afterwords

1963. "Some Reflections on Past and Future Research on Broadcasting." In *The People Look at Television: A Study of Audience Attitudes*, by Gary Steiner. New York: Knopf.

Name and Title Index

Subject Index

Academic freedom, 269, 273; social scientists and threats to, 88–105. *See also* College teachers
Achievement, and right to equality, 221–22, 224, 225, 226
Action, analysis of: disposition concept in, 58, 65, 168; interpretation in, 60–66; Lazarsfeld and, 6–10, 259; and market research, 53–69; mechanisms and motives in, 56–60, 62, 65; and time line, 58–60, 68
Advertising, 116; influence on opinion, 148, 156
Age: and effect on audience, 46; and effect on milk consumption, 63; permissiveness and, 94–95, 99, 101, 104, 104n.2; progressiveness of college teachers and, 248–49
"Allport-Vernon value test," 125
American Sociological Association, 4, 22, 257
"Anderson index," 205–6
"Apollonian pattern" (Benedict), 213, 214, 216
Apprehension: and permissiveness, 100–102; of college teachers, 88; index of, 88, 89, 90, 91, 104
Army, American: 131–47; conformity of soldier in, 138; social mobility within, 145. *See also* Attitude, of American soldier; Education, of soldier
Attitude: Allport's notion of, 168; of American soldier, 131, 132–46; basic, of family in Marienthal, 33–41; of consumer actions, 53–69; toward future, 37, 39; and open-ended interviews, 113, 114–15, 119, 128; toward political parties, 149–52; of proletarian consumer in Marienthal, 8, 272; scale analysis and, 124–26; toward United Nations, 148; Weber's concept of, 292–93; Weber and workers', 285–86, 289
Attribute: combinations of, 250; as index of different phenomena, 136; mu-

tual effects of two, 199. *See also* Dichotomous systems
Attribute-space, 15, 17, 260, 261; and reduction, 159–67; and typologies, 260
Audience: criteria of classification of, 43–47; effect of age on, 46; effect of education on, 44–45; interrelation between kinds of, behavior, 49–52; personality characteristics of, 44, 47–49; primary characteristics of various, 43, 44–47, 49; research, 42–52, 112; Summers and Wahn's study of radio, 47
Authoritarian personality, 244; in army, 137
Authority: Fromm's types of, in family, 163–65, 260; physical confidence and, 163–65; and school system in Soviet Union, 228

Bureau of Applied Social Research (BASR), 4, 147n.2, 272
Buying behavior. *See* Consumer, behavior

Case studies, in social research. *See* Deviate case analysis
Catholics: and education, 148; and Protestants in Western Europe, 276, 277, 278; and Senator Black, 150; and voting behavior, 79, 80–81, 118
Causal: analysis, 15, 190, 251; factors, 210, 227
Cause, and effect, in survey analysis, 131, 135–40, 147
"Center and periphery" (Shils), 226
Checklists, in questionnaire, 113, 120, 122–23, 128
Chicago school, 10, 23, 266, 271
Choice: Lazarsfeld and his Austrian program of, 259, 271; Weber and modern approaches of, 289. *See also* Communication; Consumer; Voting behavior

327